SCOTTISH NATIONAL PARTY
LEADERS

SCOTTISH NATIONAL PARTY LEADERS

EDITED BY

James Mitchell and Gerry Hassan

Biteback Publishing

First published in Great Britain in 2016 by
Biteback Publishing Ltd
Westminster Tower
3 Albert Embankment
London SE1 7SP
Selection and editorial apparatus copyright © James Mitchell and
Gerry Hassan 2016

ISBN 978-1-78590-092-1

10 9 8 7 6 5 4 3 2 1

A CIP catalogue record for this book is available from the British Library.

Set in Bulmer by Adrian McLaughlin

Printed and bound in Great Britain by
CPI Group (UK) Ltd, Croydon CR0 4YY

CONTENTS

AUTHOR BIOGRAPHIES

PROFESSOR EWEN CAMERON is the Sir William Fraser Professor of Scottish History and Palaeography at Edinburgh University. His four interrelated interests are the history of the Scottish Highlands, the 'land question', Scottish political history and the debates on Scotland within the Union from the late nineteenth century. His publications include *Impaled Upon the Thistle: Scotland since 1880* (Edinburgh University Press, 2010).

EWEN ANGUS CAMERON graduated in 1984 from the University of Glasgow with a degree in Scottish history and politics. He is currently preparing a PhD thesis entitled 'Putting Scotland First: The Rise of the Scottish National Party 1966–1974' at the University of Strathclyde. He has followed Scottish nationalism with interest since his school years in East Perthshire.

ROBBIE DINWOODIE joined *The Scotsman* in his native Edinburgh in 1974, going on to cover the Falklands War, the miners' strike and the conflict in Northern Ireland. Joining the *Glasgow Herald* in 1988, he became a political correspondent in 1994, reporting on the creation of the Scottish Parliament in 1999 through to the independence referendum of 2014. He now contributes as a freelance writer and blogger.

PROFESSOR RICHARD FINLAY is head of the School of Humanities at Strathclyde University and author of a number of books on modern Scottish history. Among his work, he wrote *Independent and Free* (John Donald, 1994), the standard work on the origins and early years of the SNP, and *Modern Scotland: 1914–2000* (Profile, 2003).

DOUGLAS FRASER is BBC Scotland's business and economy editor. Previously he was political editor of *The Herald* and prior to that the *Sunday Herald*, after working for *The Scotsman* from 1989 to 1997. He is co-author (with Gerry Hassan) of *The Political Guide to Modern Scotland* (Politicos Publishing, 2004).

PROFESSOR CHRISTOPHER HARVIE was Professor of British Studies at the University of Tübingen in Baden-Württemberg, Germany, for over twenty years. He is the author of several of the standard reference books including *Scotland and Nationalism: 1707–2004* (Routledge, 2004, 4th edition) and *No Gods and Precious Few Heroes: Modern Scotland in the Twentieth Century* (Edinburgh University Press, 2016, 4th edition). He served as an SNP MSP from 2007 to 2011.

DR GERRY HASSAN is a writer and commentator. His PhD was on the Scottish political commentariat and its relationship with the public sphere. He is the author and editor of over twenty books on Scottish and British politics, social change, policy and ideas. These include *The Strange Death of Labour Scotland* (with Eric Shaw) (Edinburgh University Press, 2012), *Caledonian Dreaming: The Quest for a Different Scotland* (Luath Press, 2014) and *Independence of the Scottish Mind: Elite Narratives, Public Spaces and the Making of a Modern Nation* (Macmillan, 2014).

ISOBEL LINDSAY was a lecturer in sociology at Strathclyde University. She was a national office-bearer of the SNP during the 1970s, convener of the cross-party Campaign for a Scottish Parliament and an executive member of the Scottish Constitutional Convention, and is currently a board member of Common Weal and *Scottish Left Review*. She has contributed widely to the debate on self-government, independence and the SNP, writing in *The Radical Approach: Papers on an Independent Scotland* (Palingenesis Press, 1976), *Nationalism in the Nineties* (Polygon, 1991) and *The Modern SNP: From Protest to Power* (Edinburgh University Press, 2009).

DR PETER LYNCH is Senior Lecturer in Politics at Stirling University and specialises in Scottish politics, nationalism, political parties and devolution. He maintains the Scottish Political Archive and is the author of the only single-volume history of the SNP, *SNP: The History of the Scottish National Party* (Welsh Academic Press, 2013, 2nd edition).

DR MARGERY PALMER MCCULLOCH is Senior Honorary Research Fellow at Glasgow University, an elected member of the Council of the Association for Scottish Literary Studies and former Honorary Secretary of the Saltire Society. Her publications include works on significant figures in Scottish literary life, including Neil Gunn, Edwin Muir and Lewis Grassic Gibbon, as well as *Scottish Modernism and its Contexts, 1918–1959: Literature, National Identity and Cultural Exchange* (Edinburgh University Press, 2009).

DR CATRIONA MACDONALD is Reader in Late Modern Scottish History at Glasgow University. Her research interests focus on Scottish socio-political and cultural history after 1832 and Scottish society and culture, especially Scottish literature. Her publications include *Whaur Extremes Meet: Scotland's Twentieth Century* (John Donald, 2009).

DR EILIDH MACPHAIL lectures at Lews Castle College in Stornoway in the University of the Highlands and Islands. She completed a PhD on the Europeanisation of Scottish government. Her specialist areas of research include devolution and regional government and politics.

PROFESSOR JAMES MITCHELL is Professor of Public Politics and director of the Academy of Government at Edinburgh University, having previously held similar posts at Sheffield and Strathclyde universities. His works include *The Scottish National Party* (with Rob Johns and Lynn Bennie), *The Scottish Question* (both Oxford University Press, 2011, 2014) and *Takeover: Explaining the Extraordinary Rise of the SNP* (Biteback, 2016) (with Rob Johns).

DR GORDON PENTLAND is Reader in History at Edinburgh University. His main interest is in British political history since the French Revolution, especially in radical politics. He is co-editor of the *Oxford Handbook of Modern British Political History, 1800–2000*. Among his publications is *Radicalism, Reform and National Identity, 1820–1833* (Royal Historical Society Studies, 2008), which won the Hume Brown Senior Prize in 2010.

DR MALCOLM PETRIE is a Leverhulme Fellow in Edinburgh University's School of History, Classics and Archaeology. He specialises in twentieth-century Scottish and British history and is currently working on a project on Liberalism, Unionism and Nationalism in Scotland, 1945–83.

MANDY RHODES is managing director of Holyrood Communications and managing editor of *Holyrood Magazine*. She has worked for nearly thirty years in journalism in Scotland, in newsprint, television and radio broadcasting, was *Scotland on Sunday*'s social affairs correspondent, and has won numerous awards including PPA Magazine Editor of the Year, Feature Writer of the Year and Columnist of the Year.

MURRAY RITCHIE worked for forty-five years in journalism in Scotland, thirty-two of them on *The Herald*, and was the paper's Scottish political editor from 1997 to 2003. He is author of *Scotland Reclaimed: The Inside Story of Scotland's First Democratic Parliamentary Election* (Saltire Society, 2000).

MIKE RUSSELL was SNP chief executive from 1994 to 1999 and has been a Member of the Scottish Parliament from 1999 to 2003 and from 2007 to the present. He served as a Minister in the SNP government, including serving in the Cabinet as Minister for Culture, External Affairs and the Constitution during 2009 and Cabinet Secretary for Education and Lifelong Learning from 2009–14. He has been Chair in Culture and Governance at Glasgow University since 2015 and is the author of numerous books, including *Grasping the Thistle* (Argyll Publishing, 2006).

DR PAULA SOMERVILLE completed her doctorate at Strathclyde University History Department and is the author of *Through the Maelstrom: A History of the Scottish National Party, 1945–67* (Scots Independent, 2013), the authoritative work on this period in the SNP's development.

PROFESSOR RORY WATSON is a poet and Professor Emeritus in English Studies at Stirling University. He is a Fellow of the Royal Society of Edinburgh and was general editor of the Canongate Classics reprint series. Among his work are studies of the poet Hugh MacDiarmid. He is the son of Bruce Watson, SNP leader from 1945 to 1947.

DR CLIFF WILLIAMSON is a lecturer at Bath Spa University, where he specialises in religious belief and popular culture and is an authority on radical politics in twentieth-century Scotland. His recent book, *The History of Catholic Intellectual Life in Scotland, 1918–1965*, was published in June 2016 by Palgrave Macmillan.

CHAPTER 1

LEADERSHIP OF THE SNP

JAMES MITCHELL AND GERRY HASSAN

The Scottish National Party operated on the fringe of Scottish politics, not to mention UK politics, for most of its existence. Interest in and writings about the SNP have waxed and waned with support for the party since its breakthrough in the late 1960s. There have been a number of histories,[1] including memoirs by some of its leading figures and a few rather hagiographical works, but the current position and power of the SNP is relatively recent, and studies of the party and its leading figures have been struggling to keep up.[2] There is, however, a burgeoning literature emerging of pro-SNP and pro-independence publications relating to the SNP's recent electoral success in the 2015 UK election and 2016 Scottish Parliament elections.[3]

The current SNP leadership are still in many respects a work in progress, and will undoubtedly be the subject of books and study for years to come. Its current and immediate past leaders have been the focus of book-length

---

1   These include works by contributors to this book – Richard J. Finlay, *Independent and Free: Scottish Politics and the Origins of the Scottish National Party 1918–1945* (Edinburgh: John Donald, 1994); Paula Somerville, *Through the Maelstrom: A History of the Scottish National Party, 1945–1967* (Stirling: Scots Independent, 2013); Peter Lynch, *SNP: The History of the Scottish National Party* (Cardiff: Welsh Academic Press, 2002); Gerry Hassan (ed.), *The Modern SNP: From Protest to Power* (Edinburgh: Edinburgh University Press, 2009); Rob Johns and James Mitchell, *Takeover: Explaining the Extraordinary Rise of the SNP* (London: Biteback Publishing, 2016). Others have written about the wider national movement including Jack Brand, *The National Movement in Scotland* (London: Routledge and Kegan Paul, 1978); Christopher Harvie, *Scotland and Nationalism* (London: Routledge, 2004); James Mitchell, *Strategies for Self-Government: The Campaigns for a Scottish Parliament* (Edinburgh: Polygon, 1996).

2   R. B. Cunninghame Graham has been the subject of a number of works including some focused less on his political activities. John MacCormick's *The Flag in the Wind* (London: Victor Gollancz, 1955) is semi-autobiographical and has had more influence on subsequent publications than it deserves, given its subjectivity. Gordon Wilson has written three books of memoirs, two covering SNP history.

3   See as an example Josh Bircham and Grant Costello, *We are the 56: The Individuals Behind a Political Revolution* (Glasgow: Freight Books, 2015).

treatments, but these are by their nature instant and immediate judgements – 'the first rough drafts of history'[4] – and no less interesting, being part of the making of the record of political reportage.[5]

This book attempts something different – presenting essays on all the SNP's leaders as well as other prominent figures, putting them in the context of the development of the party and its place in Scottish politics, along with the country's increasing self-government. It brings together a range of authors from different backgrounds reflecting the diversity of subjects. It sits as the companion to already published volumes on Tory, Labour and Liberal (Democrat) leaders.[6]

LEADERSHIP AND CULTURE

Leadership has to be seen in context, history and traditions – and the SNP, like all parties, has its own take on each of these. The SNP is a conventional political party in many respects – one with a relationship to a wider, looser nationalist movement, which has gone through different phases in the history of both. Sometimes one has prospered and the other hasn't; at times the focus of self-government has been political, at other times cultural; and at other unique times, such as the independence referendum, both have prospered. The SNP, like Labour, as a party often invokes and uses the language of a 'movement', but the two are not synonymous, and this has mattered post-referendum, as the SNP has increased its membership.

The SNP can be seen in its attitudes and feel as an extended family. Up until the 2014 independence referendum, the party was dominated by several generations of activists who had grown up together and collectively experienced rites of passage, including births, deaths, marriages and divorces. This shared history and identity was exemplified by the inclusion in the 2011 SNP

---

4   This remark was first attributed to Philip L. Graham, *Washington Post* publisher, 1946–63.

5   See for example David Torrance, *Salmond: Against the Odds* (Edinburgh: Birlinn, 2010) and *Nicola Sturgeon: A Political Biography* (Edinburgh: Birlinn, 2015).

6   Charles Clarke et al. (eds), *British Conservative Leaders*; Charles Clarke and Toby S. James (eds), *British Labour Leaders*; Duncan Brack et al. (eds), *British Liberal Leaders* (London: Biteback Publishing, 2015).

manifesto (which resulted in a parliamentary landslide) of a photographic section featuring such personal moments for prominent SNP leaders, conveying a 'We Are Family' sense of affirmation and togetherness.[7] This indicates how the SNP saw itself and, importantly, how it wanted to be seen by others.

That is not to say that, like all families, the SNP doesn't have its quarrels, fallouts, historic enmities and fault lines. It does. But this over-arching collective identity and belonging has carried it through many lean periods and difficult times to its present position. Now, post-independence referendum, the party has morphed dramatically from one of 25,000 members to nearly 120,000 – which in a nation of 5.3 million people per head dwarfs all of the Westminster-based parties. One long-standing SNP member, when faced with their local branch suddenly full of new, unfamiliar faces, reflected, 'It is like we have been a family for years and now we have a whole host of strangers who have gatecrashed the party, and we have to welcome them.'[8]

Many aspects of the SNP have been written about and studied throughout its existence. But like most political parties, beyond formal structures and arrangements, something much more intangible and at least equally important has mattered – ethos and culture. This is a rarely examined attribute across the political spectrum – with the one notable exception being Henry Drucker's *Doctrine and Ethos in the Labour Party*.[9] His study stressed the importance of the party's ethos in everything it did – its defensiveness, conservatism and inward-looking character – shaped by past working-class experiences, defeats and memories. These influences shaped attitudes – such as the extent to which a Labour leader can assume loyalty from colleagues even in the midst of crisis, or the importance of the rulebook and procedure originating in trade union practices. Both of these attributes (and their continued power or otherwise) have been on display in the internal Labour battles over Jeremy Corbyn's leadership during 2015–16.

---

7   SNP, *Re-elect a Scottish Government: Working for Scotland* (Edinburgh: SNP, 2011).

8   Private interview, June 2015.

9   Henry Drucker, *Doctrine and Ethos in the Labour Party* (London: George Allen and Unwin, 1979).

The SNP's current ethos is informed by the party's long journey from its marginal status for several decades to its present-day position. Many of its longer-term and most committed members see it through the perspective of this earlier experience. Thus, they continue to define the party as outside the mainstream, as anti-establishment and as standing up to bigger, longer-established parties. In so doing they refute the assertion by opponents that they are in any way an establishment party and therefore insiders – often making the point that for as long as the SNP faces opposition from the main Westminster based parties, it will always be seen as a 'David taking on Goliath'. Such an attitude carries with it an advantage in campaigning politics, as witnessed in the independence referendum, which had a distinct anti-establishment ethos on the Yes side. But it also carries tensions, as the SNP becomes more a party of government and is identified increasingly with, and accountable for, policy delivery and its record.

THE ROLE OF LEADERS IN THE SNP

The SNP, unlike the main Westminster parties, has been led by a wide array of personnel, ranging from poets to, in recent times, more conventional politicians. The very notion of a party leader has been disputed over the decades. Determining who should be included in this book was less straightforward than in accompanying volumes in this series. It may be easy to identify the SNP leader today, but the party has only formally had a leader since 2004, according to the SNP constitution. Before then it had a convener and before that a chairman.[10] The SNP chair/convener was usually only *a* leader and not *the* leader in a party that was suspicious of leaders and preferred collective leadership.

There are many people who might have had a claim for inclusion in this book. A case could be made for Roland Muirhead (SNP president from 1936 to

---

10   Throughout the book we will use the terms adopted by the party at the time. The official title of chairman was used for most of its history, then was abandoned in favour of convener, a convenient Scottish term that also suggested a subtly different role and had no gender implications.

1950), who bankrolled various nationalist organisations, as well as the socialist newspaper *Forward*, and had been a stalwart of the national movement from the end of the nineteenth century through to his death in 1964 – still taking part in sit-down protests against nuclear weapons in his nineties.[11] T. H. (Tom) and Elma Gibson, husband and wife, each played significant parts. He served as party president from 1950 until 1958, and together they contributed hugely to the SNP's development in these difficult years. Many of the party's national secretaries might have been included given the service they performed. Muriel Gibson, for example, wielded considerable power as national secretary during the 1970s and was there at the birth of the party. Gibson served as an officer during the war – 'gaining a reputation for leadership', according to her obituary in the *Herald* newspaper[12] – though not before she was arrested with others, in the paranoid state of wartime politics, because she was a supporter of a party that wanted to break up the state. Gibson interpreted her role more as SNP chief executive, long before Mike Russell formally took up that position in 1994.

Twentieth-century Scottish politics was male-dominated, as reflected in the chapters in this volume, although this did not mean that women did not hold important and influential positions and leadership roles, including in the SNP – and in this case often at pivotal times. For example, we include a chapter on Margo MacDonald by Isobel Lindsay. Isobel herself might merit a place in the book, along with Margaret Ewing (previously Bain) and Janette Jones. None ever became party leader but each contributed in important ways to the party's development.

In addition to an ideological disposition favouring collective leadership, such a style suited the circumstances when the party operated as an 'amateur activist' party[13] with, at most, a handful of full-time politicians. Prior to devolution, the party relied heavily on voluntary support with leadership supplied by people in full-time jobs. This meant that the various

---

11 James Mitchell, *The Scottish Question* (Oxford: Oxford University Press, 2014), pp. 94–5.

12 Muriel Gibson, 'Soldier nationalist and country dancer', obituary, *Herald*, 4 November 2005.

13 James Mitchell, Rob Johns and Lynn Bennie, *The Scottish National Party: Transition to Power* (Oxford: Oxford University Press, 2012), Chapter 3.

strategic and governance functions were shared among a range of individuals. It was not until 1979 that the SNP had a full-time politician as its chairman. Of course, while the party membership, or at least its activists, saw leadership as a collective endeavour, this was not always how it was seen by some of its key figures. John MacCormick was never more than a national secretary but he shaped the party more than many who held more senior offices in the party and could be rather imperious. Others were accused of being dictatorial, especially when the party was divided. Robert McIntyre faced a split party during his period as chairman (1947–56) and was accused of behaving like a dictator and decided to stand aside. He was replaced by James Halliday, who, at twenty-eight, was the youngest leader the party has ever had.

As in any organisation, there has been considerable scope for interpreting the leadership role. Among those discussed in this volume are some who emphatically saw their role as part of a team, and others who interpreted their position more in the traditional way of British party leaders as *primus inter pares*. We have included chapters on all those who have formally held office as party chairmen, conveners and leaders as well as others. It is the destiny of politically active people that those holding formal office are generally listed before those who may have been most influential but not held office. Grounds for inclusion in the latter group have inevitably been subjective and open to challenge. In a party with a strong tradition of collective leadership it would be impossible to include everyone who has been significant. Our choice of others reflects those who may not even be recognised as formal SNP leaders, nor held the highest office, but have been key to the party's evolution – in terms of how it perceives itself and how it is viewed by the public.

Robert Bontine Cunninghame Graham, for example, deserves a chapter even though he was largely a figurehead. He was eighty-one when he became SNP president at its foundation, representing an important radical strand that has run throughout the party's existence. He was a colourful figure, still speaking at rallies in the last few years of his life. John MacCormick's role in the foundation of the SNP is generally exaggerated in most accounts of the party's foundation largely because so many were based on MacCormick's own account published in 1955. There can be no disputing his importance, however, and throughout his life he struggled with the relationship between the SNP and the wider national movement.

No book on SNP leaders could omit Winnie Ewing, though she never held any major office other than the figurehead position of party president. Winning the 1967 Hamilton by-election, defeating the Secretary of State for Scotland Gordon Campbell in February 1974, becoming the first SNP Member of the European Parliament and entering the first Scottish Parliament in 1999 as its oldest Member, more than earn her a place. As mentioned, Margo MacDonald is included, though she too was never a party chairman, but served as senior vice-chairman (1974–79) at a critical period for the SNP in which she was probably better known than any other party member and was the key strategist in determining attitudes towards devolution. Her relationship with the party was always difficult, but her absence from this book would have been as odd as Winnie Ewing's, though neither were ever comfortable in the other's company, politically or otherwise. Both also went a long way to challenge the male-dominated nature of Scottish politics, attracting much interest by being women and often being subjected to sexist, derogatory and patronising commentary. Scotland has travelled a long way since then, and the public roles of Winnie Ewing and Margo MacDonald played a small part in changing this, although clearly there is still much more progress to be made.

Along with Winnie Ewing and Margo MacDonald, Jim Sillars is forever associated with winning a historic by-election for the nationalists which shook Scottish (and also British) politics. This alone might not warrant him inclusion in the book, with his formal contribution to leadership being a brief period as senior vice-convener (deputy leader) from 1991 to 1992, followed by over twenty years as a fairly semi-detached member of the SNP. But he warrants inclusion for how his contribution changed not only the SNP, but how voters saw the party, and highlights the complex relationship between the SNP as a party and the wider nationalist movement, as well as the key dynamic and tension between the nationalist and labour movements.

LEADERSHIP AND THE 'NATURE OF THE TIMES'

There are no shortages of writings about leadership. Memoirs by or observers of leaders in politics and business offer advice aplenty. Much, though not all, of this work fails to take account of changing contexts. This was well understood by Machiavelli writing in the sixteenth century. In the penultimate chapter, 'Fortune', of his most famous work, Machiavelli noted that a prince may be successful one day but ruined the next 'without appearing to have changed in character or any other way'.[14] Successful leadership may be achieved in different ways at different times. Sometimes it may call forth a leader who acts 'with circumspection, another impetuously; one uses violence, another stratagem; one man goes about things patiently, another does the opposite; and yet everyone, for all this diversity of method, can reach his objective'.[15] This, he maintained, arose from 'nothing except the extent to which their methods are or are not suited to the nature of the times'.[16]

Political leadership must take account of the different phases in a party's development. The foundation of a political party requires very different leadership skills from a period when it aspires to and holds national office. Party leaders operate in a different arena. The relationship between the leader and party membership is different from that between leader and the wider public. Political parties that hope to do well electorally must take account of societal changes. Leadership demands during significant disruption are very different from periods of relative calm. Leaders may contribute to ideological or policy development, to party management and internal reforms, to electoral appeal and to relations with other bodies, especially within the broader movement of which the party is a part. No leader can hope to perform all of these roles equally well.

This becomes evident in reviewing the history of leadership in any

---

14   Niccolò Machiavelli, *The Prince* (Harmondsworth: Penguin Classics edition, 1975), p. 131.

15   Ibid.

16   Ibid.

organisation, including a political party. There is no single skill set or con-firmed list of characteristics for successful leadership. The 'nature of the times' matters. If we could transplant Alex Salmond (leader from 1990 to 2000 and 2004 to 2014), arguably the SNP's most successful leader to date, into the party in the early 1950s it is quite possible he might not have been the right leader for the party then – when it came as close as any time to fold-ing. Equally, either Robert McIntyre (1947–56) or James Halliday (1956–60) might have been the party's most successful leader had each had the oppor-tunity to lead it at a more opportune moment. The context needs to be taken into account when understanding the challenges faced, and goals and expec-tations and qualities required. The opportunities available to the SNP and its leaders have changed, most notably with the establishment of a Scottish Parliament. For the first three decades of its existence, the main goal was keep-ing the flame alive. The prospect of electoral success was remote, and while those engaged in politics on the fringe might have been motivated by ideal-ism, it must have been dispiriting to campaign for survival and that would have required particular strengths.

We include a chapter on Bruce Watson (1945–47) – unusual in that the author is his son, who gives a unique insight into growing up in a political household during a volatile and challenging time. Bruce Watson warned the small 1946 annual SNP conference that there were no shortcuts. He maintained that try-ing to win a Scottish Parliament through the established British parties was a series of 'wasteful, exhausting, maddening processions of deputations, prayers, appeals, protests, agitations, and so on, followed inevitably by a series of prom-ises, assurances, safeguards, and sometimes cynical rebuffs, with frustration, futility, and miserable compromise at the very most'. It would be a long hard road.[17] He did not live to see the opening of the Scottish Parliament in 1999 but, as recounted in the chapter, his widow and son were present.

The nature of the times may have been against an electoral breakthrough but, as Machiavelli noted, even when a violent river floods the plain, tears

---

17   Mitchell, *Strategies for Self-Government*, p. 195.

down trees and buildings, washes soil from one place and deposits it else-where, it does not mean that precautions could not have been taken, dykes and embankments constructed when waters were flowing quietly. These preparatory tasks can be thankless, appear unproductive and provoke criti-cism, but are a measure of leadership. The electorally successful party that the SNP has become was built on foundations and leadership that is little appreciated, or even known, to most of its supporters.

TRAITS AND CHARACTERISTICS OF LEADERS

In his classic account of political leadership, Fred Greenstein – after stud-ying the US Presidency from Franklin D. Roosevelt to Barack Obama – identified six qualities required in successful leaders: to be a public com-municator; have organisational capacity; political skill; vision; cognitive style; and emotional intelligence. We might measure each of the leaders discussed here in these terms and all would be found wanting in respect of some, but each showed at least one of these traits.[18]

In the previous volumes in this Leaders series on the Tory, Labour and Lib-eral parties, the concept of statecraft was used to assess the leadership qualities and successes or not of each party's leading personnel. The definition of state-craft used has five criteria: winning electoral strategy, governing competence, party management, political argument and hegemony, and, finally, the ability to bend the rules of the game.[19] These factors were less applicable to the SNP for a large part of their history and so cannot be used as a gauge across its entire existence. However, since the SNP became a serious electoral force and then a party of government, the notion of statecraft has become more relevant.

Turning to Greenstein's criteria first, the demands of public communication

---

18   Fred Greenstein, *The Presidential Difference: Leadership Style from FDR to Barack Obama* (Princeton, NJ: Princeton University Press, 2009, 3rd edition).

19   See Jim Buller, *National Statecraft and European Integration: The Conservative Government and Euro-pean Union, 1979–1997* (London: Bloomsbury, 2000); Jim Buller and Toby S. James, 'Statecraft and the Assessment of National Political Leaders: The Case of New Labour and Tony Blair', *The British Journal of Politics and International Relations*, 14/4, (2012): 534–55.

have changed over the party's history. Radio was relatively new when the party was founded and while some of its leaders had access to this new medium they engaged with it not because of their status as leaders of a new party but because many were significant public figures in their own right – some even now might be termed celebrities. The main means of communication at that time however was the written word and the party's leadership included many talented wordsmiths. The SNP might have been a fringe party but its leadership was well represented among Scotland's writers, poets and journalists. Some could command attention on public platforms in the days when public meetings were well attended, and effective oratory could inspire and mobilise support. John MacCormick (founding secretary of the SNP) was a powerful public speaker, as was R. B. Cunninghame Graham (founding president of the SNP), while Arthur Donaldson (1960–69) and Jim Sillars (deputy SNP leader 1991–92) were among the best public speakers of later generations of party leaders. Many were pamphleteers, while others wrote articles and books making the case for Scottish self-government. Sir Alexander MacEwen (the SNP's first chairman) wrote books making the case for home rule and William Power (1940–42), founder of PEN in Scotland, contributed numerous writings making the case for the cause. As the broadcast media grew in importance, leadership focused as much on campaigning for access to the new media as well as actually broadcasting. Gordon Wilson (1979–90) was involved in Radio Free Scotland, a pirate radio station launched in 1956 four years after the first BBC Scotland television broadcast, and he and other SNP leaders spent much time and energy arguing for access to television and radio.[20]

Organisational concerns were a heavy responsibility of SNP leaders given the absence of resources available to the party until devolution. In some cases, this could be delegated to others and at least for much of its history the party was so small that organisation was not so burdensome. James Halliday (1956–60) included a picture of all those attending the party's 1956

---

20   Gordon Wilson, *Pirates of the Air: The Story of Radio Free Scotland* (Stirling: Scots Independent, 2011).

annual conference on the cover of his memoirs.[21] This portrayed a handful of delegates, far fewer than the picture on the back cover showing the group of SNP MPs elected to Holyrood prior to the publication of these memoirs. Managing that number should have been relatively easy, though the size of a party tells us little about its fissiparous tendencies. One leading wit in the national movement offered the view that he regretted compromising the unity of his party by admitting a second member. Two key leaders stand out in the SNP's history for their role in the party's organisation. Gordon Wilson's key internal role came before he became party leader, but his ideas, as set out in the early 1960s, would influence the development of the party over the period to and beyond his own period as SNP convener. The other was John Swinney (2000–2004), who may be viewed as a failure as party leader by many within and outside the SNP, but reforms he made to the constitution and organisation proved important for his successors. These transformed the SNP from an amateur–activist party into a professional organisation[22] and Swinney's interest in organisational matters has continued to be evident in his ministerial career.

A politically skilful leader can achieve goals despite limited resources and contextual challenges. Retrospective judgments are easily made and political skills, therefore, are often more recognised in hindsight after goals have been achieved. Leaving a party in a healthier state than when first becoming its leader may be a key measure, though this may not account for changing context beyond the control of the leader or party – especially as SNP leaders have often held office for long periods.

Greenstein linked political skill to vision. In common with all parties, the SNP has had a broad idea of its objective but has often disagreed on the routes to achieving it as well on what its supporters saw as subsidiary goals. It is commonly assumed today that the SNP is a party of independence but rarely appreciated that this goal was only very recently formally

21   James Halliday, *Yours for Scotland: A Memoir* (Stirling: Scots Independent, 2011).

22   Mitchell, Johns and Bennie, *The Scottish National Party*.

TABLE 1.1: SNP CHAIR/CONVENER/LEADER

SNP Chair/Convener/Leader	Years
Sir Alexander MacEwen	1934–36
Andrew Dewar Gibb	1936–40
William Power	1940–42
Douglas Young	1942–45
Bruce Watson	1945–47
Robert McIntyre	1947–56
James Halliday	1956–60
Arthur Donaldson	1960–69
Billy Wolfe	1969–79
Gordon Wilson	1979–90
Alex Salmond	1990–2000
John Swinney	2000–2004
Alex Salmond	2004–14
Nicola Sturgeon	2014–

written into the SNP's constitution. It is more widely understood that the meaning of independence has changed over time. The first time flesh was put on the constitutional bones of independence was when the SNP government produced its independence white paper in November 2013. Until then, independence was more a mobilising idea than a fully worked out constitutional option. At its establishment right through to 2004, the SNP's formal objective was self-government, a term that had allowed for various interpretations. It could mean a Scottish Parliament within the United Kingdom – some of the many variants of home rule – through to a Scottish Parliament as part of the British Empire, or independence within the European Union but outside the UK. There were contemporary examples on which to draw and the party leadership considered them but mostly preferred to maintain unity by treating its objective as a means of drawing support from as wide a field as possible. Given that the goal was a distant prospect there was little to gain from detailed definition and much to lose if it provoked internal dissent.

For most of its history, SNP leaders interpreted the party's role as an existential campaign. It may be difficult to imagine today but for much of the twentieth century there was a fear that Scottish identity and culture were threatened by encroachments that came with changes in the state, society and the economy. This was not just the view of a paranoid few but a dominant theme among many twentieth-century scholars who saw sub-state identities, such as Scottish identity, as antediluvian throwbacks, backward and standing in the way of 'progress'. A Scottish Parliament was the response of those who saw centralisation, integration and acculturation as threats to the very existence of Scotland. Hence, the form that the Scottish Parliament should take was secondary for those who saw the need for some institutional expression of Scottishness as primary. It was little surprise in the century that saw the rise of both the state and democracy that nationalists should alight upon Scottish self-government.

SNP leaders have rarely engaged with the meaning of self-government or independence, preferring instead to maintain unity around an objective that was sufficiently powerful to mobilise members while imprecise enough to contain a range of views. Leadership in the SNP, therefore, has required evading the precise definition of its objectives. It has not required clarity of definition, as it has been an objective that has rarely appeared in immediate sight. The party's leaders have had to play the same two-level game that leaders of all membership parties play: keeping the faithful content by articulating a position that appeals to hardliners while simultaneously winning electoral support from a more sceptical public.

The vision was on the horizon, visible but still some distance away. But the party soon discovered that standing on a platform at elections required it to outline its position on the key issues of the day. In Scotland's dominant two-party system – between Labour and the Scottish Unionist Party (sister party of the Conservatives) – the SNP found itself much like the Liberals through most of the twentieth century, seeking to find a position that distinguished itself from the two main parties while confronting the issues that the two-party system threw up. It was not for the lack of trying to outline a series of policy positions, a contribution notably engaged in by Robert McIntyre

(1947–56), but how to present these in a manner that would capture the public's imagination. There was less disagreement on policy than there was on how it should be packaged. Billy Wolfe (1969–79) was keen to describe the party's programme as social democratic. Many of its leaders were more in the traditional vein of radical liberalism (Sir Alexander MacEwen being a notable example) while some were clearly more on the right. Andrew Dewar Gibb had been a Unionist candidate before joining the SNP and his views were very much at odds with Cunninghame Graham on a range of matters. The latter was the first MP of any party to describe himself – when a Liberal – as a socialist in the House of Commons many years before the SNP was set up.[23] James Halliday was emphatically a man of the left though his Atlanticist outlook and fondness for the USA meant that he was often portrayed by internal critics as being on the right.

Greenstein referred to the way in which leaders process the 'Niagara of advice and information'[24] that comes their way. In the case of most SNP leaders this has meant processing political information while in full-time employment outside politics. Robert McIntyre was an eminent surgeon as well as party leader. Dewar Gibb held the Regius chair in law at Glasgow University. Bruce Watson held a chair in Chemistry. James Halliday was a young school teacher when he became leader. When the party made its breakthrough in the 1970s, Billy Wolfe was trying to run a business in difficult economic times while being party leader. It was not until Gordon Wilson took the job in 1979 that an SNP leader could devote themselves full-time to politics, but he was an MP and spent much of his time in London – far from the party's headquarters and membership and the electoral terrain on which the party fought.

Some leaders are better at dealing with the avalanche of conflicting advice and papers, and sifting through and identifying what is important and valuable. Others simply become overwhelmed. Leadership requires an ability to

---

23   Chris Bryant, *Parliament: The Biography* (*Vol. II – Reform*) (London: Transworld Publishers, 2014), p. 199.

24   Fred Greenstein, '"The Qualities of Effective Presidents": An Overview from FDR to Bill Clinton', *Presidential Studies Quarterly*, 30/1 (2000), p. 180.

set priorities and not simply become responsive to events. That is not always easy as 'events, dear boy, events' (in Harold Macmillan's memorable phrase) often have a habit of undermining strategies and plans. It is very difficult for the leader of any small fringe party to set external agendas, with the only real influence being over internal purposes: so it proved with the SNP over the first half of its existence. Making an impact, challenging other parties and setting the political agenda requires daring and imagination by small parties and their leaders. Alex Salmond became a master of the art of attention-grabbing, much to the annoyance of his opponents. In public office, the issue often becomes one of choosing and prioritising areas of activity on which a leader will focus. Micro-managers rarely make good leaders but the temptation to get lost in the detail can be great and is sometimes unavoidable.

The final characteristic identified by Greenstein is 'emotional intelligence' – the ability to manage emotions and turn them into an advantage – reaching out to those whose support, whether in the immediate circle or the much wider electorate, is required. The inner circle needs to be inspired. Some leaders are more like the lone wolf, perhaps because often these very public people are in fact quite shy and reserved, preferring to maintain a distance from those with whom they work most closely. Others favour, even need, a team of close confidantes with whom they privately share ideas and consider options. The challenge for strong leaders is that they may listen too intently to a very small core group who may be unrepresentative, or owe their inner status to the leader. There is a tendency among the inner core or other followers to bring the leader only news that will please and avoid inconvenient facts and messages.

The above examination of Greenstein's five principles covers much of the same ground as the concept of statecraft. However, statecraft carries with it a sense of the art and diplomacy of government, along with the notion of politics as theatre and drama, with much of the action being undertaken on a public stage by its leading protagonists. Any assessment of the five criteria of statecraft used in the companion volumes in this series – electoral strategy, governing competence, party management, political argument, and ability to bend the rules of the game – would have to mark clear distinctions over different periods of the SNP.

In summary, the SNP for the first forty years of its existence, 1934–74, was a small electoral force, who occasionally made an impact in a by-election or single contest, but until 1974 had only won a single parliamentary seat at a Westminster general election: Western Isles in 1970. Post-1974, the SNP has increasingly become a serious electoral force, with that year's two UK general elections something of a watershed, introducing multi-party politics to Scotland, and the SNP to British politics as more than a transient force. There were many ups and downs in the party's fortunes in the decades since (the 1979 *annus horribilis*, 1983), but it was always a permanent feature of Scottish and Westminster politics, and organised and competed on those terms. Moreover, after the 1974 breakthrough, retreats and lean period of much of the 1980s, came the second and third watersheds, which even more fully transformed the party; the first of which the establishment of the Scottish Parliament in 1999, where the SNP became the main opposition to Labour, with more parliamentarians than in all the party's history added together; while the second was the 2007 election and achievement of an SNP government, which lay the groundwork for the 2011 landslide, 2014 independence referendum, and subsequent commanding position.

The SNP's culture of leadership has unsurprisingly altered dramatically as the fortunes of the party have; and while the pre-1974 party leaders were often significantly focused on internal matters such as party management and organisation – and even at points such as the 1950s, sheer survival – this has altered subsequently, first, from 1974 onwards, and increasingly from 1999. The SNP has in this latter period professionalised to the extent that it was able to position itself as the main challenger to Labour and then defeat and replace it as the party of government. It reveals much about the evolution of the party that some of the leading figures of the party who became active in the 1970s and 1980s have adapted so fully to the new environment. That has been aided by the fact that Alex Salmond and others – including John Swinney and Nicola Sturgeon – were orchestrators of this transformation in the party's fortunes and its position in Scotland. A new kind of SNP leadership has been required for a politics based around the Scottish Parliament, where the party is in power, and then has become the dominant party of the country. There have been birth pains and difficulties in such a transition with internal challenges, all of which are detailed in this book, but the bigger picture has been the ease of change given its scale.

One indication of many which could be given has been the tone and content of Nicola Sturgeon in the weeks after the 2016 European Union referendum – where the UK as a whole voted for withdrawal yet Scotland voted for Remain. This has proven a hazardous climate for much of the Westminster political leadership, leading to the resignation of David Cameron as Prime Minister and Theresa May swiftly elected by Tory MPs as his successor, but Sturgeon with what seemed consummate ease positioned and spoke not as a party leader, or the spokesperson of the 62 per cent Remain vote, but as a national leader, aspiring to speak above party interest. SNP leaders, in the recent past and certainly again in the future, will resort as all politicians do to being transparently partisan leaders, but such leadership attributes would have been unimaginable even a decade ago. Such is the scale of change which occurred in the nationalist position in Scotland and the kind of leadership it has embodied.

THE CONTEXT OF LEADERSHIP

This wider terrain of leadership is a critical arena for understanding the modern SNP and Scottish politics. Pre-devolution, the SNP operated at a significant disadvantage to the main Westminster-focused parties. The SNP were by their nature across this period bit players at Westminster, who were often treated post-1974 equally in terms of how Scottish politics was covered, but then ignored when the attention moved to the bigger canvas of British politics. This structural disadvantage was further reinforced by the nature of Labour's dominance of Scottish politics. Labour engaged in a two-front strategy: of selling the benefits of the United Kingdom (and with it Westminster largesse) to Scottish audiences, while informing British elites of the need to give Scotland preferential treatment.[25] This approach was one of acute bridge-building, reinforcing a Scottish–British, unionist–nationalist politics that outmanoeuvred its opponents, and in particular the SNP, as it could not compete on the same dual strategy. However, devolution altered this picture to the SNP's benefit. The Labour approach became increasingly a liability as the party's ability to stand up for Scottish interests was increasingly questioned and it became more and more perceived as 'London Labour' – all of which made the bridge-building strategy less plausible. The SNP's status as a Scottish-only party became a virtue, rather than a negative, as the party articulated itself as the voice of Scottish interests in the plural, but also the collective Scottish interest. This has left the nationalists commanding both the centre-left and middle ground of politics and, hence, in the powerful place it is today.

One part of the SNP's public profile and its leadership that has attracted little study has been the party's relationship with the public sphere of the nation.[26] This is an increasingly critical arena of political mobilisation, communication and dissemination of ideas and exchange, and one that is more problematic in Scotland than elsewhere in the developed world. One obvious characteristic is that the Scottish public sphere sits in a semi-autonomous political space, intersected by the discourses and dynamics of the British media, politics and public life.[27] Some of these areas in Scotland have been the subject of debate and controversy, from the decline of the mainstream print press to issues around broadcast media and coverage of politics, particularly, but not exclusively focusing on the BBC. Yet, such concerns sit in a wider landscape informed by the contours of the public sphere: its semi-autonomy, the nature of civil society, the relative absence of bodies such as think tanks, and the influence of a UK, London-based public sphere.

25   Gerry Hassan and Eric Shaw, *The Strange Death of Labour Scotland* (Edinburgh: Edinburgh University Press, 2012), Chapter 17.

26   The definitive study of the public sphere is Jurgen Habermas, *The Structural Transformation of the Public Sphere* (Cambridge: Polity, 1989).

27   Gerry Hassan, *Independence of the Scottish Mind: Elite Narratives, Public Spaces and the Making of a Modern Nation* (London: Macmillan, 2014), Chapter 4.

A detailed set of observations is beyond the remit of this study, but suffice to say these dynamics have had a significant effect on how the SNP has gone about its politics, and the style and approach of its leadership.

CONCLUSION

The extent to which luck plays its part in politics is often overlooked. Machiavelli thought that it was equally important as leadership in determining the course of events. Often enough what may retrospectively be claimed to have been good leadership has simply been good luck, and we only call it sound leadership because success has followed. The real test of a leader is whether they are able to make the best of whatever the circumstances happen to be. Equally important is noting when power is beginning to drain away and at what point the countdown to the end days of a political leader begins: something which became obvious in the UK premierships of Margaret Thatcher and Tony Blair. Jonathan Powell, assessing modern leadership through the gaze of Machiavelli's *The Prince*, sensed 'the beginning of the end' of the Blair premiership as early as 2002, but that others, including Blair, were much less sure and convinced.[28] Most leaders do not get to choose the time of their own departure, but so far, the SNP has managed two Salmond departures (as well as one return), along with the succession from Salmond to Sturgeon with a smoothness beyond the ability of older, Westminster-based parties.

It is easy to fault leaders, easy to identify mistakes, but we must not ignore the importance of simply making a decision in the first place. Difficult decisions involved in leadership invariably involve some degree of chance – otherwise the decision would not be difficult. Being willing to take a chance – and make a choice – must ultimately be a key measure of leadership. Those who put themselves forward for leadership roles in any context

---

28   Jonathan Powell, *The New Machiavelli: How to Wield Power in the Modern World* (London: Bodley Head, 2010), p. 296.

are by definition making difficult decisions, inviting criticism and opposition. The SNP's leaders included in this book have navigated the party through the most varied political fortunes it is possible to imagine, from near-irrelevance to its current impressive state. That makes any overall assessment between, say, the leaders of the 1950s and today virtually impossible, as present SNP leaders operate in a more favourable environment. Therefore, any analysis should 'reward' those leaders who have made some impact in much more difficult circumstances, while putting more in context those who did less well when they had the wind at their back.

The vast body of people involved in politics refuse, or fail, to show the basic leadership qualities of making decisions and putting themselves on the line day in, day out. All of those discussed in this book have made this call, have contributed richly to the public life of Scotland and the character of the SNP, and have therefore set themselves apart from most of us.

CHAPTER 2

LEADERSHIP IN PERSPECTIVE

MIKE RUSSELL

Billy Wolfe, the leader of the SNP from June 1969 to September 1979, used to categorise those in leadership positions in the SNP as being either 'leaders of power' or 'leaders of influence'.

That categorisation was of particular importance to him as he grew older. He had been a significant 'leader of power' within the SNP, repeatedly elected by delegates of an increasing membership to take the party in a clear political direction and away from see-saw disputes about alignment with either left or right.[1]

However, after his unwise remarks about the papal visit in 1982, his star in the party, already on the wane, plummeted and he spent a period of time in semi-exile, neither consulted nor included in the party debates of the time.

The memory of Billy's presence, though, remained strong. He had been the mentor of the young Alex Salmond in West Lothian and when Salmond became SNP leader (or National Convener as it was called) in 1990, Billy resumed a leadership of influence among the young Turks who surrounded Salmond – the so-called Salmondistas. His unfinished business of taking the party into the mainstream of left-of-centre politics in Scotland was completed by Salmond and that group, a move that eventually led to government after a period of political and administrative learning during the first decade of the devolved Parliament's existence.

Wolfe's formulation can be applied to all the figures in this book, but they

---

1   'Billy Wolfe: Politician who played a crucial role in the transformation of the Scottish National Party', obituary, *The Independent*, 20 March 2010 [http://www.independent.co.uk/news/obituaries/billy-wolfe-politician-who-played-a-crucial-role-in-the-transformation-of-the-scottish-national-1924380.html]

cannot be as clearly defined by it as he would have thought. For example, Wolfe himself was both but he also demonstrated a range of other leadership traits.

French and Raven's five bases of power originally described in 1959 – legitimate, reward, expert, referent and coercive – and added to with a sixth (informational) five years later, give a better exposition of the positional and personal nature of political leadership.[2]

In those definitions it is possible to see Wolfe's contribution more clearly. He had legitimacy, demonstrated expertise and was clearly referent in that he had an engaging personality worthy of respect. However, it was not in his character to reward for compliance nor to be coercive or withhold vital information.

Max Weber's earlier analysis of political legitimacy,[3] applied to Wolfe, would lead to a similar conclusion. Wolfe had legal and charismatic but not traditional authority.

The SNP has spent very little time thinking and writing about itself and still less analysing its leaders and their background, influence and motivations, though it has been subject to an increasing degree of academic analysis. This book is therefore a welcome contribution to the overall literature on the SNP and, given the present standing of the party and the international interest it is currently receiving, the book is also timely.

My own collaboration with Winnie Ewing[4] was one of the first serious attempts to tell the story of a key individual in the party from within the party but also counterpointed with the growth and change of the party and Scottish, UK and European politics.

Although Andrew Dewar Gibb, William Power and others in the pioneering phase of party leadership set down their political views (sometimes at considerable length), in more recent times there has been a dearth of literature emerging on leading party figures.

---

2   J. R. P. French Jr and B. H. Raven, 'The Bases of Social Power', in D. Cartright (ed.), *Studies in Social Power* (Ann Arbor, MI: Institute for Social Research, 1959).

3   Max Weber, 'Politics as a Vocation' (1919), in Gerth and Mills (eds), *From Max Weber: Essays in Sociology* (New York: Oxford University Press, 1958).

4   Winifred Ewing (ed. Michael Russell), *Stop the World: The Autobiography of Winnie Ewing* (Edinburgh: Birlinn Ltd, 2004).

Works by Donald Stewart (an incomplete autobiography finished by his sister)[5] and Dick Douglas (a sketchy biography of Dr Robert McIntyre)[6] were slight and anecdotal, while Wolfe's own political memoir[7] was published too early to take account of the sea change brought about by the two elections of 1974, which propelled the party into the centre of Scottish, and at times British, politics. Jim Sillars's account of his own journey to support the nationalist position[8] is a stronger contribution but inevitably focused very much on himself and on his voyage away from Labour, while Alex Salmond's recent bestselling memoir of the referendum,[9] while informative and entertaining, does not seek to analyse the event in the context of the party, its growth and the political climate of the times.

This book therefore breaks new ground and presents to a wider public a range of figures in the SNP who have shaped the party into what is now the dominant force in Scottish politics, whose agenda has defined recent history in Scotland and, on occasion, in the UK.

Of course, the leadership of the party, up at least until the SNP's entry into the Scottish government in 2007, was in the greatest part unknown outside the country and there are many figures in this book whose names will still only be recognised by very few, and most of them academics specialising in Scottish affairs. The vast majority of party members – of whom there are now more than 110,000 – are unlikely ever to have heard of Douglas Young or even Jimmy Halliday, let alone William Power or Sir Alexander MacEwen. Yet, they created a movement that, over the course of eighty years, became a party that became a government and which still aspires to create a new nation.

---

5   Donald Stewart, *A Scot at Westminster* (Sydney, Canada: The Catalone Press, 1994).

6   Dick Douglas, *At the Helm: The Life & Times of Dr Robert D. McIntyre* (Portessie, Buckie: NPFI Publications, 1996)

7   William Wolfe, *Scotland Lives: The Quest for Independence* (Edinburgh: Reprographia, 1973).

8   Jim Sillars, *Scotland: The Case for Optimism* (Edinburgh: Polygon, 1986).

9   Alex Salmond, *The Dream Shall Never Die: 100 Days that Changed Scotland Forever* (London: William Collins, 2015).

In this introduction I want to consider five aspects of SNP leadership, which, taken in summation, may not only give some understanding of the progress that has been made and the role of leaders in helping to make it, but may also suggest where the next generation of SNP leaders may come from and what their task might be.

LEADERSHIP OF WHOM?

The first issue to consider is who the party actually consists of, in terms of both numbers and types of individuals.

There is a wonderful image, much-shared on Twitter during the membership surge after the 2014 referendum, of an SNP annual conference, most probably the one held in Bridge of Allan in June 1956.

A small group of individuals face the camera, standing on the steps of a hotel. They are mostly in their twenties and thirties and they could be mistaken for a church or literary group. They have an air of both enthusiasm and expectation. They look like people with a mission but who are also capable of enjoying themselves.

Membership of a political party at that time was not as unusual as it is today. Although claims that party membership throughout the UK peaked at over 3 million in the early 1950s are now thought to be exaggerated, it is true that membership – like engagement with politics – was much higher at that time. It has been in decline since then at least until the 1997 UK general election, when Labour experienced a considerable rise in membership (placing it ahead of the Conservatives for the first time since the Second World War), and then again in Scotland after the independence referendum in 2014.

In addition, there is also some international evidence that membership of political parties in the UK was and is lower than in other countries.

Parties are not compelled to publish their membership data and there is no consistent method of defining membership, but figures from accounts filed with the electoral commission and press reports suggest that total membership of the main parties in the UK (defined as Conservative, Labour, Liberal,

SNP, Green and UKIP) as of 2015 was around 700,000. The Scottish total approached 150,000, of which 105,000 were members of the SNP. Those figures imply a higher percentage of political party membership within the Scottish population than in the UK at large.[10]

In the 1970s, when the SNP experienced its first significant national electoral success, it was said within the party that no seat could be won without a membership of 1,000 or more, and that anecdotal view is significant because it suggests that the reality of constituency membership was very much less than this. In addition, as the SNP only took eleven seats in October 1974, if this rough guideline is true the total membership at that time must have been somewhat and possibly well below later estimates of 50,000 or more.

That assumption may also be buttressed by the fact that the SNP did not stand parliamentary candidates in every Scottish seat until the 1970s. As the branch structure of the party is based upon electoral boundaries, it can be inferred that the membership of the party was not capable of and could not afford such challenges until that time and effort was therefore concentrated mostly in those areas where electoral activity had been longest lasting and the membership highest – for example in West Lothian, Dundee and parts of Glasgow.

The total membership at the time that photograph was taken in Bridge of Allan must have been very much lower even than in the 1970s. Size is not all but accordingly for the first forty years of its existence the SNP membership was a small – a very small – political party and on the fringes of mainstream political activity.

Membership dipped again in the 1980s as the party languished on the polls and in electoral contests. By-election success at Govan and the emergence of a new leader in Alex Salmond, who had popular appeal and dynamism compared to his lacklustre predecessor and who aimed to recruit from Labour constituencies in particular, resulted in some modest growth, though Salmond never fully embraced the need for targeted membership drives nor the need for reform of structures in order to encourage membership participation.

---

10   Richard Keen, House of Commons Library Briefing Paper No. SN05125, 11 August 2015.

In my period as the SNP's first full-time chief executive from 1994 to 1999, membership therefore rose only slowly, from a low of around 8,000 to something over 10,000 by the time of the elections to the first Scottish parliament.

That number continued to rise thereafter – for example, Mitchell records it as being 13,203 at the time of his membership survey in 2007[11] – until it reached around 25,000 at the time of the independence referendum in September 2014 (boosted by electoral success in 2007 and 2011), but in the weeks following the referendum it increased very rapidly, reaching 85,000 by the end of 2014 and 100,000 by March 2015.

Membership of a political party is always subject to attrition for political and administrative reasons. Individuals can become alienated from parties for very particular and narrow reasons and resigning membership is often the only protest they can make. In addition, party mechanisms – particularly in parties that have grown very quickly – may not be accurate enough to contact every person whose annual membership is due for renewal and that will have been particularly true of the SNP, which maintains a branch membership structure even if it is now partly administered from party HQ.

It is therefore likely that membership declined during 2015 but increased again in the immediate aftermath of the EU referendum in June 2016. Estimated membership at that time was around 115,000, which is probably the highest total the party has ever had.

Prior to that time, building membership – and by so doing building the prospect of electoral success as a result of having more activists on the ground – was only spasmodically a priority for the leadership of the party and even when it was, specific and effective actions to achieve that aim were often lacking.

Many of the individuals examined in this book did attempt to build membership when they led the party and with it political credibility. Some of those

---

11   James Mitchell, 'Who are the SNP Members?', paper delivered at the Elections, Public Opinion and Parties Conference, Manchester, November 2008.

were figures of substance and achievement in other fields and sometimes even in politics – the Duke of Montrose, Sir Alexander MacEwen (who had been provost of Inverness), Robert Cunninghame Graham and of course Hugh MacDiarmid as founder members, to mention only a few.

Yet, these individuals were far from representative of Scotland as a whole at that time, being – as the party itself was – largely professional, university-educated, interested in literature and culture and, although from across the traditional spectrum, often at the extremes of it.

Perhaps that was why the leadership itself on occasions espoused positions that made its own progress and the attraction of support and new members even more difficult – Douglas Young, for example, in opposing conscription and Dewar Gibb in flirting with fascism – though that tendency to put foot in mouth at crucial moments continued into the modern era, as Billy Wolfe's remarks about the papal visit in 1992[12] and even Alex Salmond's about the NATO bombing of Serbia during the 1999 Scottish election campaign demonstrate, no matter how right Salmond's position now seems in hindsight. Resignations from membership and political setbacks followed any and all such incidents.

Many early and long-lasting members of the party were motivated as much by cultural considerations as by political ones. The description of SNP members as being 'monomaniacs and poets' came from an early commentator and right up until recent years it was not uncommon for the front row of an SNP conference to be occupied by several kilt-wearing old men, or one or two matronly women in tartan skirts. A certain eccentricity of manner hung about them, which was often re-enforced if they managed to get to the rostrum to speak. I remember one annual conference at which I watched, horror-struck, as one of those women denounced 'white settlers' in a Margaret Rutherford accent on the monitor in the press room. This was someone who had been a Westminster parliamentary candidate in my own party lifetime.

---

12   http://davidtorrance.com/letters-reveal-snp-crisi-over-bigoted-presidents-anti-catholic-diatribes-from-the-times-11-9-2010/

Of course, membership of any party does require a level of commitment well above that of the average voter, so party members who make it to conference as delegates from branches (the SNP maintains a delegate system for participation in all party structures above branch level, which is the basic building block of party democracy and decision-making) are likely to be particularly interested in politics, have particularly intense views and be particularly keen to make themselves heard. They may not be entirely representative of the membership itself.

Indeed, a detailed survey of the party membership by Mitchell, Johns and Bennie, undertaken in 2007 and which included not only a questionnaire to all members (which had a 50 per cent response rate) but also in-depth interviews with key party figures, found that

> the most noticeable feature of the results so far is precisely the lack of striking findings. The profile of SNP members in terms of age, social class, education and religion is not markedly dissimilar to the Scottish population, and quite similar to most other parties based on previous membership studies.[13]

Further study by the same authors of the membership of the SNP is now underway and given the remarkable rise in membership it will be interesting to see what conclusions they draw. It may be that the new members come, disproportionately, from sectors unrepresented in party membership before the referendum. It is likely that the gender imbalance within the party membership (a feature of all political parties before the referendum) is in the process of being corrected, too. Indeed, the party itself has sought to address this through a variety of mechanisms put in place for the selection of candidates and also through the leadership example of Nicola Sturgeon, whose first actions included selecting a gender-balanced Cabinet.

However, the conclusion we may be entitled to draw for the purposes of

---

13   Mitchell, Johns and Bennie, 'Who are the SNP Members?', in Hassan, *The Modern SNP.*

understanding the leadership of the SNP is that, firstly, membership was very much lower for almost the entire history of the party than it is now and up until the first significant electoral successes of the party in the 1970s; secondly, that the party's membership level confirmed the fringe status of the SNP during that time; and thirdly, the nature of the membership was much less typical of Scotland as a whole until that time.

LEADERSHIP TO WHERE?

The second issue to consider with regard to leadership in the SNP is the *purpose* of the party. Where exactly were leaders to lead members? The current assumption that the purpose of the SNP has always been to achieve independence – that is, a fully sovereign state – is open to question. Indeed, it was at least in part a confusion about what exactly the SNP wished to achieve – and the means by which political progress would be made towards whatever that goal was – that held back progress not just in the early years but in the 1970s and beyond. Only with the advent of a devolved Scottish Parliament did both a goal and a route become clear and achievable.

The founding members of the party came together in an uneasy alliance in 1934 for pragmatic reasons rather than those of political policy. John Mac-Cormick's desire for unity in the movement for what was then seen as 'home rule' or 'dominion status' for Scotland, as opposed to the then vaguer concept of independence, remained a key element in the party for the next decade and, in another guise, right up until 1997, when the SNP resolved to contest the elections for the first Scottish parliament.

Goals in politics are one thing; means of achieving them are another. The gradualist/fundamentalist divide in the SNP that was of great importance in the 1980s after the failed devolution process of the 1970s was in essence the same issue as this home rule debate, which eventually split the SNP in the 1940s when MacCormick left to found the Scottish Covenant Association.

Alongside these issues were others which also impeded the progress of the SNP as voters rarely favour parties that appear disunited or unable to agree on objectives. The ideological fissures in the SNP between left and right – almost completely resolved in the '80s and '90s and then finally by the need to have a clear manifesto for government – were clear from the beginning and were apparent in the backgrounds of some of those who held prominent positions in the party in its early stages. Dewar Gibb, for example, had been a Conservative candidate, while MacDiarmid later stood for the Communist Party.

Regular and bitter disputes about leadership positions – something that intensified in the 1980s – were also problematic even though they were good illustrations of Sayre's law given that what was at stake was often so small.

All these issues, churning within the same organisation, not only give an impression of disunity but also leave very vague the exact definition of the ultimate destination of not only leaders and activists but also the voters who put their trust in them. The task of recruitment and electoral persuasion consequently becomes all the more difficult.

Within this, however, it is possible to identify a progress from early disunity through attempts at defining a purpose and platform to what some have regarded as over-conformity within the Scottish Parliament.

The massive rise in membership after the independence referendum in 2014 confirmed that members of the SNP are now unified in their objective: independence. Home rule – that is, the control by an elected Scottish Parliament of some but not all matters of governance – is no longer an objective because it has been achieved, and while there is always a desire for more of those matters to be devolved, the campaign for such increased devolution is now normally a 'catch-up' proposed by non-independence-supporting parties when confronted with strong and increasing backing from Scottish voters for independence.

The 'settled will' of the SNP to use the Scottish Parliament as a stepping stone to independence, seeking to show that the country could run some of its own affairs competently and therefore encouraging Scots to give more powers to the Parliament over time, came about in the late 1990s and specifically after a commitment entered into by Donald Dewar that the Scotland Act would contain nothing that prevented such progress. That commitment was given to Salmond and the author in a meeting in the House of Commons in June 1997 and underpinned the decision of the SNP National Council to campaign for a double 'Yes' vote in the referendum in September of that year.

This meant that for the party there was now not only a clear objective – independence – but also a clear route to it, through success in Scottish parliamentary elections and then the accrual of more powers by the Parliament over a period of time.

The two areas that still required clarification in this formulation were the means to achieve more powers and the mechanism by which independence could be gained by the Parliament.

The second of these was the subject of considerable debate in the run-up to the first parliamentary election and in the first parliament itself, particularly within a deeply fissured SNP group. The formulation of the need for a referendum arose from that process.

The first has been less clear and has usually been as a result of success by the SNP – for example, in 2007 and 2014, the establishment of the Calman and Smith processes were in response to firstly the SNP election victory and then to the referendum outcome.

Earlier, from the late 1960s – and primarily from the victory of Winnie Ewing in the Hamilton by-election in 1967 and the subsequent surge in support in local elections – the SNP had veered between supporting cross-party attempts to establish a devolved Parliament and at least flirting with a rejection of any constitutional status short of independence.

In reality, however, most party members were suspicious of an 'independence nothing less' stance that was never fully established party policy, preferring the formulation that Winnie Ewing claimed had been expressed by Gwynfor Evans, the leader of Plaid Cymru, when he advised her never to vote against 'half a loaf' for Scotland because the country was, in democratic terms, starving.

This duality led to some difficulties for the SNP, particularly during the establishment of the Constitutional Convention, devised by Labour in response to the SNP victory at the Govan by-election in 1988 but supported widely across politics and civic society. The SNP National Executive agreed that the party should participate in the Convention and appointed the then leader Gordon Wilson along with the deputy leader Margaret Ewing and Govan MP Jim Sillars as its delegation.

However, Sillars quickly bounced the party into abandoning membership after only one initial meeting, ostensibly because the Convention would not consider independence as a legitimate option for Scotland's constitutional future. In fact, Sillars and Wilson were more concerned that the Convention would tie up the SNP and its limited resources at a time when electoral advantage might be made by the party. They were also concerned that that involvement in the process would play into the hands of Alex Salmond and supposed 'gradualists'.

The SNP accepted the withdrawal from the Convention after a bitter debate at a National Council in Port Glasgow that precipitated some resignations. The whole episode stalled the SNP's electoral progress for some time and weakened its initial period in the Scottish Parliament. The party looked to many to be one that could not cooperate with others (something the public claims to like in politicians) and that was reluctant to take responsibility.

Prior to the late 1960s, the party had gone through regular disputes about what its aims should be. The departure of John MacCormick to found the Covenant, the work of former party president and financial benefactor Roland Muirhead in the Scottish National Congress, the emergence of the '55 Group and the 1320 Club, as well as the emergence of the first Scottish Socialist Party from the membership of the SNP, all testified to fissures that were precipitated by a dispute about objectives and the means of reaching those objectives.

The Scottish playwright and poet Joan Ure once observed that in history what Scots usually wanted was not freedom of religion, but the freedom to persecute others. In political terms, that sometimes seemed the case in the SNP as well, as bitter disputes were played out with calls for expulsion and counter-claims of betrayal and – a classic insult in the '80s – failure to be a 'real nationalist'.

Yet more has united than divided the members of the party throughout its history and the key to that is in a secondary aim that was printed on party membership cards for many years – the duty of the party and its members to secure 'the furtherance of all Scottish interests'.

It could be argued that it is this long-term and close identification with Scotland that has over the years contributed most to the party's growing success and that, when such identification became associated with issues of governmental and parliamentary delivery within Scotland, lead to a sea change in the SNP's electoral fortunes.

That might be a simplistic view but the use of the term 'Scotland's Party' by the SNP in the run-up to the first elections to the Scottish Parliament (a branding first used by the author in a party political broadcast in the autumn of 1998) and the consistent strength of the public perception of the party's focus and priorities (as shown for example in opinion poll questions that ask who is best at 'standing up for Scotland's interests') both indicate that speaking for Scotland and 'putting Scotland first' are key attributes and key attractants for voters.

In their actions SNP leaders of course always recognise and act on that fact. The quiet competence and steady influence of John Swinney in his various roles over thirty years of leadership in the party is a good exemplar. As assistant national secretary, as national secretary, as MP, as MSP, as leader, as Finance Minister and as Deputy First Minister, he has consistently been an advocate of pragmatic intervention to secure improvements in many areas of national life both across the country and in his own constituency.

That type of personal service focused on improving Scotland for those who live here has been a core determinant of the political philosophy of the SNP leadership group and, indeed, has usually been the impetus that has driven them to becoming members of the party.

Alex Salmond described his own motivation in an interview with *The Independent* in 2015 in those terms, attributing the exact trigger to a row with his then girlfriend over Labour's failure to stand up for Scotland in 1973.[14]

---

14   Matt Dathan, '"If you feel like that, go join the bloody SNP": The row that made Alex Salmond join the Scottish Nationalists', *The Independent*, 16 October 2015. [http://www.independent.co.uk/news/uk/politics/if-you-feel-like-that-go-join-the-bloody-snp-the-row-that-made-alex-salmond-join-the-snp-a6697321.html]

In summary, therefore, just as the membership of the party has changed and grown over the past eighty years, so the party has clarified exactly *what* it wishes to achieve and has become explicit in *how* it is to be achieved. That has, of course, changed not only what is required from the leadership of the party but has also necessitated the development of a different type of leadership, more focused on the parliamentary route to success.

LEADERSHIP OUTSIDE AND INSIDE PARLIAMENT

The SNP was, until the 1999 elections for the Scottish Parliament, an extra-parliamentary party.

The thirty-five members of the new Parliament were double the number of Westminster parliamentarians elected in the party's entire history up until that night and although the number dropped in 2003 to twenty-seven, it rose in 2007 to forty-five and in 2011 to sixty-nine. After the Westminster election in 2015 the SNP's total of elected parliamentarians at Holyrood, Westminster and in Europe was 123, which made the SNP the third-largest parliamentary party in the UK. Fifty years before it had no parliamentary representation at all.

The role of the SNP leadership prior to 1999 was therefore very different.

In that time, the party had only been led by a sitting Westminster MP for two periods of time – between 1979 and 1987 and between 1990 and 1999. At all other times its leader had not had a parliamentary platform.

There was very considerable tension in the party when there were parliamentarians at Westminster but when the bulk of the elected leadership was not there. This situation led to some policy incoherence between 1974 and 1979, particularly over non-constitutional matters, but also resulted in a considerable degree of in-fighting and resentment on both sides. Some of the damage done resulted in a weakened party in the early 1980s.

In an attempt to avoid a repetition of that situation, and to professionalise the voluntary structure of the party, particularly after a problematic showing at the Monklands by-election of 1994, Alex Salmond moved to create a model in which there was day-to-day administrative authority in Scotland that reported to him even when he was at Westminster. That resulted in the author's appointment as the party's first full-time chief executive in December 1994, a position that he held until the Scottish Parliament elections in 1999, at which time the party leader became a Member of that Parliament.

Earlier leaders had to find a way of securing a platform without being full-time politicians, a task that was difficult given the focus of the media on Westminster up until the establishment of the Scottish Parliament in Edinburgh. The exception was during Westminster parliamentary by-elections which always gave heightened prominence to Scottish political activity in Scotland.

Billy Wolfe had a charismatic personality that secured some media attention and his work on improving and modernising the way in which the party communicated its message was more effective than that undertaken by many of his predecessors. Jimmy Halliday, although very much a stop-gap leader, did succeed in bringing a fresh face to the party not tainted by memories of wartime weakness and flirtation with fascism, while the prominence of John MacCormick and others such as the journalist and writer William Power helped the cause. But without a parliamentary platform others achieved little recognition and had no opportunity to be heard on the great issues of the day. Gordon Wilson discovered the disadvantages of that situation when he lost his Dundee East seat in 1987 but continued as National Convener until 1990.

These leaders also had to earn a living outside politics, which created another set of problems. Billy Wolfe's company eventually filed for bankruptcy and many aspirant party figures were stymied by being unable to devote the time needed to establish themselves with party members across Scotland without experiencing financial loss. Many also suffered severe tensions within family relationships – always a problem for politicians.

Extra-parliamentary parties are also ones that, perhaps because of lack of success during elections, can be attracted to fringe propositions and policies that are not properly tested by debate and public reaction. Accordingly the SNP's manifestos for repeated elections lacked both a practical cutting edge and the type of promotion that can come from the work of politicians in constituencies and in parliamentary chambers. Those politicians are also able to employ staff and the resources available are considerably greater than anything an extra-parliamentary party – or a small and declining parliamentary party, as Scottish Labour has found out – can muster.

The role and function of the leadership of such a party is therefore very different and the type of person attracted to, or chosen by, such a party will not be the same as that attracted to or chosen by a larger and more mainstream entity. That is very apparent in some of the figures examined in this book.

LEADERSHIP FROM GOVERNMENT

A further dimension in leadership comes from election to government. Up until 1999, no matter how much enjoyable speculation took place, no one in the SNP seriously expected to be in government. From 1999 onwards that situation changed, although not many thought that the SNP would win as soon as 2007.

The government that was formed in May of that year had no member who had ever served in office before. That may be what made it such an effective and popular government, as well as one of the most stable in any European democracy in recent times, despite the SNP being a minority within the Parliament.

The aim of each minister in that government was to be as accessible as possible and to be as involved as possible in direct communication with, and the decision-making for, the voters of Scotland. The First Minister was also by nature someone who directly intervened to get results, something that the ministers and civil servants quickly realised.

The future success of the party quickly became bound up with the success of the government, an entirely new situation for the SNP. Moreover, the ultimate success of the SNP in gaining independence became dependent upon the ability of the government to secure a parliamentary majority for a referendum, something that was not possible between 2007 and 2011 but which became possible because of the landslide in 2011 and the formation of a majority administration.

So, to add to the changed role of SNP leaders through the growth of membership of the party, the development of a coherent set of objectives that

could be achieved by a clearly understood route and the transfer of focus
from outside to inside a Parliament has to be added the change that comes
from leading or being a member of a government.

That change results in a wider remit, great prominence and stronger responsibility, but it also brings with it the need to differentiate between the national
interest and the party interest and to always, in government, put the national interest first, even if that might delay or derail the party's objectives.

THE UN-WON PRIZE – LEADERSHIP TO INDEPENDENCE

Owen Edwards, who in 1982 became the first chief executive of S4C,
the first-ever Welsh language TV channel, once described the job as
being to make programmes, fill television screens, save a language, promote
a nation and – if there was time – win the rugby grand slam as well.

The current expectations of the leader of the SNP are just as diverse
because she is now expected to lead a party, run a movement, govern a country,
be a role model for her gender everywhere and, of course, win independence for her nation.

There has never been a particularly collegiate leadership of the SNP,
although the party's constitutional structure which does distribute power is
still basically the same as that established by Gordon Wilson when he was
national secretary of the party in the early 1970s. This gave responsibility to
a range of elected office-bearers and empowered a variety of structures rising from branch, to constituency, to national executive, to national council
and ultimately to the party's annual national conference.

The reality of modern politics and the increased pressures of government
and a 24-hour news cycle, along with the election of Alex Salmond and then
Nicola Sturgeon, powerful personalities who expect to be decision-makers,
have, however, eroded the reality of distributed authority. For the last two
decades, decisions have increasingly been made by the leader him or herself,
working with senior colleagues whom they choose. This leadership group has

in recent years narrowed even further and now consists in the main of a small trusted group of senior figures, which includes civil servants and party staff.

That is true of every larger political party in current times and the challenge for leaders is to find ways of ensuring that party members' voices and views not only continue to be heard but are also seen by the members themselves to count. That has happened in the SNP through national conferences that are not as tightly controlled as those of some other parties (illustrated by the NATO debate in 2012) and has led to rejections of leadership positions on occasion, such as during the 2015 conference debate on land reform.

What has not been opened up for that type of debate within the party structures as yet is the strategy by which the party can achieve its ultimate aim. The 'Yes' movement was dominated by the SNP at official level but there was no wider formal discussion in the party of how that position would be used.

The White Paper on independence was produced by the present First Minister while she was Deputy First Minister without that democratic input and, indeed, there was limited opportunity for Cabinet members and ministers to influence it.

The Westminster Group has also not yet been properly engaged in a formal internal party debate with the wider membership, including the Holyrood group about its role and how it would take forward the challenging issues of using its position and size to press the independence issue at Westminster.

The SNP has always been an opportunistic party, seeking the moment at which it can make progress given the political circumstances emerging or prevailing. The first months of 2016 were focused on winning the Scottish Parliament election and although the result was spectacularly good it did not result in the absolute majority that was necessary to ensure that decision-making rested once again entirely within the SNP leadership at Holyrood.

However, before that became an issue that could have created some tension within the party and particularly within the Holyrood parliamentary group, which was indicating before the election that it wanted more influence, the European Referendum created the circumstances in which the clear and prime duty of the First Minister was to secure continuing membership of the European Union for Scotland, given the Remain vote in Scotland on that issue.

The powerful, principled and prominent leadership of Nicola Sturgeon in the days after the vote galvanised the Scottish, UK and international media. Sure-footed, concentrated on what needed to be done and clear in intention and method, this leadership not only demonstrated why she was the unanimous choice of the party at every level when Alex Salmond stepped down, but also illustrated her great physical and political strength as well as her considerable intellectual and political abilities.

The job of the leader of the SNP has always been to stand up for Scotland. Increasingly, as the aim of the party has become clearer, it has been to ensure that the country can have and will take the opportunity to vote for independence.

In late June 2016, as this is being written, Nicola Sturgeon is doing that job in exceptionally propitious circumstances, though ones that require exceptional talent and determination. It may be that she will finally be the leader who takes Scotland to independence – the leader of both power and influence who finishes the job.

Only time will tell.

CHAPTER 3

JOHN MACCORMICK

MALCOLM PETRIE

John MacCormick was a founder member of the National Party of Scotland (NPS) in 1928 (while still a student) and part of the negotiations that led to the merger of the NPS and Scottish Party to create the Scottish National Party (SNP) in 1934. He became secretary of the SNP and in that role played a pivotal part in its early years. Though never holding the most senior position, he was among its most influential members and, more significantly, of the wider national movement. He was a key player in the wartime internal battles and was involved in the breakaway when his candidate William Power was defeated for party chairmanship in 1942. MacCormick experimented with a range of strategies in pursuit of self-government, including standing as a Liberal candidate in the Paisley by-election in 1948 with the support of the Unionists (Tories) against Labour. His predilection for student politics was evident in his election as rector of Glasgow University in 1950 and involvement in the removal of the Stone of Scone from Westminster Abbey at Christmas 1950. He continued campaigning for self-government but had made little progress by the time of his early death in 1961.

·   ·   ·

Pivotal to the founding of the National Party of Scotland (NPS) in 1928, six years later John MacCormick orchestrated the merger between the NPS and the Scottish Party that produced the Scottish National

Party (SNP). And, while he never served as chairman or president, for almost a decade thereafter MacCormick used his position as national secretary to function as the *de facto* leader of the new party. Yet, despite this early prominence, the subsequent course of his career has ensured that he occupies an ambiguous position within the pantheon of SNP leaders. MacCormick renounced his membership of the SNP in 1942 following an acrimonious dispute over the party's attitude to the war effort; although he later joined the Liberals, his interest in orthodox electoral politics ebbed thereafter. His attention shifted instead to a series of endeavours intended to promote public enthusiasm for self-government, the most significant of which was the Covenant, a mass petition launched in October 1949. Intermittent flurries of publicity aside, however, such extra-parliamentary exertions achieved little, and at the time of his death in October 1961, aged just fifty-six, MacCormick was a peripheral figure in Scottish politics. Exiled from the SNP for nearly two decades, his attempts to locate an alternative to the traditional political party thwarted: for all its early enterprise, his career ended in seeming failure.

MacCormick has, in consequence, been rendered as a flawed figure: a political pioneer who lacked the discipline required to see his myriad schemes through to completion; a gifted orator and campaigner, who, though dedicated to the cause of Scottish self-government, squandered his gifts; an individualist and romantic unable to submit to the constraints of party politics; even, perhaps, a shallow politician, guilty of opportunism and naïveté.[1] Such criticism of MacCormick's leadership has been strengthened by the relative triumphs enjoyed by his successors. The first SNP Member of Parliament was returned to the Commons three years after his departure; more poignantly, the surge in support for the SNP at the polls coincided almost precisely with his passing.[2] In retrospect, then,

---

1   See, for example, the comments in: Brand, *The National Movement in Scotland*, pp. 192–5, 243–9; Michael Keating and David Bleiman, *Labour and Scottish Nationalism* (London: Macmillan, 1979), pp. 124–49; Christopher Harvie, *Scotland and Nationalism* (London: Routledge, 1998, 3rd edition), pp. 69–73.

2   In November 1961, the SNP polled 18 per cent in Glasgow Bridgeton, the party's best result in a generation. A year later, William Wolfe finished second at the West Lothian by-election. Ewen A. Cameron, *Impaled Upon a Thistle: Scotland since 1880* (Edinburgh: Edinburgh University Press, 2010), pp. 279–82.

it seems obvious that the improvements in party organisation instituted by meticulous, if rather staid, men such as Robert McIntyre and James Halliday were of greater value than MacCormick's futile attempts at building cross-party alliances.[3]

MacCormick undoubtedly embodied many of the weaknesses that bedevilled the SNP in its early years. Whether he sought a legislative assembly within the framework of the United Kingdom or something closer to dominion status was often unclear, and could alter depending on the audience he was addressing. Equally changeable was his preferred method of achieving a new constitutional settlement for Scotland; although he helped to found the SNP, the non-partisan 'convention', capable of surmounting the parliamentary barriers to self-government, was a recurring theme in his career. As Richard Finlay has underlined, it was only after MacCormick left that these questions were settled, and the SNP became a fully autonomous party explicitly committed to Scottish independence.[4] And, yet, to attribute the failure of the SNP to achieve electoral success in this period to the equivocation personified by MacCormick would be unjust. For all his flaws, MacCormick was confronted by the obstacles that faced all those who toiled outside the ranks of the two major parties in the middle decades of the twentieth century; it was only when the Labour and Conservative duopoly waned across Britain that the SNP was able to enter the political mainstream. Lacking the heritage that preserved Liberalism, and denied the foreign subventions and ideological cachet that sustained British Communism, MacCormick's achievement in establishing a political party dedicated to self-government demands recognition. Further, his ostensibly erratic career can be seen as a rational response to the political climate within which he worked. At a time when Labour and the Unionists, as the Conservatives were known in Scotland until 1965, dominated the loyalties of the Scottish electorate, his provocative methods kept the issue of Scotland's constitutional status in the public

---

3   On the SNP after MacCormick, see Paula Somerville, *Through the Maelstrom*.

4   Richard J. Finlay, 'Pressure group or political party? The nationalist impact on Scottish politics, 1928–1945', *Twentieth Century British History*, 3 (1992): 274–97.

eye, and created a heritage upon which future generations of activists could build.[5]

Rather than measuring MacCormick's direction of the SNP against a set of abstract criteria, then, this study places his leadership within the wider context of his time, assessing his decisions from the perspective of the politically possible. The portrayal that emerges is of a practical politician, skilled at garnering publicity, but ill-suited to the demands of campaigning in a mass democracy. MacCormick's essential fault was not his idealism, nor even his undeniable egotism; if anything, he could be a ruthless pragmatist, routinely prioritising tangible achievements over doctrinal purity. Instead, it was his attachment to a model of politics that valued elite opinion over popular support that proved crucial; for MacCormick, status outweighed simple numbers, and self-government was attainable if only the establishment could be converted. This perspective proved incompatible with the political culture that existed in Scotland between the 1920s and the 1960s, when Parliament's prestige was buttressed by the democratic gloss offered by the mass franchise. MacCormick's politics of alliance and intrigue, of public declarations of allegiance by the aristocracy, could not be reconciled with a representative democracy that still enjoyed the confidence of the electorate. Even so, his methods presaged those that would emerge during the 1980s, as the failure of the 1979 devolution referendum and opposition to the policies pursued by the Conservative governments led by Margaret Thatcher encouraged notions of a 'democratic deficit', and the rediscovery (or invention) of a Scottish tradition of popular sovereignty that challenged the authority of the Westminster Parliament. MacCormick's was, thus, an uncertain legacy, both anachronism and precursor; if he was redolent of an elitist political style that predated mass democracy, he simultaneously foreshadowed the broad-based civic nationalism of the final decades of the twentieth century.

---

5   These future generations included his own children. Married in 1938, MacCormick and his wife Margaret had four children – two sons and two daughters. Iain, the eldest son, was SNP MP for Argyll between 1974 and 1979 before joining the Social Democratic Party; their younger son, Neil, Regius Professor of Public Law at the University of Edinburgh, was active within the SNP and served as a Member of the European Parliament between 1999 and 2004.

THE POLITICS OF PARTY: C.1928-42

John MacCormick was born in Glasgow in November 1904 to parents of Highland extraction. This inheritance left him suspicious of those who accentuated the division between the Highlands and Lowlands, and convinced there existed an essential unity in Scottish society that transcended linguistic, class and regional distinctions. In later life he was unable to recall a time when he was not intensely proud of Scotland, and was certain that 'somehow my own country had been thwarted in the fulfilment of her destiny'. Yet, these views found no early practical outlet; indeed, MacCormick's political debut occurred, in his account at least, largely by accident. Having entered the University of Glasgow in 1923 to study law, he showed no interest in politics until some years later, when he attended a mock parliamentary debate at the student union. Intending only to spectate, he positioned himself on the Labour benches, where there happened to be space. A friend dared him to make a speech: to his surprise, his intervention drew praise, and he was asked to join the University Labour Club, swiftly becoming treasurer and then secretary. From these chance beginnings he progressed to become an active member of the Independent Labour Party (ILP), addressing meetings across Scotland and Northern Ireland.[6]

If the veracity of MacCormick's account of this formative period, offered in his 1955 memoirs, may be questioned, it nevertheless illuminates the political abilities he prized. His own effortless ease as an orator stands in contrast to the laboured interventions of the overzealous student debaters; the willingness of others to recognise his natural leadership abilities highlights the virtues of the gifted amateur, and exposes the inanity of the budding career politician. All along politics was, for MacCormick, something closer to an individual sport than a collective contest of ideologies. As such, his early membership of the ILP was largely a matter of chance, since he lacked 'any strong political convictions'; rather, he was 'in it for the fun of the game as much as because

---

6   J. M. MacCormick, *The Flag in the Wind: The Story of the National Movement in Scotland* (London: Victor Gollancz, 1955), pp. 7, 12–17.

... there were many wrongs to be righted in the world'.[7] The sole exception was his passion for Scottish self-government, and the singular nature of his political worldview aroused a distaste for unquestioning party loyalty. For MacCormick, parties were tools for the attainment of specific ends; if they ceased to perform this function, they could be discarded. Thus, as the ILP became an increasingly marginal force in Labour politics during the 1920s, and the Labour Party's support for home rule weakened, MacCormick resolved to create a new body that could make self-government an issue capable of appealing to 'Tories, Liberals or Socialists'.[8] In 1927, apparently unaware of the existence of the Scottish Home Rule Association (SHRA), he and two friends from the University Labour Club founded the Glasgow University Student Nationalist Association (GUSNA). After belatedly making contact with Roland Muirhead, the veteran radical who had re-established the SHRA in 1918, MacCormick became engaged in the moves to found a new pro-home rule party, chairing the negotiations between the Scots National League (SNL), the Scottish National Movement (SNM), the SHRA and the GUSNA that resulted in the foundation of the NPS in April 1928.[9]

That MacCormick, a student activist still in his early twenties, could play such a central role in the formation of the NPS is indicative both of his personal strengths, and of the frailty of the nascent national movement. The disparate factions that united in 1928 disagreed not only on social and economic questions, but also on what home rule meant, and how it should be pursued.[10] Precisely because he treated such questions as tiresome pedantry that only served as a barrier to self-government, MacCormick was able to position himself as an impartial broker. His objective was to find enough

---

7   MacCormick, *Flag in the Wind*, p. 14.

8   MacCormick, *Flag in the Wind*, p. 16.

9   The negotiations followed the defeat of James Barr's Private Member's Bill to establish a Scottish Parliament. It fell without a vote, after a debate lasting just forty-five minutes; the debacle convinced many in the SHRA who had previously looked to Labour to secure home rule that a new party was needed. See MacCormick, *Flag in the Wind*, pp. 18–21; Richard J. Finlay, *Independent and Free*, pp. 29–80.

10   The SNL was founded in 1920 and promoted a colonial interpretation of Scottish history, advocating separation along Irish lines, in contrast to the moderate stance of many within the SHRA. The SNM was a breakaway faction of the National League led by the poet Lewis Spence.

common ground to allow for the creation of a party 'aiming by and large at a measure of home rule', and then to commence electioneering.[11] From the very outset, he was willing to compromise on matters of policy if this enabled a wider consensus to be reached.

MacCormick's preference for action over discussion was evident at the first election entered by the National Party. This was not a parliamentary contest, but the 1928 election held to determine who would succeed the Conservative MP Austen Chamberlain as rector of the University of Glasgow.[12] The campaign was conducted along party lines, with the Unionists nominating the then Prime Minister Stanley Baldwin.[13] MacCormick responded by persuading Robert Bontine Cunninghame Graham to stand for the NPS. Then in his seventies, Graham had been a radical MP in the late nineteenth century and was a founder member of the Scottish Labour Party and the ILP; he was also a lifelong advocate of home rule.[14] Baldwin began the campaign as the clear favourite; however, Graham finished a close second, and even secured a majority among the male students; the nationalists duly dubbed Baldwin the 'lady rector'.[15] MacCormick concluded that the result had signalled the extent to which the NPS rapidly became 'a real factor' in Scottish politics.[16]

The campaign offered an early glimpse of the tensions that lay at the centre of MacCormick's political approach. He relished the public forum electoral contests offered, and his organisation of Graham's campaign and ability to acquire press coverage enabled the NPS to emerge from a

11 MacCormick, *Flag in the Wind*, p. 22.

12 Students at the ancient Scottish universities to this day elect a rector to act as their representative on the University Court.

13 Labour nominated Edward Rosslyn Mitchell, MP for Paisley; the Liberal candidate was Sir Herbert Samuel, then outside Parliament after serving as the High Commissioner of Palestine. *The Scotsman*, 16 and 25 October 1928.

14 Cedric Watts, 'Graham, Robert Bontine Cunninghame (1852–1936)', *Oxford Dictionary of National Biography* (Oxford University Press, 2004) http://www.oxforddnb.com/view/article/33504 [accessed 17 June 2016].

15 *The Scotsman*, 29 October 1928.

16 MacCormick, *Flag in the Wind*, p. 30.

position of near-obscurity with a creditable result. Yet also apparent were two recurring faults. The first was his fondness for the more theatrical aspects of student politics: the election was a raucous affair, featuring a spate of 'kidnappings' alongside heckling, disruption and an alleged 60,000 rotten eggs; MacCormick never fully lost his affection for such escapades. The second was his belief that electoral success hinged upon securing the backing of eminent figures, as evidenced by the presence of the Duke of Montrose and the novelist Compton Mackenzie, who both spoke on Graham's behalf. But if such methods were an asset in a rectorial contest – and, notably, the sole nationalist victory at the polls in the interwar period was Mackenzie's election as rector of Glasgow University in 1931 – it was increasingly irrelevant to the wider political context. During the 1920s, as Britain adjusted to the advent of mass democracy and the perceived threat posed by extremism overseas, politics began to be conducted in a more restrained and private fashion; mass rallies and public meetings were replaced by appeals targeted at individual voters.[17] Likewise, the mockery of Baldwin's support among female students indicated a failure to adjust to the extension of the franchise to women.[18] MacCormick's recollections of the NPS's first intervention in a parliamentary by-election, at North Midlothian in January 1929, suggest a similar conclusion. Despite the party's lamentable performance, he had still enjoyed the contest, since, he stated, '…we had no political ambitions and did not therefore need to take ourselves too seriously. Every campaign was to us a gay affair and wherever we went we were sure to find some *howff* where after meetings we could *ceilidh* till the small hours.'[19]

---

17 Jon Lawrence, 'The Transformation of British Public Politics after the First World War', *Past and Present*, 190 (February 2006): 185–216; Laura Beers, *Your Britain: Media and the Making of the Labour Party* (Cambridge, MA: Harvard University Press, 2010); Malcolm R. Petrie, 'Public Politics and Traditions of Popular Protest: Demonstrations of the Unemployed in Dundee and Edinburgh, c.1921–1939', *Contemporary British History*, 27/4 (December 2013): 490–513.

18 In 1918, the franchise was granted to women over the age of thirty, with some qualifications; in 1928, the voting age for women was reduced to twenty-one, in line with the qualifications for men, creating a majority female electorate.

19 MacCormick, *Flag in the Wind*, p. 40.

The inability of the NPS to rise above the level of electoral gadflies encouraged MacCormick to concentrate ever more on attracting the support of prominent individuals.[20] He had already made contact with Andrew Dewar Gibb, a lecturer in law at Glasgow University, and the Duke of Montrose before they participated in the split in Unionist ranks that produced the Scottish Party in 1932.[21] The appearance of the Scottish Party, which supported a moderate measure of home rule as a means of strengthening the imperial partnership between Scotland and England, and of protecting a distinctive Scottish identity believed to be threatened by Irish immigration, again underlined MacCormick's conditional understanding of party loyalty. Despite its right-wing origins, which contrasted with the largely radical leanings of the NPS, he assiduously courted the new body with the intention of absorbing its small but, in his view, influential membership: alongside Gibb and Montrose, its ranks included Sir Alexander MacEwen, former Liberal provost of Inverness, and the journalist George Malcolm Thomson.[22] As he suggested to the novelist Neil Gunn, if they were to have any hope of electoral success, they needed to 'do everything … to get the "Moderates" [i.e. the Scottish Party] to join with us (on our essentials) and to bring with them the prestige and the hope of financial support which undoubtedly they command'.[23]

Between 1932 and 1934, MacCormick worked to remove areas of disagreement between the two parties in order to effect a merger.[24] A crucial step was the expulsion of the 'Celtic' wing of the NPS, which MacCormick saw as essential if Scottish nationalism was to become a respectable political force. In May 1933, chastened by the dismal performance of the NPS candidate at

---

20 At the 1929 general election the NPS put forward two candidates. MacCormick stood in Glasgow Camlachie, where he polled less than 5 per cent. In 1931, when there were five NPS candidates, he contested Inverness, receiving 14 per cent of the vote.

21 National Library of Scotland [hereafter NLS], Dep. 209, Neil Gunn Papers, Box 15: letter from MacCormick to Gunn, 11 March 1931.

22 On the Scottish Party, see Mitchell, *Strategies for Self-Government*, pp. 180–83.

23 NLS, Dep. 209, Neil Gunn Papers, Box 15: letter from MacCormick to Gunn, 10 December 1932.

24 MacCormick, *Flag in the Wind*, pp. 64–71.

the East Fife by-election three months earlier,[25] MacCormick and his allies
secured backing for a restatement of policy that softened the party's stance
on the British Empire, and indicated a willingness to accept a moderate form
of home rule rather than hold out for full sovereignty.[26] The inevitable opposition this provoked from those who desired a more uncompromising brand
of nationalism provided the pretext for their removal.[27] The eventual uni-
fication of the two parties under the banner of the SNP, confirmed in April
1934, was undoubtedly a personal triumph for MacCormick, who had prevented the entrenchment of a damaging split within the national movement;
but it was also an inherently unstable one. The initial negotiations had been
conducted in secret, without the knowledge of either the party members or
Muirhead, the NPS chairman.[28] Moreover, MacCormick's expansive vision
of Scottish nationalism and deference towards those he considered his social
superiors caused him to treat the Scottish Party with a respect its paltry membership scarcely warranted; tellingly, the offices of president and chairman in
the SNP went respectively to the Duke of Montrose and Sir Alexander Mac-
Ewen. In MacCormick's view these were 'men whose names were far better
known to the public than were any [in the NPS] and who commanded the
respect which is always given, whether due or not, to rank and position'.[29]

It is, however, difficult to avoid the conclusion that MacCormick was
rather more impressed by such individuals than the wider electorate. He
considered their support vital, yet even within a Scottish context they were
relatively minor figures: who, other than MacCormick, honestly believed that
Baron Dalziel of Kirkcaldy was a man capable of influencing public opinion

---

25   The NPS candidate, the novelist Eric Linklater, polled less than 4 per cent of the vote, finishing behind
      not only the victorious Liberal National and his Labour rival, but also an 'Agricultural Party' candidate
      and Independent Liberal. For Linklater's fictionalised account of his brief political career, see his novel
      Magnus Merriman (1934).

26   On the change in policy, see Richard J. Finlay, '"For or Against?": Scottish Nationalists and the British
      Empire, 1919–39', *Scottish Historical Review*, 71 (1992): 184–206.

27   Brand, *The National Movement in Scotland*, pp. 221–7.

28   Finlay, *Independent and Free*, pp. 126–61.

29   MacCormick, *Flag in the Wind*, p. 79.

in the 1930s?[30] More than this, as well as overestimating his own standing as a political powerbroker, MacCormick treated such figures in a curiously two-dimensional fashion, neglecting to consider that they may have had interests and motives of their own. During the Kilmarnock Burghs by-election of November 1933, when the NPS and the Scottish Party put forward MacEwen as a joint candidate, thereby laying the foundations for unity, MacCormick was comprehensively outmanoeuvred by his counterparts in the Scottish Party, who forced the withdrawal of the NPS candidate. Yet, even in this instance, MacCormick believed he could still 'snatch good out of it and use the occasion to compel Sir A[lexander] M[acEwen] to leave his doubting Thomases behind and lead the worthwhile elements in the Scottish Party into our ranks'.[31] This attitude left MacCormick, and by extension the SNP, at the mercy of the whims of individuals. Montrose, an erstwhile Tory who took the Liberal whip in the Lords in 1935, and MacEwen, a Liberal, did not see the SNP as an exclusive political loyalty but as an optional adjunct. As Richard Finlay has suggested, their conversion to home rule was at least partly cynical, a means of boosting their flagging political careers: when electoral success failed to arrive, they drifted away from the SNP.[32]

Throughout the interwar period, MacCormick declined to confront the realities of politics in an era of mass democracy. To be sure, the likelihood of the SNP becoming a genuinely popular movement was always slight, but MacCormick refused even to contemplate such a path. Contemptuous of the benefits of party organisation, which he disparaged as 'machine politics', his leadership rested upon an outmoded combination of personal influence and public spectacle.[33] The contrast with the development of Labour and Conservative politics is instructive. Following the advent of universal suffrage,

---

30 Dalziel, a newspaper proprietor, had been Liberal MP for Kirkcaldy between 1892 and 1921. For Mac-
    Cormick's rather obsequious account of his dealings with Dalziel, see MacCormick, *Flag in the Wind*,
    pp. 68–71.

31 NLS, Dep. 209, Neil Gunn Papers, Box 15: letter from MacCormick to Gunn, 8 October 1933.

32 Finlay, 'Pressure group or political party?', pp. 286–7.

33 MacCormick, *Flag in the Wind*, p. 61.

the major parties competed to project an inclusive cross-class image capable of attracting newly enfranchised voters, especially women. The result was an increased focus on national propaganda and the central direction of election campaigns.[34] Within the Scottish context, this growth in centralised control saw a growing ambivalence within the Labour Party towards home rule, a trend enhanced by the economic crisis of the 1930s. Confrontational orators such as James Maxton were replaced by skilled organisers like Arthur Woodburn and Patrick Dollan, men capable of mobilising a mass electorate and maintaining party discipline.[35] MacCormick would later acknowledge that he had 'failed to appreciate the very formidable power of the professionally organised parties', having dismissed them as 'soulless' entities whose members 'lacked any real enthusiasm except for their own advancement'. Yet, even when in introspective mode, MacCormick could not resist a swipe at the limitations of democracy: 'universal suffrage' had, he suggested, granted political power to 'thousands of politically illiterate electors', making 'the evolution of the party machine inevitable'; the problem that remained was 'how to reconcile equality of citizenship with the natural leadership of men of independent mind'.[36] Little speculation is required to deduce in which camp MacCormick felt he belonged.

When the SNP failed to achieve a breakthrough at the 1935 general election, MacCormick gambled yet further on finding an alliance that would accelerate electoral success.[37] Backed by Montrose and MacEwen, but without official support from the SNP's National Council, he opened discussions with the Scottish Liberals in the hope of securing a pact.[38] The failure of these talks in the face

---

34   See: David Jarvis, 'Mrs Maggs and Betty: The conservative appeal to women voters in the 1920s', *Twentieth-Century British History*, 5 (1994): 129–52; Beers, *Your Britain*; Malcolm R. Petrie, '"Contests of vital importance": By-elections, the Labour Party, and the reshaping of British radicalism, 1924–1929', *Historical Journal* (2016): 1–28.

35   William W. Knox and Alan McKinlay, 'The Re-Making of Scottish Labour in the 1930s', *Twentieth-Century British History*, 6/2 (1995): 174–93.

36   MacCormick, *Flag in the Wind*, p. 61.

37   Unsuccessful in Inverness in 1935, MacCormick also failed at the Glasgow Hillhead by-election in 1937.

38   MacCormick, *Flag in the Wind*, pp. 88–94.

of internal opposition led MacCormick to resurrect a scheme that he had first mooted in 1932: a cross-party 'convention' in favour of home rule that would allow him to circumvent parliamentary politics entirely. The outbreak of war in September 1939, however, prevented the initial meeting of this body taking place; more ominously, the conflict released hitherto suppressed ideological tensions within the SNP. Opposition to conscription had been official party policy since 1937, but, faced with the reality, MacCormick and his supporters offered tentative support for the war effort. In contrast, many party members, led by Douglas Young, were keen to challenge the right of the UK government to conscript Scots; there was also growing discontent at MacCormick's auto-cratic leadership style. The dispute culminated at the 1942 party conference, when Young was narrowly elected chairman ahead of MacCormick's ally William Power. MacCormick promptly resigned from the SNP and, taking around half the delegates present with him, left to launch his Scottish Convention.[39]

FREELANCE POLITICS: 1942-61

MacCormick had welcomed the wartime electoral truce, hoping it might foster the atmosphere required for a non-partisan approach and allow him to build links with the Labour and Liberal parties.[40] Initially, he met with some success, leading him to believe that his cross-party approach would prove successful; as the war moved towards a conclusion, however, it became clear that Labour were once again losing interest in home rule.[41] Prior to the 1945 general election, MacCormick joined the Liberals and unsuccessfully contested Inverness before becoming the party's Scottish vice-chairman. Intriguingly, it was at this point that his politics assumed a more ideological hue. The arrival of a majority Labour government, committed to a programme of nationalisa-tion and central planning, offended his Scottish sensibilities, as he saw the

39   Finlay, *Independent and Free*, pp. 206–50.

40   MacCormick, *Flag in the Wind*, pp. 108–13.

41   Christopher Harvie, 'Labour in Scotland during the Second World War', *Historical Journal*, 26/4 (1983): 921–44, esp. pp. 931–4.

creation of the bureaucracy required to manage the emergent welfare state as a threat to distinctive Scottish institutions. For MacCormick, Labour had become a 'strictly disciplined machine', whose 'leading thinkers seemed to be more and more fascinated by the idea of a rigidly planned economy in a centralised State'.[42] His previously nebulous proclamations of radicalism now encompassed a more pronounced individualism, and he began to draw closer not just to the Liberals, but also to the Unionists, who in Scotland were opposing nationalisation on similar grounds.[43] MacCormick was a signatory to the *Design for Freedom* programme promoted by the Conservative MP Peter Thorneycroft, which called for greater protection for individual liberty. He subsequently claimed to have almost negotiated a merger of the Unionists, Liberals and National Liberals on a joint platform of opposition to nationalisation and support for home rule.[44] Yet, once more, MacCormick overestimated his ability to influence others. His decision to contest the 1948 Paisley by-election as an 'Independent National' candidate, with support from the Unionists and local Liberals but without the agreement of the Liberal hierarchy, left him open to accusations that he was a Tory stooge, and drew the lasting wrath of the Labour Party, whose candidate he unsuccessfully challenged.[45]

The contest in Paisley fatally undermined MacCormick's efforts to return self-government to the political agenda. The Scottish National Assembly, which emerged in 1947 as an extension of the activities of Scottish Convention, was intended to mobilise opinion in favour of a devolved Parliament; it began by drafting proposals, which were published a year later.[46] Mac-Cormick's aim was to present these directly to the Labour Prime Minister,

42   MacCormick, *Flag in the Wind*, p. 111.

43   Matthew Cragoe, '"We like local patriotism": The Conservative Party and the discourse of decentralisation, 1947–51', *English Historical Review*, 122 (2007): 965–85.

44   *Design for Freedom* (London: Design for Freedom Committee, 1948); MacCormick, *Flag in the Wind*, p. 119.

45   Michael Dyer, '"A nationalist in the Churchillian Sense": John MacCormick, the Paisley By-Election of 18 February 1948, Home Rule, and the Crisis in Scottish Liberalism', *Parliamentary History*, 22/3 (2003): 285–307.

46   NLS, Acc. 7295/9: *Blueprint for Scotland: Practical Proposals for Scottish Self-Government* (National Covenant Committee, 1948).

Clement Attlee. This proved hopelessly idealistic: he was unceremoniously snubbed, and directed instead to the Secretary of State for Scotland, Arthur Woodburn, who, after events in Paisley, viewed the scheme as a Tory-inspired attempt to undermine the Labour government. MacCormick, with his distaste for partisan loyalty, saw politics through an individual lens; if there was an opportunity to promote your cause, you should seize it. Unquestioning support for a single party limited such chances; in fact, parties were 'a negation of freedom ... the subordination of a man's own judgement and conscience to the will of the majority'. As such, he could never empathise with someone like Woodburn, whose profound loyalty to the Labour Party reflected a lifetime's experience, and guaranteed his resentment of MacCormick's criticism of Labour's performance in office. MacCormick simply dismissed Woodburn as a 'typical party bureaucrat', 'totally incapable of looking at anything except through the narrow eyes of party bias'.[47]

MacCormick responded to Woodburn's rebuff by attempting to appeal to the people. October 1949 saw the inauguration of the Scottish Covenant, in effect a mass petition in support of home rule, although the text itself was studiously vague, combining a pledge to 'do everything in our power to secure for Scotland a Parliament with adequate legislative authority in Scottish affairs' with an affirmation of 'loyalty to the Crown' and a commitment that Scotland would remain part of the United Kingdom.[48] In publicity terms, the Covenant was a success, attracting a reported 1 million signatures within six months. Politically, however, it was a failure, as the Labour government refused to change course, and the Unionists, who returned to office in 1951, offered only a modest expansion of administrative devolution and a Royal Commission on Scottish Affairs. Although the Covenant clearly tapped a feeling of political neglect, and perhaps even an embryonic desire for greater direct public involvement in the political process, the notion that a petition, even if its accuracy as a gauge of public opinion was accepted, could take

47   MacCormick, *Flag in the Wind*, pp. 122, 126.

48   *The Scotsman*, 31 October 1949.

precedence over Parliament remained inimical to both Scottish and British politics.[49] Thus, while it is true that the Covenant was weakened by the lack of a 'sanction clause' delineating the ramifications of its rejection, and by the failure to run candidates in support of its provisions, such criticisms overlook the more essential divide between MacCormick and his opponents.[50] MacCormick did not accept the sovereignty of Parliament, and believed that he could prevail by rallying public opinion; worse still, the campaign bore the usual traces of his hierarchical vision of society, with the Covenant being signed in the first instance by the ubiquitous Duke of Montrose, John Cameron (Dean of the Faculty of Advocates) and Reverend Neville Davidson of Glasgow Cathedral. Even if MacCormick believed that he was facilitating the expression of a consensus among the accepted figureheads of Scottish society, the result was that the Covenant could be portrayed by Labour as a reactionary measure, encouraged by a rag-bag of vested interests unwilling to accede to the authority of a democratically elected government.[51]

MacCormick's rejection of Parliament's authority was not yet echoed by any wider change in popular perceptions. This was not simply a question of the public not attaching enough importance to the issue of home rule: even if they had, there was still an expectation that such a change would be delivered from above, by government, rather than by popular pressure. This view was expressed most clearly by James Stuart, MP for Moray and Nairn and chairman of the Scottish Unionist Party, when rejecting MacCormick's calls for a plebiscite to settle the issue. As Stuart argued, 'the constitutional methods by which the people in our democracy can make their wishes known and effective are well understood, generally respected, in constant use, and available to all shades of opinion'. A similar view was articulated by Labour's Hector

---

49   Similar was the poll on Scotland's constitutional status arranged in early 1949 in the town of Kirriemuir by the Scottish Plebiscite Society. On a turnout of 86 per cent, 23 per cent voted for independence, 69 per cent for a Parliament on similar lines to that enjoyed by Northern Ireland, and just 5 per cent for the status quo. *The Scotsman*, 2 February 1949.

50   Andrew Marr, *The Battle for Scotland* (London: Penguin, 1992), p. 99; Arnold Kemp, *The Hollow Drum* (Edinburgh: Mainstream, 1993), p. 93; Mitchell, *The Scottish Question*, pp. 99–103.

51   Harvie, *Scotland and Nationalism*, pp. 171–2.

McNeil, Woodburn's replacement as Scottish Secretary, who stated frankly that the 'issues involved are complicated and cannot be dealt with by … a plebiscite … constitutional change in this country is considered and settled by the normal process of parliamentary democracy'.[52]

So long as the public continued to accept the legitimacy of representative democracy, MacCormick's efforts to shift the site of the political battle from elections and party politics to plebiscites and petitions could not succeed. Although the Covenant Association, formed in 1951 to continue the campaign for a plebiscite on home rule, toyed with the idea of running parliamentary candidates in order to exert pressure on the Labour and Unionist parties, such a move would have signalled a disheartening return to the electoral policy he had espoused and then abandoned in the 1930s. Furthermore, Mac-Cormick was aware that there was little public appetite for a competitor to the SNP, itself in the electoral doldrums; he preferred to encourage 'interest and excitement'.[53] In the end, MacCormick was reduced to calling merely for tactical voting in favour of pro-home rule candidates among the established parties.[54] The question posed by the Covenant Association, of how to 'make the people instead of the politicians … the masters of the situation', would not receive an answer until the notion of the referendum entered British politics as a result of Labour divisions over the issue of Europe.[55]

If the Covenant campaign ultimately failed, MacCormick was more successful in his other extra-parliamentary ventures in this period. Defeated six times in parliamentary elections, he was, fittingly, successful in his campaign to be elected rector of Glasgow University in 1950.[56] Always comfortable in

---

52   Quoted in MacCormick, *Flag in the Wind*, pp. 137–40.

53   NLS, Acc. 9188/8, Andrew Dewar Gibb Papers: General Correspondence, letter from MacCormick to Gibb, 5 May 1952.

54   NLS, Acc. 7295/12: The Covenant Newsletter, January 1955.

55   NLS, Acc. 7295/9: Scottish Covenant Association (n.d.). On the exceptional nature of the 1975 referendum on British membership of the European Economic Community, see David Butler and Uwe Kitzinger, *The 1975 Referendum* (London: Macmillan, 1976); Vernon Bogdanor, *The People and the Party System: The Referendum and Electoral Reform in British Politics* (Cambridge: Cambridge University Press, 1981).

56   *Glasgow Herald*, 14 October 1961.

the atmosphere of student politics, his candidacy brought him into contact with a new generation of nationalists, including James Halliday, a future SNP chairman, and Ian Hamilton, who both helped organise his rectorial campaign.[57] The close friendship he developed with the latter saw him involved in the repatriation of the Stone of Destiny, removed from Westminster Abbey by Hamilton and three friends on Christmas Day 1950, and left symbolically at Arbroath Abbey four months later.[58] MacCormick justified the stunt by stating that he and his supporters had grown 'impatient with orthodox political methods'. The government, aware of the identities of main protagonists, wisely decided against bringing charges, limiting the incident's political impact.[59]

Of greater long-term significance was the legal action that he and Hamilton, the latter now closely involved in the Covenant Association, launched in 1953, questioning the right of the new monarch to style herself Queen Elizabeth II since her namesake's reign had predated the 1603 Union of the Crowns – i.e. there had been no Elizabeth I in Scotland. Although the Court of Session ruled that the matter was one covered by royal prerogative, and could not therefore be subject to challenge, the case was notable for the *obiter dicta* it drew from Lord Cooper, who commented that the doctrine of parliamentary sovereignty was English in its derivation, and had no equivalent in Scottish constitutional law. Cooper concluded by emphasising that he found it difficult to understand why the Parliament of Great Britain, created by the Union of 1707, should inherit 'all the peculiar characteristics of the English Parliament but none of the Scottish Parliament'.[60] By eliciting such comments, the case provided the basis for the assertion of a distinctive Scottish constitutional tradition, and raised the question of whether Westminster's mandate operated uncomplicatedly in Scotland. These arguments would, of course,

---

57   Halliday, *Yours for Scotland*; Ian Hamilton, *A Touch of Treason* (Moffat: Lochar Press, 1990), pp. 37–47. Hamilton, a law student, would later become an advocate.

58   MacCormick, *Flag in the Wind*, pp. 165–76.

59   MacCormick, *Flag in the Wind*, p. 166; Mitchell, *Strategies for Self-Government*, pp. 259–66.

60   See: Colin Kidd, *Union and Unionisms: Political Thought in Scotland, 1500–2000* (Cambridge: Cambridge University Press, 2008), pp. 116–33, at p. 117. See also: Mitchell, *Strategies for Self-Government*, pp. 266–9.

return with greater urgency in the 1980s, when the growing divergence in Scottish and English voting patterns brought into question the right of the Conservative government to legislate on Scottish matters.

Yet, in the short term, these efforts failed to propel MacCormick back into the political limelight. The Covenant Association grew etiolated; if it had once enjoyed influence beyond MacCormick and his closest friends, this was no longer the case by the late 1950s. Indeed, in 1958, the Labour Party felt secure enough to officially abandon its commitment to Scottish home rule, long-theoretical in any case. In September 1961, just weeks before his untimely passing, MacCormick issued an appeal for funds, lamenting that the Covenant Association had, in recent years, been unable 'to command the widespread publicity which we were in the past able to do nor have we seemed to make the impact upon Scottish consciousness which is necessary if our aims are to be achieved'.[61] There was little intimation of the upswing in support for constitutional change that was to come in the years ahead.

CONCLUSION

How, then, should we assess MacCormick's career? His obituarists were affectionate, yet concurred in their assessments: his had been a political life devoid of any lasting achievements. For *The Scotsman*, MacCormick 'could have made his mark in either of the great political parties', but chose instead to dissipate his energies pursuing his dream of Scottish autonomy.[62] Similarly, the *Glasgow Herald* concluded that MacCormick had been blessed with 'great talent', but had enjoyed 'little opportunity' to employ these abilities for 'constructive purposes'.[63] But to criticise MacCormick for his failure to serve as an MP or hold national office would be to judge him by a set of criteria that he would not have recognised, and overlooks the single-issue nature

61   NLS, Acc. 7295/9: Scottish Covenant Association Newsletter, September 1961.

62   *The Scotsman*, 14 October 1961.

63   *Glasgow Herald*, 14 October 1961.

of his politics. He was committed to the cause of Scottish self-government; all else was detail, something for which he never had much patience. Parties were vehicles for the attainment of a Scottish Parliament, and if MacCormick was unable to best those who placed greater weight on partisan achievements, we should nonetheless judge him against what he sought to achieve.

MacCormick had substantial weaknesses. He was elitist, uncomfortable in the demotic world of mass politics; he was dismissive of those who challenged his authority; he could spectacularly misjudge his ability to convince others. Nevertheless, in what historians routinely describe as an age of unionism, he kept the Scottish question alive; whatever his faults, there were surely few who could have performed that task better. As the journalist Kenneth Roy suggested, MacCormick 'got Scotland talking about its own purpose and destiny and, once the conversation had started, it proved impossible to shut it up completely'.[64] And, crucially, although MacCormick's appeal to the institutions of civic Scotland proved impotent in the years immediately after 1945, the Covenant and the National Assembly offered a clear template for the pro-devolution campaigns of the 1980s. The 1988 *Claim of Right*, with its appeals to historical precedent and assertions of popular sovereignty, was pure MacCormick in spirit. Equally, the Scottish Constitutional Convention, formed a year later, was, in assembling an alliance of politicians, trade unions, local authorities and clergy in favour of a devolved Parliament, a direct descendant of the popular, yet deeply corporatist, Covenant campaign, marshalling the institutions of the Scottish establishment in opposition to an unsympathetic Westminster regime. The difference was, a generation after MacCormick, Labour, the Liberals, and a significant section of the public, were willing to support the movement.

As a leader of the SNP, MacCormick may be judged a failure. Despite helping to establish the party, he was unable to attract mass support, and exhausted the patience of the SNP membership, who tired of his domineering

---

64   Kenneth Roy, *The Invisible Spirit: A Life of Post-War Scotland 1945–1975* (Edinburgh: Birlinn, 2013), p. 269.

leadership and repeated policy volte-faces. Placed in the context of the wider home rule movement, however, the positive aspects of his legacy become more apparent. Never an absolutist nationalist, he bequeathed a rhetoric and a battery of tactics that could be redeployed in more propitious circumstances. As a devolutionist his place within the history of the SNP is understandably contentious; nonetheless, given the transformation of Scottish politics since 1999, and the centrality of arguments first voiced by MacCormick in making the case for devolution, he can be rightly considered as one of the most significant figures in the political history of twentieth-century Scotland.

CHAPTER 4

ROBERT BONTINE CUNNINGHAME GRAHAM

CLIFF WILLIAMSON

R. B. Cunninghame Graham was one of the most colourful and romantic figures to have played a leadership role in the SNP. He was the first Member of Parliament, then as a Liberal Member, to have described himself as a socialist in the House of Commons, though the son of senior military figures on both sides of his family. Along with Keir Hardie, he was involved in the establishment of the Scottish Labour Party, becoming its first president. He travelled extensively in South America, where he remains better known than in Scotland. Home rule was among the radical causes he espoused from the latter half of the nineteenth century right through to his involvement in the establishment of the NPS and becoming the SNP's first president at age eighty-two.

. . .

INTRODUCTION

Brendan O'Hara, the first of the new intake of SNP MPs elected in May 2016, borrowed a line in his maiden speech from that of Robert Bontine Cunninghame Graham,[1] which was appropriate, following an election that had seen the virtual wipeout in Scotland of the political party most associated with Keir Hardie, Cunninghame Graham's erstwhile

---

1   House of Commons Debates [hereafter HC Debs], 27 May 2015, c.109.

colleague in the Scottish Labour Party. After all, it was Cunninghame Graham who had turned his back on the Labour Party and seemed destined for political obscurity, he who would be vindicated in his vision of Scottish home rule as a catalyst for social change as presented by the left-of-centre SNP.

Cunninghame Graham is an enigmatic figure in the history of politics in Scotland and of Scottish nationalism. He had a hand in the formation and the leadership of three different political parties: the Scottish Labour Party (SLP) in 1888; the National Party of Scotland (NPS) in 1928; and the Scottish National Party (SNP) in 1934, and was the Member of Parliament for North West Lanarkshire from 1886–92. There is the impression that he was something of a dilettante; the *Glasgow Herald* called him a 'political freelance' while *The Times* characterised him as an 'aristocratic socialist and a cowboy dandy'.[2] At key periods in his adult life he chose adventure in the Argentine pampas or parleying in literary circles with such luminaries as Joseph Conrad and George Bernard Shaw over political action.

His friends and admirers were struck by his perceived ambivalent attitude to politics. John MacCormick said of him: '[He] was in politics (and in the best sense of the word) an adventurer who took keen delight in crossing swords with the party Goliaths who gave little thought to any of the practical considerations which might weigh with other men.'[3] Cunninghame Graham's first biographer, his close friend Aimé Tschiffely, saw Cunninghame Graham's strengths in his role as an agitator for lost causes as opposed to being a party hack. 'He was', said Tschiffely, 'one of those rare men who could never fight on the side of strength. He was one who enjoyed a losing fight…'[4] Another friend, G. K. Chesterton, thought that Cunninghame Graham's main problem was that he 'would never really be allowed in practical politics'.[5] Scholars have similarly been dismissive of his political contribution: Henry

---

2   *Glasgow Herald*, 21 March 1936, p. 11; *The Times*, 23 March 1937, p. 18.

3   MacCormick, *Flag in the Wind*, Kindle edition, loc. 558.

4   Aimé F. Tschiffely, *Don Roberto: Being the Life and the Works of R. B. Cunninghame Graham* (Kingswood: Heinemann, 1937), p. 260.

5   Ibid., p. 189.

Pelling saw him as 'quite unsuited to the political life'[6] and Peter d'A. Jones described him as 'probably never a permanent part of anything'.[7]

Yet, it would be wrong to see Cunninghame Graham as a peripheral figure. He was indispensable to both the nascent Scottish Labour Party and fledgling NPS and SNP as a marquee personality, bringing prominence and star quality to these obscure movements. However, it was not only his name recognition that was important. He was no mere figurehead. Cunninghame Graham contributed to the intellectual development of these movements through his speeches and activities. As an MP between 1886 and 1892, he was one of the few self-proclaimed socialists in the Commons, and he was to champion social justice and democracy not just in words but also in deeds, most famously when he was sentenced to prison for two months following the so-called Battle of Trafalgar Square in November 1887. He had been a supporter of Scottish home rule from 1884 onwards and was to fuse the case for self-government with advocacy for social change in a speech in 1889, presenting a vision of home rule that is arguably one of the precursors of modern commonweal and civic nationalism. His approach to Scottish home rule would also evolve. Initially an advocate of Gladstonian 'home rule all round', while keeping representation in the Imperial Parliament, by the end of his life he supported independence on the model of the Irish Free State and the 1931 Statute of Westminster, which gave legal recognition to the *de facto* independence to the dominions of the Commonwealth.

It is impossible to do justice to the extraordinary life of Cunninghame Graham in a short biographical sketch because, as his grand-niece Jean Cunninghame Graham observed, 'there seemed to be *so much* of it' (her italics).[8] Born in London in 1852, he was heir to a series of estates and titles in Scotland and went to school in England, where he attended Harrow for a couple of years. After school, he went to South America, first to Argentina, then Uruguay (where he enlisted in

---

6   Henry Pelling, *The Origins of the Labour Party* (Oxford: Oxford University Press, 1961), p. 105.

7   Peter d'A. Jones, 'Henry George and British Labor Politics', *American Journal of Economics and Sociology*, 46/2 (April 1987): 250.

8   Jean Cunninghame Graham, *Gaucho Laird: The Life of R. B. 'Don Roberto' Cunninghame Graham* (London: The Long Riders' Guild Press, 2004), p. 7.

the army), eventually settling down as a farmer in Mexico, where he gained the moniker 'Don Roberto'. He was not the best businessman and went bankrupt on a number of occasions, eventually forced to sell most of his estates in Scotland. He was kidnapped, was embezzled, became a fencing master, and had a formidable reputation as an equestrian, attracting the praise of William 'Buffalo Bill' Cody. In addition, he was an explorer, most notably following the trails of the Jesuits in central America. As well as Buffalo Bill and the future US President Theodore Roosevelt, he could count almost all of the literati of the late nineteenth century, including William Morris, George Bernard Shaw, Joseph Conrad and Oscar Wilde, as his acquaintances – and this was all before he became an MP.

Although his travel adventures and his literary life are well chronicled in biographies, his political life is less well covered, especially the last phase of his career as a Scottish nationalist. This is particularly the case in the work of Jean Cunninghame Graham, who does not even devote a single word to this period. Even his role in Labour history has been somewhat neglected. The modern incarnation of the Scottish Labour Party does not acknowledge his joint paternity in forming the original party baring its name or that he was the first socialist and Scottish Labour MP.[9] Some of the most respected studies charting the history of the Labour Party miss out both Cunninghame Graham and the SLP completely.

EARLY POLITICAL LIFE

Cunninghame Graham had gravitated towards radical politics in the mid-1880s through attending meetings of the Fabian Society, where he made the acquaintance of Beatrice and Sidney Webb; the Social Democratic Federation (SDF), founded by H. H. Hyndman, where he met George Bernard Shaw; and its offshoot, the Socialist League, where he met William Morris. His preference was for the SDF as opposed to the Fabians, whom he viewed as too

9   http://www.scottishlabour.org.uk/pages/history [accessed 16 February 2016].

'precious' as well as too 'extreme'.[10] However, his political outlook as it developed was closer to the ideals of utopian socialists such as Robert Owen than followers of Marx, such as Hyndman and Morris. It was not just in the salons of London's champagne socialists that his political outlook was being fashioned. He also read widely and, like many other radicals of the era, was profoundly influenced by the work of the American land reform campaigner Henry George, especially his 1879 text *Poverty and Progress*, which would inspire populists in the USA as well as land reform activists in Ireland and Scotland. Cunninghame Graham, however, would break with the Georgists in 1888.[11]

Cunninghame Graham was also an avid reader of the *Cumnock News*, especially the articles written by local journalist and member of the Junior Liberal Association James Keir Hardie. So impressed was he that when a meeting was arranged of the SDF in early 1885 in Cumnock, Cunninghame Graham travelled to South Ayrshire to meet the journalist. He struck up a friendship with Hardie that would last until the latter's death in 1915 as well as a political partnership that would endure until the former went on his first sabbatical from politics in 1894. The role of Cunninghame Graham in Hardie's political career was profound. He took him to the House of Commons on a number of occasions, introduced him to many of the most prominent radicals and socialists of the time, including Frank Smith, who would be his secretary for many years, and got him onto the platforms of the organised Labour movement in London, which would lead directly to Hardie becoming the independent Labour/Radical Association candidate for West Ham and an MP in 1892.[12]

Cunninghame Graham was initially, however, a Radical Liberal with socialistic leanings.[13] The politics of mid- and late Victorian Scotland had been energised through demands for radical reform covering a whole swathe of issues. There

---

10   Cunninghame Graham, *Gaucho Laird*, p. 289.

11   David Lowe, *Souvenirs of Scottish Labour* (Glasgow: W. & R. Holmes, 1919), p. 32.

12   Bob Holman, *Keir Hardie: Labour's Greatest Hero?* (Oxford: Lion Hudson, 2010), Kindle edition, loc. 54.

13   For an introduction to the Radical Liberals see T. W. Heyck and William Klecka, 'British Radical MPs, 1874–1895: New Evidence from Discriminant Analysis', *The Journal of Interdisciplinary History*, 4/2 (Autumn 1973): 161–84.

were demands for land reform and rights for tenants that culminated in the 1880 Crofters' War. Calls for church reform had stemmed from the 1843 disruption in the Church of Scotland and the end of an overwhelmingly Protestant Scotland due to influence of the Irish Catholic community, an increasing force as a result of immigration and the extension of the franchise in 1867 and 1885. There had been calls for constitutional reform, pushing for a Secretary for Scotland to bring order to the disparate administration of Scottish local government, education and justice, but also calls for reform in working conditions as the full consequences of unregulated industrialisation were exposed, as well as for moral reform, with temperance a key component in the radical tradition of the era. The main vehicle for radical opinion in Scotland at this time was the Liberal Party.

The party was, however, in a perilous state. It was, in the words of Fitzsimons, 'at best an uneasy, even tense alliance held together, as well as strained to breaking point, by the genius and prestige of one man, William Ewart Gladstone',[14] the 'grand old man' (GOM) as he was characterised. Tensions were everywhere in the party, most notably between the older Whigs and the younger radical Liberals, but also between supporters of laissez faire and those advocating state intervention, between the Liberal lairds and those that sided with the crofters, between the industrial plutocrats and supporters of organised labour. Gladstone managed to keep this dysfunctional party together until the mid-1880s, but only just. In 1886, there was the first of many haemorrhages, this one over Irish home rule, which would ultimately lead the party towards political oblivion. Tschiffely claimed that, despite sitting ostensibly as a Liberal, Cunninghame Graham 'despised Gladstone with all his heart',[15] though the GOM never seemed to show any ill-will towards Cunninghame Graham and had even sent him a 'good luck' telegram on the day of the 1886 general election.[16]

External forces were also undermining the unity of the party, with movements such as Charles Parnell's Irish Parliamentary Party. Cunninghame

---

14   M. A. Fitzsimons, 'Midlothian: The Triumph and Frustration of the British Liberal Party,' *Review of Politics*, 22/2 (April 1960): 187.

15   Tschiffely, *Don Roberto*, p. 195.

16   Cunninghame Graham, *Gaucho Laird*, p. 301.

Graham would form a close association with Parnell and often sat in the House with the Parnellites.[17] He would be a stout defender of Parnell even when his relationship with Katharine O'Shea that led to his disgrace and resignation was exposed and resulted in his untimely death in late 1891. Following Parnell's death, he lamented, 'He was human, like the rest of us.'[18] The Irish Parliamentary Party demonstrated that there was the possibility of political life outside of the two-party system that had been formulated in the 1870s with the modern incarnations of the Conservative and Liberal Parties. There was also pressure coming from within the Labour movement to abandon candidates and it too would the Liberal Party as so few working men were being selected or elected as. The founding of the Scottish Home Rule Association in 1886 can also be attributed to the success of the Irish Parliamentary Party.

MEMBER OF PARLIAMENT FOR NORTH WEST LANARKSHIRE

C unninghame Graham's long public political life began when he was elected for the seat of North West Lanarkshire at the 1886 general election. He gained the seat for the Liberals in what was otherwise a disastrous election for the party. In the UK, the Liberals lost 128 seats in 1886, including nine Scottish Liberal MPs.[19] He won the seat with a majority of 332, overturning a Tory majority of 1,103 from the previous year. He had stood in 1885 for the constituency after withdrawing from a seat in Glasgow to allow a prominent Scottish Land Restoration League (SLRL) campaigner to stand.[20] D. W. Crowley and Jones have both suggested that Cunninghame Graham's election in 1886 was largely attributable to the Land League.[21] However,

---

17 Tschiffely, *Don Roberto*, p. 255.

18 HC Debs, 10 February 1892, c.135.

19 The Liberals had won fifty-eight seats in Scotland in 1885 but seven of those were 'independent Liberals'.

20 Cunninghame Graham, *Gaucho Laird*, p. 292.

21 D. W. Crowley, 'The "Crofters" Party: 1885–1892', *The Scottish Historical Review*, 35/120 (1956): 121; Jones, 'Henry George and British Labor Politics', p. 250.

Cunninghame Graham attributed his victory to the fact that he was 'Mr Parnell's man' and 'was returned to Parliament by Irish votes'.[22]

Cunninghame Graham did not make his maiden speech until early 1887, nearly six months after his election, but he stamped an impression on Westminster as a result. The speech caused, according to the *Pall Mall Gazette*, 'a mild sensation' and suggested that he was 'no slight acquisition in these endless nights of dreary talk'; *Vanity Fair* called him a 'Scotch Home Rule Visionary'.[23] He was a frequent voice on the floor of the House, making nearly 800 contributions as recorded in Hansard over six years. This was despite spending a fair part of late 1887 and early 1888 in Pentonville Prison following the riot in Trafalgar Square on 17 November and being suspended from the Chamber twice. The first time was in December 1888 for unparliamentarily language. He accused a senior government minister of a 'dishonourable trick' in refusing to answer his question on behalf of workers in Wolverhampton.[24] His second suspension came about when he denounced 'shareholders in swindling companies' during a debate on the Local Authorities (Purchase of Land) Bill. The Speaker named and suspended him. Leaving the Chamber, he remarked, 'Suspend away … I do not care a damn.'[25] It would be one of his last contributions before losing his seat – 'a final snort of contempt at the British Legislative machine', as Jean Cunninghame Graham summarised it.[26]

He had decided to stand for the SLP in the Glasgow Camlachie constituency and not seek re-adoption as a Liberal in North West Lanarkshire. Alongside the other SLP candidates, he went down to a heavy defeat, but he was not particularly unhappy at leaving Westminster. He said, 'I have been foolish enough to soil myself with the pitch of politics, endured the concerted idiocy of the Asylum for incapables at Westminster for

22   HC Debs, 3 August 1891, Vol. 356, c.1178.

23   Cunninghame Graham, *Gaucho Laird*, pp. 306–7.

24   HC Debs, 1 December 1888, Vol. 331, c.733.

25   Ibid., 4 May 1892, c.107.

26   Cunninghame Graham, *Gaucho Laird*, p. 321.

six years … Now I think I may do my fooling alone, and leave the stage to younger fools…'[27]

There may have been another reason for leaving the Palace behind. He was going broke. Cunninghame Graham was an MP before the introduction of the payment of Members and so had to finance his own time in Westminster. He had no sponsorship so he had to rely on revenue from his estates. The original estimate of living costs made by his accountant had been too low and he could not afford another campaign.[28]

THE SCOTTISH LABOUR PARTY

The SLP has traditionally been viewed primarily as a precursor of the British Labour Party, as a regional manifestation of a larger movement, which would reach fruition in 1900 with the founding of the Labour Representation Committee.[29] Much of this has to do with the prominence afforded to Keir Hardie as the principal instigator of the party. The orthodox narrative is that, by the mid-1880s, Hardie had grown increasingly frustrated by the lack of Scottish Liberal Federation support for working-class candidates. In 1888, Hardie broke with the Liberals after he failed to gain the nomination of the party for an upcoming by-election at Mid Lanarkshire, though he had already been selected as the Liberal candidate for North Ayrshire.[30] He decided to stand as an independent 'Labour and Home Rule' candidate at the election but was defeated. He won 817 votes out of a total poll of over 7,000, but formed the Scottish Labour Party following the contest.

Hardie was certainly crucial: first as a candidate at Mid Lanarkshire and then as the organiser of the first meeting of the SLP.[31] It should be noted, though, that a 'Scottish Labour Party' was first mooted at a Miners' Conference in Edinburgh

---

27 Tschiffely, *Don Roberto*, p. 263.

28 Cunninghame Graham, *Gaucho Laird*, p. 321.

29 Pugh, *Speak for Britain!*, loc. 838.

30 Pelling, *Origins of the Labour Party*, p. 66.

31 For the main account of the founding of the SLP, see Lowe, *Souvenirs of Scottish Labour*, pp. 1–5.

in 1887 before Mid Lanarkshire, with Cunninghame Graham as its leader. The
idea predated Hardie's intervention.[32] It is important also to write Cunninghame
Graham into the story of the SLP, as he was arguably the most prominent figure
in the party throughout its short existence. In the words of the main historian
of the party, Cunninghame Graham 'alone voiced the aspiration of the workers
in the debates in Westminster'.[33] Cunninghame Graham was elected honorary
president of the new party and ostensibly was an SLP MP until 1892.[34] His role
in the SLP would be very similar to the one he would later play in the NPS and
SNP as its public face, helping to shape the message of the party and also have a
significant organisational role (though not so much that it was too demanding).
He would be elected 'president' to a number of bodies in his life. This is not to
say he did little spade work for the SLP. He was involved at Westminster pushing
legislation, most notably agitating for an eight-hour working day for miners, and
in 1890 he led an abortive attempt to negotiate an electoral pact between Radical
Liberal Associations and the SLP for future elections.[35]

The SLP only lasted for six years, from 1888 to 1894, when it voted unanimously at its conference on a motion from Hardie to wind up the party and
to join the Independent Labour Party that had been founded a year earlier in
Bradford.[36] The programme of the SLP adopted at its first conference was a
mix of ideas drawn from Radical Liberal, Land League, Fabian Socialist and
Labour reform movements. It supported reform of government; home rule
all round and disestablishment of the churches – key Radical Liberal ideas.
It called for the nationalisation of the land and minerals, which was a central demand of the SLRL, and for an eight-hour working day among other
Labour reforms. This hodgepodge of ideas was reflective of the make-up of
the party, which was drawn from all of these different groups.

---

32 Pelling, *Origins of the Labour Party*, p. 70; Cunninghame Graham, *Gaucho Laird*, p. 311.

33 Lowe, *Souvenirs of Scottish Labour*, p. 19.

34 Dr G. B. Clark, the Crofters' Party MP for Caithness, was also an SLP supporter and vice-president of
the party but he returned to the Liberal colours in 1892.

35 Pelling, *Origins of the Labour Party*, p. 102.

36 Lowe, *Souvenirs of Scottish Labour*, p. 170.

The breadth of the coalition was essential as the party sought to appeal to a very disparate electorate. The SLP could not succeed solely by appealing to working-class voters as, despite recent franchise reform in the 1884 Representation of the People Act,[37] which increased the Scottish electorate from 293,581 in 1880 to 560,580 in 1885, it only enfranchised around a third of all working men.[38] It needed support from rural voters in the Highlands and Islands, Radical Liberals from the suburbs, the Labour aristocracy, those workers affluent enough to gain the right to vote and the Irish, and used the lure of land reform and home rule to gain support from among them. It failed totally to build this coalition. The pull of the Liberal Party was still too strong, especially as it championed almost all of the same things as the SLP. Trade unions were also still close to the Liberals and when they pushed for representation they set up the Scottish United Trades Councils Labour Party (SUTCLP) as a rival party to the SLP in 1892.[39]

Of particular note for the SLP in general and Cunninghame Graham in particular was a troubled relationship with the Irish Catholic Community. As noted, Cunninghame Graham had attributed his success in North West Lanarkshire to the support he had garnered from the Irish. However, right from the start, the SLP had trouble making inroads in the Catholic community. At the 1888 Mid Lanarkshire by-election, Charles Parnell had personally intervened to urge support for the official Liberal candidate and not Hardie.[40] Ironically, it was to be Cunninghame Graham's friendship with Parnell that was to prove to be his undoing with the main newspaper of the Catholic community in the west of Scotland, the *Glasgow Observer*. It reminded voters at the 1892 general election that Cunninghame Graham had supported the Parnellite candidate John Redmond at the expense of Michael Davitt at a by-election at Waterford earlier that year and that he was a 'Scottish

---

37   Representation of the People Act 1884, 48 & 49 Vict., c.3.

38   *British Electoral Facts 1832–1987*, compiled and edited by F. W. S. Craig (Parliamentary Research Services, 1989).

39   Keating and Bleiman, *Labour and Scottish Nationalism*, p. 53.

40   Pelling, *Origins of the Labour Party*, p. 66.

Landlord'.[41] After the election, the *Observer* blamed Cunninghame Graham for acting as a spoiler candidate as he split the vote enough to allow for the Liberal Unionist candidate to defeat the Gladstonian Liberal. Cunninghame Graham, for his part, was somewhat ungracious in defeat and blamed 'the attacks of reactionary priestcraft' for his poor showing.[42]

What was the legacy of the SLP to the Scottish National Party? Cunninghame Graham's presence in the SLP establishes a link between modern Scottish nationalism and the radical politics of the late nineteenth century. It allows for the SNP to claim to be the inheritor, alongside the Liberal and Labour Parties, of a definable radical tradition in Scottish politics, rather than as an idiosyncratic narrow nationalist party only concerned with the recovery of a romantic notion of lost nationhood. Not only is it part of this tradition, through Cunninghame Graham's intellectual contribution there is also the emergence of a distinctive vision of Scottish home rule as a vital element in the achievement of social justice. This *leitmotif* will be revisited not only throughout his time in the self-government movement but will be present in the writings and approach of the likes of Roland Muirhead, John MacCormick and Jim Sillars, all of whom will journey towards Scottish nationalism from the political left as Cunninghame Graham had. Sillars would form his own version of the Scottish Labour Party in 1976 before joining the SNP in 1980.

In addition, intellectuals and activists within the SNP would interpret the state of Scotland as attributable not just to exclusively constitutional factors, but also to social and economic factors, which were exacerbated by the lack of national sovereignty. Stephen Maxwell summed it up as 'one of the most persistent strands in SNP rhetoric – the appeal to the socialist home rule traditions of Keir Hardie and the Scottish ILPers'.[43] Cunninghame Graham is in many ways the unacknowledged father of this brand of left-wing

---

41   *Glasgow Observer*, 9 January 1892.

42   J. J. Smyth, *Labour in Glasgow, 1896–1936: Socialism, Suffrage, Sectarianism* (Edinburgh: Tuckwell Press, 2000), p. 132.

43   Stephen Maxwell, 'The 79 Group: A Critical Retrospect', in *The Case for Left-Wing Nationalism*, edited by Jamie Maxwell (Edinburgh: Luath Press, 2013), Kindle edition, loc. 2021.

nationalism and the 1888–94 SLP, an unacknowledged precursor of the modern SNP.

ATTITUDE TO SCOTTISH HOME RULE TO 1894

Whereas Cunninghame Graham's commitment to socialism and liberalism were transient aspects of his political identity, there is no doubt that support for Scottish self-government was a constant feature of his politics. However, what he regarded as 'self-government' was not fixed and evolved over the course of his fifty-year association with the home rule movement. A second aspect crucial to his vision of Scottish self-government was the purpose of home rule as part of his commitment to social justice. We can trace the evolution of his approach to Scottish home rule as well as see how a commitment to social change interweaves over the course of his political life. This section evaluates his approach to home rule from the period 1886–94; later we shall look further at his pronouncements, especially in the later period of his life, when he became a pioneer figure in the Scottish nationalist movement from 1928 to 1936.

Cunninghame Graham came to the cause of self-government through the Scottish Home Rule Association (SHRA). The organisation was founded in Edinburgh in 1886 and emerged from two developments, first Gladstone's Irish Home Rule Bill and second due to the success of the Irish Parliamentary Party in Westminster elections in 1885, which effectively held the balance of power with eighty-five of the 101 Irish seats. Home rule was a key Radical demand and the Irish had shown how salient the issue could be electorally. The SHRA attracted not just Radical Liberals such as Cunninghame Graham but a whole generation of new activists who would have a major role to play in the evolving party system. Keir Hardie was a vice-president, as was Robert Smillie, another Scottish Labour pioneer and the secretary of the London Branch, where Cunninghame Graham was on the executive committee, as was Ramsay MacDonald. MacDonald would drift away from the SHRA in the mid-1890s, though he was mooted as a potential home rule candidate for one of the Aberdeen constituencies at the 1892 general election.[44] MacDonald, on behalf of the London branch of the SHRA, sent a letter in support of Hardie at Mid-Lanarkshire, in which he wrote:

> Let the consequences be what they may, do not withdraw. The cause of Labour and of Scottish Nationality will suffer much thereby. Your defeat will awaken Scotland and your victory will reconstruct Scottish Liberalism. All success be yours, and the cause you champion.[45]

This failure notwithstanding, the SHRA did succeed in bringing the issue of Scottish home rule to Westminster in 1889. In April, Cunninghame Graham and Dr G. Clark moved the motion. Gladstone also spoke in the debate, as did Arthur Balfour. The debate allows us to see not only the character of the arguments used by supporters and opponents of Scottish home rule, but also the differences of approach from within the home rule movement, including within the Scottish Labour Party, Clark and Cunninghame Graham being somewhat at odds with each other.

Clark proposed the motion and set out his terms for a Scottish Parliament based on grounds familiar to Radical Liberals of the era. First, he argued that Scottish issues were neglected. He drew attention to education as an example where reform of Scottish education had to wait until England had a national system in 1870, 'and then it was revised on English lines'[46] the following year for Scotland. His second point was that 'Scotch opinion is overwhelmed by uneducated English opinion.'[47] He drew attention to topics such as temperance and church disestablishment, where English MPs overrode the wishes of Scottish members. His solution was a federal system with home rule all round across 'every section of the Empire'.[48]

---

44   David Marquand, *Ramsay MacDonald: A Biography* (London: Jonathan Cape, 1977), p. 23.

45   Marr, *The Battle for Scotland*, p. 57.

46   HC Debs, 9 April 1889, Vol. 335, c.70.

47   Ibid.

48   Ibid., c.73.

In his contribution, Cunninghame Graham offered an alternative rationale for home rule. 'I do not wish to support this proposal specifically on national grounds.'[49] Instead, he believed that there was,

> ...a great and growing feeling in favour of home rule in Scotland [which comes] from the extreme misery of a certain section of the Scottish population ... and they wish to have their own members under their own hands, in order to extort legislation from them suitable to relieve that misery.[50]

He argued that Scotland was 'much riper', as he described it, for progressive legislation such as the 'eight hours question'.[51] In terms of the land question, Cunninghame Graham proposed that a Scottish legislature would not support a solution based on forced emigration. He also envisioned a Parliament where 'we should find the working classes much more represented than is the case here'.[52] His approach to home rule was to see it as a means to effect radical social change, promote social justice and to have a political system that was more of a tribune for the people as opposed to landed and financial interests.

There was also a memorable exchange between Cunninghame Graham and A. J. Balfour. The Conservative minister sought to use Cunninghame Graham's speech to chide Gladstone and portray home rule not only in Scotland but also in Ireland as a result of 'socialistic agitation'.[53] Balfour said, 'He wants home rule for Scotland because he wants socialism in Scotland. [Cunninghame Graham: 'Hear, hear.'] He admits, therefore, that I have not misrepresented or exaggerated his sentiments,' to which Cunninghame Graham responded, 'I always stand by my words.'[54]

---

49 Ibid., c.98.
50 Ibid.
51 Ibid.
52 Ibid., c.99.
53 Ibid.
54 Ibid.

This was the authentic voice of Cunninghame Graham expressing the cause he would devote the rest of his life to. He would grow more sympathetic to what he had previously denounced as 'sentimental grounds' for home rule and move towards separate statehood for Scotland. Joining the cause of Scottish democracy to social justice would provide a thread of radicalism that would interweave throughout the history of the SHRA, the NPS and the SNP and resonate to the present day.

The motion was defeated by 200 votes to seventy-nine. A motion on Scottish home rule would be passed in 1894 and others in 1895 and 1912, but all efforts to transform a general endorsement of the idea into legislation failed, though a Bill did get as far as a second reading in 1913. The Liberals returned to power in 1905 and, despite a commitment to home rule for Ireland, only moved on the issue when it was forced to, after the two deadlocked 1910 general elections made them reliant on the Irish Parliamentary Party. Even then support was lukewarm and they prevaricated due to Ulster resistance and threats of violence. It was no surprise that the Liberals were cold on home rule all round when trying to legislate for it in Ireland turned into a nightmare. The SHRA had done its job in pushing for the maximum support among the Liberal and the emerging Labour Parties but this had produced no tangible results. This left a major question: what was the best route to achieve home rule?

FROM THE SHRA TO GUSNA

Following the 1892 general election, Cunninghame Graham spent most of the next two decades travelling and writing. He seems to have remained involved in Labour politics until at least 1894 as he was present at the inaugural conference of the ILP in 1893 and was at the last SLP meeting the following year. During the First World War, his skills and contacts in the horse trade in South America were used to identify supplies of horses for the British Army. It seems that he did not totally abandon Liberal politics as well. He was persuaded to stand as an independent Liberal in the newly

created West Stirlingshire constituency in the 1918 general election. A Unionist, Harry Hope, and Thomas Johnston from the ILP (and a future Secretary
of State for Scotland) opposed him. He came third with 2,582 votes, with
Hope winning the seat. He confessed to Neil Munro, Scottish novelist and
writer, that he was 'sick of the infernal folly of elections'.[55]

The only political organisation Cunninghame Graham associated with at
the start of the 1920s was the revived Scottish Home Rule Association. The
SHRA had become defunct by 1914 following the failure of the Liberals to carry
the 1913 Scottish Home Rule Act in Parliament. Roland Muirhead, the secretary of the Lochwinnoch ILP, was the 'principal architect' of the new SHRA
in 1918.[56] It was becoming apparent in the early 1920s that the Liberals had
been eclipsed by an ascendant Labour Party. The SHRA was pinning its hopes
on Labour until 1924, when an attempt to advance home rule was stifled by
a combination of parliamentary procedure and Ramsay MacDonald's growing indifference. The former secretary of the London Branch of the SHRA in
a letter to Muirhead abdicated responsibility for legislative initiatives, telling
him to contact the relevant government minister rather than him in future.[57]

A further attempt in 1927 to put home rule on to the statute book was
also frustrated by obstruction and ambivalence at Westminster. However,
by 1927 there was evidence that there was momentum building for a nationalist party that sought to challenge the London-based parties electorally. In
1920, the Scots National League was founded, led by Sir William Gillies and
Ruaraidh Erskine of Mar. Richard Finlay has argued that the SNL 'was the
most important of all the interwar nationalist groups, especially with regard
to the future development of Scottish Nationalist philosophy'.[58] It championed 'independence' or separate statehood for Scotland. More important
in a practical sense was that it had 1,000 members and fifteen branches by

55   Tschiffely, *Don Roberto*, p. 380.
56   Finlay, *Independent and Free*, p. 1.
57   Ibid., p. 10.
58   Ibid., p. 29.

the mid-1920s, as well as an official newspaper, the *Scots Independent*, that acted as the mouthpiece for the movement.[59] Within the SHRA, Robert Muirhead, the brother of Roland, had helped to found the Scottish National Party Group, which was lobbying for the association to reinvent itself as a political party. Roland was himself promoting the idea of Scottish National Convention to take out of Westminster's hands the whole issue of home rule and instead vest it in a forum where partisan concerns, such as the status of Scottish MPs voting in Westminster, which had been a major stumbling block in 1924, would be less problematic. A third development in 1927 was the founding of the Glasgow University Student Nationalist Association (GUSNA) led by John MacCormick.

Cunninghame Graham's involvement in the SHRA in the early to mid-1920s was sporadic. He was often invited onto home rule platforms. In 1920, however, he refused to attend one SHRA meeting arranged in support of Irish nationalists over the violence perpetrated by members of the IRA against British soldiers. In a letter to the secretary of the association, he reaffirmed his commitment to Scottish home rule but decried Éamon de Valera and the 'international Jews' in New York who he claimed were behind the violence. He tried to mitigate his anti-Semitic remarks in a postscript to the letter by saying, 'I have, of course, no idea of imputing complicity in murder to the Jews as a race'.[60] This sort of language was not uncommon in his correspondence. It is difficult to know Cunninghame Graham's attitude to all of the machinations going on within and outwith the SHRA at this time, although he was a senior figure in the body.

Since 1648, the undergraduates of Glasgow University have elected a rector to represent them in the institution. The rector was elected every three years and 1928 was to be election year. In MacCormick's account of events, he was trying to think of who might be a suitable and substantial prospective candidate. He wrote that Cunninghame Graham 'came vaguely into mind'

---

59   Ibid., p. 66.
60   Tschiffely, *Don Roberto,* pp. 380–81.

as a possibility and then became certain after reading one of his books, *Hope*, and the preface to George Bernard Shaw's *Captain Brassbound's Conversion*, the main character of which is based on Cunninghame Graham.[61] Cunninghame Graham turned out to be an energetic candidate, despite being seventy-eight years old, and came within seventy votes of beating his rival, incumbent Prime Minister Stanley Baldwin.

CUNNINGHAME GRAHAM, NPS AND THE SNP

By the time of the rectorial election in the autumn of 1928, the final stages of a merger involving the SNL, the SHRA, Scots National Movement (a split off from the SNL) and GUSNA had taken place in time for the launch in November of the National Party of Scotland (NPS). Finlay has argued that Cunninghame Graham did not play much of a role in the negotiations.[62] Tschiffely has claimed that Cunninghame Graham had been named president of the NPS as early as March in 1928, but according to MacCormick this did not take place until the first conference in November.[63] The role he would play in the NPS was largely honorary, though he would participate in the later negotiations in 1933/34 that would see a further merging of the fragments of the national movement with the NPS to form the Scottish National Party.[64]

Although not part of the managerial team in the NPS, he was its most prominent spokesperson. His first major address for the party came following the Glasgow University campaign. He gave a typically acerbic speech, delivered in, according to MacCormick, an 'oratory of Victorian vintage'.[65] He addressed the need for a further party when there were already four. The Conservatives, he said, 'were assured that everything was alright so long

---

61   MacCormick, *The Flag in the Wind*, loc. 520.

62   Finlay, *Independent and Free*, p. 80.

63   MacCormick, *The Flag in the Wind*, loc. 520.

64   Ibid., loc. 1187.

65   Ibid., loc. 520.

as they remained in power';[66] the Liberals were too occupied with the fate and future of Lloyd George; the ILP was too pious; and the Communists too interested in bloodshed and bound to Moscow. The NPS was 'the only party fit to push on the national aspirations and regain once more control of all Scottish National affairs'.[67]

As spokesman he made a number of important statements that shaped the nature of Scottish nationalism. According to MacCormick, Cunninghame Graham was always 'at our service for big meetings'.[68] Arguably his most famous first speech was given at the annual meeting on the NPS at Bannockburn in June 1930. The speech portrays Scottish nationhood not just as an idea drawn from antiquity or from the memory of a long-ago-fought battle, but also based on modern notions of national self-determination. He pointed to the world of nation states that had emerged in the aftermath of the Great War, where, since 1919, twenty new nationalities had emerged. He described nationality as 'the atmosphere of the world' and said that it was 'a sin against political science' for Scotland to be 'subservient, [that it] should be a mere appendage of the predominant partner, a mere county of England' and be denied the same status as that enjoyed by others across the world.[69] In this speech, Cunninghame Graham was moving further towards independence than before.

CONCLUSION

R. B. Cunninghame Graham was in many ways one of the founding fathers of the modern SNP. First, he was a vital element in bringing into being a separate political party devoted to Scottish home rule. He did this by being able to lend respectability and credibility to the cause initially

---

66   *Glasgow Herald*, 29 October 1928, p. 8.

67   Ibid.

68   MacCormick, *Flag in the Wind*, loc. 520.

69   R. B. Cunninghame Graham, 'Nationality is in the atmosphere of the world', in *Great Scottish Speeches*, edited by David Torrance (Edinburgh: Luath, 2011), pp. 98–9.

through his candidature for rector at Glasgow University in 1928 but subsequently through drawing members away from the Scottish Home Rule Association and towards the National Party of Scotland. Second, his 'star power' in the late '20s and early '30s was able to bring prominence to a movement that was largely obscure and peripheral. Although he did not transform it into a mainstream party, he could at least use his celebrity, which was still considerable even nearly forty years after he had lost his seat in Parliament, to attract attention from the media and provide a platform for the NPS and the SNP, which, arguably, they would not have received otherwise.

Third, he brought with him a vision of Scottish nationalism that would connect the NPS and the SNP to the SLP and other manifestations of Scottish Radicalism that gave the movement greater depth and relevance to contemporary Scotland. Cunninghame Graham's interpretation of Scottish home rule was that it was more than just a sentimental longing for a lost nation, that it was more than just a tidy administrative change that sought to bring greater democratic accountability to pre-existing distinctive Scottish institutions, such as the legal and educational systems. He viewed home rule as a vital element in addressing the unique social and economic problems of Scotland, which had been neglected at Westminster, that he saw as representing privilege and big business. From his first statement on the issue in the House of Commons in 1889, and as a radical socialist through to his last speeches as the first president of the Scottish National Party, he maintained this analysis, and in doing so laid down a template upon which the modern-day SNP has built.

CHAPTER 5

SIR ALEXANDER MACEWEN

PROFESSOR EWEN CAMERON

Sir Alexander MacEwen was a prominent Liberal early in his life and was elected a councillor in Inverness before joining one of the precursors of the SNP, the Scottish Party, standing in the Kilmarnock by-election in 1933 with the support of the National Party of Scotland, polling a respectable 17 per cent. With the coming together of the two parties to form the SNP in 1934, he became its first ever chair, but upon the party's disappointing results in the 1935 election, he stood down.

• • •

The town of Inverness was central to the events surrounding the formation of the SNP in 1934. Many of the key negotiations that led to the merger of the National Party of Scotland and the Scottish Party took place there, or were developed through correspondence that emanated from the 'Capital of the Highlands'. The novelist Neil M. Gunn, based in his bungalow, 'Larachan', on Dochfour Drive, was an important player, not least through his relationship with the main subject of this chapter, Alexander MacEwen, who became the first chairman of the new Scottish National Party in 1934. MacEwen was an important figure in Inverness: he had been a member of the town council since 1908 and served as provost between 1925 and 1931. He was a senior partner in the legal firm Stewart and Rule and was active in the associational life of the town, such as the Gaelic Society. His contribution was marked with the naming of a street – MacEwen Drive

– in his honour. Appropriately, given his interest in public housing, this was in a new scheme of council houses constructed during his provostship.[1]

MacEwen's importance goes beyond that of a parish-pump politician who found himself on a wider stage. He was a significant figure who had clear ideas about the role of nationalism in Scottish politics in the 1920s and 1930s. His career prompts reflection on at least four important areas in the early history of the SNP and its predecessors. The first is his role in the events that led to the formation of the party in 1934. His initial involvement in nationalism was through the Scottish Party, founded in 1932 as a 'moderate' counterpoint to the National Party, established in 1928. The second area in which MacEwen deserves attention is as a parliamentary candidate. He stood in the Kilmarnock by-election in 1933, endorsed by both the Scottish Party and the National Party in a move that obviated the appearance of rival nationalist candidates; he was also an SNP candidate for the Western Isles in 1935. Thirdly, vitally important to MacEwen's identity as a politician was his thinking on the particular problems of the Scottish Highlands. In this activity he cooperated with colleagues from other parties and with non-partisan figures to argue for the reconstruction and development of the region. Finally, his role highlights the links between the nationalists and other parties, both before and after the formation of the SNP. MacEwen was, essentially, a nationalist Liberal and he remained in contact with leading Liberals in the 1930s.

Before proceeding to discuss these points, the extent of MacEwen's writings should be noted. He produced two full-length books on his approach to nationalism, both in the Scottish case and in a wider sense, and many shorter pieces on education and the condition of the Highlands.[2] Two clear themes emerge from these writings. The first is what he called the 'business case' for Scottish

---

1   Frank G. Thompson, 'A different drum: a biographical note on Sir Alexander MacEwen, Inverness', *Transactions of the Gaelic Society of Inverness*, 60 (1997–98): 108–24; *Glasgow Herald*, 30 June 1941, p. 6; *Northern Chronicle*, 2 July 1941, p. 2; *Inverness Courier*, 1 July 1941, p. 3; *Highland News*, 5 July 1941, p. 3.

2   Alexander MacEwen, *The Thistle and the Rose: Scotland's Problem Today* (Edinburgh: Oliver and Boyd, 1932); Alexander MacEwen, *Towards Freedom: A Candid Survey of Fascism, Communism and Modern Democracy* (London: William Hodge, 1938); Alexander MacEwen, *Scotland at School: Education for Citizenship* (Edinburgh: Belhaven Press, 1938).

self-government. Although he placed due emphasis on history and culture, his principal contention was that the creation of a Scottish Parliament would make Scotland a more prosperous place. When he became chairman of the SNP in 1934, his rallying call was that the party was the first to 'present to the electors a definite practical policy of reconstruction'.[3] This was more important to him than self-government as an expression of national identity. It also helps to explain why he was 'moderate' in his demands and was against 'separation': 'a moderate policy has the double advantage of being more likely to succeed in a short space of time and of offering opportunities for adjustment and improvement'. He thought complete independence was impractical and likely to 'dislocate trade and involve serious political complications'.[4] A further important theme was his emphasis on self-help. In 1938, he argued that nationalism was not a narrow concept but the best expression of the kind of democratic cooperation that was necessary to solve the economic and social problems that faced the world in the 1930s. He contrasted his conception of nationalism to the kind of patriotism demanded by dictatorships of both left and right; in his view they were 'antagonistic to individual rights and liberties'. He argued that 'deification of the state is not patriotism or nationalism', the individual was at the heart of the nation and the success of the nation could only be achieved through self-reliance, something which could not be delivered by the state in a direct way.[5] These ideas received practical expression in MacEwen's career through his parliamentary campaigns and his activity relating to the Scottish Highlands.

MacEwen was, despite his prominence, a slightly diffident and reserved figure, and his chairmanship of the party was short-lived and relatively unsuccessful.[6] George Malcolm Thomson, for example, thought him 'not harsh enough' in his approach or his rhetoric and he was sidelined in 1936 by Andrew

---

3   Alexander MacEwen, 'The National Crusade! A Rousing Call', *Scots Independent*, October 1934, p. 177–8.

4   MacEwen, *The Thistle and the Rose*, pp. 153–4.

5   MacEwen, *Towards Freedom*, pp. viii, 3–8; Alexander MacEwen, 'The Future of Scottish Nationalism', *Scots Independent*, November 1937, p. 3.

6   MacCormick, *Flag in the Wind*, loc. 65–6.

Dewar Gibb, a former Unionist who took the SNP in a different direction.[7] This mildness did not insure him against scorn from such as Christopher Murray Grieve (aka Hugh MacDiarmid), who regarded him as a moderate, hardly a nationalist at all, and one of an establishment clique who took over and corrupted the National Party in 1934.[8] MacEwen lacked the verve and hyperactivity of John MacCormick or the talent for self-publicity of Douglas Young, but he was central to the early history of the SNP and in the period from 1932 to 1936 was crucial to the establishment of even the small amount of credibility that it had, not least through his election campaigns. MacEwen, unlike most other figures in the party, had experience of executive administration, albeit at the local level in Inverness. He was, however, a significant figure in the life of the town at a point at which it developed markedly and his role in expanding the public housing stock of the burgh was very important. He was also one of a vocal and articulate group – including Dr Lachlan Grant of Ballachulish, John Lorne Campbell of Canna, Neil Gunn and Thomas Murchison – that wrote and campaigned in a way that ensured that the problems of the Scottish Highlands were part of the wider debate about the condition of Scotland in this period.

MACEWEN AND THE FORMATION OF THE SNP

I n December 1933, MacEwen fought a by-election in Kilmarnock after intense politicking had headed off the prospect of a damaging fight between rival nationalist candidates. Although MacEwen's performance at the election was scarcely triumphant, this was a significant event in the history of Scottish nationalism and it led directly to the formation of the SNP. To understand MacEwen's place in these developments, we need to examine his place in the emergence in 1932 of the Scottish Party, usually seen as a right-wing alternative

---

7   NLS, Gibb Mss, Dep 217/1/4: letter from G. M. Thomson to Andrew Dewar Gibb, 31 August 1934; George McKechnie, *The Best-Hated Man: George Malcolm Thomson, Intellectuals and the Condition of Scotland Between the Wars* (Glendaruel: Argyll Publishing, 2013), pp. 183–9.

8   Alan Bold (ed.), *The Letters of Hugh MacDiarmid* (London: Hamish Hamilton, 1984), Grieve to J. H. Whyte, 1 July 1936, p. 851.

to the National Party.[9] Along with the Duke of Montrose and businessmen like Sir Daniel Stevenson, MacEwen was prominent in what was initially known as the 'Scottish Self Government Party' when it was launched at meetings in Glasgow and Edinburgh in late 1932. At a public meeting in Glasgow, MacEwen emphasised that the new party was based on a search for individual and national self-reliance, a 'very old' Scottish tradition. The aim was to seek for Scots 'the elementary right to manage their own affairs' and, he stressed, this would not 'disrupt the Empire or cause a civil war'.[10] The approach of the Scottish Party, MacEwen included, was condemned as 'devolutionist' by many in the SNP, such as T. H. Gibson on the left of the party, who could see no distinction between the approach of the 'Montrose–MacEwan [*sic*] gang' and conventional Westminster parties, such as the Liberals, with an interest in Scottish home rule but no track record of delivery despite a history of government.[11] The difficulty for the National Party in this period was that it seemed to be making no political progress. The 1931 election, aside from a promising performance by John MacCormick in Inverness-shire, had been a disappointment, and other forays into electoral politics, such as Eric Linklater's disastrous candidature in East Fife, had been embarrassing.[12] This was the background to the opening of negotiations between MacCormick and MacEwen through the good offices of Neil Gunn and his friend Robin MacEwen, son of Alexander.[13] The difficulty with these discussions was that each party to them had a different interest. MacEwen was principally interested in creating a moderate nationalism that would steer a middle path between the

---

9   Finlay, *Independent and Free*, pp. 93–6.

10 *Scotsman*, 22 September 1932, p. 9; 2 December 1932, p. 11; 15 December 1932, p. 8.

11 NLS, Gunn Mss, Dep 209/15/2: Gibson to Gunn, 6 April 1933.

12 This provided Linklater with comic material for his 1934 novel *Magnus Merriman*.

13 Finlay, *Independent and Free*, pp. 104–8; F. R. Hart and J. B. Pick, *Neil M. Gunn: A Highland Life* (London: John Murray, 1981), pp. 112–93. Robin's brother, Malcolm, was also politically active in the Labour Party and, from 1940, the Communist Party of Great Britain; he was on the staff of the *Daily Worker* but left the party after the Soviet invasion of Hungary in 1956. He came to the attention of the security services, who monitored his activities from 1938 to 1958. See the National Archives of the UK, KV2/2985–9; Elizabeth Darling, 'MacEwen, Ann Maitland (1918–2008)', *Oxford Dictionary of National Biography* (Oxford University Press, January 2012) http://www.oxforddnb.com/view/article/99705 [accessed 20 May 2016].

'extremists on both sides', but he was disappointed that the National Party's attitude had hardened in the summer of 1933 after promising initial talks in the aftermath of a conference in Inverness in May of that year.[14] He had tried to stress that the Scottish Party was not antagonistic to the National Party but when he tried to articulate his sense of Scottish nationalism it tended to come across as rather close to a conventional home-rule position. In an article in the *Scots Independent* in 1933, he argued that the Scottish Party aimed for a Scottish Parliament with 'final legislative authority on Scottish affairs' including taxation but he stressed the importance of the Imperial Parliament for defence and foreign affairs. He went on:

> We believe that the National Spirit is capable of a richer development
> in partnership with England and the Empire than in glorious isolation.
> Nationhood depends not on guns and ships or a seat at Geneva, but on
> the extent to which a country can realise its distinctive national life, not
> only in government but in literature, art and social well-being.[15]

Gunn, on the other hand, was resistant to fusion at any price, was suspicious of the 'devolutionist' Scottish Party and regarded the National Party as the true and established vehicle for Scottish nationalism.[16]

The Kilmarnock by-election brought these matters to the fore in an unambiguous way. When the election was called, the National Party was quick to announce a candidate, John M. McNicol, and there was a degree of surprise when Andrew Dewar Gibb, a prominent academic lawyer and former Unionist candidate, came forward as a Scottish Party candidate. Neil Gunn interpreted it as a deliberate and provocative challenge to the National Party.[17] A conference was held in Glasgow in September 1933 at which the National Party and

---

14   NLS, Gibb Mss, Dep 217/1/2: letter from MacEwen to Gibb, 1 August 1933.

15   *Scots Independent*, May 1933, p. 104.

16   NLS, Gibb Mss, Dep 217/1/1, letter from Gunn to Gibb, 28 July 1933.

17   Ibid.

the Scottish Party were represented. At this meeting the National Party reiterated its fundamental principles: a Scottish Parliament with control over taxation and finance; equality between Scotland and England in the empire; joint machinery for defence and foreign policy; belief in action by an independent political party with no ties to any 'English-controlled party'. The parties agreed to work together to set up the necessary Anglo-Scottish machinery for imperial affairs; to oppose tariff barriers between Scotland and England; to gain international representation for Scotland at the League of Nations. They concluded that there should only be 'such alterations in the Union with England as are necessary to obtain the above'. On this basis both parties agreed to stand down their candidates and to allow the local representatives in Kilmarnock to nominate a joint candidate.[18] This represented a victory for the Scottish Party side in the negotiations and MacEwen was at the heart of this. One historian has called it a 'coup d'état' and it was facilitated by MacEwen's knowledge of practical politics.[19] Further, he had enough contacts in the National Party, through Gunn and his son Robin, who was close to John MacCormick, that he did not arouse the same suspicion as other leading figures in the Scottish Party, such as the Duke of Montrose or John Kevan McDowall.

If this was a coup d'état, then the next stage was the appearance of MacEwen as the candidate in Kilmarnock. The process by which this transpired was another important milestone on the path towards fusion between the two parties and the creation of the SNP. Initially, the Gaelic-speaking Liberal and former Scottish rugby international captain John M. Bannerman was suggested, but his associations with the Duke of Montrose, whose tenant farmer he was, were too much for some, who condemned Bannerman as a Tory – a clear case of guilt by association. He later became one of the key figures in the Liberal Party during its period in the wilderness, standing as a

---

18   NLS, Gunn Mss, Dep 209/15/2: minute of meeting of representatives of the National Party of Scotland and the Scottish Party, 5 September 1933.

19   Finlay, *Independent and Free*, p. 146.

candidate in their interest on no less than eight occasions from 1945 to 1966.[20] A breakdown in negotiations was only avoided when the local chairman suggested MacEwen as the joint candidate. MacCormick reported that, in view of the local popularity of this suggestion, he 'could see no way of opposing it' and that he was 'disappointed' with this outcome.[21] The lack of openness with which this decision had been reached infuriated National Party activists, some of whom felt that the Scottish Party was taking over. Even if MacEwen was seen, in the words of T. H. Gibson, as a potentially 'valuable asset to the National Party', he was regarded with suspicion because of his opposition to 'separation', which he had elevated to a bogey word, and his continuing links with the Liberal Party.[22]

MACEWEN AT KILMARNOCK, DECEMBER 1933

At this moment in the history of Scottish nationalism there was no more important person than Alexander MacEwen. He bore the nationalist standard in a crucial by-election, a contest that was vital in restoring the electoral credibility of the nationalist cause. He was the only person who had sufficient trust on both sides of the Scottish Party/National Party divide to be able to push forward the idea of fusion between the two parties and have the outcome regarded as something other than a complete takeover by the Scottish Party. He had a level of national standing and political experience that no other nationalist could command, even if this did make him look like a fully paid-up member of the establishment. As Neil Gunn noted, '[A]ll depends on Sir Alexander MacEwen. If he stands by his opening address and does not accept (1) dilution of his policy and (2) party help from any Westminster lot like the Liberals, we're right and there will be a mighty surge forward.'[23]

20   John Fowler (ed.), *Bannerman: The Memoirs of Lord Bannerman of Kildonan* (Aberdeen: Impulse Books, 1972).

21   NLS, Gunn Mss, Dep 209/15/2: letter from MacCormick to Gunn, 8 October 1933.

22   NLS, Gunn Mss, Dep 209/15/2: letter from Gibson to Gunn, 12 October & 20 October 1933; Elma Campbell (Gibson) to Gunn, 12 October 1933.

23   NLS, Gibb Mss, Dep 209/1/1: letter from Gunn to Gibb, 17 October 1933.

In his election address, where he was described as the 'Scottish Self-Government Candidate', MacEwen articulated the key points that had emerged from the Glasgow meeting in September 1933 (see above). He argued that Scottish control of Scottish affairs was necessary to stop the increasingly southwards drift of industry, especially in the cases of banking and the railway companies, and to counter very high levels of unemployment in Scotland. He also argued for greater power for the Scottish Office departments and their relocation to Scotland. His thoughts on foreign policy belied his Liberalism – an avoidance of foreign entanglements that might lead to 'the possibility of this country being involved in another European war'. The prevailing imperialism of Scottish nationalism, present in the National Party as well as the Scottish Party, although stronger in the latter, was also part of his appeal. He described membership of the 'British Commonwealth of Nations' as a 'fundamental principle', and he advocated 'all measures calculated to strengthen the friendship and commercial ties between Scotland and England and the Dominions and Colonies'. In his conclusion, he attempted to assert his independence from other parties by arguing that, although members of the Labour, Liberal and Unionist parties supported self-government, they 'are under the control of their party whips and cannot enforce a Scottish demand'.[24]

The Kilmarnock by-election was vital for the nationalist movement in Scotland in re-establishing electoral credibility. MacEwen fought a campaign of practical nationalism, emphasising such issues as the loss of Scottish economic control, exemplified by the forthcoming move of Stewarts & Lloyds, steel-tube manufacturers, to Corby; and the effect on the locomotive industry, a major employer in Kilmarnock (as in Inverness), of the amalgamation of the Scottish railway companies with English concerns. Despite the fact that free-trade views were losing their force among agriculturalists, he attempted to make an appeal to farmers.[25] This was a campaign fought in prose rather than poetry and in its competence

---

24   NLS, 6.2398, Election address of Sir Alexander MacEwen, Kilmarnock by-election, 25 October 1933; Richard J. Finlay, '"For or Against?"'.

25   *The Scotsman*, 28 October 1933, pp. 13, 14; 30 October 1933, p. 12; 31 October 1933, p. 10.

and sober appeal at the opposite end of the political spectrum to Linklater's efforts in East Fife. The *Scots Independent* felt that the ground lost on that occasion had been 'brilliantly recovered and the foundation of future progress have been securely laid'.[26] The tone may have been uninspiring but, arguably, this is what the nationalists required at this moment, and for the delivery of which MacEwen had been selected. Even one of his opponents, who derided the Scottish nationalist movement as having been 'born in an Edinburgh drawing room' and dominated by 'poets, artists and intellectual highbrows', admitted that MacEwen stood out as a practical man of administrative experience.[27] The circumstances of the election were unusual in that all of his three opponents were 'Socialists' – National Labour, Labour and Independent Labour Party – and the election was fought in the shadow of the sensational East Fulham election on 25 October, in which the National Government candidate had been defeated by a Labour opponent. Perhaps this resulted in a rallying of support for the National Labour candidate, costing MacEwen some votes.[28] In the event, on 2 November, he came bottom of the poll, but with just over 6,000 votes (compared to the 12,577 for the National Labour victor).[29] This was slightly disappointing and certainly short of the expectations indicated by a cartoon in the *Scots Independent* that showed MacEwen in a tartan plaid, driving a car with the registration 'AD1314' accelerating past his opponents.[30] It was, nevertheless, a respectable showing for the technocratic brand of nationalism articulated by MacEwen and evident in some of his publications.[31] Some Unionists, including John Buchan and Sir John Gilmour, specifically argued against separatism, perhaps in an attempt to sow discord among nationalists. MacEwen's response was both low-key – he hoped that a putative Scottish Parliament would not be a 'slavish imitation of

---

26   *Scots Independent*, December 1933, p. 1 (see also p. 25 of the same issue).

27   *The Scotsman*, 31 October 1933, p. 9.

28   Ibid., 27 October 1933, p. 8; 29 October 1933, p. 25; 1 November 1933, p. 10.

29   Ibid., 4 November 1933, p. 14.

30   *Scots Independent*, November 1933, p. 3.

31   Alexander MacEwen, John MacCormick and Thomas H. Gibson, *Scottish Reconstruction* (Glasgow: National Party, 1930).

that at Westminster' but a 'business-like assembly and not a talking shop' – and concerned to address wider issues – he declared himself surprised that Buchan, 'who realises the loss of the individuality of our national life', did not appreciate that a 'Scottish Parliament would stimulate the whole life of our nation and fire our people to greater efforts'.[32]

MACEWEN IN THE WESTERN ISLES, 1935

MacEwen had a further appearance as a nationalist candidate in the 1935 general election, this time in the Western Isles. As a Gaelic-speaking Highlander, this was more fertile territory for him than industrial Kilmarnock. Although the early nationalist parties were uncertain about the extent to which a strategy of contesting parliamentary elections was the correct one, they secured some of their best results in the Highlands. This was not an indication that the Highlands were particularly nationalistic in outlook, but, through choice of good candidates with local connections, such as John MacCormick in Inverness-shire in 1931 and 1935 or MacEwen in the Western Isles in 1935, the SNP were able to take relative advantage of three cornered contests to score respectable results. MacEwen's 28.1 per cent share of the vote, although in third place, was the best result for an SNP candidate up to that point. A more common fate was a lost deposit.[33] In making their appeal to the highland electorate, the SNP emphasised their political independence from the main parties and, on some occasions, attempted to place themselves in a direct line of political inheritance from the Crofter MPs of the 1880s.[34] Although he had notable SNP figures, such as Mrs Burnett Smith (the homely writer Annie S. Swan) and the Duke of Montrose, to speak for him, he played down the party political elements of his candidature.[35] At a meeting in Stornoway,

---

32   *Scotsman*, 31 October 1933, p. 9; 1 November 1933, p. 11.

33   MacCormick, *Flag in the Wind*, pp. 49–50, 88–9.

34   A point made by John MacCormick in a speech in Stornoway, *Stornoway Gazette*, 8 November 1935, p. 8.

35   *Stornoway Gazette*, 22 November 1935, p. 6.

he argued that his ambitions were not political but constructive. He was opposed to centralisation, evident in the 1929 Local Government Act, and argued that his 'only ambition was to try to do something useful for the Highlands, and more particularly for the Western Isles'.[36] In common with many nationalists of this period, he played down the idea of outright independence for Scotland in favour of a greater role for Scotland in the empire:

> I would never be a party to any scheme of self-government, to any scheme of devolution which was going to weaken the ties of Scotland to the British Empire, or which was going to create any hostility or animosity between England and Scotland. The self-governing communities of the Empire were knit to the mother nations by ties far stronger than any legal bonds or anything that paper or parchment could bestow. But if the present neglect of Scotland was allowed to continue, there was a grave danger that there would arise in the minds of the Scottish people a sense of injustice and inferiority to England.[37]

In the event, the election was won by the Labour candidate, Malcolm Mac-Millan, who represented the constituency until he was toppled by the SNP's Donald Stewart in 1970.

MACEWEN AND THE SCOTTISH HIGHLANDS

The prominence and prestige of MacEwen in the Highlands gave him a regional base, authority and experience unavailable to others in the nationalist parties of this period. Further, MacEwen had clear ideas on the development of the region. He had been secretary of the 'Highland Reconstruction Association' in the early 1920s, an organisation that had argued for development of the economy of the region by investment in more

---

36   Ibid., 20 September 1935, p. 6.

37   Ibid., 8 November 1935, p. 8; Finlay, '"For or Against?"', pp. 184–206.

labour-intensive industries so that the Highlands would not be left behind as the rest of the country recovered from the Great War. As one of MacEwen's colleagues in the Association later recalled, his objective was 'to make the Highlands a fit place for Highland heroes to live in'.[38] He would sustain an interest in the idea of reconstructing the economy and society of the region throughout his life.[39] The Highlands had been characterised by depopulation and underdevelopment for at least a century and, although government had intervened to try to deal with the land question from the 1880s and in the 1920s had undertaken what were, effectively, large-scale land nationalisation projects, the Highlands were in a depressed condition by the 1930s. The land settlement of the 1920s had been paralleled by very extensive emigration, which compounded the losses suffered during the Great War.[40] By the late 1930s, emigration had ceased and the land settlement operation was no longer active, and this presaged a new debate about the condition of the region, to which MacEwen contributed.[41]

During the 1930s, there was an extensive discussion about the extent to which Scotland's problems were virtually existential. The most pessimistic prognostications were put forward by Andrew Dewar Gibb, also of the Scottish Party, and George Malcolm Thomson.[42] MacEwen bought into some of this thinking; in his Kilmarnock campaign he talked of the loss of economic control and activity, the effects of emigration and the unemployment that afflicted Scotland in the 1930s. This was a view that emanated not only from

---

38   NLS, Lachlan Grant Mss, Acc. 12187/9, f. 21: letter from Donald Cameron of Lochiel to Lachlan Grant, no date but circa February 1936.

39   MacEwen, *The Thistle and the Rose*, pp. 220–36.

40   Ewen A. Cameron, *Land for the People? The British Government and the Scottish Highlands, c.1880–1930* (East Linton: Tuckwell Press, 1996); Marjory Harper, *Emigration from Scotland Between the Wars: Opportunity or Exile?* (Manchester: Manchester University Press, 1998), pp. 71–112.

41   Alexander MacEwen and John Lorne Campbell, *Act Now for the Highlands and Islands* (Edinburgh: Belhaven Press, 1939); Ray Perman, *The Man Who Gave Away His Island: A Life of John Lorne Campbell of Canna* (Edinburgh: Birlinn, 2010), pp. 68–9.

42   Andrew Dewar Gibb, *Scotland in Eclipse* (London: Toulmin, 1930); George Malcolm Thomson, *Scotland: That Distressed Area* (Edinburgh: Porpoise Press, 1935); this literature is analysed by Richard J. Finlay, 'National Identity in Crisis: Politicians, Intellectuals and the "End of Scotland", 1920–1939', *History*, 79 (1994): 242–59.

nationalist drawing rooms but also from some elements of the business community, who felt that economic policy was built around the priorities of the south-east of England rather than the industrial areas of Scotland. Organisations like the Scottish National Development Council (of which MacEwen was a member), founded in 1931, and its offshoot the Scottish Economic Committee, contributed to this body of opinion.[43] As far as MacEwen, and some within government, were concerned, initiatives such as the Special Areas Acts did nothing for the particular problems of the Scottish Highlands, which did not arise because of temporary economic circumstances but from conditions that were 'as old as the physical considerations which give rise to [them]'.[44] The debate about the Highlands revolved around two approaches. One was essentially romantic and argued that the region was separate from the rest of Scotland and that the focus ought to be on its traditional industries – agriculture and fishing – and on land reform. Initiatives along these lines would not 'spoil' the landscape and render the region unattractive to tourists. Others took a different view and argued that the benefits that would come from increased employment were as applicable in the Highlands as in Lanarkshire and that industries such as aluminium, which already had a foothold, and carbide ought to be developed, and if that meant extensive construction of hydro-electric schemes that would flood romantic landscapes then the price was worth paying for economic progress. This view was associated with Dr Lachlan Grant of Ballachulish, who was behind the establishment of the 'Highland Development League' following publication in 1936 of his *A New Deal for the Highlands*.[45] This debate was seen at its clearest in the attempts to pass the Caledonian Power Bill, which would have provided the supply

43   MacEwen, *The Thistle and the Rose*, pp. 191–7; R. H. Campbell, 'The Scottish Office and the Special Areas in the 1930s', *Historical Journal*, 22 (1979): 167–83; Angus Mackenzie, 'Self-help and Propaganda: Scottish National Development Council, 1931–1939', *Journal of Scottish Historical Studies*, 30 (2010): 123–45.

44   National Records of Scotland [hereafter NRS], DD15/12: undated [c.1939] memo concerning the Highland Development Commissioner.

45   This debate is discussed in Ewen A. Cameron, '"Outside the ranks of those who stand for the traditional and the sentimental": Lachlan Grant and Economic Development', in Ewen A. Cameron and Annie Tindley (eds), *Dr Lachlan Grant of Ballachulish, 1871–1945* (Edinburgh: Birlinn, 2015), pp. 81–93.

of electricity to the British Oxygen Company for a new factory at Fort William. This proposal was defeated by an unholy alliance of landed interests, left-wing opposition to natural resources being captured by private business interests and the coal lobby, who feared the development of alternative sources of cheap renewable energy. MacEwen argued that the Caledonian Power Scheme was defeated by English parliamentary votes, despite having extensive support in Scotland.[46] His position was highly controversial, however, as he was retained by the British Oxygen Company as their spokesman. The *Inverness Courier* was a particular critic of MacEwen in this respect.[47]

His view was more nuanced than his critics allowed, however, and owed much to his Liberal political roots. When the Scottish Economic Committee reported on the condition of the Highlands in 1938, they recommended that a 'Highland Development Commissioner' be appointed to coordinate the work of the agencies that had responsibility for the administration and development of the Highlands.[48] Despite strong support for this idea across the Highlands, MacEwen was opposed on the grounds that this was handing too much responsibility to one individual in the name of the state. He labelled the proposed Commissioner a 'dictator for the Highlands'. For MacEwen, the Commissioner would become a prisoner of government rather than an advocate of Highland interests. A permanent board led by a figure with knowledge and experience of the region was preferable, in his view. MacEwen also saw this issue in quasi-nationalist terms: 'absentee government is as bad as absentee landlords'.[49] In the event, this debate was inconclusive as the outbreak of the Second World War prevented even the government's modest response to these proposals from being implemented.

---

46 MacEwen, *Towards Freedom*, p. 109.

47 Clive M. Birnie, '"New deal" or raw deal? Public Administration and Economic Development in the Highlands and Islands of Scotland, 1929–1939', unpublished MSc thesis, University of Edinburgh, 2003, pp. 47–61.

48 Scottish Economic Committee, *The Highlands and Islands of Scotland: A Review of the Economic Conditions with Recommendations for Improvement* (London, 1938).

49 Alexander MacEwen, 'A dictator for the highlands? The strengths and weaknesses of the Scottish Economic Committee's Report', *Scots Magazine*, 30 (1938–39): 293–8.

MACEWEN AND THE LIBERAL PARTY

T hroughout his time in the SNP, MacEwen was identified as a politician
with whom other parties could do business, especially those in the Liberal Party. This became an especially pressing matter in the post-1931 period.
The formation of the National Government in 1931 and the initial participation in it of both the official Liberals under Herbert Samuel and the Liberal
Nationals under Sir John Simon sowed very considerable tension in the
Liberal movement. When, in 1932, the official Liberals resigned their Cabinet positions (they eventually crossed the floor of the House of Commons in
1933) over the traditional Liberal principle of free trade, these divisions were
deepened. In this context, the emergence of the Scottish nationalist parties was
problematic. The Liberals felt proprietorial over the idea of home rule, having
advocated it since 1886, and they resented the nationalist challenge. Further, the
Liberals performed very badly in Scotland in the election of 1935, their representation declining to only three seats and 6.7 per cent of the vote (in 1910 they
had fifty-eight seats and 54 per cent of the vote, a memory that was painful).

The Liberal leadership fell to Sir Archibald Sinclair, MP for Caithness
and Sutherland. He was both resentful and fearful of the SNP and was of the
view that it must be possible to reach out to elements within the new party to
try to prevent further electoral decline. In 1935, Sinclair told Montrose that
it 'would be ridiculous for the Nationalist and Liberal parties to be cutting
one another's throats in Scotland and at the next General Election'.[50] The
most consistent target for Sinclair and his acolytes in the development of this
self-preservation strategy was MacEwen. Throughout the period from 1930
to 1938, MacEwen was in contact with Sinclair and other leading Liberals
about a rapprochement between the two parties. As a 'moderate' nationalist
who did not believe in 'separation', MacEwen had much in common with
Sinclair, and they also shared Liberal views on the role of the state and on

---

50   Cambridge, Churchill College Political Archives Centre [hereafter CCPAC], THRS V, 13/1/5–6: letter
      from Sinclair to Montrose, 27 November 1934.

free trade. There seem to have been three phases of contact. The first came in 1932 and involved an attempt on the part of Sinclair to attract MacEwen to come to the Liberal conference and move a resolution on 'moderate' home rule, in the hope that this would widen the appeal of the policy. This initiative foundered on renewed arguments for separatism on the part of leading nationalists, much to the disappointment of MacEwen, according to Sinclair.[51] There was renewed contact in 1934, at which point Sinclair was highly complementary of MacEwen. Sinclair saw the dangers of competition between Liberals and nationalists but he was worried about overriding the autonomy of local Liberal parties and splitting the party for uncertain gains, and therefore counselled against any binding commitments.[52] There was an attempt to get MacEwen to stand in the ill-fated Ross and Cromarty by-election of 1936; this came to nothing and a brave but inexperienced Liberal candidate recorded a poor result in a contest dominated by luminaries like Randolph Churchill and Malcolm MacDonald.[53] There was a final series of contacts in 1938, when there were rumours emanating from the Duke of Montrose, whom Sinclair distrusted, that MacEwen 'was hesitating on the brink of coming over finally to the Liberal Party'. This time the obstacle was that he wanted to fight a Highland seat but was disinclined to fight against MacCormick in Inverness-shire and thought it imprudent to fight the Western Isles as a Liberal. By this time there was some weariness on the part of the Liberals with MacEwen's temporising. Sinclair felt that his stock had fallen as a result of the failure of the SNP but that if he could be tempted he would be a valuable addition to the Liberals' slate of candidates.[54]

These events are interesting as they sum up a number of themes in MacEwen's career and highlight some of the issues surrounding his politics.

51   CCPAC, THRS II, 68/3/86: letter from Sinclair to William Webster, 11 August 1932; 68/4/24: Webster to Sinclair, 26 September 1932; 68/4/39: Sinclair to Webster, 28 October 1932.

52   CCPAC, THRS II, 70/1/3/20–1: letter from Sinclair to James Scott, 9 November 1934.

53   CCPAC, THRS II, 72/3: letter from Sinclair to MacEwen, 1 January 1936; 72/3: MacEwen to Sinclair, 11 January 1936; Ewen A. Cameron, '"Rival foundlings": the Ross and Cromarty by-election, 1 February 1936', *Historical Research*, 81 (2008): 507–30.

54   CCPAC, THRS II, 74/3: letter from Sinclair to Findlay, 31 March 1938.

MacEwen's chairmanship of the SNP was not very successful. His own performance in the Western Isles notwithstanding, the 1935 election had been a disaster and MacEwen felt a degree of personal responsibility for the failure. Although not mentioned by name, a hostile article in the *Scots Independent* in early 1936 drew attention to 'weak spots' in the strategy of the party in this period. The four points of policy agreed in 1933 were attacked and, in a scarcely coded attack on MacEwen's scepticism about 'separatism', it was asserted: 'Let it be clearly stated that no limit is prescribed, that the Scottish Parliament must have as full power as other independent nations ... we narrow our policy when we say what is to be done by the Scottish Parliament.'[55] This was a direct challenge to the 'moderate' approach. The very aspects that made MacEwen a figure of some suspicion in nationalist circles – his 'moderation' and lack of enthusiasm for 'separatism' made him initially attractive to Liberals. Further, it is clear that Sinclair and his colleagues did not view the SNP as a conventional political party conforming to the customary rules of discipline and organisation, and MacEwen in his overtures to them did nothing to discourage this point of view. The impression was both given and received that the SNP was merely a vehicle for a home rule scheme and if that could be achieved through treating with other parties then such a course of action was permissible for its leading members. This ambivalence is a major theme in the early history of the SNP and, arguably, was not resolved until well into the post-war period. MacEwen in his approach to both his own party and the Liberals was a prime example of this fundamental uncertainty in the strategy of the nationalists in the 1930s.[56]

---

55   *Scots Independent*, February 1936, p. 2.

56   Finlay, 'Pressure group or political party?'; Graham Watson, 'Scottish Liberals and Scottish Nationalists and Dreams of a Common Front', *Journal of Liberal Democrat History*, 22 (1999): 3–13.

CHAPTER 6

ANDREW DEWAR GIBB

CATRIONA M. M. MACDONALD

'It has been noticed with others ... of the younger members that they take for granted positions which were long matters of heart searching to the pioneers.'

— DOUGLAS YOUNG TO ANDREW DEWAR GIBB,
4 NOVEMBER 1943

Andrew Dewar Gibb was politically engaged throughout his adult life, as well as a leading academic lawyer, becoming Regius Professor of Law at Glasgow University in 1934. He stood for Parliament in 1924 and 1929 as a Unionist, but slowly came to the view that Scotland did not gain from union with England. Realising this, he first joined the Scottish Party, and when the SNP was set up in 1934, became one of its founder members. He became its second chairman in 1936, and three times stood for the party in the Scottish Universities seat, finishing second and polling 31 per cent in the 1936 by-election, but resigned as chair in 1940 as the party's centre-left character became more pronounced. He increasingly became detached from politics after 1945, though he was president of the Covenant Association, focusing instead on cultural affairs through the Saltire Society.

. . .

n an age when many old European nations embraced leadership cults and the new nations that emerged from the Great War idolised statesmen who had been midwives at their birth, the Scottish nationalist parties of the interwar years boasted no modern martyrs, few contemporary heroes and arguably little in the way of leadership. There were, of course, individuals who adopted leadership positions in the National Party of Scotland, the Scottish Party and the Scottish National Party, but there was no consensus as to what leadership *meant* in a movement, the goals of which were disputed, its aims contested, and its strategy fluid to say the least. The early occupants of executive positions in these parties were often in practice at liberty to define their own roles; they alternately reached beyond or failed to fulfil the remit of their office; and – given the small size of party membership – they would regularly conduct business informally and behind closed doors. Perhaps as a consequence, personality was at a premium, but not necessarily of the type that was attractive to the public or that ultimately impacts upon conventional political histories.

The posthumous reputation of Andrew Dewar Gibb (1888–1974) has suffered as a consequence of his role as one of this pioneer generation, his status as an 'establishment' figure, and the unforgiving glare of hindsight, which sees little to commend in his racialist views and early fascist sympathies, even when acknowledging them to have been more common in a previous generation. Gibb entered politics as a member of the Unionist Party and unsuccessfully contested two general elections in the Tory interest in 1924 (Hamilton) and 1929 (Greenock) before becoming one of the founders of the SP, the second chairman of the SNP from 1936 to 1940, the co-founder (with George Malcolm Thomson) of the short-lived Scottish Centre in 1945, and a loyal (if ultimately disenchanted) supporter of the Scottish Covenant Association into the 1960s. A native of Paisley, and a graduate of the University of Glasgow, Gibb served in France in the Royal Scots Fusiliers during the Great War, ultimately reaching the rank of major. After practising law in England from 1919, he lectured in English law at the University of Edinburgh (1929–31), and lectured in Scots law at the University of

Cambridge (1931–34) before returning to the University of Glasgow as Regius professor of law – a post he held until 1958.[1] Posterity – at least from what may be gleaned in the current historiography of the nationalist movement – has accorded Gibb a very uncomfortable place in the succession of nationalist leaders. Some writers fail to go much beyond Gibb's racial approach to Scottish identity and his bigoted views on the Catholic Irish in Scotland,[2] while others see his views on the empire as a break on nationalist radicalism.[3] Fascist links and sympathies – both institutional and personal – have also haunted Gibb's story,[4] while the most recent history of the post-'45 SNP is perhaps kinder than most, simply by not mentioning him at all.[5]

Gibb's era as SNP chairman is regularly contrasted with that of the party secretary who replaced John MacCormick in 1942, Robert McIntyre: Richard Finlay notes that under McIntyre, party organisation and propaganda improved, membership rose and a distinctive nationalist message was presented with confidence.[6] His achievements were crowned by his success at the Motherwell by-election in 1945. Yet McIntyre did not *create* a party, he *reformed* one: he was not of the pioneer generation, and in evaluating the achievement of those who preceded him this ought to be borne in mind. For all its failings, by 1942 the SNP had survived eight years of the most challenging economic, social and political upheaval that any modern democracy had endured. Gibb is – in part – the reason why, by 1942, the party needed

---

1   Ewen A. Cameron, 'Gibb, Andrew Dewar (1888–1974)', *Oxford Dictionary of National Biography* (Oxford University Press, October 2009; online edition, September 2010) http://www.oxforddnb.com/view/article/58792 [accessed 5 April 2016].

2   Patrick Hossay, 'Partisans and Nationalists: Rethinking Cleavage Formation and Political Nationalism in Interwar Flanders and Scotland', *Social Science History*, 27/2 (2003): 186–7; R. M. Douglas, 'The Swastika and the Shamrock: British Fascism and the Irish Question, 1918–1940', *Albion*, 29/1 (1997): 72–3; Tom Gallagher, 'Political Extremism in Urban Scotland 1930–1939: Its Growth and Contraction', *Scottish Historical Review*, 64/2 (1985): 146.

3   Kidd, *Union and Unionisms*, p. 290.

4   Gavin Bowd, *Fascist Scotland: Caledonia and the Far Right* (Edinburgh: Birlinn, 2013), pp. 124–5; Stephen M. Cullen, 'The Fasces and the Saltire: The Failure of the British Union of Fascists in Scotland, 1932–1940', *Scottish Historical Review*, 87/2 (2008): 320.

5   Somerville, *Through the Maelstrom*.

6   Finlay, *Independent and Free*, pp. 235–43.

McIntyre, but how and why the party survived into the 1940s is – in part – also Gibb's story.

By focusing on the history of the interwar nationalist parties from the Tory perspective of Gibb much is to be gained, as, to date, the history of the SNP has largely been seen through the prism of NPS interests and in the spirit of its antecedents in the early Labour movement and the Scottish Home Rule Association. Seen in this light, the merger in 1934 looks very different, and the elevation of SP leaders to prime executive positions in the new party more than simply fortuitous for the smaller party's interests. That said, it is impossible to judge Gibb's chairmanship and his electoral defeats as a candidate for the Scottish universities in 1935, 1936 and 1938 as anything other than missed opportunities for the party: at root, they reveal a failure of leadership and an inability to see party unity as facilitative of wider ambitions rather than an end in itself.

Yet, Gibb's wartime role in the SNP is certainly in need of revision: his stance on the declaration and execution of war and his relationship with Douglas Young, anti-conscription campaigner and party chairman from 1942, call in to question common distinctions made between party moderates and radicals in these years, and cast a new (if hardly forgiving) light on

TABLE 6.1: SCOTTISH UNIVERSITIES ELECTION RESULTS, 1935, 1936, 1938

Year	Electors	Turn-out (%)	Candidate (Party)	Votes
1935	52,981	51.2	Prof. J. G. Kerr (C)	8,252
			Dr G. A. Morrison (NL)	7,529
			A. N. Skelton (C)	7,479
			Prof. A. D. Gibb (SNP)	3,865
1936	52,981	54.8	Rt Hon. J. Ramsay MacDonald (NLab)	16,393
			Prof. A. D. Gibb (SNP)	9,034
			D. C. Thomson (Lab)	3,597
1938	55,272	52.1	Rt Hon. Sir J. Anderson (Nat)	14,042
			Dr Frances H. Melville (Ind)	5,618
			Prof A. D. Gibb (SNP)	5,246
			Sir P. C. Mitchell (Ind Prog)	3,868

Gibb's fascist leanings. Finally, Gibb's role in the Scottish Centre and in the Covenant Association speak to changes in Scottish politics and the role of the British state that demanded leadership of a type the ageing pioneer generation lacked, and energy which – as the survivors of two world wars and far more numerous internecine party conflicts – they had exhausted.

ECLIPSE AND EMPIRE

Richard Finlay has explained Gibb's apparent disgruntlement with the Scottish Unionist Party in the late 1920s as being driven by thwarted ambition, when 'there appeared no prospect of a safe seat as a reward for faithfully representing the Conservative cause on the Red Clyde'.[7] Yet even the most naïve of Scottish nationalists would have acknowledged that there was far less chance of election as a representative of a movement as yet in its infancy than as one of the established parties, if this was one's sole ambition. Rather, Gibb's departure from the Unionist fold was rooted in a fundamental ideological crisis, which remained unresolved during the entirety of his political career. The dilemma was simple: for one who – like Gibb – saw no incompatibility between conservatism and Scottish nationalism, there was no obvious party to support.[8] In the north, the Tories were represented by the Unionists, whose commitment to the Anglo-Irish union, threatened by Gladstone in the 1880s, had been lazily transferred to the older Anglo-Scottish Union of 1707, partly in recognition of long-established support for the British Empire it had secured, and partly as a response to home rule tendencies in the Labour movement.[9] When, by 1930, the strict (non-legislative) limits of the Unionist Party's devolutionary sympathies had been revealed and shown to be incapable of protecting Scotland from the ravages of the

7   Finlay, 'Pressure group or political party?', p. 287.

8   NLS, Dep 217/21L: Scottish National Assembly, Report of Proceedings, 22 March 1947, pp. 19–20.

9   Margaret Arnott and Catriona M. M. Macdonald, 'More than a Name: The Union and the Un-doing of Scottish Conservatism in the 20th Century', in David Torrance (ed.), *Whatever Happened to Tory Scotland?* (Edinburgh: Edinburgh University Press, 2012), pp. 44–5.

global depression, Gibb had no alternative but to reshape the party political environment of Scotland.

In *Scotland in Eclipse* (1930), Gibb refined his vision of a Scotland suffering more than its English neighbour in the Union state, its spirit 'deadened' as a consequence of 200 years of English cultural and spiritual overlordship, its laws 'warped and mutilated' by the incompetence of the Westminster Parliament, and true Scots dispossessed and forced on board emigrant ships as Irish settlers, created a 'deplorable colony' in the spaces left by the best of the race.[10] The advance of administrative devolution – much of it under Tory-led governments – had done little to halt the diminishment of the Scottish nation, and, beyond gestures (the elevation of the Scottish Secretary to Cabinet rank and the restructuring of the Scottish administrative boards), it was clear that the Unionists would go no further. The stumbling block, according to Gibb, was the 'ruling caste' of Scottish Conservatives.[11] In stark contrast, he noted confidently, 'It can be unchallengeably asserted, that there exists at the present moment in Scotland a majority formally if tepidly in favour of Home Rule and a minority earnestly and actively in favour of independence.'[12]

As late as September 1930, George Malcolm Thomson was encouraging Gibb to stand at the next general election as a Tory nationalist; whether within or outwith the Tory fold it is unclear, as Gibb was still at that point a member of the Unionist Party.[13]

The deciding factor in Gibb's abandonment of his original party is also unclear, yet a second publication in the 1930s clarifies the wider context within which Gibb appreciated the limiting impact of the Union on Scotland's future. In *The Scottish Empire* (1937), Gibb showed how, despite obvious Scottish success abroad, the imperial relationship with England mediated through

---

10   Dewar Gibb, *Scotland In Eclipse*, pp. 65, 131–72, 93, 57. Gibb's text was one of many in the '30s that addressed the apparent malaise in Scottish society: see Finlay, 'National Identity in Crisis', p. 247.

11   Ibid., p. 180.

12   Ibid., p. 181.

13   NLS, Dep 217/1/3: letter from George Malcolm Thomson to Andrew Dewar Gibb, 13 September 1930 & 26 September 1930.

the Union had cost Scotland its nationhood: 'The will, the policy, the direction, the philosophy of the Empire have been all but wholly England's.'[14] Six years after the Statute of Westminster, guaranteeing the legislative independence of the Dominions, the future lay with the 'young nations' letting go of imperial apron strings.[15] Scotland – the unappreciated mother nation of the empire – was being left behind. Gibb – even on VE Day (1945) – would admit to having 'no British patriotism', and when his son Nigel joined the navy, he 'grudged him every second to the british [*sic*] raj'.[16]

Colin Kidd has correctly observed that a central tenet of Gibb's nationalism was his realisation that the Union had failed to generate any genuine 'dualism' at the heart of the British state.[17] Counter to contemporary Unionism, Gibb identified Scottish legislative competence within the framework of a reformed empire as the most convincing way of making the Union fit for purpose. According to Gibb, it was by this means that a genuine partnership would be created across the nations of the UK. The creation of a new party – the SP – was a means of giving practical expression to this ideal in 1930, yet even in 1945 Gibb had not left his conservatism behind. In May, anticipating a general election in the summer, Gibb thought he might stand as an 'Independent Conservative or Scottish Independent or Scottish Conservative. However, nobody has asked me.'[18]

TORY ENTRYISM

The SP, of which Gibb – alongside George Malcolm Thomson, Alexander MacEwen, Kevin McDowall and the Duke of Montrose – was a co-founder, has been variously referred to as an imperial reform party (Kidd), a badly organised elite pressure group, and a loose collection of inconsistent

14   Andrew Dewar Gibb, *Scottish Empire* (London: Alexander Maclehose, 1937), p. 312.

15   Ibid., p. 3.

16   NLS, Dep 217/19: Diary 1939–47, 8 May 1945; Diary 1947–58, 1 August 1951.

17   Kidd, *Union and Unionisms*, p. 289.

18   NLS, Dep 217/19: Diary 1939–47, 22 May 1945.

individuals (Finlay).[19] All of these descriptions certainly fit the SP experience at various times in its short history (it lasted four years), yet together they fail to reveal two important features of the party that would have a long-lasting impact on the future of the SNP: its goal of unity for its own sake, and its role as a Tory entryist party that was from its foundation determined to take over the NPS. Looking at the merger of 1934 from the position of the SP – the 'gospel' of which was to be 'Nationalism for Tories ... a synthesis of Toryism (real Toryism) and nationalism' – resets uncomfortably our current understanding of the early years of the SNP by pointing to the ways in which John MacCormick was as used by the SP as he, in turn, used it.[20]

Having mooted a 'large respectable non-party association' in the summer of 1930, George Malcolm Thomson wrote to Gibb in August that 'the raison d'être of the society should be to unite those who feel there is something wrong but are not sure of the exact spot or cure but mean to find out'.[21] This society would become the SP, a party, according to Thomson, 'wide and ... hospitable to different interests and stages of opinion' but with a narrow support base, consciously restricted ('sifted') to ensure the party kept the applicants 'worth keeping', while directing the others to the NPS – a party that he would soon join himself.[22] The 'tendency towards vagueness' that Finlay identifies in the early SNP thus emerged as a direct result of the minority progenitor party's deliberate avoidance of contentious issues that would destabilise the consensus in support of putting Scotland first – whatever that meant.[23] As late as 1933, Neil Gunn (NPS) would confess to Gibb that 'I could not swear to it what it is precisely that you do desire!'[24] The very vagueness of party ambition was both policy and strategy. For a mature party, its colour established in the spectrum of

---

19   Kidd, *Union and Unionisms*, p. 290; Finlay, *Independent and Free*, p. 157; Finlay, 'Pressure group or political party?', p. 284.

20   NLS, Dep 217/1/3: George Malcolm Thomson to Andrew Dewar Gibb, 15 August 1930.

21   Ibid., 26 August 1930.

22   Ibid., 26 September 1930; see McKechnie, *The Best-Hated Man*, p. 182.

23   Richard J. Finlay, '"For or Against?"', p. 200.

24   NLS, Dep 217/1/1: Neil Gunn to Andrew Dewar Gibb, 8 January 1933.

party allegiances, the approach makes little sense; for an embryonic movement, however, it has more merit than historians have accorded it to date.

The opaque nature of the SP's vision also performed a further function: for a party intent on infiltrating and taking over the NPS, the ability of SP members to identify themselves as NPS 'fellow travellers' (no matter how ill-defined) was essential. In August 1930, Thomson was explicit: '[O]ur job is to collect a few men[,] all of whom have a certain reputation or position and who agree to act together and, when the time is ripe, to make a spectacular embracement of the NPS (which will probably be profoundly embarrassed).'[25] A month later, Thomson highlighted Gibb's central role in these machinations: 'When we do get to the length of joining that disastrous body ourselves ... you will be our sole political brain actually on the spot. Obviously we shall have to work through you.'[26] Having Thomson eventually 'on the inside' also helped. In December 1932, it was clear that Gunn's view was that differences between the SP and the NPS were 'fundamental', but by mid-1933 – the NPS purged of its more militant members – Thomson would encourage Gibb to talk Gunn round, reaffirming that 'until we get the union we can do absolutely nothing with Scotland'.[27] Despite Gibb's misgivings (he seems to have thought about leaving the SP as early as 1932 and considered transferring to the NPS as late as September 1933), Thomson urged Gibb to push himself forward, ahead of MacEwen ('an ambitious man' according to Thomson) and abandon his 'diffident' nature.[28]

Ultimately the resolution of conflicts surrounding the Kilmarnock by-election of 1933 – when for a time it appeared the SP and the NPS would both contest the seat – was to be the 'stepping stone to complete unity'.[29] Gibb by this time was liaising personally with Neil Gunn, even to the extent of

25   NLS, Dep 217/1/3: George Malcolm Thomson to Andrew Dewar Gibb, 15 August 1930.

26   Ibid., 13 September 1930.

27   Ibid., 30 December 1932; 5 June 1933; 10 July 1933; 30 March 1933.

28   Ibid., 26 December 1932 & 31 August 1934; Dep 217/2/2B: Andrew Dewar Gibb to George Malcolm Thomson, 30 September 1933.

29   Ibid., 30 September 1933.

recommending the NPS candidate, J. M. McNicol, who would appear on the final joint shortlist.[30] The NPS were also courting Gibb himself: approaching him about the prospect of contesting the universities seat in their interest.[31] By October 1933, Gunn was emphatic: 'I cannot impress sufficiently upon you now', he wrote Gibb, 'the need for immediate fusion.'[32] The NPS had come round to the SP plan hatched years before. In December 1933, Neil Gunn confirmed in correspondence with Gibb how earlier 'fundamental' differences now appeared as nought:

> I am definitely out for immediate complete fusion or no working arrange-
> ment between the parties whatsoever ... Either there is a fundamental
> difference in the parties upon which fusion is impossible, or there is none.
> If there is none, why mutually destroy by keeping apart? If there is a fun-
> damental difference, what is it?

What was needed, he emphasised, was 'some fair-minded fellow like yourself'.[33]

Commentators have mused on the high proportion of senior executive offices taken up by former SP members following the merger in 1934 (Montrose became president of the SNP[34] and MacEwen became chairman), with Finlay explaining that the 'mergerites in the NPS were only interested in attaching the personnel of the Scottish Party for prestige purposes and, perhaps, most importantly, to give a new sense of leadership and direction'.[35] If this perspective is the best from which to judge the merger, then hindsight reveals how foolish it was to presume that trading leadership positions would not, as a corollary, demand the ceding of power. If, however, one acknowledges that this state of affairs is

---

30   NLS, Dep 217/1/1: Neil Gunn to Andrew Dewar Gibb, September 1933.

31   NLS, Dep 217/2/2B: C. Stewart Black to Andrew Dewar Gibb, 29 April 1932 & 11 May 1932.

32   NLS, Dep 217/1/1: Neil Gunn to Andrew Dewar Gibb, 17 October 1933.

33   Ibid., 20 December 1933.

34   He does not mention this in his autobiography: see The Duke of Montrose, *My Ditty Box* (London: Jonathan Cape, 1952).

35   Finlay, *Independent and Free*, p. 157.

the predictable outcome of entryist tactics on the part of the SP, the early history of the new party is seen in a fresh light and, with it, Gibb's role as a pioneer.

SOMETHING LIKE HARMONY

Having secured the senior positions within the SNP, it is clear that former SP
members had little idea of what to do going forward. In part this was down
to the vague nature of the policies that had secured the new partnership in the
first place. More than this, however, the SP brought no clear vision of leadership
and little in the way of organisational competence: McDowall left in 1935; Mac-
Ewen offered his resignation as chairman in February 1936; and three months
later, Montrose joined the Liberal Party. Perhaps because he had nowhere else
to go, or because at last he had got close to securing parliamentary office (his
performance in the 1936 by-election in the Scottish universities constituency
was the SNP's best performance to date), Gibb was one of the few high-profile
former SP leaders who remained in the SNP at the end of the 1930s. Yet, it was
with some reluctance that Gibb replaced MacEwen as party chairman in 1936,[36]
and at the universities by-election in 1938 Gibb's share of the poll fell. The party
moved to the left under his chairmanship, and there seemed little he could do
about it: executive members were leaving as the 'socialist' sympathies of the party
became more apparent and party finances limited action.[37] In March 1939, Gibb
was thinking of resigning the chairmanship: he wrote to the party secretary, John
MacCormick, whose role he wished to see more clearly defined (that is, restricted):

> ...I feel just as much responsible for the state of matters ... as I can hold
> anyone else. I feel that I should have somehow got these matters put to
> rights long ago. And feeling so I can't believe that some other person would
> not do my job infinitely better.[38]

---

36   Ibid., p. 189.

37   NLS, Dep 217/2/2B: David Dewar to Andrew Dewar Gibb, 2 March 1939.

38   Ibid., Andrew Dewar Gibb to John MacCormick, 21 March 1939.

In January 1940, Gibb confessed (at least to his diary), that 'the handling of men bores me', and despaired at the end of that year that council meetings were becoming the 'usual leftist farce'.[39] Yet his resolve to seek unity at all costs remained the guiding principle. In correspondence in 1940 with A. Rugg Gunn, a Harley Street doctor and party member contemplating resignation, Gibb asked Gunn to hold off for a month or two: 'I may say that I and other conservatives have time after time sunk our individual point of view in order to achieve something like harmony. We have done all the conceding, and up to now I have no regrets.' But, 'I think there will be changes', he noted, adding tellingly, as it would prove: 'If not I am afraid (strictly *entre nous*) that I shall have to go.'[40] Gibb offered his resignation as party chairman that same month.

During Gibb's years as SNP chairman, the avoidance of division was bought at any cost, even at the cost of discipline, making for a very weak form of unity. It is a period of drift and dissipation often blamed on Gibb's lack of control and the re-emergence of factions that had dogged the NPS. But, unlike the National Association for the Vindication of Scottish Rights of the previous century, and the SHRA of the 1880s, re-birthed by Roland Muirhead in 1918, the SNP was heading towards a decade on the political stage. How long the party might have limped along in this fashion we will never know: war intervened, and Scottish nationalism was forced to confront British patriotism in ways that no one could have predicted.

WAR

On 7 April 1934, Gibb recorded, in German, the foundation of the SNP in his pocket diary: '*Endlich ist alles sehr gut gelungen und die Scottish National Party existiert*.'[41] This private entry reveals Gibb's sympathy

---

39   NLS, Dep 217/19: Diary 1939–47, 1 January 1940 & 2 November 1940.

40   NLS, Dep 217/2/2B: Andrew Dewar Gibb to A. Rugg Gunn, March 1939.

41   'Finally, everything is fine and the Scottish National Party exists', NLS, Dep 217/19: 1934 pocket diary, 7 April 1934.

with German culture – he regularly wrote in German in his diaries over the years. In this regard he exemplified strong Germanophile sympathies shared by many Scottish intellectuals in the late Victorian period and beyond.[42] Yet in the circumstances of the interwar years, and up to 1945, such empathy would be controversial: Gibb was the party chairman when Britain declared war on Germany in 1939, and issues relating to the conflict would be crucial features of his time in office.

Until 1941, Gibb's sympathies with Germany remained relatively secure, though earlier fascist leanings were less pronounced after the fall of France. Gibb's admiration for Hitler in the interwar years was well known: in speeches in 1935 he quoted more than once Hitler's perspective on the political endurance of minority movements: 'Facts are <u>concealed,</u> and those who reveal them like us are <u>abused</u>. But every day on which we are not abused, insulted and attacked is a day lost.'[43] Beyond this, Gibb was clearly sympathetic to Nazism as a bulwark against communism (or at least as the lesser of two evils), and shared its anti-Semitic anxieties, even if he did not support its approach to dealing with them.[44] It is also notable that it was only following government raids on the homes of some SNP members in 1941 that Gibb wrote to a government official regarding a pre-war visitor to Scotland, Gerhard von Tevenar, whom Gibb (rather belatedly) suspected of ulterior motives.[45] The year before, Gibb had taken umbrage when – somewhat reluctantly – he had been interviewed by the intelligence services, who had found his German language skills only 'fair to good' and could offer him nothing above the rank of lieutenant.[46]

---

42 Peter Hume Brown (1849–1918), the first professor of Scottish history at the University of Edinburgh, for example, was a biographer of Goethe. See Dauvit Broun, 'A forgotten anniversary: P. Hume Brown's 'History of Scotland, 1911', in N. Evans and H. Pryce (eds), *Writing a Small Nation's Past: Wales in Comparative Perspective, 1850–1950* (Farnham: Ashgate, 2013), pp. 267–82.

43 NLS, Dep 217/4/1: notes for speech, Neilston, 5 November 1935. In this I take issue with Finlay's observation that Gibb kept his fascist tendencies 'quite secret from others in the SNP': Finlay, *Independent and Free*, p. 197.

44 NLS, Dep 217/2/2B: Andrew Dewar Gibb to A. Rugg Gunn, March 1939.

45 NLS, Dep 217/19: Diary 1939–47, 11 May 1941. See also Bowd, *Fascist Scotland*, pp. 146–51.

46 NLS, Dep 217/19: Diary 1939–47, 7 September 1940.

Gibb's stance on the war, however, is far more complex than these episodes suggest. While offering his services to Churchill on the day war was declared, Gibb feared that war 'must mean the end of Scotland', and confessed in his diary that 'I don't care who wins'.[47] On 12 October, he offered to resign from the SNP, explaining to Bob Hurd of the Edinburgh branch that at the council meeting he had 'made no secret of my distinct Fascist leanings', but he stayed in post for the time being.[48] Throughout the war, Gibb remained critical of the British government, referring to ministers as nonentities and 'third rate confidence men' in January 1940.[49] Yet, one ought not to conflate criticism of the government with support for the enemy. A critical turning point for Gibb in this regard was the Clydebank Blitz of 1941. Gibb was in Glasgow when the bombs started to fall:

> ...they came every 3–5 minutes, seemingly in droves, & dropped stuff all over, at Govan, Hyndland, Park, Dalmuir, near BBC, u.s.w., u.s.w. (Tonight I renounced the Germans definitely) ... about 2 I thot [sic] my number was on one. The whole place shook & glass was heard crashing all about ... windows out all over the Quad & curtains flying in the brilliant moonlight a most sinister scene.[50]

Gibb could no longer in good conscience maintain the intellectual distinction between Germany and the Nazi state: a month later he noted, 'My attitude of rational understanding of Germany as distinct from the Nazis is being put to a severe test these days.'[51]

In April 1940, Gibb had offered to resign (again) owing to party discord over his war views – the *Scots Independent*, for example, was becoming

---

47   Ibid., 3 September 1939.

48   NLS, Dep 217/19: Andrew Dewar Gibb to Bob Hurd, 12 October 1939.

49   NLS, Dep 217/19: Diary 1939–47, 1 January 1940.

50   Ibid., 13 March 1941. ['u.s.w. (*und so weiter*), German, meaning and so on (etc.).]

51   Ibid., 7 April 1941.

reluctant to publish the party chairman's 'injudicious' critical wartime reflections, and Gibb was kept at arm's length when the party contested the Mid-Argyll by-election that year.[52] Gibb, replaced by William Power as chairman, nevertheless remained on the party's council until 1943 and would play an important role in the party when its more radical members seized control at the annual conference in 1942 and MacCormick left the party in protest. It would be another instance when Gibb sought to put unity above all else.

Gibb's consistent criticism of the British government, even in wartime, made him an important, if unusual, confidante of Douglas Young, who replaced Power as chairman in 1942. Young's accession to the chairmanship has been seen as confirmation of the rise to power of the party's fundamentalist lobby at the expense of moderatism. Gibb's approach to the fissure in 1942, however, ought to make us more sceptical about the ease with which such positions or factions are identified. As early as October 1940, Gibb referred to Young as 'very witty ... a great fellow', and in March 1942, the month before Young went on trial for refusing conscription, Young visited Gibb: 'Amusingly defeatist as ever,' Gibb noted. 'Some people object. I can't say I do. I sympathise with the mainspring of action tho' not with his ultimate wish.'[53] Young at this time was taking a determined stance against conscription on the grounds that, in the strict terms of the Union of 1707, the British state had no right to conscript Scots. Gibb's scepticism about the government's war strategy and Young's objection to the state's right to force Scots to take up arms meant they were united in the qualified nature of their patriotism, if nothing else: even in 1940, for example, Gibb (a fire warden at Glasgow University for the duration) was giving speeches asking, 'Is it Scotland's War?'[54]

In 1942 – despite knowing it would be futile – Gibb sought to mediate

52   NLS, Dep 217/19: Andrew Dewar Gibb to John MacCormick, 21 April 1940; NLS, Dep 217/2/2B: Macdonald to Andrew Dewar Gibb, 11 June 1940.

53   NLS, Dep 217/19: Diary 1939–47, 11 October 1940 & 12 March 1941.

54   Ibid., 18 December 1940.

in the dispute between MacCormick and Young, writing separately to each man, asking MacCormick to return to the fold and Young to step down as the newly appointed chair.[55] In a letter to MacCormick, Gibb showed the conciliatory tactics that had been his default leadership strategy:

> There were faults on both sides at the Conference. Young's supporters weary of the people who ran the party did, by way of protest, but rashly and impetuously what I think was a disservice to the party by electing as Chairman a man who, brilliant and charming as he is, holds views which are irreconcilable with the prosecution of the war. That was a mistake, but pretty clearly it was rather impetuous than studied.
>
> Your reaction to it struck me as equally impetuous and unwise, if you will allow me to say so. You should have remained in the party and sought to remedy matters instead of creating a split.[56]

While the approach got nowhere – MacCormick set up the Scottish Convention and Young stayed put – correspondence at the time shows that Young had regretted Gibb's resignation in 1940, was hopeful that Gibb might have accepted the presidency in 1942, and would regularly go to the elder politician for advice.[57] Indeed, a year after the split, Young was willing to step down as chairman if Gibb accepted the nomination of the Edinburgh branch, and in November 1943 Young was even encouraging Gibb – who left the party the month before – to draft 'a well-grounded systematic exposition' of the party's vision.[58] Gibb, for his part, was resolved that Young should maintain the chairmanship in 1943, knowing that as chairman of an anti-conscription party, his position as a supporter of the war effort

---

55   NLS, Dep 217/2/2B: Andrew Dewar Gibb to Douglas Young, 8 June 1942; Dep 217/19: Diary 1939–47, 11 June 1942.

56   NLS, Dep 217/2/2B: Andrew Dewar Gibb to John MacCormick, 8 June 1942.

57   NLS, Dep 217/1/4: Douglas Young to Andrew Dewar Gibb, 13 June 1942 & 27 June 1942; Dep 217/19: Diary 1939–47, 11 June 1942.

58   NLS, Dep 217/1/4: Douglas Young to Andrew Dewar Gibb, 6 May 1943; Dep 217/2/2B, Douglas Young to Andrew Dewar Gibb, 4 November 1943.

in the interests of Scotland would have been one of 'mere uncomfortable futility'.[59]

It is more than simply coincidence that Gibb left the party following the split of 1942: but he left, not because a cadre of fundamentalists had taken over, but because the fragile unity he had sought since 1934 had been lost, and there appeared little chance of it re-emerging, at least not in a form that could have sustained nationalist conservatism. After 1942, while encouraged to resign from the party by George Malcolm Thomson, Gibb remained for a short time, and even flirted with the presidency of the party in May 1943. The 1945 general election, however, would find him with 'no party, no organisation, no time, and no demand'.[60] Young offered some party support – 'assistance with addressing and filling envelopes' – should Gibb contest the Scottish universities seat in the nationalist interest, but Gibb did not stand.[61]

CODA: CENTRE AND COVENANT

In 1945, Thomson and Gibb founded a new society – Scottish Centre. It survived beyond the general election of that year, but the initial aim of the Centre was simply to survey the views of candidates on the question of home rule, with the hope of forming a parliamentary lobby that would, in addition to securing administrative improvements, support the principle of Scottish self-government.[62] Thomson attempted to pull the strings from London, acknowledging Gibb's 'lamentable tendency to regard newspapers as a mysterious, malign and alarming institution', but despite their efforts the initiative failed to bear fruit: the landslide Labour victory was secured in part by promising post-war reconstruction in the northern kingdom that

---

59 NLS, Dep 217/2/1: Andrew Dewar Gibb to Mr Aitken (Edinburgh branch, SNP), 9 May 1943; Andrew Dewar Gibb to Douglas Young, 9 May 1943.

60 NLS, Dep 217/1/3: George Malcolm Thomson to Andrew Dewar Gibb, 2 June 1945.

61 NLS, Dep 217/1/4: Douglas Young to Andrew Dewar Gibb, 5 June 1945. It is worth noting that at this election MacCormick stood in Inverness as a Liberal.

62 NLS, Dep 217/2/2A: circular, June 1945.

would ultimately be secured by loans against the collective resources of the Union state.[63]

Instead, Gibb redirected his efforts to MacCormick's non-party Convention and ultimately the Covenant Association. Gibb had been a sponsor of Mac-Cormick's proposals for a convention in 1939 (shelved during the first years of war),[64] had met with the Liberal Lady Glen Coats in 1941 when MacCormick was exploring cross-party collaboration as SNP secretary,[65] and in 1947 represented Scottish Centre at the National Assembly, noting still his persistent ideological dilemmas: 'I find myself in the awkward position that, while I am on the extreme left so far as national aspirations are concerned, I am on the extreme right so far as politics are concerned.'[66] For the rest of his active political career, Gibb proved a loyal servant of the Covenant, proposing the major resolutions at the fourth National Assembly in 1950, and reaching the position of honorary president: this did not, however, make him a loyal servant of its leader.[67] While Gibb defended MacCormick against criticism from Eric Linklater following the leadership's American tour in May 1950; applauded MacCormick's successful rectorial campaign at the University of Glasgow that same year; and delivered a moving eulogy at MacCormick's funeral in 1961, Gibb thought MacCormick cowardly when it came to the return of the Stone of Destiny, constantly bemoaned the tiresome executive meetings, and was critical of MacCormick's resistance to contesting elections and his increasingly dictatorial style. Gibb noted in his diary how, in July 1950, MacCormick had stood up at an executive meeting and asked '"Who made the Covenant?", then he answered himself, "I did: I am the Covenant. Damn you." Not very pretty.'[68] With each year Gibb grew more discontented with the lack of direction in

---

63　NLS, Dep 217/2/3: George Malcolm Thomson to Andrew Dewar Gibb, 5 July 1945.

64　NLS, Dep 217/21: 'The Scottish National Convention, 1939'. This meeting, planned for 29 September/1 October 1939, was never held.

65　NLS, Dep 217/19: Diary 1939–47, 29 January 1941.

66　NLS, Dep 217/21: Scottish National Assembly, Report of Proceedings, 22 March 1947, p. 19.

67　*The Scotsman*, 24 April 1950.

68　NLS, Dep 217/19: Diary 1947–58, 12/13 July 1950.

the Covenant Association following the initial burst of national enthusiasm: MacCormick's plans for a plebiscite seemed pointless to Gibb. After all, had the Covenant itself not shown that the strategy simply did not work? Non-aligned home rule sympathies could not dissolve the harsh divisions of left and right that seemed to be imbedded in the post-war political environment.

Already, by the 1950s, Gibb was a living ancestor in the national movement, and a discontented one at that: called on most often to lecture on the history of the movement rather than its future.[69] There also are signs in his diaries that even during the war years, Gibb suffered from debilitating bouts of depression, and following the death of his mother in 1948 ('I feel disgust with life') these seem to have worsened.[70] In July 1950, he noted in his diary: 'I feel chronically depressed tho [sic] I don't quite know why – very easily tired – "lassitude". If this is old age I don't think I am going to like it. Today has been a bit of a nightmare.'[71] Sedatives made little impression on his symptoms, and it is hard to avoid the conclusion that Gibb ended his political and professional careers unfulfilled, his ambitions thwarted.

By the mid-1940s, Gibb had been overshadowed by John Boyd Orr as the home rule movement's celebrity academic: one can only imagine how Gibb felt when Orr won the Scottish universities seat in 1945 and, in 1951, beat him to secure the presidency of the Covenant Association.[72] Unlike Orr, Gibb would never acquire a title, not that that probably affected him: he had never been an uncritical supporter of the royal house of Windsor, bemoaning the displays of public mourning on the death of George VI and referring to the expectant Princess Elizabeth as a 'puppet'.[73] At the University of Glasgow, Gibb loathed his principal, Sir Hector Hetherington,[74] whose period in office

---

69 NLS, Dep 217/19: Diary, 1947–58, 29 November 1952, 10 April 1953.

70 NLS, Dep 217/19: Diary 1939–47, 6 July 1940 & 18 July 1945; Dep 217/19: Diary, 1947–58, 19 May 1948, 4 July 1950, 16 July 1950 & 7 October 1953.

71 NLS, Dep 217/19: Diary, 1947–58, 16 July 1950.

72 NLS, Dep 217/19: Diary, 1947–58, 27 October 1951.

73 NLS, Dep 217/19: Diary, 1947–58, 7, 9 & 10 February 1952 & 28–29 May 1953.

74 NLS, Dep 217/19: Diary, 1947–58, 7 June 1951. In this diary entry, Hetherington is described as a 'god-awful bore'.

coincided with Gibb's time there: indeed, Gibb appears to have applied unsuccessfully for the principalship of the University of St Andrews. In 1953, Gibb admitted that he was 'still looking for a suitable occupation': his repeated attempts to secure a principal sheriffship had shown him to be a reliable but hardly stellar legal professional. Finally, Gibb's last major work on nationalism, *Scotland Resurgent* (1950), proved to be anything but as optimistic as its title. Instead, Gibb was looking back, and the refrain was by now familiar:

> In general ... the division of the nationalist forces has weakened the move-
> ment. The advantage gained by the existence of a moderate devolutionary
> body has not compensated for the weakening of the fighting party which
> has found itself on that account less capable of turning to account the great
> increase in really national sentiment brought about by the arrival in power
> of a collectivist government with strong centralising tendencies and a more
> than usually profound ignorance of the Scottish way of life.[75]

Elsewhere in this volume, readers of his earlier works would have heard echoes in his reference (although more muted) to the racial characteristics of Scots and the violence and disorder of the Irish (Protestant and Catholic). This is certainly not Gibb's whole story, but it was a consistent aspect of his narrativising of Scottish interests. Since 1930, everything had changed and nothing had changed; in 1952, Gibb decided that he might well be more suited to the short story genre.[76]

In 1942, George Malcom Thomson confessed to Gibb that, 'I have come to recognise that it will not be my generation but [the] one following it which will shape the coming Scotland. I am passé.'[77] To date, the controversies caused by war have diverted our attention from a generational shift in the

---

75   Andrew Dewar Gibb, *Scotland Resurgent* (Stirling: Eneas MacKay, 1950), p. 260.

76   NLS, Dep 217/19: Diary, 1947–58, 9 June 1952.

77   NLS, Dep 217/1/3: George Malcolm Thomson to Andrew Dewar Gibb, 2 June 1945.

national movements in Scotland at mid-century: it was the passing of the pioneer generation – more than questions of conscription, the Stone and the naming of the new queen – that had the most long-lasting consequence for nationalism, and Gibb's story affirms this. There is little for pioneers to do when the frontier lies always out of reach.

CHAPTER 7

WILLIAM POWER

MARGERY PALMER MCCULLOCH

William Power was a prominent and influential writer and journalist of the interwar years, rising to be leader writer for The Herald *and then editor of the* Scottish Observer. *He was deeply involved in Scottish cultural debates in the 1930s, and was a founding member of Scottish PEN and its president from 1935 to 1938. He became chairman of the SNP in 1940, at a difficult time for the party, after polling impressively in the Argyll by-election, winning 37 per cent and second place. The Second World War was a period of acute pressures on the party, and in 1942 Douglas Young stood against Power and defeated him for the leadership on the issue of the party's attitude to the war, which then led to a split in the party.*

•   •   •

T he journalist and author William Power followed Andrew Dewar Gibb as chairman of the Scottish National Party in 1940. Power was born on 30 August 1873 in the family home in Arlington Street in what he calls in his autobiography 'the inner West End of this big, inscrutable city' of Glasgow.[1] Both parents had come to Glasgow from Brechin, Forfarshire and had belonged 'to families that had dwelt from time immemorial in the region comprising the Braes of Angus and the Howe of the Mearns'.[2] His father was a shipmaster who sailed mostly to the Baltic and

---

1   William Power, *Should Auld Acquaintance* (London: Harrap, 1937), pp. 11–12.

2   Ibid., p. 13.

Mediterranean, and as the first child of the family Power travelled with both parents or with his father alone to various places on the cargo steamer's route before formal schooling claimed him. He attended Woodside School in Glasgow, where his progress would most probably have led him to university had his father not suddenly died in Gibraltar from West African fever when he was just over thirteen, and he had to leave school and find a job. He became an apprentice at the Gallowgate Branch of the Royal Bank of Scotland and was transferred to the chief Glasgow office when he was eighteen. Encouraged by the Head Teller, he returned to studying: re-reading the Romantic poets and taking classes in French and English literature where his blank verse poem 'Clutha', written for an essay assignment, so impressed the class teacher that he had it printed – Power's first publication. He also began to travel again – sometimes alone, mostly with the various friends he had made – in Scotland, England and Europe. What changed the course of his inherited political thinking was his conforming to the established custom for young men to join an organisation known as the Volunteers, with battalions established throughout Scotland. As news of the relief of Mafeking reached his 1st Lanark battalion one evening meeting in 1900, he found himself questioning his previous 'Tory Imperialist' beliefs. He realised how these beliefs had been gradually and unwittingly modified by his travels in the Highlands, with their evidence of poor stewardship by landlords; and how in his involvement with the Volunteers he had been

> struck by the absence of anything that linked on with native tradition [...]
> no one seemed to know anything about Scots history or Scots books; the
> spiritual home of our officers was Aldershot or Pirbright; and an English
> adjutant spoke of 'the people in these parts', as if we had been Hottentots.

And he concludes: 'I slipped my political cables and drifted into the open sea.'[3]

Power's life changed in other ways in the early years of the new century. He

---

3   Ibid., pp. 68–9.

married in 1906 and, having for some time contributed reviews and literary articles to the *Glasgow Herald*, he decided to give up his post in the bank and ask the editor of the *Herald* for 'an inside job'. He writes in his autobiography: 'I had taken a big risk, but it came off. A fortnight later I was at a desk in Buchanan Street.'[4] This move to full-time journalism, together with the change in his political beliefs and his conviction of the need for Scotland to become aware of its history and present-day needs, led to his prominence in the Scottish cultural movements of the interwar period, and to his eventual overt involvement with Scottish national politics in the early years of the Second World War.

A SCOTTISH RENAISSANCE?

Power continued with his *Glasgow Herald* employment during the First World War, being at the age of forty-one outside conscription age. His involvement with the new movement for Scottish regeneration in the postwar period came when a friend drew his attention to 'an extraordinary young man named C. M. Grieve, who had been in the Army and had settled down as the editorial factotum of a Montrose paper. He was bringing out a series of modern Scots poetic anthologies, *Northern Numbers*, and editing the *Northern Review*.'[5] From the beginning, Power was supportive of Grieve (later better known as the poet Hugh MacDiarmid), endorsing his belief that 'a Scots poet should have the same range in the vernacular or in Gaelic as, say, T. S. Eliot or Ezra Pound has in English; that Scotland should express the whole of world thought with its own particular accent and interpretation'.[6] Power's support in the *Glasgow Herald* was particularly helpful in the early days of what popularly became known as the Scottish Renaissance, and was due both to his genuine appreciation of the quality and modern direction of the new writing and to his own increasing aspiration 'to lend a hand in the

---

4   Ibid., p. 76.
5   Ibid., pp. 115–16.
6   Ibid., p. 116.

organising of a new Scotland'.[7] His next opportunity to aid regeneration in Scotland came when a chance arose for him to become editor of a new paper supported by the Scottish churches. He decided to take this, and resigned from the *Herald* in 1926 to become editor of the *Scots Observer*.

Like most people in his time, Power accepted the place of the various religious denominations in the wider life of Scotland. In his view, a paper such as the new *Scots Observer* could give the churches a higher profile in the life of the country, while at the same time help to promote more widely much-needed social and cultural change. The paper's success in his second aim was demonstrated by the quality of its wide range of contributors, including many of the writers associated with the Scottish Renaissance movement, and by the equally wide range of topics put forward for discussion. Power wrote that 'a sign of the liveliness of the paper was the number of letters to the editor. We could have filled half the paper with them, and we had to do a lot of sub-editing to get most of them in.'[8] On the other hand, what became clear as the paper progressed was that its backers, the Scottish Protestant churches, were less interested in schemes for renewing Scotland generally than they were in promoting the Protestant churches at a time when Catholicism and Irish immigration appeared to be threatening Scotland's historical traditions and way of life. Power's realisation that his new paper could never play the role he had envisaged for it probably hardened after the formation of the National Party of Scotland in 1928, especially after dissatisfaction was expressed by his employers in relation to his published account of a nationalist meeting in St Andrew's Hall after Cunninghame Graham had come close to being elected rector of Glasgow University. For one of the *Scots Observer*'s directors, Power's account of the St Andrews Hall meeting was 'preaching Scots Nationalism', something, Power admits in his account of the incident in his autobiography, he 'had been doing ever since I began journalism'.[9] This political dissatisfaction

---

7   Ibid., p. 121.

8   Ibid., pp. 126–7.

9   Ibid., p. 128.

on the part of his employers may also have been behind the letter he wrote on *Scots Observer* notepaper to R. E. Muirhead on 19 November 1928, saying: 'Many thanks for your very kind letter. I am sorry that since I wrote to you circumstances have emerged which will make it impossible for me to publish the items about which I wrote to you. So please do not bother in the meantime.'[10] He gives no further details about the 'items', but it seems likely these may have been connected with the new nationalist politics. Power left the editorship of the *Scots Observer* in 1929 and commented that he was not sorry when his term of office expired. On the other hand, as one door closed, another opened, when he was asked to become a regular contributor to newspapers in the Associated Newspapers group (now DMG Media).

SCOTLAND, EUROPE AND THE NEW POLITICS

Power's resignation from the *Scots Observer* marked the beginning of a more public and eventually more overtly political part of his life. He had been one of the writers who supported MacDiarmid in his establishment of Scottish PEN in 1927, and he was now able to play a larger part in the organisation. In 1928, when he was still editor of the *Scots Observer*, he had attended the PEN International Congress in Oslo as one of the Scottish delegates, only to find the Germans and French questioning Scotland's right to national representation, as 'Scotland had no distinctive national culture.'[11] Power's indignant arguments for Scotland's right to inclusion succeeded in having the matter deferred, and at a subsequent conference full national rights were granted. Power's next PEN Congress was in Warsaw in 1930 where 'world literature was congratulating Poland on her rebirth as a nation',[12] followed by the Congress at The Hague in 1931. Tensions in Europe were becoming increasingly apparent at the 1932 PEN Congress in Budapest, where Edwin and Willa Muir were the official Scottish

---

10   NLS, Acc. 3721, Box 5, File 87: letter from William Power to R. E. Muirhead, 19 November 1928.

11   Power, *Should Auld Acquaintance*, p. 143.

12   Ibid., p. 151.

delegates, with Willa writing that 'this was the first time in our lives we experienced political fear'.[13] After the Dubrovnik Congress in 1933, at which the German delegates would not accept the passing of a resolution condemning intellectual persecution, including the burning of books by the Nazis in Germany, Power reported that German PEN, which in Germany had been replaced by a society of Nazi authors, would in future be represented by exiles from Germany such as Thomas Mann, Ernst Toller and Lion Feuchtwanger. So far as Scotland itself was concerned, the country's inclusion in the International PEN organisation was endorsed by the holding of the Annual PEN Congress in Edinburgh in 1934, with delegates attending from all over the world. Power (who would himself be president of Scottish PEN between 1935 and 1938) writes:

> There was a garden party at Holyrood, where the delegates were received by the Secretary of State for Scotland [...] Edinburgh Castle was floodlit. There were receptions by the municipalities, the universities, the RSA, and other bodies. There were tours to the Borders, the Highlands, and the Land of Burns. [...] These things helped to convince our foreign guests that Scotland was not an English county.[14]

National affairs were not so settled in Scotland's political arena. The year 1934 also marked the formation of the Scottish National Party as a result of the merger of the National Party of Scotland and the right-wing Scottish Party. These parties were not completely in agreement as to their political aims, however, and the marriage was one of convenience rather than choice and was uncomfortable from the start. Power's books *Scotland and the Scots* and *My Scotland* were also published in 1934, with his *Literature and Oatmeal: What Literature has Meant to Scotland* in Routledge's 'Voice of Scotland' series appearing in 1935. These books were on the whole optimistic in that they were based on his belief that there was a new readiness in Scotland to

---

13   Willa Muir, *Belonging* (London: Hogarth Press, 1968), p. 157.

14   Power, *Should Auld Acquaintance*, p. 177.

explore and further the country's own native resources and talents. He was well aware of the economic and social decline discussed in George Malcolm Thomson's *Caledonia* (1927) and Andrew Dewar Gibb's *Scotland in Eclipse* (1930), and he himself contributed to that exploration of decline in his writings. He believed, however, that the mood in the country had changed and that Scotland was now prepared to take a hand in its own future.

From his interwar writings and comments in his autobiography, it is clear that Power was both nationalist and internationalist in his thinking, but it is not clear from these writings exactly when he decided to add involvement in Scottish politics to his preoccupation with Scotland's renewal. In his book *George Malcolm Thomson: The Best-Hated Man*, George McKechnie discusses the gradual conversion of Andrew Dewar Gibb and George Malcolm Thomson to the nationalist cause (although Thomson had to keep this conversion hidden from his employer Lord Beaverbrook). Gibb, a strong Unionist and Conservative Party supporter, appears to have been the first to realise the necessity of a nationalist dimension in Scottish politics, and Thomson followed with his pamphlet *The Kingdom of Scotland Restored*, published in 1931. The introduction to the pamphlet was jointly written by George Blake, Moray McLaren, Andrew Dewar Gibb and William Power. McKechnie discusses a letter from Thomson to Gibb in which the former suggests that Blake and McLaren were prepared to join the National Party of Scotland, and that 'at some point "they" would need to take editorial control of the party newspaper, the *Scots Independent*, with William Power earmarked as the potential editor'.[15] Thomson, however, would appear to have decided not to tell William Power about this: '"Power was down last week. I thought it more tactful not to mention our *Scots Independent* intrigue," he cautioned Gibb.'[16] McKechnie adds:

All of the scheming proved to be neither fanciful nor wishful thinking on Thomson's part. In March, 1931, John MacCormick, the secretary of the

15   McKechnie, *The Best-Hated Man*, p. 156.

16   Ibid.

NPS, told Gunn that Blake had become a member and that he had also had a 'long talk' with Power: 'I think that very soon he will follow the same course.'[17]

It appears likely, therefore, that William Power became a member of the National Party of Scotland in 1931 and subsequently of the Scottish National Party when the National Party of Scotland merged with Dewar Gibb's Scottish Party in 1934. His formal participation in the leadership group of the party would appear not to have taken place until the end of the decade. His name does not appear in the list of office-bearers or conveners of committees in the minutes of the 11th annual conference of the Scottish National Party held on 27 May 1939. Here Professor A. D. Gibb is still chairman with Mr Robert Maclauren and Mr D. H. McNeill vice-chairmen. Power is, however, mentioned as 'our Vice-Chairman' by John MacCormick in *The Flag in the Wind* during his discussion of the Argyll by-election candidacy in April 1940.[18]

The outbreak of war in September 1939 found the nationalists unprepared, with unresolved tensions evident in the party and division between those who thought that Hitler's aggression had to be confronted and those whose view was 'We will fight no more in England's Wars', as Wendy Wood had proclaimed in 1938 in MacDiarmid's *Voice of Scotland* magazine.[19] Douglas Young, a member of the Aberdeen branch, had nonchalantly departed on a visit to Greece in August 1939, 'thinking on the whole there would be no war, and even if there were still I would have had a little try while the going was good'.[20] Young was one of the strongest anti-conscription protesters, arguing not on a pacifist basis as did the poet Norman MacCaig, but on the basis of the Westminster government having no right to conscript Scotsmen for war. The September 1939 issue of the *Scots Independent* itself appeared

---

17   Ibid.

18   MacCormick, *The Flag in the Wind*, p. 98.

19   Wendy Wood, 'We Will Fight No More in England's Wars. Eirich Alba', *Voice of Scotland*, 1/1 (June–August 1938): 15–17.

20   NLS, Acc. 6419, Box 4: letter from Douglas Young to Rupert Allan, 20 January 1940.

transitional, with on the one hand its advertisement for the Welsh nationalists' inauguration of an anti-conscription fund to 'give assistance to young men who refuse to be conscripted for military service'[21] and its call to the Scots to do likewise; and on the other contributions such as an article praising William Power by MacDiarmid, together with a companion review of MacDiarmid's recent book *The Islands of Scotland,* and an advertisement for a new literary magazine, *The New Alliance, a Quarterly of Scottish and Irish Writing.* A letter written by R. E. Muirhead to MacDiarmid dated 23 October 1939 confirms a change in direction for the *Scots Independent,* advising him that since receipt of his last article (i.e. the Power article in the September issue), there had been at the request of the annual conference a change of control in regard to the journal, with its becoming again, from the October issue, a Scottish National Party organ. He tells him that he hopes that the new editors will continue to 'accept articles from independent Scottish writers such as yourself', but he is clearly intimating a changed and more focused party political direction.[22]

The new direction for the paper is marked immediately in the October issue with Andrew Dewar Gibb's front-page article 'Scotland and the War: Difficult Future Challenges: Vigorous Nationalist Effort', and with his status in the party clearly signalled by 'Chairman, Scottish National Party' under his name.[23] William Power was also a regular contributor to the reorganised paper, with front-page or other prominently placed articles. As was Power's custom, these articles were thoughtful, even philosophical, rather than politically polemical, but they addressed questions that were especially relevant to the time. In the section titled 'Rival Imperialisms' of his October 1939 article, he writes (in an argument that might well be applied to our own recent times): 'The present war is being waged for the liberation of nations cruelly suppressed by Germany. This is a legitimate object; the overthrow

---

21   'Anti-Conscription Funds', *Scots Independent,* September 1939, p. 7.

22   Letter from R. E. Muirhead to C. M. Grieve, *Dear Grieve: Letters to Hugh MacDiarmid,* selected and edited by John Manson (Glasgow: Kennedy & Boyd, 2011), p. 255.

23   Andrew Dewar Gibb, 'Scotland and the War', *Scots Independent,* October 1939, p. 1.

of Hitlerism is not, for no country has a right to interfere with the internal affairs of another country.' And he continues: 'For most people, Poland has gone out of sight [...] It is a contest of rival Imperialisms.'[24] This uncertainty about what is legitimate in relation to taking up arms was reflected in the arguments of the nationalist branches as they tried to work out their response to the war and especially to the question of Scottish conscription. Alongside such arguments was the equally vexed question of by-elections: did the outbreak of war mean that they should now cease attempts to challenge the government candidate when vacancies arose? Was this likely to damage the nationalist cause, making them appear unpatriotic in the wider British sense when the country was in danger? Or was it more important to keep the nationalist cause in the public eye?

In the spring of 1940, the argument about fighting by-elections became critical when a vacancy arose in the constituency of Argyll. John MacCormick, the party's honorary secretary and principal decision-making member of the leadership group, was especially anxious that the party should continue to fight by-elections if there was a chance that they could poll well and so increase the party's visibility and status. It was agreed that the party should put forward a candidate in Argyll, but there was uncertainty as to finding a candidate suitable for the challenge. MacCormick describes the party's dilemma in his account of the by-election in *The Flag in the Wind*, where he writes: 'In all the circumstances, however, we knew that it was essential to choose someone who was widely respected and could not be accused of even the slightest disloyalty to the war effort.' He continues:

> Fortunately, we had such a person readily to hand. He was William Power, who, ever since his retiral from the Editorship of the Scot Observer some years before, had taken an active part in all our work and was now our Vice-Chairman [...] He had written so much and for so many years to

---

24   William Power, 'Scotland and the Wealth of Nations: Mr William Power Looks at Post-War Future', *Scots Independent*, November 1939, p. 2 (1–2).

the popular Press that his name was a household word and although his nationalism was profound and sincere no one could suppose for a moment that he would countenance any folly of extremism. The only difficulty was that he was now sixty-nine years of age and Argyll was so extensive and scattered a constituency that we hesitated to ask him to undertake such a strenuous campaign.[25]

Power agreed to stand, his only hesitation being that as a journalist and a literary man – and therefore unaccustomed to electioneering – he might be found disappointing on an election platform: a fear that proved to be unfounded.

Writing from his home address of Corra Linn, Stirling, Power produced an outstanding 'Address to the Electors of Argyll'. He began by referring to his acceptance of the invitation to be their candidate and wrote that he had been moved 'chiefly by my life-long interest in the Highlands, and by the conviction that the lamentable conditions revealed in the 1938 Report of the Committee on the Highlands and Islands will not be remedied unless and until the Scottish people have charge of their own affairs': thus immediately headlining these three important references before moving on to develop them more fully. He took up the question of the 'so-called "Political Truce"', but responded that his 'faith in democracy enables me to believe that it can operate in war-time as well as in peace'; and that 'the "Truce" is a subtle belittlement of your right to vote, to criticise and to make constructive proposals'. He made it clear that 'the war and its conduct is not an issue in this election, since I will support any necessary war effort as readily as the Government candidate'. And he emphasised that the Scottish National Party 'has always proclaimed the right of small nations to their freedom and is wholly devoted to the democratic principle'. He argued that while 'my election for Argyll will not overthrow the Government nor weaken the war effort', it 'will compel the Government to give serious attention to the immediate and most

---

25   MacCormick, *The Flag in the Wind*, p. 97. Power was in fact aged sixty-six not sixty-nine in April 1940, having been born on 30 August 1973.

clamant needs of the Highlands and Islands, needs that have been rendered tragically urgent by war-time conditions in regard to freight, transport and restrictions on access'.[26]

Power's election address moved on to list and discuss several proposals for the future of the Highlands, including the establishment of a University of the Highlands and Islands (which has now come to fruition after Devolution in this twenty-first century). While the address is too long for detailed examination in the context of a chapter such as this, it is worth studying for the continuing relevance of its content, its crispness of presentation and the writer's capacity to address his readers as if they were participants in the new road forward, working *with* the candidate as opposed to being told what *he* thinks is good for *them*. A particularly significant comment is his closing promise: 'It will be my endeavour, if I am elected – *or whether I am elected or not* [my italics] – to help you, with all the means at my command, to build up a social and economic future worthy of your august Traditions.'[27] The communication here, and throughout his substantial address, is that this speaker is someone whose interest is genuine and long-lasting, not acquired merely for electioneering purposes.

Despite MacCormick's fears concerning his age, Power survived and appeared to enjoy the traverse of Argyll during the by-election process, writing to Douglas Young from the Temperance Hotel in Inveraray: 'We have had great meetings here [...] we have deserved success.'[28] In the end, the Scottish National Party did not succeed, but Power polled a sizeable 7,308 votes against the government candidate's 12,317. It was thought by many that the party might even have won had not the news of Hitler's occupation of Norway been broadcast the evening before the poll. The reorganised *Scots Independent* responded ecstatically to the result, declaring in its May 1940 issue: 'Argyll Sets Heather Afire: United Highland Demand for Action',

---

26   William Power, 'To the Electors of Argyll', election address, County of Argyll parliamentary by-election, 10 April 1940 (Lochgilphead: J. M. MacCormick, 1940).

27   Power, election address, final paragraph.

28   NLS, Acc. 6419, Box 4: letter from William Power to Douglas Young, 9 April 1940.

followed by: 'Mr Power struck the first blow'.[29] Power himself contributed a lengthy article, 'The Significance of Argyll', to this celebratory issue.[30] The *Scots Independent* itself shared in the praise when a reader wrote in its July 1940 issue: 'May I congratulate you on the very inspired "Scots Independent". It has grown up, become a dignified voice speaking for Scotland. More power to it.'[31]

Power's reward for his efforts and achievement in Argyll was his election to the chairmanship of the Scottish National Party at the annual conference in 1940, Andrew Dewar Gibb having recently resigned from the position. This was a poisoned chalice, however, as despite the euphoria caused by the strong result in Argyll, the disagreements within the party about policy, and especially about conscription and by-election issues, were coming to the surface again. Such disagreements were particularly strong in the Aberdeen branch. In June 1940, Douglas Young received a letter with the news that 'MacCormick has just written to say that, with the Authority of the Executive, he has excluded all the Aberdeen Resolutions at the Conference as he thinks they might cause the Party to be involved in Police Action, the Conference being a public one.' The letter writer, who signs himself 'Dear old Murelieson', urges Young 'to carry out at once your intention of writing to the papers about the Party's statement on the election at Montrose'.[32] A Westminster by-election had been called for the summer at Montrose, but the National Council of the party was evenly divided in relation to fielding a candidate. Young then received a letter from MacCormick, dated 27 June, saying: 'I met some of the Montrose people myself at Stirling on Saturday and found, as you did, that they are not very keen on an election. In these circumstances possibly we shall have to revise our decision.'[33] From this it would appear that MacCormick (who remained the principal action planner

---

29 'Argyll Sets Heather Afire', *Scots Independent*, May 1940, p. 2.

30 William Power, 'The Significance of Argyll', *Scots Independent*, May 1940, p. 7.

31 Conagh Cole, *Scots Independent*, July 1940, p. 6.

32 NLS, Acc. 6419, Box 4: letter from 'Dear old Murelieson' to Douglas Young, 22 June 1940.

33 NLS, Acc. 6419, Box 4: letter from John MacCormick to Douglas Young, 27 June 1940.

in the leadership group after Power's election to the chairmanship) had initially supported the fielding of a candidate (as he had in Argyll), but that a lack of enthusiasm from the people who would have to run the by-election had made him rethink his decision. In the end, the realisation that party funds were not strong enough for another election led to a decision against putting forward a candidate.

Another interesting point in this letter of 27 June is MacCormick's thanking Young for an earlier letter and saying that he 'suspected that your nomination for the Chairmanship had been made without your knowledge, but in the absence of definite information, I had no option but to let it go forward'. He adds: 'I shall, of course, arrange to have it withdrawn on the final list of nominations submitted at the Conference.'[34] Given Young's challenge to Power two years later for the chairmanship of the party, and his letter to MacDiarmid of 3 July 1940 (i.e. shortly after the 'Montrose' letters discussed above), in which he disparages the leadership generally and refers patronisingly to Power himself, it would not be surprising if he had indeed intended to put in a bid for the chairman's position in 1940, but had decided against it when he saw the support Power achieved after the Argyll by-election. He writes in his July letter to MacDiarmid:

> Please do not trouble meantime with the articles for the organ of the N.B. Devolutionaries [...] Poor misguided creatures, they have no convictions to have the courage of. I was at their annual conference last Saturday and it was a pitiable affair. Of all that crew the only man I really respect is R. E. Muirhead.

Then he adds – perhaps because he knows MacDiarmid has a strong respect for Power: 'although of course one has an affection for some of them, such as old Willie Power, now styled the "hero of Argyll"'.[35]

---

34   Ibid.

35   NLS, Acc. 6419, Box 4: letter from Douglas Young to C. M. Grieve (Hugh MacDiarmid), 3 July 1940.

The 'hero of Argyll' did not have an easy time during his period as chairman of the SNP, and one finds few direct or expanded references to him
in political history writings about the period. In his account of the SNP in
Independent and Free, Richard Finlay describes Power as 'pliant' and refers
to 'the clique that had gathered around MacCormick and William Power'.
Both characterisations are unfair to Power, and do not represent the character of the man as it appears in his earlier life and work, or in what can be
found out about his chairmanship period. It is thought-provoking to realise
that Power took over the chairmanship of the SNP around the same time in
the year of Dunkirk, as Winston Churchill replaced Chamberlain as Prime
Minister of Britain; and both men were in their mid-sixties as they took office.
In very different ways, each would appear to have been the right man for the
task before him. Churchill's ebullient character, which had won him many
enemies in his pre-war political career, has been acknowledged as the essential quality needed for his wartime role. Power's war work was of a different
nature, and required a leader who could be 'pliant' in the positive sense of
the word, who could mediate between opposing sides and sense when it
was more productive to avoid an irreparable collision. Power's 'leadership' was
in reality a 'holding operation' under wartime conditions; and reading the
fractious arguments between the various factions of the party during this
period, it is difficult to comprehend that such bitter internal disputes were
actually contemporaneous with the evacuation of troops from Dunkirk, the
air battles over the English Channel, the bombing of London and the south
of England, and, in Scotland itself, the Clydebank Blitz in the spring of 1941.
Power continued to contribute to the *Scots Independent* during his leadership
period with articles which avoided current internal disputes but looked forward to questions of how Scotland might be governed after the war if home
rule were to be achieved. Some articles ranged beyond Scotland, such as
his 'My View of "The New World Order": The Nation and the Federation',
which seemed to anticipate future developments similar to that of the European Community. One potential contributor who does not appear in the *Scots
Independent* in these early war years as often as one might have expected is

Douglas Young, who, as previously discussed, was one of the strongest protesters against the conscription of Scots for war service. His personal refusal
to register for service would result in his imprisonment in the autumn of 1942.
In the summer of that year, however, he was instrumental in bringing to an
end William Power's role as chairman.

In their accounts of events leading up to the annual conference in 1942,
both MacCormick's *The Flag in the Wind* and Finlay's *Independent and
Free* stress the part that Young's anti-conscription campaign played in keeping alive the contentious atmosphere in the party. Young's arguments before
the Conscientious Objectors' Tribunal were based on his belief that, 'as a
Scotsman, no Government of the United Kingdom had power to impose
conscription upon him'.[36] When his case was rejected and he was sentenced
to one year's imprisonment, he became a heroic figure to supporters of the
anti-conscription position. Other party members, including MacCormick
and the leadership team, were unhappy about the unpatriotic image that
was increasingly being attached to the party through such anti-war publicity. Intermingled with these anti-conscription concerns was the recurring
disagreement over whether or not to fight by-elections in order to bolster
the party's image, with William Whyte, who was defeated in the by-election
in Cathcart in April 1942, blaming his defeat on the negative publicity
received as a result of Douglas Young's trial, which unfortunately occurred
at the same time.

Such divisions came to a head at the June conference in 1942, when Young,
despite his approaching imprisonment, stood for election as chairman against
William Power and was elected with a small majority of four votes. The meeting itself would appear to have been something of a rabble, and there are
contradictory accounts of it in MacCormick's *The Flag in the Wind* and in
the official party account published in the *Scots Independent* of July 1942.
John MacDonald, editor of the newspaper, was shouted down as he attempted to make his editorial report in protest against a leader in the paper,

---

36   MacCormick, *The Flag in the Wind*, p. 103.

which Young and his supporters considered 'prejudiced and inaccurate'.[37]
According to the *Scots Independent*, after Power's defeat by Young, 'Mr
Muirhead then proposed that Mr Power should be elected Hon. President
according to the Constitution, and thanked him for his outstanding services
to the Cause.' MacCormick then rose to 'implore' Power not to accept this
offer, saying that 'for too long the Party had tried to face both ways [...] But
this was too important an occasion to do so any longer.'[38] It was then reported
that there was 'a hubbub', which, after some further speech by MacCormick,
ended with him being asked to 'desist' by the new chairman, who 'bade him
farewell in Russian'. As for William Power, he 'accepted Mr MacCormick's
advice and declined the Office of Hon. President'.[39] In this account, as in
MacCormick's own more conspiratorial version of events, Power appears
sidelined, with the stage given over to more dramatic personalities. Mac-
Cormick's version, on the other hand, gives Power a dignified exit in what
is presented as his closing speech:

'Mr Chairman,' he said,

> I congratulate you on your election, I bear you no ill-will and, while I do
> not agree with the position you have taken up about war service, I admire
> your courage in defying popular opinion. But it seems to me that a deci-
> sion has been taken not on persons but on a principle. I, therefore, will go
> with John MacCormick. I, too, resign.[40]

Power appears to have left no written record of his own thoughts concerning his two-year chairmanship of the SNP or his 1942 election defeat by
Young, just as he seems to have left no account of his earlier involvement with
nationalist politics. He followed MacCormick and some other Nationalist

37   'Report of the Annual Conference 1942', *Scots Independent*, July 1942, p. 2.
38   Ibid.
39   Ibid.
40   MacCormick's communication of William Power's resignation speech, *The Flag in the Wind*, p. 107.

Party members into the wider grouping of Scottish Convention where he became vice-chairman, then chairman, and he was later president of the newly formed Covenant Association. As he had intimated in his farewell speech, he genuinely appeared to bear Young no ill-will, writing to him during his imprisonment in Saughton Prison, as can be seen from a series of letters between Muirhead and Power in late 1942.[41] He continued to write about Scotland after his departure from the SNP. In 1943, his short book *The Culture of the Scot: Its Past and Future*, with an introduction by Neil M. Gunn, was published for Scottish Convention by William MacLellan and his final publication, *Kelvingrove Jubilee*, appeared in 1952, a year after his death. This is a fine account, beautifully illustrated with photographic material, of the history of Glasgow's Fine Art Collections and their various museum homes, ending with the present Kelvingrove Art Gallery, and it reminds readers that Power was a knowledgeable and appreciative art lover as well as journalist and author. He died on 13 June 1951 in hospital in Alloa, near Stirling. His obituary in the *Glasgow Herald* emphasised his intellectual curiosity and his creativity, citing early books such as *The World Unvisited* (1922) and *Robert Burns and Other Essays* (1926), and suggested that this 'was his metier rather than the field of politics'.[42] Obituaries in several newspapers stressed his sociability and popularity and his helpfulness to young writers, while a letter writer to the *Glasgow Herald* of 15 June 1951 reminded readers of his international interests, affirming that his idea of Scottish nationalism was broad and without xenophobia, judging him to be both a good European and a world citizen. Although his leadership of the SNP was a brief one, he kept faith with his concept of nationalism and internationalism in difficult and dangerous times.

---

41   NLS, Acc. 3721, Box 5, File 87: letters between William Power and R. E. Muirhead, 25 & 30 November 1942, 5 & 7 December 1942.

42   *Glasgow Herald*, 14 June 1951, p. 3.

CHAPTER 8

DOUGLAS YOUNG

GORDON PENTLAND

'You speak of Wallace. I am not to be compared with Wallace, perhaps rather with Jimmie Maxton. But I would make this point about Wallace. He chose his time to fight.'[1]

Douglas Young joined the SNP in 1938, while still a member of the Labour Party, and became chair in 1942, when he defeated William Power, leading to a split in the party. Young's election as chairman was owed to his opposition to conscription. He maintained that the UK government had no right to conscript Scots into the war effort. This led to Young being jailed. Upon his release, he stood in the Kirkcaldy by-election in 1944 and won 42 per cent of the vote, assisted by a wartime truce between the main parties that meant there was no Unionist. When the SNP banned dual membership in 1948, Young chose Labour over the SNP despite misgivings about Labour's commitment to home rule.

. . .

So wrote Douglas Young (1913–73) to Robert McIntyre in 1948, just ahead of quitting his membership of the Scottish National Party. It was both a perceptive and a revealing comment. Across his

---

1   NLS, Acc. 10090/15, Papers of Dr Robert McIntyre: letter from Douglas Young to Robert McIntyre, 4 April 1948.

longer political life and as chairman of the SNP himself between 1942 and 1945, Young had indeed shared much common ground with Maxton. Like Maxton, Young had an uneasy relationship with a changing Labour Party and was a committed opponent of conscription (albeit with a very different rationale), who actively courted legal trials to dramatise and publicise his own beliefs. Like Maxton, Young advocated maximum unity of a wider movement, while his own actions helped to make this unity difficult or impossible to engineer. Like Maxton, it might also be argued that Young achieved very little in conventional political terms, but was, nevertheless, a charismatic figure capable of inspiring considerable loyalty and securing a berth in the folklore of a wider movement.

Among the many differences between the two was the impact of the 'Devil's Decade' of the 1930s on their developing politics. While both were firmly internationalist in general outlook, for the older Maxton, the interwar years saw a pivot away from nationalist and home rule positions, with the characteristic affirmation that 'the general social problem always takes the premier place in my mind, before the nationalist'.[2] For Young, this formula was reversed, as nationalism became the ever more dominant ingredient in his composite and shifting political philosophy. Indeed, in the closest approximation to an autobiography, Young provided a similar ranking of political priorities:

> It struck me that, if one was to be serious at all about self-government for Scotland, it was only proper to be most serious about the most serious aspect of the question. Accordingly the question of Scotland's position in a war as of more importance than the incidence of infantile mortality, overcrowding in slums, electrification of railways, construction of road-bridges over the Forth and Tay estuaries, digging of a mid-Scotland ship-canal, and all the other stock-in-trade of nationalist platforms.[3]

2   Finlay, 'Pressure group or political party?', p. 282; William Knox, *James Maxton (Lives of the Left)* (Manchester: Manchester University Press, 1987), p. 122.

3   Douglas Young, *Chasing an Ancient Greek: Discursive Reminiscences of a European Journey* (London: Hollis & Carter, 1950), p. 56. See also NLS, Acc. 6419/39/1, Papers and Correspondence of Douglas C. Young: letter from Douglas C. Young to John MacDonald, July 1939: 'You are not a Labour or Liberal Home-ruler, even though you may be a socialist and a democrat. You are primarily a nationalist.'

There is a consensus that the experience of the Second World War played a pivotal role in the painful birth of a recognisably 'modern' SNP.[4] As befitted someone of Young's temperament, his period of leadership within the SNP was brief but eventful. This essay will trace Young's political career, paying especial attention to the period of his election to and holding of the SNP chair between 1942 and 1945. In particular, the fractious politics of the war years forced partial resolutions to two questions that had dogged the party from its earliest days. The first was a tactical and strategic question: was the SNP a conventional political party aiming for mass membership and electoral success or was it primarily a pressure group? The second was an ideological and intellectual question: what was the precise content of the nationalism it espoused? Young's leadership had important implications for both these questions.

EARLY YEARS

Young was born in Tayport, Fife, to Stephen and Margaret Young. It would be tempting to ascribe some of his outlook, both his sense of national attachment to Scotland and his local patriotism for Fife, to the influence of his father. Stephen Young was a jute salesman and clerk for a Dundee firm and the family was based in Jagatdal near Calcutta. Young insisted, however, that all of his children be natives of Tayport, involving his wife in a number of gruelling return trips.[5] Young spent his early life in India, before attending Merchiston Castle School in Edinburgh from 1921. Intellectually very able, Young passed the entrance exams for the universities of Oxford, Cambridge and St Andrews. Whether his decision to attend St Andrews was motivated by a kind of formless 'nationalist instinct' (the gloss that Young himself later gave to the decision), to an early enthusiasm for golf, to St Andrews's

---

4   Finlay, *Independent and Free*, Chapter 6; I. G. C. Hutchison, *Scottish Politics in the Twentieth Century* (Basingstoke: Palgrave, 2001), pp. 83–7; Peter Lynch, *SNP: The History of the Scottish National Party*, Chapter 3.

5   Clara Young and David Murison (eds), *A Clear Voice: Douglas Young, Poet and Polymath: A Selection from his Writing with a Memoir* (Loanhead: Macdonald Publishers, 1977), p. 9.

reputation in the Classics, or to a mixture of all three, any preference for Scottish universities did not prevent him attending Oxford after St Andrews, though it perhaps explains his lack of enthusiasm for the English institution.[6]

Young's early political life was a microcosm of the different streams that were, in Compton Mackenzie's apposite verb, 'kneaded' into the National Party of Scotland and subsequently the SNP.[7] While later biographical sketches tended to highlight a conversion to nationalism evinced by support for the SNP's first contested election in 1929 or by Young's own involvement in Eric Linklater's 1933 campaign in East Fife, his path, like those of others, was messier and more meandering.[8] Indeed, another point of commonality with Maxton was juvenile beginnings on the conservative right of politics. At school, according to the recollections of a contemporary (the High Court of Justiciary judge Lord Robertson), he scorned modern Scottish nationalism and spoke and voted against it in a debate as 'the honourable member for Wormit', while later at St Andrews he became president of the Conservative Club. It was perhaps in Oxford that both his political engagement and his nationalism really crystallised through his presidency of the Bryce Society and, more importantly, the ubiquity of large and urgent political questions during the 1930s. This led to his joining the Labour Party in 1935, an association that was not incompatible with support for nationalist candidates at the polls, but that would ensure that the increasingly vexed debate around 'dual membership' within the SNP would affect him very personally.[9]

There are things worth noting about these youthful experiences. Young was clearly intellectually first-rate, winning armfuls of prizes wherever he went. His interests were wide-ranging and eclectic and translated into a certain eccentricity in personal dress and style. The combination of his upbringing and his education ensured that he was able to cultivate a wide and learned

---

6   Young, *Chasing an Ancient Greek*, pp. 5–7 & 55.

7   Compton Mackenzie, *On Moral Courage* (London: Collins, 1962), p. 147.

8   *The Free-Minded Scot: Trial of Douglas C. C. Young in the High Court of Edinburgh* (Glasgow: Scottish Secretariat, 1942), p. i; Young, *Chasing an Ancient Greek*, p. 55.

9   Young and Murison, *A Clear Voice*, pp. 10–12.

network and had provided opportunities, through student activism and associational life, to develop leadership qualities, as an organiser and an orator,
that would help to shape his adult political life.

NATIONALISM, SOCIALISM AND DEMOCRACY

Following Oxford, and declining other superficially more attractive career
opportunities in both Oxford and the USA, Young took up a position
as assistant to the professor of Greek at the University of Aberdeen. And it
was from Aberdeen that the more systematic and practical engagement with
nationalist politics began, when Young became secretary of the Aberdeen
branch of the SNP. These political steps ran in tandem with, and remained
intimately connected to, Young's literary activities. The latter were focused
on poetry (critiqued over breakfast sessions with Edwin and Willa Muir)
and his developing experiments with Scots verse in *The Auld Aiberdeen
Courant and neo-Caledonian Spasmodical: A Political and Literary Galli-
maufry*.[10] Young's cultural nationalism was a constant across his career and
became evermore central to his concerns following the war, from his defence
of the achievements of and rationale for the Scots renaissance in *Plastic Scots*
through to his attempts to expand these achievements through his own collections of verse and translations of other poets and dramatists into Scots.[11]

It was not his poetry, however, that elevated him to a leadership position
within the SNP, and around the outbreak of the Second World War Young
was restlessly thinking through and writing about political and constitutional
nationalism. Young, who was cosmopolitan in spirit and outlook and had a
ready command of ancient and modern European languages, was well qualified

---

10 Young, *Chasing an Ancient Greek*, pp. 174–5; NLS, Acc. 12944/41, Frank Cameron Yeaman Papers: *The
Auld Aiberdeen Courant and neo-Caledonian Spasmodical.*

11 Douglas Young, *'Plastic Scots' and the Scottish Literary Tradition: An Authoritative Introduction to a
Controversy* (Glasgow: William Maclennan, 1947). Probably the most celebrated translations were those
of Aristophanes plays *The Frogs* and *The Birds*, Douglas Young, *The Puddocks: A Verse Play in Scots frae
the Auld Greek o Aristophanes* (Tayport: Douglas Young, 1957); Douglas Young, *The Burdies: A Comedy
in Scots Verse* (Tayport: Douglas Young, 1959).

to scan and analyse the troubled state of European politics. Efforts to gauge the possibilities these opened up for Scottish nationalism can send a chill up modern spines. The least attractive examples would include articles for the *Scots Independent*, with titles such as 'Scotland and the New World Order', or bloodless and Olympian assessments of the possibilities opened up by a (possibly unsuccessful war) against Hitler's Germany: 'The SNP must not be thirled to democracy in case democracy should be the wrong camp.'[12]

Such statements make for uneasy reading and reveal an apparent 'dark side' to Young's nationalism, but they formed part of a more complex whole. They were enough to ensure that Young's home, along with those of Donaldson, Muirhead and others, was raided in a notorious wartime sweep.[13] Nevertheless, Young was far from alone in his efforts to struggle with the kaleidoscopic international possibilities of the 1930s in an effort to find a stable compound of Europe's dominant political ideologies. To pluck but one example, around the same time William Beveridge speculated to Beatrice Webb along similar lines: 'I would very much like to see Communism tried under democratic conditions.'[14]

A letter to a divinity student at the University of St Andrews, who had written to the *Scots Independent*, provides a neat summary of Young's political outlook at this stage. He wrestled with how Scotland might blend nationalism, socialism and democracy in a way that avoided the 'repulsive features' of the German variant, which ought to be discountenanced on both pragmatic and ideological grounds:

> Now abideth these three, Nationalism, Socialism, Democracy. Any one is
> good, any two are better, and happy they who achieve all three together.
> I maintain that we Scots are among the few human communities who at

---

12   NLS, Acc. 6419/39/1–2, Young Papers: letter from R. E. Muirhead to Douglas Young, 30 March 1939; Douglas Young to John MacDonald, July 1939; Douglas Young to R. E. Muirhead, 1 August 1940. Maximum polemical value has been squeezed from these sorts of assessment in Bowd, *Fascist Scotland*, Chapter 4.

13   Mitchell, *The Scottish Question*, pp. 97–8.

14   Mark Mazower, *Dark Continent: Europe's Twentieth Century* (London: Allen Lane, 1998), p. 190.

this stage of history can achieve all three together. Scotland with social-democratic nationhood will be a model-unit for a new world order. That, sketchily, is my philosophical justification for my faith and works as a member of the Scottish National Party.[15]

For the illustration of a felicitous combination of these features, Young recommended (and would not be the last within the SNP to do so) Sweden, which was increasingly brought to the attention of the British left during the 1930s.[16] So Young, in common with many others, regarded the Nazi regime in the 1930s as an illustration of the brutal efficiency of state control. What was sometimes expressed as a mere preference for democracy, however, hardened into an article of faith.

OPPOSITION TO WAR

In terms of practical political action, it was as secretary to the Aberdeen branch that Young became a kind of lightning conductor that channelled various tensions within the party. These were pre-eminently raised by, if they were not entirely created by, the outbreak of war. One broad set of problems was essentially ideological and rested on differing visions of the relationship between Scotland, the United Kingdom and the empire. When such questions were coupled with various positions on conscription, always a complex issue within nationalist politics, they presented a series of delicate challenges for the leadership of a motley and fissile party. While a balancing act (or fudge) could be maintained in the 1938 manifesto, the outbreak of the war brought such issues to a head.[17]

The response of John MacCormick and others was to try to maintain the pre-war balancing act under wartime conditions. The SNP announced general support for the war effort, including the offer of its offices to government,

---

15   NLS, Acc. 6419/39/1, Young Papers: letter from Douglas Young to R. Y. Drummond, 25 February 1939.

16   Bjarne Braatoy, *The New Sweden: A Vindication of Democracy* (London: Thomas Nelson, 1939).

17   Mitchell, *Strategies for Self-Government*, pp. 184–7.

in return for a clear definition of war aims and for some commitment to put into effect in its own back yard those principles of self-government for which it was fighting on the European continent. When, unsurprisingly, the government felt safe in completely ignoring this ultimatum, the SNP withdrew the offer (a gesture that was similarly ignored). Its leaders were driven into increasingly uncomfortable positions: 'The Party merely supports the war effort of the Government which does not necessarily mean that we range ourselves alongside the Government on all issues. Indeed, we claim the right to oppose the Government.'[18]

As MacCormick's defensive tone indicates, the second set of tensions was driven by strategic and by personality differences, which interacted with the more ideological ones. By facing both ways, critics could argue, the party went nowhere. The sense that the outbreak of war created strategic opportunities, coupled with a contemporary focus on the need for political 'movement', could be brought together and aimed at the leadership. Even before the war, Young openly expressed discontent with the inertia of the SNP: 'The Scottish National Party is not a wholly useless organisation, but woefully woolly witted. It is full of complaint and analysis, but its constructive programme seems lacking in realism.'[19] It was through the conscription issue that Young rose to the leadership of the SNP, having led the Aberdeen branch to disaffiliate over the issue in 1941. As a key issue at annual conferences, conscription remained as a stalking horse for all sorts of intra-party grievances.[20]

The 1940 conference had urged government to expand the criteria for conscientious objection to include nationalist political convictions. This presented one route to refusal, that a Scot had a moral right to oppose conscription. Young's position echoed aspects of that argument and, indeed, his completed National Service (Armed Forces) Act pro forma rested almost entirely on such grounds:

---

18   *The Scotsman*, 8 December 1939; NLS, Acc. 6419/39/2, Young Papers: letter from John MacCormick to Douglas Young, 10 December 1940.

19   NLS, Acc. 6419/39/1, Young Papers: 'Authoritarian Antics in Scotland', February 1939.

20   Finlay, *Independent and Free*, pp. 206–13 & 227–9.

> Having regard to the self-evident truth that it is a prior moral obligation
> to secure the independence of one's own nation before embarking on
> war for that of other nations ... makes it ethically inadmissible for a Scot
> to take part in this war as a conscript of the Westminster Government.[21]

There were, however, other intellectual resources with which to oppose conscription. At an Aberdeen May Day meeting in 1939, Young had answered a heckler by asserting a legal and constitutional rather than a moral point: that it was *ultra vires* for the Westminster Parliament to impose conscription for foreign service on Scottish subjects.[22] Young evidently tested this point on the legal expert and nationalist Andrew Dewar Gibb, whom Young had met at the party conference of 1939 and who attempted to burst his bubble with a statement of the Diceyan orthodoxy that 'Parliament can do anything'.[23] Undeterred, Young went on to restate this approach and in November 1940 three nationalists came before Glasgow Sheriff Court and justified their failure to register on the grounds that the military service act did not apply to Scotland, because it breached the treaty of Union.[24] Young was, therefore, not the first Scot to refuse conscription on these constitutional grounds. His significance and notoriety stemmed rather from his having the abilities to conduct and to publicise his own trials as a dramatisation of the complex issues involved. Trials and imprisonment were invited for purely propagandist purposes.

The first in a cycle of trials and confinements that would last until 1944 took place at Glasgow Sheriff Court in April 1942. Young refused to comply with the conscription scheme because he was not British but Scottish, and highlighted the distinctly ethnic basis of his own nationalism. As a practical man,

---

21 NLS, Acc. 6419/39/2, Young Papers: National Service (Armed Forces) Act 1939: Application to local tribunal by a person provisionally registered in the register of conscientious objectors, 11 April 1940.

22 Young, *Chasing an Ancient Greek*, p. 57; Mackenzie, *On Moral Courage*, p. 148.

23 NLS, Acc. 6419/39/1, Young Papers: letter from Andrew Dewar Gibb to Douglas Young, 27 October 1939.

24 NLS, Acc. 6419/39/2, Young Papers: letter from R. E. Muirhead to Frank Yeaman, 10 December 1940.

he did not wish to be conscripted in support of a war being conducted with 'fusionless incompetence'. He could not bear to see Scots men and women transported 'like coolies, to labour for an alien imperialism furth of Scotland, while Scotland is invaded by a swarm of miscellaneous foreigners'.[25] These were only preludes to Young's legal argument – an elaborate, erudite and often witty constitutional essay, which forwarded a number of related points. Young's key propositions were that conscription law was incompatible with the common law of Scotland and that absolute parliamentary sovereignty was a doctrine utterly irreconcilable with the Treaty of Union. From these flowed contentions that the sheriff substitute could not execute a statute unknown to the law of Scotland and that the British state was 'a legal non-entity'.[26]

It was heady stuff, and the sheriff substitute for Lanarkshire was the first of a number of Scottish judges who would have cause to congratulate Young on his great learning and erudition, before sentencing him to prison. From sheriff court, an appeal took him to the High Court in Edinburgh, in July 1942, where he presented substantially the same case. Here his learning met with less indulgence and the judges dismissed 'an argument of considerable length which had the misfortune to be mainly irrelevant'.[27]

Young and those from whom he sought legal and constitutional advice had, of course, laboured under no illusions that the defence would be successful, though Young certainly believed his defence was valid from an intellectual point of view. As Colin Kidd has indicated, at root the argument involved a kind of analytic unionism and rested on a strict construction of the settlement of 1707 rather than a fundamentalist nationalism. Certainly, it helps to explain the congratulations Young's father, a church elder in Fife, received from ministers and elders enamoured of his son's defence of Scottish rights.[28]

---

25   *The Free-Minded Scot*, pp. 4–5.

26   See the different versions of *Free-Minded Scot*, offering accounts of the trial in Glasgow and the appeal in Edinburgh, for summaries of the issues involved. See also, Young, *Chasing an Ancient Greek*, pp. 55–60.

27   *The Free-Minded Scot*, p. 30.

28   Kidd, *Union and Unionisms*, pp. 293–5; Young, *Chasing an Ancient Greek*, p. 62.

We might speculate that fewer of the Cupar presbytery would have agreed with the intentions behind such arguments, which were to render plain the absurdities and inconsistencies of the British constitution and to undermine or substantially remodel the Union rather than to facilitate its strict enforcement. Young embodied a kind of old-style radicalism, one stretching back to the state trials of the 1790s, which had allowed activists to use courtrooms and legal reporting as a soapbox for their views.[29] He was not beyond drawing comparisons with that period of Scottish history himself and at a later trial denounced the 'Tyrannous power' of conscription not seen 'since the dark days of Henry Dundas, the most powerful and reactionary Scottish Quisling of the last two centuries'.[30] From his dramatisation of trial and imprisonment, through his use of constitutionalist languages, to the elaborate and choreographed procession that marked his release, Young tapped into a long and rich radical tradition.[31]

PARTY CHAIRMAN

Between the trials in Glasgow and in Edinburgh, Young had become chairman of the SNP. While it suited MacCormick to present the outcome of the party conference in May 1942 as down to the machinations of a fundamentalist 'faction', sponsors of 'a truculent sort of nationalism which is far more concerned with its own purity of expression that with its relations with a real and sometimes not very romantic world', all of the cross-cutting tensions outlined above played roles.[32]

Ideological issues and the SNP position on the war were prominent, but

29   James Epstein, '"Our real constitution": trial defence and radical memory in the Age of Revolution', in
      James Vernon (ed.), *Re-reading the Constitution: New Narratives in the Political History of England's
      Long Nineteenth Century* (Cambridge: Cambridge University Press, 1996), pp. 22–51.

30   NLS, Acc. 10090/15, McIntyre Papers: Imprisonment of Douglas Young, Glasgow, 20 October 1944.

31   Young, *Chasing an Ancient Greek*, p. 61.

32   NLS, Acc. 6419/39/3, Young Papers: letter from John MacCormick to Andrew Dewar Gibb, 15 June
      1942; MacCormick, *Flag in the Wind*, pp. 102–7. A good modern account of the split can be found in
      Finlay, *Independent and Free*, pp. 227–31.

so too were tactical and organisational matters. MacCormick's preferred, and incumbent, candidate, the writer William Power, had polled an impressive 37 per cent at the Argyll by-election in April 1940. Since that point, however, seven by-elections had gone by uncontested and the one recent effort, William Whyte's candidacy in Glasgow Cathcart one month before the conference, had been a dismal failure and Whyte polled only 5.5 per cent. An additional cause for concern was that this inertia was evident at a time when genuine grievances, especially around the wartime 'shift south' of both industries and conscripted female workers, were causing lengthy debates in Parliament and seemed promising issues on which an active SNP might capitalise.[33] Young's recent performance in the sheriff court, speedily circulated in pamphlet and press, provided a contrasting picture of dynamism to set against the trimming of the existing leadership. Having declined to be nominated against Power in 1940, Young saw the course in 1942 and was elected by a margin of two votes. With a Presbyterian sense of theatre, one year away from the centenary of the disruption in the Church of Scotland, MacCormick and his supporters walked out of the conference and reassembled over the road at the Rutland Hotel to establish the Scottish Convention.

For Young, the showdown was about the nature of the party and how it conducted itself: 'whether policy should be responsible, consistent and democratic, or whether it should be conducted on the "opportunist" principles of the North British Cripps and his caucus'.[34] Indeed, in both ideological terms and strategic ones, Young was a lot closer to MacCormick than any idea of a fundamental schism would suggest.[35] Though he did certainly peddle a kind of anti-colonialist rhetoric – as his references to the Scots as a 'coolie people' would suggest – he was not a fundamentalist on the idea of separation, regularly thinking through and discussing various federal or devolutionary arrangements

---

33   HC Debs, 12 May 1942, Vol. 379, cc.1575–702.

34   NLS, Acc. 6419/39/4, Young Papers: letter from Douglas Young to Andrew Dewar Gibb, 13 June 1942.

35   Finlay, *Independent and Free*, pp. 229–30; Mitchell, *Strategies for Self-Government*, p. 186.

in a pragmatic way.[36] A similar pragmatism coloured his strategic thinking. While he certainly pushed in 1942 for a more active electoral policy, he discussed with MacCormick a kind of SNP-led Scottish Convention project from as early as 1940 and conceded that the Convention actually established might well have some value. Nevertheless, the sense of a conscious new direction was plain: 'If we seek practical results, we must build up an independent political party. No use putting our wine into old leaky moribund bug-ridden bottles.'[37]

Young's immediate principal value to the SNP was as a propagandist and figurehead rather than a strategist. His high-profile martyrdom was the reason that sufficient levels of support coalesced around him and generated column inches for the party. Almost immediately the new chairman was put out of action, when his appeal was dismissed in July 1942 and he went to spend his first stint in prison and to badger the Scottish Secretary, Tom Johnston, for a typewriter, a lamp and other privileges that would allow him to continue his commentary on Theognis from within Saughton Prison.[38]

It was not a beginning conducive to active chairmanship and in May 1943, his health impaired from incarceration, Young offered to step aside and allow Gibb to take the role, on the proviso that he adhere to Young's positions on conscription and defence. As well as his delicate health, Young was also concerned that his leadership was doing some harm to the party. His carefully researched and crafted constitutional arguments did nothing to dispel the idea that his election marked the SNP as a 'pacifist' party, a damaging charge in the midst of an existential war.[39] Where he did keep up his activity was in his natural *métier* as a propagandist, and there was a steady stream of pamphlets from Young's pen to supplement the accounts of his trials. *Quislings in Scotland*, for example, provided a populist nationalist history

36　Douglas Young, *William Wallace and this War (Speech at Elderslie Commemoration, 1943)* (Glasgow: Scottish Secretariat, 1943), p. 3.

37　NLS, Acc. 6419/39/4, Young Papers: letter from Douglas Young to Andrew Dewar Gibb, 27 June 1942.

38　NLS, Acc. 6419/39/4, Young Papers: letter from Douglas Young to Thomas Johnston, 27 July, 12 August, 11 September & 3 December 1942.

39　NLS, Acc. 6419/39/5, Young Papers: letter from Douglas Young to Andrew Dewar Gibb, 6 May 1943; Finlay, *Independent and Free*, pp. 231–2.

of Scotland from Wallace onwards. It was an attempt at a nationalist version
of Tom Johnston's phenomenally popular *Our Scots Noble Families* (1909)
and identified the 'anti-national' elements in Scottish life, a fifth column
marking in three files 'Privilege', 'Religion', 'Money'.[40]

On his release, however, there were early signs in Young's leadership
of the direction in which the party would move, under the influence of
men like Robert McIntyre and Arthur Donaldson. Individual campaigning issues were identified and pressed, such as opposition to the Scottish
Council of State's plans for hydroelectric schemes in the Highlands as part
of post-war reconstruction.[41] Efforts were made to reorganise internally
and to provide 'a comprehensive statement of policy', dealing with not only
the question of Scottish sovereignty, but what the SNP would do with this
in relation to defence, banking, emigration and other issues.[42] And there
was some clarification on the precise shape of the SNP's ultimate goal.
At the annual conference in 1943, a rewritten constitution highlighted the
party's aim as:

> Self-government for Scotland. The restoration of Scottish national sover-
> eignty, by the establishment of a democratic Scottish government, whose
> authority will be limited only by such agreements as will be freely entered
> into with other nations in order to further international co-operation and
> world peace.[43]

The natural accompaniment to this was a renewed seriousness around electioneering. Here, Young very much led from the front, and on the suggestion

---

40   Douglas Young, *Quislings in Scotland* (Glasgow: Scottish Secretariat, 1942), pp. 1 & 32.

41   Douglas Young, *'Fascism for the Highlands': Gauleiter for Wales?* (Glasgow: Scottish National Party,
     1943).

42   NLS, Acc. 6419/39/5, Young Papers: letter from R. Gibson Sinclair to Douglas Young, 5 July 1943.

43   Lynch, *SNP: The History of the Scottish National Party*, p. 58. This was a significant change from earlier
     formulae such as 'It is pledged to secure NATIONAL FREEDOM by the achievement of responsible
     government through a Scottish Parliament which shall be the authority on all Scottish affairs.' Young,
     Quislings, p. 35.

of council undertook to contest the Kirkcaldy Burghs seat at a by-election in February 1944.[44] Having contested only two of the twelve Scottish by-elections since the beginning of the war, it was an opportunity for the SNP to gulp down some of the oxygen that the electoral truce between the major parties had afforded to smaller outfits.

Young, a passionate and effective speaker and physically imposing at 6 ft 6 in. (he wrote during the campaign to an editor to commend his paper's impartial reporting but to point out that 'your reporter has deprived the constituents of two inches of their candidate'), was made for the platform. With Arthur Donaldson as his election agent, the campaign had a certain professionalism to it, something demonstrably lacking in many previous efforts. Election literature could repeat Douglas Young's '12 demands for Scotland', which embodied a distinctively Scottish programme for post-war reconstruction. Different sections of the electorate were cleverly appealed to with squibs and songs in Scots: 'When you reach the polling-booth, / VOTE FOR YOUNG and Scotland's Youth.'[45] The attempted association of the SNP with youth may have been something of an own goal, when young nationalists in Glasgow were associated with an explosion at ICI offices in Blythswood Square and other acts of theatrical violence against property.[46]

Young was presented as the local man, 'a Fifer', against the Labour candidate Hubbard and the Christian Socialist Henry Hilditch, and ran Hubbard very close with 41.3 per cent of the vote, the best performance in the party's history, albeit in the peculiar circumstances of wartime. The success can partly be explained by the fact that Young and the SNP had latched onto an emotive and popular issue ahead of the Kirkcaldy campaign war production. Topping the list of Young's 'demands for Scotland'

44 NLS, Acc. 6419/39/5, Young Papers: letter from Douglas Young to Andrew Dewar Gibb, 13 October 1943; NLS, Acc. 3721/100/165, Papers of Scottish Secretariat and R. E. Muirhead: Kirkcaldy By-election, 1944.

45 *When you reach the polling-booth, VOTE FOR YOUNG and Scotland's Youth* (Kirkcaldy: Arthur Donaldson, 1944).

46 NLS, Acc. 6419/40/1, Young Papers: Information sheet for branch secretaries and others, 1944; *Evening Times*, 4 January 1944.

was an end to the 'shift south' of young female workers and Scottish industries, which had been a widespread cause of concern and debate from
1942 onwards.[47]

Young shackled this issue to his existing concerns in his final propaganda
campaign as chairman, this time directed at industrial conscription and the
evils and illegality of 'Bevinism'. Young actively courted another trial in which
to air his political and constitutional arguments and, by refusing to present
himself at an employment exchange in March 1944, Young was brought to
trial at Paisley Sheriff Court. The Scottish legal system proved far less indul-
gent than it had been in 1942. His judge in Paisley, whom Young claimed was
hard of hearing, was perhaps simply incredulous and the trial report includes
some healthy doses of humour:

> *Accused:* ...I show, having regard to the Constitution of the United King-
> dom of Great Britain, as instituted by the International Treaty of Union
> between Scotland and England in 1707, that this regulation is ultra vires.
> *Sheriff:* What?
> *Accused:* A term meaning 'beyond the powers of'.
> *Sheriff:* I understand that simple Latin expression. I was merely manifest-
> ing astonishment.[48]

His appeal was rejected by the High Court with the rationale that the judges
believed it to be based on essentially the same grounds as his previous effort.
For someone as loquacious as Young, not being heard was an exquisite punishment, especially when he had been gearing up for another propaganda
effort and a set-piece speech: 'On Friday 6 October at 10.15 a.m. the Parliament House will hear some remarks by me worthy of Saltoun or at least of

---

47   *Kirkcaldy Burghs By-election: Douglas Young's Demands for Scotland* (Kirkcaldy: Arthur Donaldson,
     1944).

48   *British Invasion of Scottish Rights: Douglas Young's Speech in Paisley Sheriff Court on 12th June 1944.*
     Why Industrial Conscription and Delegated Legislation are Unconstitutional in Scotland (Glasgow:
     Scottish Secretariat, 1944), p. 3.

Belhaven. There are a great many bees which I shall liberate from under my bonnet at the marionettes.' Even the presiding presence of Lord Cooper, who would famously open the door to similar arguments with his opinion in the 'royal numerals' case in 1953, could not secure Young a hearing.[49]

His second stint in Saughton was not quite the end of his tenure of the chairmanship, which lasted to witness the election of his collaborator Robert McIntyre for Motherwell in April 1945. Following the election of another Aberdeen University academic, Professor Mearns Bruce Watson, as chairman, the general election of 1945 burst any bubbles about an imminent uptick in SNP electoral fortunes.

DUAL MEMBERSHIP

Young's drift to the fringes of and eventual exit from the SNP had already begun by 1945. The issue of dual membership was the final precipitant. Having resisted efforts within the SNP executive to settle the issue against membership of more than one party, by 1946 Young was frustrated by the internal sectarian witch-hunting the issue generated: 'Unless the Council or Conference decides on what grounds it admits or excludes individuals, and treats other organisations as 'political parties', I for one shall waste no more time on the SNP.'[50] Conference did decide, and the embodiment of its decision in the revised party constitution voted in at the annual conference in May 1948 was Young's exit ticket.[51]

Impatience had bred a more general disenchantment and a sense that the SNP was not making the most of available opportunities. In his analysis, the problem lay not so much in the party having made a single wrong choice from the menu of strategies for self-government, but in the fact that it was failing on all possible fronts: 'Frankly I cannot disguise from myself the conviction

---

49   Kidd, *Union and Unionisms*, pp. 116–20 & 294–5.

50   NLS, Acc. 10090/15, McIntyre Papers: letter from Douglas Young to Robert McIntyre, 23 April 1946; Lynch, *SNP: The History of the Scottish National Party*, pp. 70–72.

51   Mitchell, *Strategies for Self-Government*, p. 195.

that the SNP has got nowhere and will get nowhere either in practical politics or in academic doctrine about Nationalism. Even as a publicity organisation, it is still most inadequate.'[52] As a pressure group, as a party, and as a propagandist body, the SNP was still not an effective vehicle.

Young's mind was turning to other opportunities and contexts for nationalism. As in the aftermath of the First World War, the period following the Second World War saw a fertile discussion about the role and position of nation states old and new, within which Young sought an inflated role for Scotland: 'The world-wide importance of Scottish Nationalism, and its possibilities for the whole future of Humanity, are scarcely imagined as yet.'[53] Debates around some form of European federation and Labour's mandate to build the post-war world were both lining Young's route out of the SNP and back towards a more consensual and cross-party approach. He was quite content to work with MacCormick's Scottish Convention and, by the end of 1948, having left the SNP, Young sought a role as the Scottish conscience of the Labour Party.[54]

Young had also been trying to end the professional disruption of the war years and developing passions other than strictly political ones, in particular his poetry and involvement with PEN. He filled with distinction university posts at Dundee (1947–53) and St Andrews (1953–68), before his academic career took him overseas to McMaster (1968–70) and finally North Carolina (1970–73). The interest in nationalist politics did not fade, but as a leader within the nationalist movement his influence was, after the 1940s, indirect – the influence of the writer, poet and 'elder statesman'.[55]

In the final analysis, we might ask whether Young offered to the SNP any more than the *Perthshire Advertiser*'s assessment of him: 'Mr Young is a

---

52   NLS, Acc. 10090/15, McIntyre Papers: letter from Douglas Young to Robert McIntyre, 11 December 1947.

53   Douglas Young, *The International Importance of Scottish Nationalism* (Glasgow: Scottish Secretariat, 1947), p. 1.

54   Douglas Young, *Labour Record on Scotland: Unfulfilled Pledges Exposed* (Carlops: Scottish Secretariat, 1949).

55   Young and Murison, *A Clear Voice*, pp. 18–34.

brilliantly clever loon, and he has the courage of his convictions.'[56] Certainly, his leadership did little to overturn the impression that had seen Patrick Dollan famously dismiss the early party as 'a mutual admiration society for struggling poets and novelists'.[57] Nor can Young reasonably be claimed as the leader of a 'fundamentalist' position within the party. Indeed, in his open-mindedness about the specific political and institutional content of 'national independence', in continuing to see the SNP as a vehicle for holding Labour, Liberal and Unionist feet to the fire, and in his readiness to work pragmatically with other organisations and approaches, Young was much closer to MacCormick than to the leadership group headed by McIntyre and Donaldson that emerged under his own chairmanship.

Young's political achievement was to help to keep the SNP in existence at a moment fraught with political difficulties. While not a 'fundamentalist' himself, his election and his self-conscious dramatisation of certain issues did help to crystallise those challenges that faced the party during and immediately after the war years. In his flamboyant performances in sheriff and high courts, Young generated publicity and opened a rich vein of legal and constitutional theatrics that would stretch from the royal numerals case to the poll tax and beyond.[58]

Young himself was perhaps too restless to provide settled or consistent direction to the party as a whole, but he did have one great practical leadership virtue: the sense to allow other individuals with greater organisational ability and a clearer sense of direction, such as McIntyre and Donaldson, to work unimpeded. Young was thus on the ground floor of the SNP's (long and painful) development as a 'modern' political party. At the same time, he also suffered from one perennial sickness within the nationalist movement and frequently succumbed to overly optimistic prognostications and a sense that sweeping nationalist successes were just around the corner. This

56 *Perthshire Advertiser*, 9 January 1943.
57 Finlay, 'Pressure group or political party?', p. 283.
58 Kidd, *Union and Unionisms*, Chapter 3; Rodney Barker, 'Legitimacy in the United Kingdom: Scotland and the Poll Tax', *British Journal of Political Science*, 22 (1992): 531.

could naturally breed resignation, impatience and a search for alternative strategies. His own promising performance at Kirkcaldy and McIntyre's successful showing at Motherwell were false dawns in a rapidly emerging 'moment of British nationalism'.[59] Alienation from the party itself began quickly thereafter.

Towards the end of his life, in a 'Sketch History' of the nationalist movement, Young glimpsed another potential moment of 'take-off':

> It is possible that the revived SNP, with its predominantly young membership, is replacing Labour today as the main radical force in Scottish politics, as Labour replaced the Liberals between 1922 and 1924. On recent form, at a general election in 1970 or 1971, the SNP might win a dozen or so seats, perhaps even 40 out of the whole 71.

It was another false dawn, though this time the direction of travel, in the medium term, was accurate. Young, who died on 23 October 1973 with his copy of Homer on the desk in front of him, would not live to see the partial fulfilment of his prophecies in the general elections of 1974.[60]

---

59   Christopher Harvie, 'The Moment of British Nationalism, 1939–1970', *Political Quarterly*, 71/3 (2000): 328–40; Ross McKibbin, *Parties and People: England, 1914–1951* (Oxford: Oxford University Press, 2010), pp. 185–7.

60   Douglas Young, 'A Sketch History of Scottish Nationalism', in Neil MacCormick (ed.), *The Scottish Debate: Essays on Scottish Nationalism* (London: Oxford University Press, 1970), p. 19; Young and Murison, *A Clear Voice*, p. 31.

CHAPTER 9

BRUCE WATSON

RODERICK WATSON

Bruce Watson was Professor of Organic Chemistry at Aberdeen University. He became chairman of the party towards the end of the Second World War, following the resignation of Douglas Young. Watson maintained that there were no shortcuts to self-government and that the cause of self-government would not make real progress without electoral pressure. He held office for only two years and stepped aside to allow his friend Robert McIntyre, who had a higher profile, to become chairman.

. . .

I can remember a time when saying that you believed in the future of Scotland as an independent democratic country would produce an uneasy silence in polite company. When I was a small boy and overly sensitive to such things, it seemed like one of those family secrets best kept at home. Hence my occasionally ironic but friendly smiles at the enthusiasm of young people outdoing each other to call for a 'Yes' vote in the 2014 Scottish independence referendum campaign. Out of the closet and on to T in the Park, perhaps, and with more than 110,000 members after the event, the SNP has now become by far the largest party in Scotland.[1]

I was barely two years old when Bruce Watson was elected party leader at the annual national conference on 9 June 1945. Douglas Young had to stand down as chairman when the party ruled that he could no longer be a member

---

1   'In numbers: Scottish political party membership', *The Scotsman*, 2 October 2015.

of both the Labour Party and the SNP. At that time, Robert McIntyre was vice-chairman, but having taken the Motherwell by-election from Labour with over 50 per cent of the vote that April, he was famously engaged as the party's first MP at Westminster. It was a short-lived victory, though, for he lost the seat that July when the Scottish electorate delivered what would soon become a familiar strategy in general elections: voting Labour to keep the Tories out. My father and Robert McIntyre were close friends, and I guess he looked like a safe pair of hands by Robert and served as leader from 1945 to 1947. When McIntyre succeeded my father and took up the post again, he held the chair for the next nine and a half years and went on to lay the foundations for what the modern SNP was to become.

It was a difficult time, for, with the threat of war and then throughout the 1940s, there had been much debate, not to say turmoil, in the SNP when pro- and anti-conscription factions were arguing about what was best for Scotland and the party, not necessarily in that order. As a medical man and a pacifist, McIntyre was opposed to conscription, though not as vehemently as Douglas Young and Arthur Donaldson. We must remember that after the exhaustion of 1914–18 and the depression years that followed, many people throughout the UK were strongly opposed to the prospect of war in those early years. Socialists saw war as the tool of imperialism and isolationists thought that what happened in Europe was no business of ours. Naomi Mitchison never doubted the need to fight Hitler, but she spoke for many thousands of people when she observed 'Two wars in a lifetime. It seemed unfair. Such a short time since 1918.'[2] In January 1939, Arthur Donaldson predicted that 'everything that Hitler has done and is said to have done against humanity and democracy will be done by our dictators within a month or two after the first gun, and worse before it is all over.'[3] He went on to imagine, prophetically as it happens, the horrors of the mass bombing of civilian targets. With their strongly socialist leanings, Donaldson, Douglas Young and Oliver

2   Naomi Mitchison, *You May Well Ask: A Memoir, 1920–1940* (London: Victor Gollancz Ltd., 1979), p. 222.

3   *Scots Independent*, January 1939, p. 8.

Brown were in no hurry to support what they saw as another imperial conflict, while their nationalist sympathies seized on the opportunity to highlight what they saw as a democratic crisis in Scotland.

At that time, Douglas Young was the new assistant in the university Greek department at King's College, Aberdeen. Tall, bearded, confident, erudite and loquacious, he was a natural speaker, ready to hold forth on any topic at the drop of a hat, whether in large public meetings or over the breakfast table, all to great effect and at some length. Also on the committee of the Aberdeen SNP branch, along with my father, was David Murison, yet another young academic in the Greek department, who married Hilda Angus, one of my mother Jo's older sisters, in 1940. My own parents married in December 1939 – one of many ceremonies, I suspect, prompted by the times.

The Aberdeen branch of the SNP seems to have been a lively place in those years, even if its committee must have looked a little esoteric, with two Greek scholars and an organic chemist among its ranks. Young was speaking on 'The Future of Scottish Socialism' to packed audiences in the YMCA hall in Union Street, and Oliver Brown toured on a similar platform in the summer of 1939 and again in 1940. John MacCormick was invited to speak at yet another mass meeting in the YMCA and even David Murison, pretty severely reticent by nature, was contributing to the public debate. In due course my father became president of the Aberdeen branch, Douglas Young became the Aberdeen District representative on the National Council and David Murison was elected to the National Council as well.

The conscription issue continued to divide an already furiously fissiparous party, and Young continued to press the case for a declared policy of resistance, with the Aberdeen branch demanding a national debate on the topic in December 1939. To the relief of John MacCormick and others of a more moderate opinion, the motion was defeated, although the meeting conceded that 'profound political conviction' would still be allowed as grounds for conscientious objection.[4]

---

4   See Finlay, *Independent and Free*, Chapter 6 for a full account of this period.

This helped with how the party was being perceived at large, but it also allowed Young and Donaldson to pursue the same course under their own steam. In particular, Young argued that since the Treaty of Union had long been broken under English hands, it followed that conscription could not be legally imposed by Westminster, or not, at least, until the rights of an independent Scotland had been conceded by HM Government. This was an unlikely outcome, when all was said and done, in the face of what was happening in Europe. Still the internal debate rumbled on, and of course the redoubtable and radical C. M. Grieve (who had served with the Royal Army Medical Corps (RAMC) in the First World War) was always ready to stir the pot. When Young, rather than the moderate William Power, was elected as chairman of the party at the National Council in 1942, it prompted a walk-out by Power and John MacCormick and their supporters, which led to the establishment of the National Convention, whose aim was to create an alliance that would make a common, cross-party declaration broadly in favour of self-government.

HM Government had its own view on the matter and, along with many other households throughout the country, our bungalow home at 65 Craigton Road was raided by members of MI5 in May 1941. They came looking for subversive literature and weapons and left, frustrated but doubtless newly enlightened, with bundles of SNP pamphlets. 'Is there a Gestapo in Scotland?' was the headline in the *Scots Independent*. Young's considerable correspondence was confiscated – some of it in Greek. Arthur Donaldson was detained under wartime regulations before his release was secured by a general petition and the intervention of Tom Johnson, the Secretary of State for Scotland. Nevertheless, the SNP broke all ties with Donaldson's United Scotland group and its more extreme opposition to conscription, not to say the prosecution of the war.[5]

These were difficult issues and some of the greatest Scottish poets of my

---

5   For a further insight into the relationship between MI5 and the SNP, and in particular its concerns about C. M. Grieve, see Scott Lyall, '"The Man is a Menace": MacDiarmid and Military Intelligence', *Scottish Studies Review*, 8/1 (Spring 2007): 37–52.

later acquaintance had felt similarly divided. Norman MacCaig absolutely refused to kill or to support the war effort as a matter of primary conscience and duly served time in prison for his views. Under the same misgivings, Edwin Morgan specifically chose to join the RAMC. George Campbell Hay took to the hills of Argyll to avoid conscription before surrendering to the inevitable. Sorley MacLean finally conceded that his hatred of fascism was marginally stronger than his dislike of English imperialism and went on to fight in the North African campaign. My uncle, David Murison, later to be the most distinguished editor of the *Scottish National Dictionary*, was a conscientious objector too, and he served out the war as a forester in the north-east and, latterly, tending greenhouses and goats in Stirling.

Young's refusal to be conscripted, and a failed appeal against the ruling, finally led to his arrest and eight months' imprisonment at Saughton on the outskirts of Edinburgh. He is said to have remarked that the experience was not very different from his school days at Merchiston, even as he read Homer and wrote poetry in his cell. Demonstrators gathered to the skirl of bagpipes outside the jail. It speaks volumes for Young's capacity and his public persona that, when he contested a Labour seat at the Kirkcaldy by-election in 1944, he only narrowly lost to Labour despite his spell in prison, his continuingly intemperate remarks over a contentious issue, and a further brush with a spiteful magistrate.

I have no clear sense of how strongly my father supported Young's case against conscription, but as an organic chemist working at Aberdeen University, he was exempted from the army in any case, and accepted service instead as gas protection officer for the whole north of Scotland. I remember the yellow helmet he had, and tales of his guarding the roof of Marischal College armed with a bucket and a stirrup pump, or being called out to muddy fields in Orkney or darkest Donside to examine what turned out to be oxygen bottles dropped or lost from passing aircraft.

While he was intensely proud of, and widely read in, Scottish history and culture, my father's nationalism was always based on demographic and economic grounds. He argued passionately that the electoral imbalance across the so-called United Kingdom meant that Scotland's interests, and its election results, would always and inevitably be subservient to the balance of power south of the border, under policies 'framed by an English majority opinion which is completely out of touch with, if not wholly unsympathetic to, Scottish needs, conditions and aspirations'.[6] He deplored the consequent neglect of native initiative and industry (not to mention its later dismantling) and the slow attenuation of the Highlands and Islands in particular, subject to feudal land ownership and starved of transport links and proper development. He liked to cite Norway as an example in this regard and frequently spoke and wrote of how Scotland should embrace its own 'smallness', and its admirably democratic tradition, to be more confident and more self-sufficient in every sense of the word. I remember a family holiday in Mull in the mid-1950s, when he spoke passionately about how damaging the Clearances had been to this island, pointing to the acres and acres of bracken that were poisoning decently fertile, but long-abandoned ground. He was passionate, too, about the continuing ideological influence of the media, prophetic of what we now call the 'cultural cringe', which 'has created a political atmosphere such that many otherwise intelligent Scots regard an interest in Scottish affairs as evidence of a reprehensible and narrow parochialism'.[7]

In the early 1940s, he wrote a set of lectures called 'Whither Goes Scotland?', dense with historical information, to be delivered in what must have been three particularly long and rather demanding talks to young people in Aberdeen, taking them through Scottish history and historiography, from earliest times to what he freely declared to be the present pressing need for self-government. In such views he was very much in tune with Robert McIntyre's left-of-centre stance and his vision of social democracy and civic nationalism, and the two became close friends. Robert was godfather to my sister Alisoun when she was born in 1947, and my father was Robert's best man when he married Letitia ('Lila') Macleod in 1956.

6   Dr M. Bruce Watson, 'Foreword', in *Whose Country? An up-to-the-minute plea for the Democratic Government of Scotland* (Glasgow: Scottish National Party, 1947), p. vi.

7   Ibid.

The families visited regularly and took occasional holidays together. To entertain us children, Robert's party trick was to make strangely deep grunting noises in his chest, which we took to be the authentic sound of the griffon from *Alice's Adventures in Wonderland* – 'Do the griffon, Robert', and he would duly oblige. He had a genuine talent for meeting and talking with people from every walk of life, and a lesser talent for time-keeping, perhaps. I remember a camping holiday at Achiltibuie, when Robert and my father were sent off to see if they could buy some kippers for tea, only to sail into view, to the fury of the women folk, many hours later. The kippers were cooked and eaten in the dark.

Robert cared greatly for public health – it was his special field after all – and he served as consultant chest physician at Stirling Royal Infirmary for almost all his professional life. As a politician he was particularly passionate about Scotland's dreadful health record, especially in urban areas, where the rates of infant mortality and the short life expectancy of working people in crowded and insanitary slums was a national scandal. I remember him telling me, in my teenage years, how grim it had been for him, as a specialist in tuberculosis, to see so many patients die – at least until the advent of penicillin.

I think my father's chief achievement at political meetings might have been his skill as a chairman, for in that role he managed to remain controlled and lucid when all around him were in freefall. (He had a temper, too, when needed, and he knew the rulebook.) I remember his stories about the liveliest of meetings coping with what John MacCormick called the party's 'wild men', each of whom 'was a party in himself'.[8] At one such event he recounted Chris Grieve being particularly disruptive, interjecting at every conceivable point, until Archie Lamont (I think it was) rose wearily to his feet to complain, beginning: 'Mr Chairman, I have been a member of this party longer than Mr Grieve…', whereupon Grieve again leapt to his feet. Lamont cut him off before he could speak, but, saying, 'I said *longer*, Mr Grieve, not *oftener!*' Scotland's greatest poet could only concede to general laughter.

8   MacCormick, *Flag in the Wind*, Kindle edition, Chapter 17, loc. 1448.

At home in Aberdeen, as a child in bed, I can remember loud voices and hilarity downstairs when the Aberdeen branch was in full swing. Oliver Brown, Arthur Donaldson, and no doubt George and Mary Dott, must all have been there, at one time or another, though I did not know them and never really met them. I was close to David Murison in later years, of course, and recall some vivid encounters with Douglas Young. I remember, too, the genial interest and approval that was generated by the 'theft' of the Stone of Destiny and the excitement about Radio Free Scotland, moving from location to location like the Scarlet Pimpernel. And my mother was very fierce in her objection to 'E II R' on the letterboxes, although she did (just about) draw the line at blowing them up.

In the wider scene, I consider myself fortunate to have known or to have become friends with many of the poets of the literary renaissance, and Sorley MacLean and Chris Grieve in particular remembered my father fondly from the wartime and post-war years. As a schoolboy I was encouraged to recite MacDiarmid's Scots lyrics in place of the usual tim'rous beastie fare when the annual Burns Competition came around, and I ended up making friends with Grieve and visiting him on many occasions when I was working on what was certainly the first ever PhD on his poetry at Cambridge. It was during my time in Cambridge that I met and became friends with John Herdman, whose memoir *Another Country* is such an entertaining account of the Scottish literary political scene in Edinburgh in the 1960s and 1970s.[9]

The Watson family had been city-dwelling Aberdonians for five generations when my father was born. (In later years, he took up serious genealogical research to trace his own and my mother's family trees.) His father, also Mearns Bruce Watson, was the third child and the second son in a family of five to Alexander Giles Watson, who had started life as a weaver before building a large and prosperous business as a fruit and flower wholesaler. There are photographs of the family standing in front of seriously impressive

---

9   John Herdman, *Another Country: An Era in Scottish Politics and Letters* (Edinburgh: Thirsty Books, 2013).

motorcars, but AG died of chest complications at forty-four, and for whatever reasons the firm did not prosper under the hands of his second son, and the business declined in the 1920s. When my dad was about thirteen, his father left for South Africa to try his luck. But he never sent for his family and never came home, leaving his wife, Bruce and his young sister Rhona in very hard circumstances. We think Mearns died in Australia in 1948 and drink was involved. My father never spoke of this. The family moved to live with their mother's mother who kept a pie shop at Holburn Junction and Bruce studied for his exams by the light of a candle in the attic. He did well, though, gaining a scholarship and going on to graduate in Chemistry at Aberdeen University in 1933, followed by a PhD on the effect of light on vitamin C in milk, and an assistant lectureship at Aberdeen University in 1935. Ten years later, he moved to Robert Gordon's technical college (now Robert Gordon University), where he developed his department from scratch and was Head of Chemistry until he retired in 1975.

My parents were keen hill walkers in their youth and all our family holidays were spent in Scotland. After I was born, when my mother left her job as an accountant, we took regular summer vacations in Corgarff, in an isolated shepherd's cottage west of the Lecht, without electricity or running water. Sanitation was an earth closet at the foot of the tangled garden. (This is now a listed building, as it happens, still in its original state, and still in the care of the family who succeeded us as renters.) Throughout the long summer weeks (in those days of extended academic vacations) we fetched water in buckets from the burn while my mother cooked heroically on a paraffin-wick stove under Tilly lamps. My sister and I roamed outside all day in what was a really special experience of late-eighteenth-century Scottish rural life—without its backbreaking labour of course. Dad fished and helped out with the local farmer's harvesting and shearing tasks, and over something like eleven years at Loinherry I became an expert dam builder in the burn and a fluent speaker of broad Aberdeenshire Doric.

As my sister and I grew older we travelled further afield on our family holidays, especially to the west coast and the Highlands, where my father was keen to learn and practise speaking Gaelic. This could be difficult at times, for when addressed by a stranger in their mother tongue, the first impulse of many Gaels in those days was to reply politely and firmly in English. My father's commitment to Gaelic was strong, however (he was a life member of An Comunn Gaidhealach), and when he retired and left Aberdeen with my mother to live at Saasaig in Skye in 1975, he worked for ten years as a tutor for *Gàidhlig Bheo* from the National Extension College at Cambridge, receiving written exercises and cassette tapes from learners all over Britain and Europe. The founding of the Sabhal Mòr Ostaig in 1973, just down the road from where he lived, gave him great satisfaction.

Bruce enjoyed his retirement to Skye on the Sleat peninsula. He could tell a good Doric joke, and appreciated a good single malt, and, just as they did in Corgarff, my parents fitted into the community, making many close friends and contributing to local life. Dad spoke at various social events, and on one occasion used his expertise as a chemist to experiment with traditional dyes made from lichen and roots, cutting up blankets to show the local ladies what their garments might have looked like in the eighteenth century. A workshop in the garage attached to the single-storey Finnish house they built at Saasaig allowed him to continue with his hobbies in carpentry and, for one summer only of terrible smells of boiling sheep's horn in the kitchen, making traditional shepherd's crooks.

These activities were not a new thing, for dad had a wide and esoteric range of interests beyond his actual profession. He was a Fellow of the Royal Society of Chemistry and the Royal Institute of Chemistry, but as a man with lasting antiquarian and historical interests he was proud to be a Fellow of the Society of Antiquaries (Sco), and amassed a considerable library of rare books, especially ones to do with the history of Aberdeen and 'twal mile roon'. I remember him reading and writing in Latin and studying classical civilisation when we were living in Aberdeen, and this passion shook hands with an interest in bookbinding when he re-bound dozens of paperback volumes from the Penguin Classics library with hard covers in matching red cloth. And it was his interest in collecting Roman and Greek coins that took him into carpentry to make a rather fine coin cabinet with panelled doors and many slender drawers. He was genuinely creative in his way and, when it was time for a coffee break or lunch at the chemistry department, he would sit with his friends the painters Ian Fleming and Bobby Henderson Blyth, who worked next door at Gray's School of Art.

My own generation has been much more mobile than our parents ever managed, and I regret that my father never got to visit the great art galleries in Italy, nor to see the ruins of Pompeii or ancient Rome, which I know he would have loved.

But, always and above all else, his commitment was to Scotland and to Scottish life, language and culture. 'There's still so much to see in Scotland,' he would say, unconsciously echoing, perhaps, MacDiarmid's poem, 'Scotland small? Our multiform, our infinite Scotland *small*?' This love was what fuelled his political commitment, enthusiastically fierce and occasionally impatient as he was. My sister and I were lucky, I think, to grow up with such a perspective, with such confident and committed parents who were not afraid to stand up and be counted, and to ask more of democracy than the status quo was delivering. It makes me sad to reflect, however, that neither Jo nor Bruce lived long enough to witness the referendum result in 2014. My mother lived until she was ninety-two (the Anguses were sturdy stock) and wept at the reconvening of the Scottish Parliament on the Mound in 1999. But by then my father had been dead for eleven years. It still felt like a family thing.

CHAPTER 10

ROBERT MCINTYRE

RICHARD FINLAY

Robert McIntyre became one of the earliest nationalist trailblazers even before he became chair of the party, winning the Motherwell by-election in April 1945 against Labour. Subsequently, he became chair in 1947, after already serving as National Secretary from 1942 to 1945, and held the post for the next nine years, during which he helped draft the party's revised new policy document of 1948, and oversaw the organisational overhaul of the party. After his period as chair, he served as president of the SNP from 1956 to 1980, as well as provost of Stirling. He was involved in the intense internal battles of the early 1980s but latterly became a father figure in the party.

. . .

The period from the mid-'40s to the late '70s was a distinctive phase in terms of the development of the identity and ideology of the SNP, in which Robert McIntyre was one of a handful of individuals who was profoundly influential in shaping the modern party.[1] British identity had been re-forged in the furnace of the Second World War around the idealism of the welfare state. This would prove remarkably stony ground for the flower of Scottish independence to grow as the whole notion was presented

---

1   The early history of the SNP is covered in Finlay, *Independent and Free*; Somerville, *Through the Maelstrom*; Peter Lynch, *SNP: The History of the Scottish National Party*; Hassan, *The Modern SNP*; and Mitchell, Johns and Bennie, *The Scottish National Party*.

in the media as backward-looking, romantic and the province of cranks.[2] Although the party made an electoral breakthrough in the mid-'60s and '70s, the period before was one marked by impotence and frustration in which a major challenge was to keep the faith and hold intact the seed that one day would flower into Scotland's most successful political party and protect it from the chill wind of irrelevance in a British political system dominated by class allegiance and loyalty. Gestation periods and origins are important in tracking the history of political parties and form a considerable core of the historiography as historians often use this period of formation as marking the essence and character of that particular movement. In a British context, the origins of both the Liberal and Conservative parties are rendered complex by eighteenth- and nineteenth-century roots in the pre-democratic era, whereas Labour, the Communist Party and Plaid Cymru can be clearly dated and charted.[3] The period from the late 1880s until the end of the First World War usually marks the origins of the Labour Party and the years covering a similar length of time between 1928 and the mid-'60s takes the SNP from its inception to its establishment on the British political stage. One of the reasons that it is important to put the origins of political parties under the historical microscope is that it often marks the 'making' of the movement, and this becomes the subsequent benchmark for assessing whether or not the party has remained true to its origins or forgotten its roots. Consider the contemporary debate surrounding the Labour Party, in which left and right fight for its soul and contest the very nature of its political being.

2   For the reshaping of British identity after the Second World War see Richard Weight, *Patriots: National Identity in Britain 1940–2000* (London: Macmillan, 2003). For the legacy of the war in British culture see Mark Connelly, *We Can Take It! Britain and the Memory of the Second World War* (London: Pearson Longman, 2004).

3   British historiographical benchmarks in terms of party origins include Pelling, *The Origins of the Labour Party*; David Howell, *British Workers and the Independent Labour Party, 1888–1906* (Manchester: Manchester University Press, 1984); Ross McKibbin, *The Evolution of the Labour Party, 1910–1924* (Oxford: Oxford University Press, 1984); Duncan Tanner, *Political Change and the Labour Party 1900–1918* (Cambridge: Cambridge University Press, 2008); Richard Wyn Jones, *Plaid Cymru: The History of the Welsh Nationalist Party, 1925–98* (Cardiff: Welsh Academic Press, 2005); and James Klugmann, *The History of the Communist Party of Great Britain (Vol. I – Formation and Early Years, 1919–24)* (London: Lawrence & Wishart, 1987, new edition).

The career of Robert McIntyre is interesting because it bridges the gestation of the party and its subsequent development into the Scottish political mainstream.[4] McIntyre is noteworthy in that – even at a British level – few political leaders' careers coincide with such a critical period in terms of the party's development. An obvious comparison in the Labour Party would be Ramsay MacDonald. This is not to say that McIntyre's legacy to the SNP is the same as MacDonald's is to Labour, but it does demonstrate how founders can influence contemporary debate in terms of establishing legitimacy as Labour's first Prime Minister is variously characterised as either a pragmatic realist or a class traitor.[5]

The development of the nationalist or independence movement in Scotland as it emerged in the twentieth century did so at a time when arguably it was least opportune. In many respects, the nationalist movement in Scotland was a latecomer and arrived after the heyday of European nation-state nationalism. Unlike Irish nationalism, which had at least a century of grievance to fuel it, the Union had been remarkably successful for the Scottish political classes and, in the period after the First World War, Scotland largely mirrored the rest of the United Kingdom in that class was the primary focus of political allegiance and loyalty.[6]

The Labour Party had the institutional backing of trade unions in its quest for working-class votes, while the Conservatives could rely on the support of the myriad business- and property-owner institutions and networks in buttressing its middle-class vote. The principal difficulty facing the nationalist movement was the lack of a natural constituency to appeal to, especially in

---

4   For an accessible biography see Dick Douglas, *At the Helm*, available online at
      http://www.electricscotland.com/history/mcintyre/preface.htm

5   Lauchlan MacNeil, *The Tragedy of Ramsay MacDonald: A Political Biography* (London: Secker & Warburg, 1938) was the classic account of his betrayal until rescued by Marquand, *Ramsay MacDonald*, which did much to rehabilitate his reputation.

6   For a history of Irish nationalist ideology see Sean Cronin, *Irish Nationalism: A History of its Roots and Ideology* (London: Academy Press, 1981); D. George Boyce, *Nationalism in Ireland* (London: Routledge, 1995, 3rd edition) and countless others on the nationalist movement per se. Scotland has Harvie, *Scotland and Nationalism* (London: Routledge, various editions), which does not really focus on nationalism as either a movement or ideology, and recently T. M. Devine, *Independence or Union: Scotland's Past and Scotland's Present* (London: Allen Lane, 2016) tries to marry a predominantly unionist historiography to a contemporary history that seems to be moving in the opposite direction.

the era after the Second World War, when nationalism lost much of its intellectual credibility on account of its association with fascism. Furthermore, the objectives of the nationalists were far from clear. In particular, there were two issues facing the nationalist movement which needed to be resolved.[7] Firstly, there was the issue of whether the goal should be independence or some form of devolution, and the lines were blurred by the fact that the direction of political travel was the same for most of the way for both objectives and many independenistas believed that devolution was a necessary constitutional prerequisite; the so-called stepping stone path to independence. Secondly, there was the issue as to whether the movement should act as an independent political party committed to achieving an electoral mandate or whether it should act as a pressure group designed to push the existing political parties towards devolution, which in turn would lead to independence.

The period in the 1930s and '40s witnessed the party and movement oscillate around and between these objectives. Although the party in 1942 formally committed itself to a policy of independence and securing a mandate by winning a majority of Scottish parliamentary seats, this issue was by no means settled, as evidenced by the popularity of John MacCormick's National Covenant movement in 1948/49 and his flirtation with the Liberal Party at the Paisley by-election.[8] Part of the difficulty was that because the road of devolution and independence followed the same route, a primary focus on the former, it was believed, picked up supporters of the latter by default, whereas a commitment to independence was just as likely to deter supporters of devolution. In the era of the centralising British state after 1945, the Covenant seemed the best way to maximise support and the fact that it was able to gather 2 million signatures showed it had the potential for success. Likewise, many believed that the issue of independence or devolution was a single issue that did not necessitate the apparatus of a separate political party, especially when devolution had regularly appeared on both the Liberal and

7   Finlay, *Independent and Free*.

8   See Michael Dyer, "'A Nationalist in the Churchillian Sense'".

Labour agenda. Indeed, contesting elections against devolutionist parties was only likely to create more hostility to the policy. Arguably, it took the collapse of the National Covenant to establish the SNP position as the default for the nationalist movement. That said, the British parties' flirtation with devolution in the '60s and '70s and the anti-Conservative Scottish Convention of the late 1980s and '90s demonstrated the vulnerability of the SNP to marginalisation whenever devolution entered the mainstream of British politics.[9]

Robert McIntyre played a pivotal role in holding the SNP to both its position as an independent political party and its commitment to Scottish independence from the British state. This was especially important during a period when the party had no real success as its membership dwindled, the number of seats it contested declined and the volume of votes attained remained stubbornly minuscule. As much as anything, McIntyre and his band were 'keepers of the faith' in the sense that holding to this position at a time when it paid no, and looked unlikely to pay any, electoral dividends was their contribution to the history of the party. To keep the idea smouldering until more propitious times is rarely acknowledged as a major achievement in history, but that was a key part of McIntyre's legacy and his experience of the oscillations in the party during the 1940s was a significant factor in keeping him on this straight and narrow path. McIntyre's other major legacy was to try to carve out an ideological position that would have the potential to win over a majority of the population to the core principle of independence and, at the same time, distinguish itself from the left and right, middle- and working-class polarities that dominated the British political system. In essence, McIntyre worked on a philosophy for the party that would help to distinguish it from the established British parties, but without simply occupying the centre ground between them. As will be seen, some elements have stood the test of time, and some proved more problematic.

---

9   See David Denver, James Mitchell, Charles Pattie and Hugh Bochel, *Scotland Decides: The Devolution Issue and the 1997 Referendum* (London: Frank Cass Publishers, 2000), pp. 1–27.

McIntyre's political career began as a student in Glasgow University in the Labour Party.[10] This was a trifle unusual in that Glasgow University had been at the heart of the formation of the National Party of Scotland in 1928 and had almost ousted Stanley Baldwin as student rector when the nationalist candidate, R. B. Cunninghame Graham, stood against him in 1929 and Compton Mackenzie actually won in 1931.[11] It was after graduation and during the war as a medical official that McIntyre gravitated to the national party, although it was possible for nationalists to be members of other parties at this time. He joined the party on Bannockburn Day in 1940 and was shortly afterwards asked to become the national secretary, in charge of the day-to-day running of the party. According to McIntyre, he believed that there was a need for 'an independent political party committed to self-government' and when a motion appeared in conference in 1942 stating that the party should not contest elections, he voted against it: 'It was to keep a fighting Scottish political party that made me take the side I did ... having just joined the blessed organisation for that reason I wasn't wanting to see it disappear.'[12] Another point worth stressing, because it tends to be taken for granted – though in the context of the times the SNP emerged, it should not – was a commitment to non-violent and democratic means. For McIntyre, a functioning political party committed to Scottish independence was the best way to ensure a 'peaceful democratic avenue open to the people of Scotland so that you would not have any violence in our midst'.[13] McIntyre stood as a candidate in the Motherwell by-election just before the Second World War, which he won, only to lose months later at the general election in July 1945. He was leader of the party from 1947 to 1956 and thereafter SNP president until 1980. In local government, he was provost (Lord Mayor) of Stirling from 1967 to 1975. Rather than a blow-by-blow account of McIntyre's

---

10   NLS, Acc. 12509: Robert McIntyre Collection, undated typescript of a speech.

11   MacCormick, *The Flag in the Wind*, Chapter 5 for the election; Compton Mackenzie, *My Life and Times, Octave 7, 1931–38* (London: Chatto, 1968) and *Scots Independent*, December 1931.

12   NLS, McIntyre Collection, 25, undated speech.

13   Ibid.

career, however, this chapter will focus on his intellectual contribution to modern Scottish nationalism.

McIntyre did not publish a lot of material and his ideas have to be picked out from the various pamphlets, short articles and speeches that are scattered in his manuscript collection.[14] In essence, the issue for McIntyre was that Scottish members of British political parties would always be bound by the majority English interest and that this would work against the possibility of the implementation of home rule. An essential cynicism about the ability of the British political system to cater to Scottish needs entailed the creation of a Scottish party dedicated to Scottish interests. Although McIntyre believed in independence, he held that devolutionists could not rely on the Labour or Liberal parties to fulfil their commitments. Originally propounded by Tom Gibson back in the 1920s, the legitimacy for a mandate for Scottish independence and, by default, devolution, could only be demonstrated when a political party attained a majority of Scottish parliamentary seats by contesting an election on that specific issue.[15] For McIntyre, an independent political party was essential, which meant building up an apparatus, membership, branches and all the work that this entailed. It is easy to see why for some, such as John MacCormick, the temptation to rely on petitions and other political parties to deliver home rule might seem attractive and more realistic than the painfully slow road undertaken by the SNP. But, for McIntyre, whatever the attraction of pressure-group politics, it would turn out to be a waste of time, as was demonstrated both by the failure of the Scottish Home Rule Association, which collapsed in 1928 leading to the formation of the National Party of Scotland in 1928, and the ultimate failure of MacCormick's Convention, when the Scottish Secretary of State simply called upon its followers to attain an elected mandate for home rule.[16]

---

14   NLS, split over two deposits: Acc. 12509 and Acc. 10090: Scottish National Party.

15   Finlay, *Independent and Free*, p. 59.

16   See Richard J. Finlay, *Modern Scotland: 1914–2000* (London: Profile Books, 2004), p. 231.

As was pointed out, the objective of independence was a single issue that sat awkwardly with party politics in the sense that the normal expectation of a political party was that it served the interests of a constituency based on class and economic interest and that was held together with an ideology that had to appeal to (ideally) the majority of the electorate. In order to become a credible political party, it was necessary to arm itself with an ideological base and a set of policies that would garner enough support to win a mandate. For the nationalists this presented an intellectual dilemma in that the principle of independence was believed to be of such paramount importance that it ought to garner support from both the left and right and that once independence was established it would be left to the electorate to decide what direction to take. A move to either the left or right had the danger that it was just as likely to alienate as attract support. The history of the SNP showed that there was a natural tendency for the left and right to divide and compromise party unity, hence the necessity of trying to steer a middle course.[17] Furthermore, the raison d'être of independence, that Westminster rule was ineffective, meant that it was subject to differing interpretations from a left and right perspective, and an inevitable tendency to see all policy through the prism of the left or right tended to highlight these divisions. But eschewing the politics of both the left and right entirely ran the danger of an ideologically anaemic organisation. For both the cause of independence and the SNP to be credible, there would need to be a coherent intellectual case that had the potential to appeal to a majority of the Scottish electorate. For a party that was renowned for its lack of discipline, the imposition of policy was problematic for those who argued that the party's role was to deliver independence and leave policy up to the electorate once that had been achieved. For realists, however, the cause of independence as a philosophic matter of principle may be fine and well, but unless it could be demonstrated that it would

17   For an overview of the history of the SNP see Lynch, *History of the Scottish National Party* and for a discussion of the issue of ideology, although more in the context of the later period, see his 'From Social Democracy back to No Ideology? – The Scottish National Party and Ideological Change in a Multi-level Electoral Setting', *Regional & Federal Studies*, 19/4–5 (2009), Special Issue: New Challenges for Stateless Nationalist and Regionalist Parties: 619–37.

produce tangible socio-economic benefits for the electorate, it was unlikely to
garner any support.

In broad terms, these were the issues that McIntyre faced as a leader of
the SNP and resolving them in a coherent way that could hold the disparate elements of the nationalist movement together was no easy task. In a
practical sense, one part of the legacy left by McIntyre was an insistence on
party discipline, as enshrined in the party's conference in 1947, which was
designed to keep it purist in terms of the objective of independence and
free from other political organisations.[18] As the party evolved in the 1960s
and '70s, it was dominated by procedures, standing orders, committees and
constitutional regulation all designed to maintain party discipline and good
governance.[19] A young Alex Salmond fell victim to the party's monotheism
in 1982 when he and fellow left-wingers in the 79 Group were expelled.[20]
In more recent times, the SNP has been accused of being a 'cult' that opposes
free thinking and imposes iron discipline. Yet, although probably forgotten
by most, it is the fissiparous early history of the movement, in which having
one key objective makes unity vulnerable to the oscillations of the normal
ideological shifts between left and right, that necessitates a strong sense of
party discipline. While McIntyre recognised that Scottish nationalists had
to work within the ideological world of the left and right, he held that this
had to play second fiddle to the ambition for independence.

While there is a growing historiography on the intellectual development
of unionism, nationalism has remained the poor Scottish cousin.[21] Unionism has a longer pedigree that can be artificially stretched back into the
sixteenth century and a similar form of intellectual connectivity has not been
made for the opponents of the Union, rather, it has been treated as epi-
sodic. Furthermore, in an endeavour to escape its ethnic variant, modern

---

18   NLS, McIntyre Collection, 13, Policy Committee 1949.

19   Evidence of this can be seen in Gordon Wilson's account, *SNP: The Turbulent Years 1960–1990* (Stir-
     ling: Scots Independent Publications, 2009).

20   Torrance, *Salmond: Against the Odds*, Chapter 3.

21   See Kidd, *Union and Unionisms*.

nationalism has been cast as civic and while there is much to commend this as an analytic model, it does have the effect of blurring the lines between the devolutionist and independence movements.[22] Its primary use has been as an ideological glue to bond the anti-Conservatives in Scotland in the 1980s and '90s. With independence at the top of the Scottish political agenda, civic nationalism has lost some of its explanatory power and it is perhaps now an opportune moment to reconnect the current protagonists with their intellectual forerunners to chart the evolution of the philosophy and ideology of Scottish nationalism.

McIntyre set down some of the basic elements in determining policy that has held the SNP to a left-of-centre, middle-ground platform.[23] In part, a key factor in positioning the party at this point in the ideological spectrum is that it was and is believed to represent the majority view of the Scottish electorate. The middle ground in British politics, however, is a hotly contested arena and a key issue for the SNP was to somehow make a distinctive play for it that distinguished the nationalist position from the consensus politics of Labour and the Tories.[24] A thorny issue for Scottish nationalists was that although both Conservatives and Labour accepted the principle of state intervention, this was the British state and state intervention tended to be the benchmark in defining the ideological boundary between left and right. Given the widespread acceptance that state intervention was the best mechanism to achieve social justice, Scottish nationalists were caught in a quandary of either supporting the extension of the power of the British state or appearing as politically conservative. How to square the circle? McIntyre published *Some Principles for Scottish Reconstruction* in 1944, which sought

22   The classic exposition of civic nationalism in Scotland is Graeme Morton, *Unionist Nationalism: Governing Urban Scotland, 1830–1860* (East Linton: Tuckwell Press, 1998), which has been developed to account for the growth of the self-government movement in the Thatcher era, see Owen Dudley Edwards, *A Claim of Right for Scotland* (Edinburgh: Polygon, 1989).

23   The clearest of McIntyre's exposition on these principles was published during the war as *Some Principles for Scottish Reconstruction* (Glasgow: Scottish National Party, 1944).

24   The best synoptic account of post-war consensus is David Dutton, *British Politics Since 1945: The Rise and Fall of Consensus* (London: Blackwell, 1991).

to carve a distinctive niche for the SNP by pursuing a centrist position while at the same time warning about the threat of big government to democracy. As a policy document, it was not original and many of the ideas had been part and parcel of the nationalist programme, but what McIntyre was able to do was give it an intellectual coherence and the left-of-centre ground was occupied, not as a means to balance the left and right factions, but because it was believed.[25] This process was assisted by the fact that it tended to be the right-leaning that lost in the 1942 split and went off with MacCormick's National Covenant and tended to belong more to the devolutionist wing. Perhaps the distinctive feature that McIntyre hoped would give the party its sense of identity was its suspicion of big monolithic organisations, be they private or state. It also chimed in with a wider view in British society that there should be a middle way between the excesses of state socialism and unbridled capitalism:[26]

> Is it to be the happy hunting ground for big business and unscrupulous monopolies? Is it to be a bureaucratic state in which we are labelled and controlled from the crèche to the crematorium in the name of all but for the good of none?[27]

McIntyre was an active Christian with a Presbyterian heritage and his politics were informed by a strong sense of individual social responsibility that was suspicious of bureaucracy and excessive collectivism. In many respects his political philosophy was not too dissimilar from the mainstay of Liberalism

---

25   McIntyre published a series of articles and letters during the second half of 1944 and the first half of 1945 in the *Motherwell Times and Wishaw Advertiser* that reinforced the message of *Some Principles for Scottish Reconstruction*, Acc. 12509, p. 25.

26   Harold Macmillan's *The Middle Way* (London: Macmillan, 1938) helped popularise the term, which gained considerable intellectual currency during wartime Britain in which the post-war settlement would be able to combine the best of socialism with the best of capitalism; see Peter Hennessy, *Never Again: Britain 1945–51* (London: Penguin Books, 2006), p. 2; and Kenneth O. Morgan, *Britain Since 1945* (Oxford: Oxford University Press, 2001), pp. 1–5.

27   McIntyre, *Some Principles for Scottish Reconstruction*, p. 1.

that dominated Scotland before the First World War.[28] State intervention was necessary to guarantee a minimum socio-economic and educational attainment before an individual could make the most of the freedoms espoused by classical liberalism.[29] Direct government intervention in the economy such as nationalism was regarded with suspicion, but the welfare state was easier to accommodate because it was based on universalism, which accorded benefits on an individual basis.[30]

Localism was an ingredient that featured more heavily in the nationalist policy in that giving a voice to the community in a world that was subject to wartime central control, and the likelihood that this would not diminish to any great extent during the peace, was one that chimed in naturally with nationalist suspicion and hostility to London control.[31] The SNP used this to good effect in the Kirkcaldy by-election of 1944 by denouncing the policy of female conscripted labour in which young Scottish women were sent south to work in the munitions factories.[32] The growth of the centralised state, particularly in matters relating to the economy, formed a key part of the SNP message that London control was damaging the nation's material wellbeing as it was too remote and bureaucratic. Indeed, this became a mantra to be repeated as the economy failed in the '60s and '70s. For McIntyre, the community was the essential link between the individual and society.

Scotland has no need of a highly centralised state interfering in the private

---

28 This is an area that has been under-researched. The transition from a Liberal political culture to a Labour political culture and the implications for individualism and its relationship to collectivism has been glossed over and the success of the Labour Party after 1964 and the decline of the Conservative Party has probably inclined people to accept the idea that Scotland has more of a collectivist rather than an individualist political culture. This is assumed rather than tested.

29 The classic intellectual account is Michael Freeden, *The New Liberalism: An Ideology of Social Reform* (Oxford: Clarendon Press, 1986).

30 In this context it is worth pointing out the continuing support for welfare universalism in the SNP and how this may be construed as an example of 'state individualism'.

31 A good example of this is D. C. C. Young, *Hitlerism in the Highlands* (Glasgow, 1944), which was an attack on the plans for the hydro-electrification of the Highlands.

32 NLS, Acc. 3721: Muirhead Collection, 100, manifesto of Douglas Young, Kirkcaldy by-election, 1944.

lives of the people. We have seen enough of that kind of thing whereby homes are broken up at the behest of officials of one kind and another during the war. A self-governing Scotland would depend on the natural organisation of the family and the local community for its stability. The vigour and integrity of local authority in Parish and Burgh must be restored and control of affairs brought as near to people as possible. Let the community of Scotland be reborn.[33]

This faith in local democracy was demonstrated in his career in local government and it was his belief that the community could provide a collective political counterweight to the state.

Nationalism as a philosophy has not had much in the way of discussion by members of the SNP. Echoing Archie Lamont, McIntyre argued that there was a fundamental difference between the nationalism of small nations and big nations in that the former could not constitute a threat to world peace and that the world's greatest evils, such as imperialism, stemmed from the latter.[34] It rather glossed over any philosophical difficulties and more often than not the defence of 'small-nation nationalism' was no more than a litany of the achievements of individuals who happened to be born in small countries and hence their contribution to world civilisation.[35] The definition of what and who constituted a Scot was historically constructed rather than ethnically defined. The way that McIntyre chose to demonstrate this was in terms of how he expressed his loyalty: 'To the English-controlled parties I owe no allegiance. My loyalty is to Scotland and her people.'[36] This was done to great effect when he was elected to the House of Commons in 1945 and refused to take sponsors as all the other MPs were from 'English-controlled' parties and without sponsors he was forbidden to take

---

33 NLS, McIntyre Collection, election pamphlet, Motherwell by-election, 1945.

34 Archie Lamont, *Small Nations* (Glasgow: William MacLellan, 1944).

35 Ibid., pp. 75–80.

36 NLS, McIntyre Collection, manifesto, Motherwell by-election, 1945.

his seat.[37] He was eventually sponsored under protest, but the 'sad nuisance' had made his point.[38]

The one area in which McIntyre left his intellectual stamp on the SNP was a strong commitment to pragmatism that was fuelled by a suspicion of ideology. McIntyre did not share in the enthusiasm for Soviet planning that spread throughout Britain during the war and, indeed, his scepticism was based on the way that nationalities were treated and swallowed up within the USSR.[39] In many of his speeches he made frequent reference to the work of George Orwell (1984), Aldous Huxley (Brave New World) and Neil M. Gunn (The Green Isle of the Great Deep), all of which warned against the dangers of totalitarian thought and the notion that the means justify the ends, because, for McIntyre, there were no ends, only means.[40]

The Scottish National Party was often accused in the past by those thirled to orthodox socialist conceptions of being reactionary and chauvinistic, and by those of the right of being another type of socialist party. Instinctively the National Party kept clear of the tentacles of either of those parties or their ideologies, representing as they did the opposing economic forces within industry and the economy fighting for its control.[41]

McIntyre argued against the black-and-white political analysis of capitalism and socialism and believed that the nation and the individual were the antidotes to the economic conflict.

> We beware of ideologies ... in the beginning they may have a fine ideal.
> The ideologies produce a scheme, a system, a faith, with or without works
> which they believe will bring their ideal about. In due course they get stuck
> with the system of thought rather with the original ideal and you have an

---

37   Ibid., collection of press cuttings. McIntyre was the subject of a *Punch* cartoon.

38   Sir Harold Nicolson, *Diaries and Letters, 1939–45* (London: Collins, 1967), p. 449.

39   NLS, the McIntyre Collection has an extensive number of magazines, newsletters and paraphernalia from nationalists movements that were contained within the Soviet Union.

40   NLS, McIntyre Collection, undated speech.

41   Ibid.

ideology for its own sake. Its original purpose goes, the human reasons and moral considerations which initiated the process become lost and forgotten ... the ideology becomes the god and everything that serves it becomes justified.[42]

This scepticism against ideology meant that for most of the post-war era it worked against the left because of its association with state intervention and this arguably diminished the SNP's stance as a left-of-centre party. If anything, it pushed them closer to the Liberal Party, which equally had a strong sense of localism, and the frequent ponderings about a merger was a factor that emerged from time to time.[43] This idea of steering a distinctive path between the Tories and Labour determined the actions of the parliamentary SNP in the 1970s in that they supported and opposed in equal measure both the Labour government and the Tory opposition. This almost became an ideology in itself and militated against a pragmatic course of action in the British Parliament, which made it easy for opponents to say that the SNP favoured the Tories against Labour.[44]

McIntyre was a strong constitutionalist whose vision of sovereignty was formed by his reading of Scottish history. For him, the seventeenth-century jurist George Buchanan formulated the notion of the sovereignty of the people which was used in contradistinction to the Westminster concept of the sovereignty of Parliament.[45] This was brought to light in the 1950s when John MacCormick launched a legal challenge against Elizabeth's use of the 'numeral II' in Scotland when Lord Cooper ruled that parliamentary sovereignty was a peculiarity of English law.[46] In many respects, this was largely

---

42   Ibid.

43   See Fowler, *Bannerman*, p. 116; and Jo Grimond, *The Liberal Challenge* (London: Hollis & Carter, 1963), p. 59.

44   Perhaps best exemplified when the SNP voted against the Labour government in 1979 leading to Prime Minister James Callaghan's comment that this was the first time in recorded history that turkeys have voted for an early Christmas, 28 March 1979.

45   NLS, McIntyre Collection, 28, undated speech from 1978.

46   Lord Cooper, Lord President of the Court of Session, MacCormick *v.* Lord Advocate (Edinburgh, 1953).

an unintended by-product of the debate. It was McIntyre who heroically plugged the distinctive constitutional nature of Scottish nationalism and placed it at the centre of the debate. Legal scholars such as Andrew Dewar Gibb, D. H. McNeill, H. J. Paton and Neil MacCormick provided a strong constitutional backbone for the case of Scottish nationalism, but McIntyre was responsible for enshrining it in party policy and brought it to a wider audience of activists.[47] Scottish history, he argued, from the Declaration of Arbroath in 1320 onwards, had limited the role of the monarchy and laid the basis for the supremacy of the law in which no one was above.

> Any threats today do not, of course, come from the monarchy. The Scottish people have always supported the monarchy and do so today. The danger can come from the overweening power of the executive and the bureaucracy. This [proposed] constitution seeks as far as a constitution can, to keep that power within the rule of law. The very fact of a written constitution which can be appealed to over the heads of government is a step in that direction.[48]

McIntyre was a passionate advocate of a Bill of Rights that would have the same standing as the European Convention of Human Rights. The legalist and constitutional nature of the SNP owed a lot to McIntyre's philosophy. He believed that the SNP was an outgrowth of the nation's 'liberal human tradition' and argued that dictatorship in Nazi Germany and the Soviet Union could be explained by those respective nations' historical experiences.[49] At the party's annual conference in 1977, the rationale for a strong constitutional basis for Scottish government was set out by McIntyre as something that only the Scottish people could decide on because constitutionalism had

---

47   There is a strong legal/historical dimension in SNP thought as can be shown by the prominence of the following texts: Dewar Gibb, *Scotland Resurgent*; H. J. Paton, *The Claim of Scotland* (London: George Allen & Unwin, 1968); D. H. McNeill, *The Historical Scottish Constitution* (Edinburgh: Albyn Press, 1971); J. N. Wolfe (ed.), *Government and Nationalism in Scotland* (Edinburgh: Edinburgh University Press, 1969); and MacCormick, *The Scottish Debate*.

48   NLS, McIntyre Collection, 5, speech at annual conference, 27 May 1977.

49   Robert McIntyre, 'How the SNP See Politics', *Glasgow Herald*, 25 July 1968.

its roots 'deep in our history and its struggle for humanity and freedom from the Declaration of Arbroath onwards. They are … a defence against arbitrary power and provide freedom within the law and use the law as a protector of freedom and justice.'[50]

The issue of contesting elections was finally enshrined at the party conference in 1947, though remained a thorny issue more on the grounds of practicality than principle. With limited funds and members, contests were confined to a handful of constituencies and, more often than not, a saved deposit was considered a good result.[51] Contesting elections for a mandate to attain independence was a cornerstone of SNP policy designed to build up credibility as a serious electoral force, but the dismal showing at elections arguably had the reverse effect and demonstrated just how far off the SNP were in terms of their objectives. In many respects it was a catch-22 situation and the preceding history of the party had shown that there was little prospect of any shortcut. Furthermore, the ideological climate in the late '40s and '50s was against the movement, with nationalism associated with the Axis powers during the war era.[52] The centralised roll-out of universal benefits associated with the welfare state and Keynesian demand management economics established as orthodoxy meant that nationalism was presented as a romantic and backward-looking movement that had little relevance to the socio-economic aspirations of the majority of the electorate.[53] In many respects, the most important role that McIntyre and others played during this period was holding the faith and sticking to the policy of independence and contesting elections despite the lack of progress.

As was alluded to earlier, the legalist, democratic and constitutional route to independence has very much been taken for granted and it is worth

---

50   McIntyre, conference speech 1977.

51   Somerville, *Through the Maelstrom.*

52   Both Scottish and Welsh nationalism suffered from this identification; see Richard Wyn Jones, *The Fascist Party in Wales?: Plaid Cymru, Welsh Nationalism and the Accusation of Fascism* (Cardiff: Cardiff University Press, 2014), which shows how the myth was perpetuated. Recently Bowd's *Fascist Scotland* has reiterated the connections between some in the SNP and the far right.

53   Anthony D. Smith, *The Ethnic Revival* (Cambridge: Cambridge University Press, 1981), p. 178.

remembering that, in the period of the Cold War, practically all nationalists and independence movements had a violent and revolutionary wing that was able to tap into the neo-Marxist narrative of liberation from capitalist imperialism.[54] The history of Scottish nationalism has a constitutional probity that makes it more of the exception than the rule in this period.[55] The flirtation with violence was not far away, especially when the party was unable to make any electoral progress. The furore around Elizabeth's use of the numeral 'II', which ignored that there had been no queen of that name in Scottish history, and this making it plain that the British monarchy was the continuation of the English monarchy inflamed passions to such an extent that post boxes baring the offending number were blown up and shop windows were broken for selling souvenirs that were insensitive to Scottish regnal propriety.[56] The fact that the government removed the offending numeral was taken by some as a sign that violence did work. Rumours of infiltration by MI5, the easy publicity of direct action, such as stealing the Stone of Destiny or William Wallace's sword, and the appearance of radical wings, such as the 1320 society in the mid-'60s or Siol nan Gaidheal in the late '70s, demonstrate that the constitutional legal route was by no means a foregone conclusion. McIntyre's antipathy to ideology can perhaps be explained by the fact that he recognised the vulnerability of the nationalist movement to an association with either left- or right-wing radicals prepared to use direct action to circumvent the democratic process.

This was particularly apparent when the SNP made its breakthrough in the late '60s as commentators looked for and found more militant voices. The 1320 Club was only too happy to oblige in presenting a much more macho and militant nationalist movement.[57] Although the leaders of the 1320 Club were known, its membership was secret and had clear fascist overtones

54 Closest to home the example of Ireland, see Alan O'Day (ed.), *Political Violence in Northern Ireland: Conflict and Conflict Resolution* (London: Praeger, 1997).

55 Luis de la Calle, *Nationalist Violence in Postwar Europe* (Cambridge: Cambridge University Press, 2015).

56 Finlay, *Modern Scotland*, pp. 231–2.

57 Mitchell, *Strategies for Self-Government*, pp. 266–9.

as many of its spokesmen clearly had no time for party politics. The club attracted the support and endorsement of the cranky wing of the nationalist movement and Christopher Grieve (Hugh MacDiarmid) was quoted in the *Sunday Telegraph* as saying,

> I don't know any country that has got its freedom without bloodshed. I am
> not advocating it – it may be imposed on us by the English. I look towards
> it with equanimity, remembering the physical nature of our country. The
> military leadership exists already – large numbers of Scots are ex-soldiers.[58]

The Scottish Liberation Army was also a focus of interests and the same issue of the *Sunday Telegraph* photographed two of its members removing the Union flag from Stirling castle.[59] The continued emphasis on constitutional, democratic and non-violent means was arguably the most important legacy of this period.

By the mid-'60s, the political environment changed and produced a more favourable climate for the SNP. State planning was failing to deliver and centralised Westminster control of the economic levers of power no longer had the same unquestioning ideological acceptance. It is no surprise that the nationalists won the Hamilton by-election at a time when unemployment was high and the government had suffered the indignity of the devaluation of sterling. Social change worked to diminish the power of the traditional blocs of Conservative and Labour electoral power as new towns destroyed old political loyalties and social mobility and new types of employment blurred traditional class loyalties. The diminution of tradition provided an opportunity for the SNP to break into new territory where no traditional political loyalty had been established.[60] Ideologically, the counter-culture and neo-Marxist theories of colonialism and imperialism helped to dent the traditional

---

58   'Who are the Scottish Nationalists?', *Sunday Telegraph* (supplement), 9 February 1968, p. 15.

59   Ibid.

60   See the introduction of James Mitchell in *The Scottish Question* for background to the emergence of
     the SNP.

assumption that nationalism was an ideology of the right. The fact that the SNP opposed nuclear weapons gave the party a distinctive edge that became pertinent following the decision to base Polaris in the Holy Loch.[61] This helped fuel a growth in new members who were younger and more dynamic and injected a new lease of life and enthusiasm into the party, all of which was vital in making the party electable. As a political movement, the danger of drawing on the electorate's discontent with British parties was that the SNP would find it difficult to be anything other than a protest movement.[62]

For McIntyre and leaders of the SNP, the problem was that the discontent with the Conservative and Labour parties may well pay electoral dividends in the short-term but it was not a sustainable base for long-term political success. In the period from the late '60s until the late '70s, the Scottish electorate used the SNP as a vehicle of protest against what was perceived to be the failure of the British parties to deliver in terms of socio-economic advancement.[63] While the SNP positioned itself as a centrist party, the reality was that that was the position of all the parties and the issue facing the nationalists was what the Scottish state could do that the British state could not. McIntyre did try to pose a philosophic distinction that tried to bypass the traditional differences of ideology associated with the left and right. As he put it in an article in the *Glasgow Herald* in 1968:

> The Scottish National Party is not just a coalition of left and right. Members may have been in other political parties but the Scottish National Party has its own distinctive policies related to the new political alignment. For example, it is against any further nationalisation and was against the nationalisation of steel. It wishes to encourage owner occupation of land, and of houses. It wishes to remove the stranglehold of widespread private land monopoly in many parts of the country. It believes in a social as

61   Brian P. Jamison (ed.), *Scotland and the Cold War* (Dunfermline: Cualann Press, 2003).

62   See Mitchell, Johns and Bennie, *The Scottish National Party*, p. 41.

63   A key argument in William Miller's *The End of British Politics?: Scots and English Political Behaviour in the Seventies* (Oxford: Oxford University Press, 1981).

well as a political democracy. There is not much room for left and right extremists in this.[64]

For McIntyre, the national freedom he sought for Scotland should be extended to the individual and social responsibility and individual responsibility went hand in hand. As has been mentioned before, McIntyre saw a Scottish political tradition that was based on individual liberty and freedom that could be mobilised against the threat from both big business on the one hand and an over-powerful state on the other. In terms of the ideological position of the SNP, its rhetoric against the encroachments of the British state pushed it more from the centre towards a right-leaning individualism that was more in tune with the politics of North America than Europe.[65]

McIntyre believed that the paradigm of the left/right political axis based on class was being replaced by the growth of state power, which was combining and operating with financial and industrial complexes, and that the real conflict was between the 'robot state' and the individual and communities that were being controlled for its benefit. For McIntyre, a new political alignment was necessary to provide communities and individuals with more democratic power to 'unify communities and remove false class prejudices'. The success of the Liberals at Orpington and the growth of Plaid Cymru were, he believed, evidence of this realignment. In retrospect, what contemporaries like McIntyre believed to be a political realignment was in fact evidence that the post-war consensus was breaking down. The crises that engulfed the British state in the second half of the 1970s arguably led to a greater degree of political polarisation based on class that culminated in the respective rightward and leftward swings of the Conservative and Labour parties in the early 1980s. Arguably McIntyre's centrist and anti-ideological

---

64 *Glasgow Herald*, 25 July 1968.

65 Perhaps some of this can be traced back to the Douglas Social Credit movement, which had a number of adherents in Scotland in the interwar era. It was a redistributive economic philosophy that stressed the priority of the individual and argued that economic systems ought to serve society and not the other way round. According to Douglas, consumers acted like voters in favouring producers and providing access to credit ought to be the state's priority.

position was overtaken by events as radicals within the SNP sought to position the party more to the left and reflect the growing anti-Thatcherite mood of the Scottish population. Unfortunately, his warnings against the invidious presence of the British state sounded too similar to that of the Iron Lady, and although there were substantive differences in outlook and philosophy, there was enough of an overlap in Thatcher's neo-liberalism and McIntyre's new liberalism to make it awkward. The emphasis on individualism and social responsibility bore an uncanny resemblance to 'standing on one's own two feet' and hostility to the 'nanny state', while suspicion of 'robot government' was echoed in the promise to 'roll back the state' and free the people. McIntyre had not been a noted advocate of trade union power and his reluctance to accept the paradigm of class as a factor in political behaviour left him at odds with what was happening in Scotland as Thatcher stuck the boot into state industries and their unions. In the polarised times of the mid-1980s, the centre was not a comfortable place to be and McIntyre's philosophy seemed to belong to a gentler time in the past. That said, his ideas are probably now closer to the political mainstream than ever before and his quest to square the circle of individual rights and responsibilities with the obligations of the state is one that still preoccupies politicians to this day.

CHAPTER 11

JAMES HALLIDAY

PAULA SOMERVILLE

James Halliday followed Robert McIntyre's near-decade-long leadership after the latter fell foul of internal dissent. He joined the SNP in 1943, aged sixteen. He was a historian, teaching history in schools and later further education college. Along with McIntyre, he had been the SNP's sole candidate in the 1955 election, and he was a candidate in the following 1959 election, on both occasions. At twenty-nine, he was the second youngest SNP leader in its history (Douglas Young was younger by a matter of months). Halliday's success was maintaining the independent existence of the SNP in the post-war height of British nationalism and laying the groundwork for the breakthroughs of the next decade.

. . .

James 'Jimmy' Halliday was born on 27 February 1927 in the coastal village of Wemyss Bay, Scotland, as the only child of parents James Wightman Halliday, a gardener, and Mary Halliday. For as long as he can remember, Halliday always regarded himself as a nationalist, a view that was instinctive – 'inborn' rather than taught. His family certainly expressed no such nationalist desires. His parents if anything discouraged his nationalist outlook, his mother in particular believing it could harm his prospects in life.[1] At school there was little in the way of nationalist influence either.

---

1   Halliday, *Yours for Scotland*, p. 1.

His teachers and his peers did not share his nationalist viewpoint and for the most part looked upon notions of Scottish nationalism with indifference, ridicule or antagonism. For the young Halliday, it seemed, he stood alone in his beliefs.

Despite discouragement at home and at school, Halliday supported nationalist ideals throughout his formative years and officially joined the SNP in 1943 at age just sixteen. In Halliday's mind, he was already a member, having psychologically joined the party at eleven, when he purchased an SNP badge from a stall at the Empire Exhibition in Glasgow in 1938.[2] Halliday spent these early years satisfying his inquisitive appetite for nationalist writings. Journals such as the *Scots Independent* provided the eager young Halliday with information about the goings-on of the SNP and key players within the national movement, which only seemed to solidify his nationalist ideals. But it was not until he entered university in 1944 that he began to play an active role in nationalist life.

On becoming a student at Glasgow University, Halliday soon joined the Glasgow University Scottish Nationalist Association (GUSNA). At GUSNA it was something of a revelation for Halliday as he met other like-minded nationalists who shared his ideology. There were also nationalists of varying degrees: those who supported devolution, others who sought federalism and separatists like himself. Halliday embroiled himself in GUSNA activities, including taking on the posts of secretary and president, participating in its many debates (for which he won the prize for best speaker), and even becoming joint chair of John MacCormick's successful rectorial campaign in 1950. He also became involved with MacCormick's Scottish Covenant Association, though he supported neither its devolutionary aims nor its sanctionless strategy, which gathered petition signatures but failed to contest elections. GUSNA was invaluable in introducing Halliday to active political life. It provided him with important debating skills as well as organisational and leadership insight and introduced him to a network of nationalists of

---

2   Ibid., pp. 4–5.

all parties. Not insignificantly, it was also where he met Olive Campbell, his future wife and mother of his two sons.

Halliday graduated late from university in 1952, having developed tuberculosis of the spine in his first year, which immobilised him for eighteen months. After leaving university and establishing his professional career as a history teacher, Halliday was approached to stand at the 1955 general election as the parliamentary candidate for the SNP in the constituency of Stirling and Falkirk Burghs. He quickly took up the challenge and was one of only two candidates to stand, the other being then leader Robert McIntyre. Up until this point, Halliday had not been an important player in the SNP or even well known within the party, but with other SNP figures declining to stand themselves, Halliday's candidature came as welcome news, particularly for McIntyre, who intended to withdraw from the campaign if no second candidate agreed to stand. The result of the election, however, was disappointing for Halliday. While McIntyre increased his share of the vote to almost 23 per cent, Halliday obtained less than 7 per cent, or just 2,885 votes. Though Halliday had played a prominent role in MacCormick's rectorial campaign as well as Robert McIntyre's 1950 election campaign in Motherwell, beyond this he had little campaign experience nor adequate resources or activists to sufficiently canvass the constituency. On a positive note, he was the first to use the distinctive black and gold colours in his election material during the campaign, which later came to be adopted as the party's official colours.[3]

Despite Halliday's poor result, standing as an SNP parliamentary candidate brought him to prominence within the party. Soon after the election, Halliday was appointed to the SNP's National Council and National Executive Committee, then, following McIntyre's resignation from the chair and with no other contenders for the position, he was unanimously elected party chairman at the SNP's annual conference in 1956. McIntyre had given up the chair and moved to the role of president following internal discord within the party with the establishment of the '55 Group. This group, which subsequently became the Nationalist Party of Scotland, had challenged McIntyre for his alleged dictatorial style of leadership and the lack of electoral progress the SNP had made during his tenure. The appointment of Halliday as the new chairman, it was hoped, would turn the focus away from the previous year's disputes and factious elements and help rejuvenate the party. Halliday's appointment was thus broadly welcomed within the party, though a few did look upon him as McIntyre's young upstart.[4] At just twenty-nine, Halliday became the SNP's second youngest leader (Douglas Young taking the title by a few months) and it presented him with the unique opportunity to shape the party and steer its future direction.

A key focus for Halliday as chairman was to recover the SNP from the Nationalist Party of Scotland debacle and expand. To help do this he sought to increase the party's membership and branch network, which, according to the SNP's report on the state of its branches in 1955, was less than 1,350 members,[5] a figure that Halliday believed himself to be vastly inflated.[6] He visited different areas of the country, first focusing on places where organisation already existed, notably in Perth and Stirling, before looking to new areas such as Dumfries and Galloway. He visited constituency associations and branches to energise them and encourage their work and spoke at public meetings to spread the party's ideals and entice new members to join. A 'Choose Scotland Campaign 1957' was also launched in Halliday's first year, which was essentially a recruitment drive to capitalise on the 250th anniversary of the Treaty of Union. It sought to advance the notion that Scotland was a separate entity, not simply 'North Britain', by tapping into sentiments of nationhood that may be roused by the anniversary date. Halliday's efforts produced some results. Some new branches were formed and the party did recruit some talented new members, not least Ian Macdonald, who would go on to become national organiser and see the SNP through a period of rapid

---

4   Halliday, *Yours for Scotland*, p. 56.

5   NLS, McIntyre Mss, Acc. 10090, File 44: Report of the SNP 'State of Branches as at 9-4-1955'.

6   According to James Halliday there were only about 250 fully fledged SNP members around the time he became chairman. Interview with James Halliday, 13 March 2008.

growth in the 1960s. Halliday's hopes for expansion, however, did not amount to much beyond this and the 'Choose Scotland Campaign' failed to attract the 1,000 new members optimistically hoped for.[7] The rate of party membership when Halliday left the chair was in fact not much more than when he had first taken up the role and it was one of his major regrets as chairman that he did not 'carry out proper evangelising work throughout the country' as his successor, Arthur Donaldson, would go on to achieve.[8]

But it was not just about membership numbers. Halliday also saw his leadership role as upholding the SNP's constitution and rules and providing strong party discipline. This he achieved with significantly more success. From the outset, Halliday instilled the strong hand of discipline. This was shown at his first annual conference in 1956, just after taking the chair, when he called to order veteran nationalist Roland Muirhead for not following the standing rules while speaking in a debate.[9] Muirhead had been a founding member of the SNP and involved in its forerunners and had also been party president as well as a frequent benefactor to the party's coffers in times of need. But he was increasingly at odds with the SNP's strategy and in 1950 he formed his own organisation, the Scottish National Congress (SNC). This was modelled on Gandhi's Indian National Congress, which sought home rule through extra-parliamentary means, such as civil disobedience. As Muirhead had established the SNC, it was tolerated within the SNP and was not classed as a political party, which, under the party's dual membership rule would have automatically banned SNP members from joining it. Halliday and other leaders within the party did not view the SNC as helpful to the SNP's cause as its civil disobedience tactics harmed the image of the national movement and by association the SNP itself. For Halliday, it was important for the party and party members to portray a respectable imagine of nationalism and to disassociate it from unconventional or disorderly behaviour. In

---

7   NLS, McIntyre Mss, Acc. 10090, File 56: SNP statement by John Smart: 'Choose Scotland Campaign', 1957.

8   Halliday, *Yours for Scotland*, pp. 73–4.

9   Ibid., p. 51.

essence, he sought 'to establish in people's minds the fact that it was wholly ordinary and normal' to support the SNP and to counteract the commonly held view of those outside the party that it was 'daft, eccentric, obsessive, lawless, and may be dangerous'.[10] Halliday's opportunity to outlaw the SNC came in 1958, when it made an appeal to the USSR requesting that it raise the issue of the 1707 Treaty of Union with the United Nations. This so-called Russia Resolution was a step too far for Halliday and the SNP, who strongly opposed the USSR's foreign policy and viewed it as hostile to the interests of smaller nations. The SNC was now incompatible with the policy of the SNP and the SNP duly banned its members from holding SNC membership.[11] This included Muirhead, the 'grand old man' of nationalism, whose quarter-of-a-century-long affiliation with the SNP now came to an end.

In the same year, Halliday also grasped the nettle and expelled other members from the party who had supported an independent candidate at the Glasgow Kelvingrove by-election. The SNP had decided not to contest the seat on the advice of local officials due to a lack of resources and organisation in the area – a decision that was not universally welcome. David Murray put himself forward as an independent nationalist candidate but agreed to take the Liberal whip if he was elected. Some members of the SNP actively campaigned for Murray and even printed unofficial slogans such as 'SNP for Murray' despite the party's opposition. For Halliday, this directly contravened party discipline and he argued, 'If they worked for Labour, Unionist or Liberal candidates their position would be obvious. In my opinion they have offended just as seriously by working for Mr Murray.'[12] Halliday was resolute in what had to be done; he expelled the offending members from the party, displaying again his commitment to instilling discipline and protecting the party's governing rules. To confront this issue head-on and expel members from the party so swiftly and resolutely, and, more importantly, take on

---

10   Ibid., p. 59.

11   NLS, McIntyre Mss, Acc. 10090, File 180: Scottish National Party's *The Scottish Newsletter*, March 1958.

12   NLS, McIntyre Mss, Acc. 10090, File 56: letter from James Halliday to SNP Executive Members, 12 March 1958.

the issue of Muirhead's SNC, which had plagued the party for the last eight years and had not been dealt with by his more experienced predecessor, was no mean feat for the SNP's second youngest leader. Halliday's ability to take tough decisions and command control was a leadership attribute he had in spades. He possessed the killer instinct for the role of chair.

Under Halliday's leadership, the party also busied itself in campaigning initiatives. Given the factions and internal turmoil the party had wrestled with in the '50s, it was important for Halliday and the SNP to look outwards in their efforts to advance the party's cause. One important campaign was party political broadcasting, which the SNP and other smaller parties believed to be unfair. Halliday played a prominent role in the campaign and, just prior to becoming chair, represented the party at a public rally the SNP held in Trafalgar Square with other small parties – Plaid Cymru, Common Wealth and the Independent Labour Party (ILP) – to demonstrate against current broadcasting rules.[13] The SNP also set up a BBC Committee within the party to take forward its broadcasting policy and strategy and sent a deputation to the BBC in Scotland. Halliday, alongside David Rollo and Robert McIntyre, put the party's case before the BBC's Controller in Scotland, Melville Dinwiddie, though he was less than receptive to their requests.[14] Nationalists in Scotland also set up a pirate radio station, Radio Free Scotland, in 1956 in protest against broadcasting policy. It was not established or run by the SNP, but SNP members were largely involved and its broadcasts included topical issues and recorded interviews of leading nationalists, not least James Halliday. But, despite these efforts and the time that was heavily invested in campaigning, Halliday failed to gain an improved broadcasting settlement for the SNP during his time as leader. However, these efforts set the groundwork for later success, when party political broadcasts were finally granted to the SNP in 1965.

---

13   NLS, McIntyre Mss, Acc. 10090, File 58: press statement, 'Break the Radio Ban on the Smaller Parties', 21 March 1956.

14   NLS, Halliday Mss, Acc. 13417, Item 3: minutes of meeting of the National Council of the SNP, 7 November 1956.

With Halliday at the helm, the SNP also became involved in topical issues such as new towns and energy, which similarly helped focus the party's attention outwardly. In the case of new towns, the party did not support their creation and argued that the government's overspill policy only added to the issue of population density across central Scotland, whereas policy should be focused on disseminating people to towns and villages throughout Scotland, particularly areas that were suffering population decline.[15] Ironically, the SNP would later shore up support in new towns as residents increasingly turned to the SNP as an alternative party in the 1960s. On energy, the SNP called for a relaxation in taxation policy for shale oil to encourage the industry to grow and it claimed that Scotland was being treated unfavourably compared to England as a rise in taxation on diesel fuel would have a larger negative impact in Scotland, where consumption was proportionally higher.[16]

These issues were significant in concentrating the party's efforts on current subject matters and redirecting its attention away from the infighting that had gone on within the party. They were also important in developing the party's position on a range of topical areas. However, despite their significance, it is important to note that there was no serious attempt by Halliday to overhaul the party's existing policy during his time in the chair. Halliday was ideologically committed to independence and viewed it as the key tenet on which the party must fight, whereas other policy strands were an aside and should in no way undermine the SNP's core principle. During Halliday's time as leader there was also less cohesion in the party on wider policy values, and not everyone shared his left-of-centre ethos or his views on areas such as defence. For the most part, Halliday's focus was restricted to a theme of protest against what he saw as the neglect or exploitation of Scotland by the UK government. But not updating the party's policy was a missed opportunity for Halliday, who could have taken advantage of the so-called post-war

15   NLS, McIntyre Mss, Acc. 10090, File 56: SNP statement by John Smart, 'Glasgow's Overspill', 28 February 1957.

16   *Scots Independent*, 22 December 1956 & 29 December 1956.

consensus that was emerging in British politics at the time between the two main political parties by offering an alternative set of policies to the Scottish electorate. The SNP's first official policy statement adopted in 1946 indeed remained the cornerstone of party policy throughout the '50s and it was not until the run-up to the 1964 general election that a new policy statement and manifesto, *SNP and You*, was finally published.[17]

Halliday's leadership also marked the beginning of a change in the SNP's general election campaigns. With Halliday in the chair at the 1959 general election, small improvements to the SNP's campaigning efforts began to be made. The party fielded five candidates, which in itself was an achievement compared with only two candidates at the previous election, not least because party membership had been fairly static over that time. The SNP's 1959 campaign was also more organised and developed than its campaigns had been in the past. A National Election Plan had been drafted which proposed a number of strategies to enhance the party's performance and, significantly, election manifestos were also produced as part of the Plan. *This Can Be The New Scotland* set out the SNP's long-term vision of what an independent Scotland could be,[18] while a shorter manifesto focused on more immediate concerns and what the party would seek to achieve in the short-term with its MPs at Westminster, notably greater devolved administration for Scotland.[19] These election manifestos were an important development in the party's campaigning efforts and provided voters with a more informative picture of the SNP than the simple election pamphlets and leaflets that had gone before. They were also the closest the SNP came to policy-making during Halliday's time as leader.

Despite improved organisation and strategy at the general election, the SNP still had a long way to go translating its campaigning efforts into votes. It obtained only 21,738 votes in total, which was less than 1 per cent of

17   It was produced by the party's vice-chairman for publicity and future leader Billy Wolfe.

18   Printed in full in the *Scots Independent*, 14 February 1959.

19   NLS, Acc. 6038, Scottish National Party Mss, Box 1, File 15: SNP Manifesto 1959.

the overall vote. Of the five candidates, Halliday's own campaign was perhaps the most disappointing. Though not the lowest vote (Sandy Milne in Aberdeen North took that prize), Halliday obtained only 2,983 votes, which in percentage terms was slightly less than he had achieved in 1955. Given that Halliday had contested the seat before and he now stood as leader of the party, it is surprising that he did not poll more than he achieved particularly as the SNP had made progress in Stirling's municipal wards with McIntyre and others in the party winning seats, which had familiarised the local electorate with the SNP, and there was no Liberal or other fourth candidate standing in the constituency. Thus, while the general election of 1959 demonstrated the progress the SNP had made in terms of planning for its campaigns, it also highlighted Halliday's own lack of ability to attract voters and enthuse support for the party, or to project a sense of presence, a necessary attribute for any leader.

Shortly after the result, Halliday announced his intention to leave the chair. His poor election result was not the main reason. He had moved from Glasgow to Dunfermline the previous year for a teaching opportunity and his move meant that he was no longer located near its headquarters in Glasgow, making his duties as chair logistically more difficult.[20] Halliday's other commitments to his family and his teaching profession also influenced his decision that it was time to stand aside. At the party's 1960 annual conference he duly passed the reigns of chairmanship to Arthur Donaldson.

It was rather unfortunate for Halliday that he stepped down from the chair just as the party entered the '60s, the decade in which the SNP would make its breakthrough. In just a few short years, the party's membership and support grew exponentially, from around 2,000 members in 1962, 8,000 in 1964 and 42,000 in 1966[21] to winning representation in Parliament in 1967 with Winnie Ewing's historic by-election victory in Hamilton. On giving up the chair, Halliday took on the far less active role as party vice-president and his involvement in party life at the national level became substantially reduced and

---

20   Halliday, *Yours for Scotland*, p. 72.

21   NLS, McIntyre Mss, Acc. 10090, File 98: memorandum by the SNP to European states, 31 May 1967.

more centred on local constituency matters. Halliday's retreat from national activities consequently meant that he missed out on many of the important developments that were occurring within the SNP in the '60s as it began its transition from a fringe to a mainstream political party in Scottish politics. But as the party contested and won more seats in the '70s, Halliday's position on the SNP's Election Committee necessitated that he became more involved in the party's national affairs.

Halliday had sat on the SNP's Election Committee from the 1950s, but as the SNP had fought few seats before the '70s, it only came to life when contesting an election was in the offing. With the party's unprecedented level of growth and support the Election Committee became a permanent fixture of the party's committee structure to allow it to be better prepared at election times. The importance of its work grew when more candidates were required during the '70s as the party was able to contest more seats. The prospects of a Scottish National Assembly becoming a reality also increased the number of potential candidates required. Halliday, as Convener, built up a bank of potential candidates from which constituency associations could draw. Candidates were vetted and interviewed for suitability, then trained. Many of those who did not meet the criteria did not take kindly to Halliday's selection interview. A National Council member described potential candidates being put through 'Jimmy Halliday's mincer'.[22] Halliday indeed took his role very seriously and saw it as of fundamental importance to weed out any prospective candidates who may disgrace or embarrass the party in any way. It was certainly in Halliday's fashion to discourage dissent and ensure all toed the party line. Halliday and other members of the Election Committee can take some credit in helping the party obtain its electoral successes in the '70s by its proactive approach to candidate selection and election preparedness. It was in some measure the organisational work that went on within the Election Committee that enabled the SNP to stand a record number of candidates and win a record number of seven seats at the February 1974

---

22   Halliday, *Yours for Scotland*, p. 104.

general election; then by October that year, with very little time to prepare in between, stand candidates in every constituency in Scotland for the first time and win four more seats in the second general election of 1974. Halliday was invited to stand himself as a candidate in Fife West at the 1970 general election. Though he polled better than his previous elections gaining 11 per cent, he still failed to inspire voters or save his deposit. When it came to elections, Halliday's strength lay behind the scenes.

While Halliday took on a more active role in the party during the '70s, power struggles were also emerging that dismayed Halliday. A power struggle between the newly established parliamentary wing of the party and the National Executive arose following the 1974 general elections. The return of seven then eleven SNP MPs meant that the party was able to form a parliamentary group for the first time, but issues of governance and accountability soon surfaced as the National Executive and the parliamentary group jostled for power. Halliday, as Convener of the Election Committee, felt pressure from some MPs to speed up the selection process of his committee and he came to look upon them as impatient, possibly even arrogant. He also viewed some MPs as 'talking down' to fellow colleagues and party Executive members.[23] This he believed undermined the importance of the party's officials and tensions between the groups only intensified as the '70s progressed.

Other tensions had also been building within the SNP which left Halliday feeling increasingly marginalised. The dramatic expansion of the SNP in the '60s had resulted in many people on the left joining the party, people who would otherwise have voted Labour. Individuals such as Margo MacDonald, Isobel Lindsay and Tom McAlpine, who were clearly identifiable on the left, now graced the SNP's top ranks. Party chairman Billy Wolfe also stood solidly on the left of the political continuum. Consequently, the influence of socialism became more prominent within the party and socialist values came to occupy more attention. While Halliday had always viewed himself as a

---

23   Ibid., pp. 113–14.

social democrat and agreed with many social justice arguments advanced by the left, he did not identify with the term 'socialism' and resented the importance being placed on it by some leading individuals within the SNP. He regarded himself as belonging to the 'old left' that supported redistribution and high taxation in order to assist and advance the underprivileged.[24] But in his eyes the rise of the 'new left' was watering down the party's main goal of independence as debates increasingly focused on achieving a socialist society even if that meant working within a devolved structure. For Halliday, independence was the main issue and should be placed above all other sectional interests, whereas focusing on socialism, particularly for those who were willing to accept a constitutional settlement within a Westminster framework in order to achieve it, diminished the standing of the party and only made the SNP resemble the Labour Party.[25] Halliday regarded socialism as a vote loser and believed the implementation of a devolved settlement in Scotland would be a stumbling block that in the long-term would only hold back the party's pursuit of independence. The emergence of the 79 Group dismayed Halliday. Its socialist ideology and the gradualist outlook of many of its members, he believed, diverted attention and energy away from nationalist attitudes and policies and he consequently gave his support to a rival group, the 'Campaign for Nationalism in Scotland' in an effort to raise the profile of Nationalism (with a capital 'N') within the party.[26] Despite the 79 Group being forced out of the SNP by the old guard traditionalists, including Halliday, many within the party still remained sympathetic to its ideas and some of its members would later rise to prominence within the party.

But it was not just these issues. Halliday's strong held views on foreign and defence policies also put him at loggerheads with many in the party. Halliday was given the role of Convener of the party's External Affairs Committee, which was a strange appointment given that his views on defence and

---

24 'James Halliday in Conversation with James Taggart', *Scots Independent*, January 2006.

25 Halliday, *Yours for Scotland*, pp. 114–15.

26 The Campaign for Nationalism in Scotland was formed as a reaction against the 79 Group. See Lynch, *SNP: The History of the Scottish National Party*, pp. 172–3.

foreign policy were very much to the right of the party. Halliday believed that Scotland should forge strong ties with the USA and should stand firmly with the USA in the Cold War. As a lecturer in history, he had a special interest in the USA and was particularly scathing of anti-American and non-alignment rhetoric from some members of the party. For Halliday, the USA and Western Europe shared close cultural and political ties and he believed it was important to associate with countries that most reflected Scotland's social and political outlook.[27] He was resolutely against disarmament and was critical of the increasing influence that pacifism and the Campaign for Nuclear Disarmament (CND) were having on the party. Halliday had long held these views and even as a teenager during the Second World War he had rejected the notion of neutrality or pacifism and had duly registered for war service viewing it as a war worth fighting, whereas staying neutral, he believed, offered no defence to small nations like Scotland.[28] His appointment unsurprisingly was short lived and only served to widen the gulf between party colleagues and himself over defence and foreign policy matters. Because of his views, Halliday was unpopular among some of his SNP peers and he felt increasingly alienated and disillusioned with the party and came to question why he should continue to serve on it. By the early '80s, despite the demise of the 79 Group, Halliday felt worn down by the unpopularity of his views and of him as an individual and he ceased to be an active member of the SNP other than helping out at election times or at events. It was with great disappointment that he came to withdraw from the party as he entered his retirement years from his teaching profession, just at a time when he had envisaged devoting much more time to SNP activities, not less.[29]

Halliday continued to work in his own way for an independent Scotland. He was involved with the 1820 Society that sought to raise awareness and commemorate the Radical War, which had strong associations with

27   James Halliday, 'Dealing with Defence', in David Rollo (ed.), *The Scotland We Seek* (Stirling: Scots Independent Publications, September 1987), p. 7.

28   Halliday, *Yours for Scotland*, p. 8.

29   Ibid., p. 141.

nationalism.[30] Most of his energy, however, was channelled into the pro-independence journal, the *Scots Independent*, which he had been involved with since it had become an independent limited company back in 1955. Working at the *Scots Independent*, he was among kindred spirits who benefited from his experience and his witty humour and he advanced the arguments for Scottish statehood through its newssheets. Halliday, who had authored several books on the topic of Scotland and Scottish nationalism, also published some of his works through the journal. He carried on having disagreements with some of the SNP's leaders, not least those 79 Group members who now emerged among the party leadership. He disagreed with what he saw as peripheral issues pursued by the party at the expense of the key issue of independence and he also fought to retain the independence of the journal itself from the control of the SNP's National Executive which sought to rein it in from producing what it viewed as 'counter-productive' articles.[31] The *Scots Independent* was an important outlet for Halliday that allowed him to articulate his nationalist expressions and pursue his self-determination ambition for Scotland without denigration from within the party. Halliday remained involved with the paper for almost sixty years, serving as chairman of its board right up until his death on 3 January 2013, aged eighty-five.

What then of Halliday? On the face of it, Halliday's term as leader was not a successful one. Fundamentally he failed to grow the party to any great extent either in membership numbers or at the polls and his tenure ended much as it had begun, with the SNP remaining insignificant in numbers and as a small irrelevant fringe party that hardly registered on the political landscape. Fractious elements and expulsions within the party also continued under Halliday's leadership, which gave the SNP the appearance of a party that suffered from perpetual internal conflict. Its campaigns during Halliday's leadership failed to deliver on their objectives. The policy positions it adopted had no impact. Halliday also neglected the important area

---

30   Halliday authored a book on the subject: Halliday, *1820 Rising: The Radical War* (Stirling: Scots Independent Publications, 1993).

31   Halliday, *Yours for Scotland*, p. 150.

of policy during his time as leader. With no new serious effort to develop its policy in over a decade other than a few single-issue campaigns and election manifestos, the SNP failed to take advantage of the post-war consensus and undermined its ability to be relevant to the Scottish electorate. For Halliday, independence was the key issue and all other policy issues were secondary. The ability to win over many voters or attract much support to the party was an essential leadership quality that Halliday also did not seem to possess and his inability to connect with voters and sway them over at the polls did not play well for a party leadership role. Halliday's time in the chair of only four years also limited his ability to accomplish much as leader or leave a lasting legacy for the party.

But, for all that, it has to be recognised that Halliday did take on the chair at a particularly low point in the party's history. Blighted by the remnants of civil war, low in numbers and chronically underfunded, Halliday faced an uphill struggle from the start. In a wider context, the environment in which Halliday and the SNP operated when he became leader was not conducive to nationalism. With rising living standards since the Unionist party had been returned to power in the '50s and an increase in British identity cemented by war and the advent of planning and nationalisation, Unionism was on the rise in Scotland. Supporting a nationalist party was far from appealing against this backdrop. During his time as chairman, Halliday had to earn a living in his day job as a teacher which meant that time constraints also hampered his leadership not to mention the professionalism of the party. There were also clear achievements that Halliday did make during his time as leader despite his party's lack of progress. Most notably Halliday showed strong leadership in terms of discipline and was prepared to protect the party's governing rules and tackle dissent head on even if it meant forcing out important figures in the national movement, such as Roland Muirhead and his Scottish National Congress. It also showed that Halliday had the strength of character that was required for the chairmanship role. The campaigns and debates undertaken during Halliday's leadership also kept the party active, even dynamic, and early work on issues like broadcasting would bear fruit in later years. In terms of membership, even though the party failed to recruit many new members during Halliday's term, some talented new members did enter the party, not least future organiser Ian Macdonald. It was under Halliday's leadership that the party also went on to increase the number of candidates it stood at general elections even though Halliday himself proved not to be such a successful candidate, and the manifestos it produced for the 1959 general election were also important developments from the election literature that had gone before.

Halliday's style of leadership in many respects resembled his predecessor, McIntyre, in terms of upholding the party's governing rules, challenging dissent and taking a long-term approach towards the party's goal of Scottish independence. Both leaders viewed independence as a long hard war to be won with no short cuts to success, exemplified by the Scottish Covenant's failure. Though lacking originality, this continuity in Halliday's leadership helped sustain the SNP through fractious periods and the bleak years of the '50s when it could very well have been taken over by more extreme elements of the party or disintegrated altogether or been swallowed up by the many competing nationalist organisations around at the time. Halliday's greatest leadership achievement was simply his ability to keep the party going through these incredibly tough years and maintain an unwavering long-term strategy underpinned by discipline and rules and a steadfast commitment to the fundamental principles of the SNP. It is on these foundation stones that the SNP's future success as a political party has been built.

CHAPTER 12

ARTHUR DONALDSON

EWEN ANGUS CAMERON

Arthur Donaldson was involved in the SNP from the very beginning, joining its predecessor, the National Party of Scotland, while working in the USA. Upon his return to Scotland in 1937, he became active. He was arrested and briefly detained in the Second World War when the state was highly suspicious of any person or organisation deemed insufficiently loyal. He became chairman of the party in 1960, by this time retired and able to devote more time to the cause, and contributed significantly to the first major upswing in the party's fortunes, seeing impressive by-election campaigns and support, the Hamilton victory and increases in membership and branches. This was aided by Donaldson's leadership style, and his persuasive speaking and impressive energy, leaving the SNP in a much stronger place than it was when he first became leader.

·   ·   ·

During a tour of Africa in early 1960, Prime Minister Harold Macmillan remarked, 'The wind of change is blowing through this continent, and, whether we like it or not, the growth of national consciousness is a political fact.'[1] There was an even wider international context, observing events in Quebec, the Basque, Catalonia, and Eastern Europe alongside the African 'wind of change' when Gordon Wilson, a later chairman of the SNP, remarked, 'The decade was a struggle against authoritarianism from which

---

1   Brian MacArthur, *The Penguin Book of Twentieth-Century Speeches* (London: Viking, 1992), p. 289.

many political movements, including the SNP in Scotland, were beneficiaries.'[2] How much did Arthur Donaldson contribute in this decade of change?

Arthur Donaldson occupies a unique place among the leaders of the Scottish National Party. He led both a small outfit on the fringes of Scottish politics and a mass party. A year before Donaldson became chairman, an internal party report showed that the SNP had twenty-six branches with an average membership of twenty-seven.[3] This made barely 700 members in 1959, yet at the end of 1968 the party claimed 125,000 members and in early 1969 decided to award a banner to Tarbert on Loch Fyne for becoming the 500th branch.[4] This transformation had a clearly visible impact on the ability of the SNP to field candidates in a general election, only five in 1959 but sixty-five in 1970, and the increase in candidates in turn contributed towards a substantial rise in the numbers who voted SNP; 21,738 in 1959 to 306,802 in 1970.[5]

Arthur Donaldson was born in Dundee in 1901. He went to school at Harris Academy and then spent the years 1918–20 as an assistant registrar recording births, deaths and marriages in Dundee. His next employment was as a reporter for *The Courier*. In this capacity he had to write daily reports and specialised in court cases.[6] In November 1922, one month before the young Donaldson became eligible to vote, a major political event occurred in Dundee when Winston Churchill, then a Liberal, was unseated by Edwin Scrymgeour, who became the first and, it subsequently turned out, only ever, MP for the Scottish Prohibition Party. It had been Scrymgeour's sixth attempt to become an MP. In the first three attempts he kept getting around just 5 per cent

2   Wilson, *SNP: The Turbulent Years 1960–1990*, p. 74.

3   NLS, Acc. 6038, Scottish National Party correspondence of and to Arthur Donaldson, Box 1: reports to Annual Conference 1959.

4   NLS, Acc. 11987, Scottish National Party Papers, Item 30: minutes of Organisation Committee, 16 November 1968; Item 31: minutes of National Executive Committee, 11 April 1969.

5   See F. W. S. Craig, *British Parliamentary Election Results 1950–1970* (Chichester: Parliamentary Research Services, 1971) for the full sets of election results for each constituency.

6   NLS, Acc. 6038, SNP, Arthur Donaldson, Box 1: a CV outline written in 1955.

of the vote and then improved his share to the point when he got elected.[7] *The Courier* reported a victory rally at which Scrymgeour remarked, 'So great a victory after a life's work should be an inspiration to every young lad and girl in Dundee ... that the world's greatest powers were of no account against perseverance.'[8] The report may have been written by the young Donaldson, but even if not he would likely have been aware of it, and it presages his own perseverance with the SNP. Just over a year later, he wrote a letter in which he praised successful people who were 'try-ers again' and mentioned Edwin Scrymgeour in the same sentence as Robert the Bruce.[9]

In 1923, Donaldson moved to the United States and spent most of the 1920s in Detroit. He was employed by Chrysler as secretary to the head of an engineering department, which prompted the young Donaldson to study engineering at Detroit technical college. He remained in touch with Scottish affairs and became an overseas member of the National Party of Scotland as soon as it was founded in 1928 and acted as a sales agent in the USA for the *Scots Independent* newspaper. He also met Violet Bruce, a woman from Forfar, whom he married in 1932. The Donaldsons' first home together was in Washington DC, where Arthur was employed as part of a Chrysler effort to motorise the US Army. By 1937, the Donaldsons had started a family and decided at this point to return to Scotland. Arthur Donaldson became a poultry farmer in North Ayrshire and then in 1944 moved to Forfar, where he settled for the rest of his life, earning a living by a combination of retail business and freelance journalism.[10]

Donaldson was one of the earliest Scottish nationalists to get a mention in the House of Commons. On 3 May 1941, the homes of seventeen persons were searched by the police; eleven were taken to their local police station for further

---

7   F. W. S. Craig, *British Parliamentary Election Results 1885–1918* (London: Macmillan, 1974) and *British Parliamentary Election Results 1918–1949* (Glasgow: Political Reference Publications, 1969).

8   *The Courier*, 20 November 1920.

9   NLS, Acc. 6038, SNP, Arthur Donaldson, Box 1: 'Random Reflections of an Exile', Detroit, 24 January 1924, p. 11. On p. 8 he said Prohibition was working well in the USA.

10   NLS, Acc. 6038, SNP, Arthur Donaldson, Box 9: a summary of his life experience written for Galloway constituency association in July 1969.

questioning and three were jailed. One of the imprisoned was fined for illegal possession of arms. Arthur Donaldson was one of the other two.[11] James Maxton, one of the 'Clydesider' Labour MPs elected in the general election of 1922, and by this time an Independent Labour Party MP, twice raised what was happening to Donaldson in Parliament. At the second, he asked the Secretary of State for Scotland if Donaldson would be given a chance to appeal against his imprisonment in Barlinnie. Secretary Tom Johnston replied:

> I have fully considered all the available information relating to this case and while I am satisfied that the information then available was sufficient to justify the making of an Order for provisional detention I have reached the conclusion after reviewing all the circumstances that this man's indefinite detention is not necessary in the interests of national security and I have accordingly authorised his release.[12]

What was the reason for his imprisonment? Donaldson himself was told by the police that he was being detained 'not for anything I had done but what I might do'.[13] Donaldson also said he believed the British government expected to uncover a connection between him and Germany because they could not understand him giving up a good life in the USA to return to Scotland. He was grateful to James Maxton for raising his position in Parliament as up until that point his prison wardens were unpleasant to him because they thought he was a German spy.[14]

The arrest of Arthur Donaldson in 1941 continues to be a matter of occasional controversy even in the twenty-first century, with opponents of the SNP calling Donaldson a fascist sympathiser. How accurate is this? In 1994, MI5 released papers on Donaldson's arrest. The explanation given was that there

---

11   HC Debs, 27 May 1941, Vol. 371, cc.1696–8; *Scots Independent*, June 1941.

12   HC Debs, 12 June 1941, Vol. 372, c.352W.

13   NLS, Acc. 9178, William Oliver Brown, Item 12: 'Police Raids of 1941' by Arthur Donaldson, 1944.

14   Ibid.

was 'a considerable body of evidence highlighting subversive activities over a long period'.[15] The evidence had been collected by a government agent who after the war became a Conservative MP.[16] A point detailed in the 1994 revelations was that the person leading the team that arrived at Donaldson's home in Ayrshire to arrest him was a Major. This is interesting because when James Maxton first raised the arrest of Donaldson in the House of Commons, he questioned whether it was valid for soldiers to be used in a civil case and was given the assurance by the Solicitor General for Scotland that no military were present.[17] Hence the official government statements on the arrest of Arthur Donaldson have not been consistent.

Part of the supposed evidence against Arthur Donaldson is a quote attributed to him in which he claimed England would be crushed by Germany, so Scots should try to make their own deal with the Germans.[18] However, this particular claim looks more like hearsay than reliable evidence and even if accurate does not constitute proof that Donaldson had any intention or desire to assist the Germans to invade.

Nevertheless, Arthur Donaldson's own writing illustrated that he had no loyalty to the British state. In 1942, he commenced a pamphlet by describing three possible outcomes to the war: defeat, victory or negotiated stalemate. He believed that any of the three would leave Scotland in a better position than the slide towards exploited colony that he regarded the pre-war years as having been.[19] He clearly had no grasp of what a Nazi occupation would have looked like and consequently held both sides in the war in equal contempt. For Donaldson, the British Empire was certainly not a force for good. It was not just about the countries within the empire but the power of London as the financial centre of the world and a ruling elite he described as a 'master class', which reads like a sneering term comparable to master race. He even

---

15   *Glasgow Herald*, 25 August 1994.

16   Ibid.

17   HC Debs, 27 May 1941, Vol. 371, cc.1696–8.

18   Bowd, *Fascist Scotland*, p. 171.

19   Arthur Donaldson, *Scotland's Tomorrow: Our Fight to Live* (Glasgow: Scottish Secretariat, 1941), p. 6.

scornfully added that this master class was happy to see Hitler emerge in Germany as they believed he would help contain Soviet Russia.[20]

The intensity of Donaldson's dislike of the British state explains the side he took in the conscription debate, which split the SNP down the middle. For many Scottish nationalists, it was logical to resist being conscripted by a state they did not believe in, and, given the Scottish casualty rate in the previous war, being potentially sent to death by said state. The pro-conscription side argued that this was misguided, that it was logical to support the British state as a lesser of two evils when compared to Nazi Germany. As one pro-war Scottish nationalist put it, 'Imagine German soldiers goose-stepping down Argyle Street.'[21] Reflecting years later, Arthur Donaldson said of conscription that it was 'immoral to compel such a sacrifice from young men on behalf of a society which had over many years denied them even a fair opportunity to win a decent job'.[22] This raises the question: who has the right to decide whether a cause is worth dying for? The state or the individual? Donaldson supported the rights of the individual against the state, a position which is the opposite of fascism. Donaldson became a parliamentary candidate for the first time in the general election of 1945, standing in Dundee, but he lost his deposit along with five of the other seven SNP candidates. Although unsuccessful as a Scottish National Party candidate, Donaldson was successful standing as an Independent in council elections; he was elected to Forfar Town Council in 1945 and to Angus County Council in 1946. He remained on Angus's council for nine years and on Forfar's for twenty-three.[23]

It should be noted that standing as an Independent was normal for a council election in a rural area, and it did not mean Donaldson was any less committed to the SNP. During the 1950s, the nationalist movement had fragmented

---

20   Ibid.

21   *Scots Independent*, February 1941.

22   *Scots Independent*, March 1982.

23   NLS, Acc. 6038, SNP, Arthur Donaldson, Box 1: CV outline, 1955; Box 6: resignation letter to Forfar town clerk, 16 January 1968.

into a number of components, the Scottish Covenant Association, the Scottish Patriots and the Scottish National Congress. None of these organisations believed that contesting general elections was the way to achieve progress, but Arthur Donaldson did. In 1957, he was invited to join National Congress and replied, 'I am so convinced that the Scottish National Party is the real hope for Scotland that I am unwilling to do anything which can in any way impair its effectiveness or damage its unity.'[24] This was despite the party not yet exceeding 1 per cent of the Scottish vote.

In May 1957, Arthur Donaldson became a vice-chairman of the SNP.[25] Two and a half years later, in October 1959, he was a parliamentary candidate for a second time. This time he was the first ever SNP candidate for Kinross and West Perthshire, saved his deposit with 15 per cent of the vote and came third. During the course of the four general elections in the 1950s, the SNP had only managed to save four deposits (three with Robert McIntyre in Perth and East Perthshire). Hence, by saving this deposit, Donaldson emerged as the second most credible parliamentary candidate the party had.

The general election of 1959, although one of negligible progress for the SNP, was a turning point in Scottish electoral history, which changed the political environment into one potentially more fertile for Scottish nationalism. For a period of thirty-five years, Scotland had been a Conservative country, with the Conservatives having more MPs than Labour for all but eight years in the period from 1924 to 1959.[26] Even the famous Labour landslide of 1945 was a smaller event in Scotland than it was in England (52 per cent of the Scottish seats, 65 per cent of the English). In 1951, the voters of both Scotland and England turned from Labour to Conservative; in 1955, both re-elected Conservative by an increased margin; but then, in 1959, England re-elected the Conservatives with yet another increase in the margin of victory while Scotland turned toward Labour. The Conservative Prime Minister

---

24   Ibid., Box 1: letter from Arthur Donaldson to R. E. Muirhead, 21 January 1957.

25   Ibid., letter from national secretary John Smart to Arthur Donaldson, May 1957.

26   See Alice Brown, David McCrone and Lindsay Paterson, *Politics and Society in Scotland* (London: Macmillan, 1998), Table 1.1, pp. 8–9 for a comprehensive list of general election results in Scotland.

Harold Macmillan had famously declared Britons had 'never had it so good' and the electorate of England responded as if in agreement, but north of the border, in the words of Chris Harvie, 'The Scottish electorate announced to Prime Minister Macmillan that it had had it better.'[27] The economy was perceived to be going wrong in Scotland; shipbuilding in decline, train building in decline, unemployment at 4 per cent in Scotland while only at 2 per cent in England.[28] It was ironic that it was a Prime Minister with a Scottish surname who stamped upon the Conservative Party the image of being a party of English interests and as a result the Conservatives never again had it so good in Scotland.

In 1960, the SNP had a change of chairman. Jimmy Halliday decided to step down as he felt he no longer had enough time for the role, whereas Donaldson was now retired and had more free time than previous leaders to get around the country and help build the party up.[29] Donaldson turned out to be the only nominee and so acquired the chairmanship unopposed on 5 June 1960.

An early expression of the new chairman's came in an article in the *Scots Independent*:

> The achievement of self-government is not an end in itself but a means to an end. It is the instrument through which great things can be done for Scotland. But it can be no greater than the men who will be trying to make use of it. We must see these men greatly changed before that day arrives. What Scotland will need is not only to achieve self-government but to create a party capable of putting it into real effect. There will be at least a ten years job for that National Party as a National Government to put the new Scotland on its feet and the right path.[30]

---

27   Harvie, *Scotland and Nationalism*, p. 179.
28   Miller, *The End of British Politics?*, p. 27.
29   Halliday, *Yours for Scotland*, p. 73.
30   *Scots Independent*, 4 March 1961.

Donaldson continued by saying that it would be necessary to break the hold of the big two political parties in Scotland, create a Parliament which is less dominated by party politics, and eventually a self-governing state that would be both a good neighbour and a dependable friend.

A few months later, the SNP decided to contest Glasgow Bridgeton, its first by-election in nine years, with Ian Macdonald, a young Ayrshire farmer, as candidate. Born in Japan in 1934, Macdonald's first involvement with Scottish politics was as a member of the Glasgow University Scottish Nationalist Association. After national service, he acquired a farm in North Ayrshire and contested the council ward of Galston and Loudoun. As the SNP candidate for the by-election in Glasgow Bridgeton on 16 November, Macdonald finished third with 19 per cent of the vote. Both he as an individual and the nationalists as a party felt encouraged by this result. Macdonald gave up his farm in Ayrshire to become a fully paid official in the SNP, taking the newly created post of national organiser in June 1962.[31]

After two months in his new post, Ian Macdonald was interviewed for the *Scots Independent* by another young nationalist, the 24-year-old Gordon Wilson, who had written his first article for the newspaper in 1961. Wilson asked Macdonald why he gave up his farm to become national organiser. Macdonald answered that Scotland's freedom was much more important than any person's career and that Bridgeton showed there was a political opportunity. He was convinced of the tremendous future of the National Party and that coordination would be all-important. He wanted to see branches in every constituency, strong enough to fight every seat in Scotland in a general election. He believed this position would be reached in a comparatively short time and that membership drives and increased finance would be the twin keys to success.[32] Macdonald seemed to sense that a transition from fringe to mainstream was imminent and he would play a key part in it as national organiser.

---

31   Ian Macdonald, 'The SNP Story', in the *Scots Independent*, 11 June 1966.

32   *Scots Independent*, 11 August 1962.

In June 1962, William Wolfe finished with 23 per cent of the vote and second place in a by-election in West Lothian. Labour still had a safe majority but the SNP had replaced the Conservatives as the potential challenger to Labour. Another important development was an organisational innovation introduced during the by-election campaign. Wolfe realised that the constitution of the SNP had no provision for constituency associations – the only unit of local organisation was the branch.[33] Consequently, Wolfe set up a local structure providing a forum for the coordination of a single campaign instead of several smaller campaigns lacking cohesion.

At the end of 1962, Arthur Donaldson made his first appearance on television. A BBC series entitled *Patterns For Prosperity* saw Esmond Wright, later Conservative MP for Glasgow Pollok, interview key figures in all political parties, including the SNP. The interview covered a range of topics: whether independence would mean border posts or staying in a customs union, internationalism, bureaucracy, nationalisation, the economy and defence. At one point Donaldson confirmed that he was expressing a vote of no confidence in Scotland's current seventy-one MPs. At the end of the interview, Wright asked if Donaldson was saying that the fundamental thing is a Scottish Parliament, which received the reply, 'You cannot avoid a Scottish Parliament if you are going to do anything useful at all for Scotland.'[34] In the days and weeks that followed this interview, Donaldson received many congratulations from SNP supporters and others. C. M. Grieve, then in the Communist Party, sent his 'heartiest congratulations'. In reply to congratulations from Wendy Wood, leader of the Scottish Patriots, Donaldson emphasised what he saw as his role in the SNP:

> I think you know that as Chairman I am only one of the office-bearers of the National Party and not, as Esmond Wright said in the broadcast, its leader. I do not presume therefore to claim that I can speak for the National

---

33   Wolfe, *Scotland Lives*, p. 17.

34   *Scots Independent*, 16 & 23 February 1963, published the BBC transcript in two parts.

Party except on matters which have been normally considered and decided
by the Party Executive.[35]

In other words, it was the National Executive Committee that actually ran
the Scottish National Party, with the chairman not necessarily the most influential figure.

At a meeting of the party's National Executive Committee in August 1963,
Gordon Wilson was given the post of assistant national secretary and three
months later was asked to review the party's organisation. One of his first
questions, in a letter to Donaldson, was who the party's chief executive was.
Was it the president or the chairman? And could the chairman confirm it
was him?[36] The move towards a reorganisation followed a disappointing by-
election. Donaldson had been the candidate in Kinross and West Perthshire
but had finished in fourth place with a lost deposit and only 7 per cent of the
vote. He had finished third at the previous general election when there was
no Liberal candidate.[37] It had been a high-profile by-election, as it allowed
Sir Alex Douglas-Home to take up a seat in the Commons having resigned
from the Lords as newly appointed Prime Minister. Early in 1964, Gordon
Wilson submitted his report. It proposed to clarify the powers and responsibilities of different party bodies and offices. Wilson later observed that the
new organisation remained largely in place for forty years[38] and acknowledged that the best advice he received prior to preparing the report came
from Donaldson. Wilson reckoned the advice was a consequence of Arthur
Donaldson's years of working for Chrysler in the USA, where he had experienced a structure of executive vice-chairmen with specific responsibilities.[39]

---

35   NLS, Acc. 6038, SNP, Arthur Donaldson, Box 2: letters from C. M. Grieve to Arthur Donaldson,
     7 December 1962; Wendy Wood to Arthur Donaldson, 15 December 1962; and Arthur Donaldson to
     Wendy Wood, 8 January 1963.

36   Ibid., NEC, 16 June 1963 & 22 November 1963; letter from Gordon Wilson to Arthur Donaldson,
     27 November 1963.

37   Craig, *British Parliamentary Election Results 1950–1970*.

38   Wilson, *SNP: The Turbulent Years 1960–1990*, p. 12.

39   Conversation between the author and Gordon Wilson, 7 December 2015.

The Conservatives under Home lost the 1964 election, marking an early stage in the decline of Scottish Tories even with a Scottish Tory as leader of the party across Britain. England returned more Conservative MPs than Labour but decisive wins for Labour in Scotland and Wales overturned the narrow Conservative victory in England. This had the effect of giving the English electorate a Labour government that they had not elected. Donaldson contested Kinross and West Perthshire again with almost the same result as in 1959 with no Liberal candidate, but doubling his share of the vote compared with the by-election. The SNP saved three deposits, a feat achieved as far back as 1931, which showed how little progress had been made in a third of century. However, the fifteen candidates fielded was almost double its previous high of eight, hinting at an improvement in party organisation.

In the month after the election, a review of constituency organisation was submitted to the party's National Council.[40] A sense of the party's organisation can be gleaned from this. There were only five with a constituency association in place, four with three or more branches, five with two branches, twenty-three with just one branch, and thirty-four with no branches at all.

The SNP constitution required a minimum of twenty members to form a branch and a minimum, preferably more, of two branches to form a constituency association. Ian Macdonald, as national organiser, viewed forming the first branch in a constituency as usually the most difficult step. Macdonald travelled all over Scotland organising the delivery of cards inviting interest in forming a branch. Even if only 1 per cent replied after 2,000 had been delivered, that would be enough to form a branch. A meeting would be arranged to set up a branch and elect a chair and other positions. The chair of these meetings, at least until the branch chair was elected, would usually be someone from SNP HQ, often Macdonald. After the first branch in a constituency came into being, the national organiser could step back and let the locals take the initiative. This resulted in more branches formed in the constituency and

---

40   NLS, Acc. 6038, SNP, Arthur Donaldson, Box 2: 'Review of Constituencies' by Alan Niven.

in time to the branches getting together to form a constituency association.[41]
By 1965, the SNP was beginning to feel more confident in its branch-
building skills. A booklet on *How to Build up Your Constituency* described
how to go from no organisation to a constituency association fighting a general election in three years. By December 1965, Donaldson reported that
over a million television viewers had seen Billy Wolfe in the SNP's first ever
party political broadcast in September. This had been followed by a successful membership drive, taking the total number of members to 20,000 for the
first time in the party's history.[42]

Wolfe observed that a new branch formed every week in the early months
1966.[43] The party had an additional paid organiser in Hamish MacQueen
from Glasgow, who was employed by the party as 'branchmaker' in the west
of Scotland for a year from 1965.[44] Another reason for expansion at this time
was expressed in a letter by Douglas Drysdale, vice-chair for organisation,
'...the most important single contribution to the party over the last two
years has been Mr Gordon Wilson's non-stop attempts to infiltrate into TV
and wireless'.[45] Wilson had been writing letters every few weeks to broadcasting authorities and senior politicians and to increase the SNP's profile.
In addition, Rosemary Hall, national organising secretary, had issued 100
press releases over the previous year.[46]

In February 1966, Harold Wilson announced that there would be a general election on 31 March.[47] The SNP was allowed a party political broadcast
for the first time during an election campaign, having fulfilled the condition
of contesting a minimum of one-fifth of the seats in Scotland. In addition,

41   Ibid.; Box 3, 'How to Build up Your Constituency' by Russell Thomson.

42   NLS, Acc. 11987, SNP Papers, Item 2: minutes of National Council, 4 December 1965.

43   Wolfe, *Scotland Lives*, p. 77.

44   NLS, Acc. 11987, SNP Papers, Item 75: minutes of Organisation Committee, 29 May 1965–28 May 1966.

45   Ibid., Item 107: Organisation Correspondence: letter from Douglas Drysdale to members of Organisa-
     tion Committee, 28 February 1966.

46   Ibid., Item 3, NC, 5 March 1966.

47   David Butler and Anthony King, *The British General Election of 1966* (New York: St Martin's Press,
     1966), p. 43.

the party was represented on four televised debates during the campaign, with Donaldson making two appearances. Gordon Wilson wrote to Donaldson offering advice, including the need to be more aware of which camera was operating to avoid facing the wrong way, and to mention the party's name more often as the public was not yet familiar with the SNP.[48]

With twenty-three candidates in place, the SNP conducted its biggest campaign yet. Many activists had little campaigning experience. After the election, an editorial in the *Scots Independent* maintained that 80 per cent of activists had not campaigned before.[49] The SNP election manifesto was entitled *Putting Scotland First*. It asserted that Scotland should not become part of the EEC while still part of the UK but might become a member after independence, and also made policy statements on transport, education, housing and employment.[50]

Labour improved its performance in Scotland while the Conservatives continued to decline. It was also the SNP's best result to date.[51] The SNP was seriously threatening to replace the Liberals as the third party in Scottish politics in votes, though still far behind in seats. In the rural parts of Scotland, the Liberals were well ahead of the SNP, but in the central belt the SNP were ahead of the Liberals. The best SNP result in a rural constituency was for Donaldson, who won 21 per cent of the vote in Kinross and West Perthshire and ended in second place, narrowly ahead of Labour though still well behind Conservative. Richard Finlay noted on the Scotland-wide picture, 'The fact that the party was in a position to organise and fund such an extensive campaign should have sent alarm bells ringing in the Scottish political establishment.'[52]

The death of a recently returned Labour MP caused a by-election in

---

48   NLS, Acc. 6038, SNP, Arthur Donaldson, Box 3: papers from March 1966.

49   *Scots Independent*, 16 April 1966.

50   Somerville, *Through the Maelstrom*, pp. 161–2.

51   Compiled from data in Craig, *British Parliamentary Election Results 1950–1970*.

52   Richard Finlay, 'The Early Years: From the Inter-War Period to the Mid-1960s', in *The Making of the Modern SNP*, p. 30.

Carmarthen in Wales within weeks of the general election. Plaid Cymru, the SNP's sister party in Wales, was in third place behind Labour and the Liberals in the general election but ahead of the Conservatives and needing a 15 per cent swing to win the seat. The by-election was held in July 1966, with Gwynfor Evans, Plaid Cymru president since 1945, as candidate. Evans had contested Carmarthen in the 1964 and 1966 elections. He won the seat with a swing of 18 per cent, finishing with 39 per cent of the vote to Labour's 33 per cent. This had an impact in Scotland. Prior to Carmarthen, there was no evidence that a nationalist candidate could win a parliamentary contest with more than one of the main British parties on the ballot paper. Carmarthen encouraged the belief that it could be done. The *Scots Independent* called for similar in Scotland under a front-page headline 'The Challenge of Carmarthen'.[53] At the SNP National Council in September 1966, Donaldson suggested that Carmarthen was a portent of similar success for the SNP, regardless of how 'safe' any seat appeared to be. The result in Wales combined with the continued growth of the SNP led him to see an opportunity.[54]

Another development during the summer of 1966 was a census of where the SNP stood as an organisation. The party prepared a table listing how well organised it was in each constituency.[55] The map below is based on the detail in the report and illustrates the areas of strength and weakness of the SNP organisationally in summer 1966.

There had been significant growth in just twenty-one months. There were fourteen constituency associations, eight constituencies with three or more branches, seven with two branches and twenty-eight with just one branch. Perhaps most important of all, by August 1966 there were only fourteen constituencies with no branches compared to thirty-four twenty-one months earlier.

Encouraged by the summer's developments, the SNP had an autumn

---

53 *Scots Independent*, 23 July 1966.

54 NLS, Acc. 11987, SNP Papers, Item 3: NEC, 3 September 1966.

55 Ibid., Item 28: NEC, 12 August 1966. Part of the table was published in Brand, *The National Movement in Scotland*, pp. 289–91.

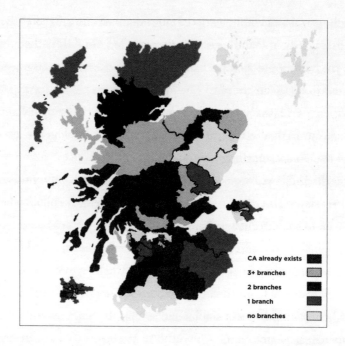

campaign aimed at recruiting more members and building up the party organ-isation. Gwynfor Evans was invited to speak across Scotland. Donaldson also went on a speaking tour. In December 1966, he reported that he had attended twenty-three branch meetings from September to December, with about 100 people on average in attendance. Donaldson observed that sup-port was beginning to snowball, and it was reported that membership had passed 40,000.[56]

By the end of the first quarter of 1967, the SNP had 254 branches and twenty-seven constituency associations.[57] The *Scots Independent* noted that nineteen of every twenty SNP members had not been a member four years earlier, a sign of how much the party had grown.[58] One of those nineteen in every twenty was George Leslie, the SNP candidate in the Glasgow Pollok by-election held

---

56   NLS, Acc. 11987, SNP Papers, Item 3: NEC, 3 December 1966.

57   Ibid., Item 29: NEC, 17 March 1967.

58   *Scots Independent*, 18 March 1967.

in March 1967. Leslie had decided to join the party in 1964 after living for three years in England and, as he put it, seeing Scotland from the outside.[59]

The SNP mounted its most vigorous campaign yet in Glasgow Pollok. It claimed to have canvassed every house in the constituency and 60 per cent of them twice (this likely means doors knocked rather than voters spoken to). It was in this by-election that the SNP first developed what would become trademarks of SNP campaigning: car cavalcades, jazzy literature and fly posting.[60] The by-election ended with victory for Esmond Wright of the Conservatives, but the Conservative share of the vote in Pollok fell from 48 per cent to 37 per cent and Labour's fell from 52 per cent to 31 per cent. The SNP's, however, rose from 0 to 28 per cent, while Liberal and Communist each received 2 per cent. The SNP had achieved a 25 per cent swing from Labour, larger than Plaid Cymru's in Carmarthen. Donaldson wrote in the *Scots Independent* that Pollok had burst a few bubbles and remarked, 'A movement does not march from 2,000 members to 50,000 members in six years without having thrown up capable leadership.'[61]

In early 1967, leadership was a subject being given thought by Douglas Drysdale, by this time vice-chairman for finance. He wrote to Donaldson outlining his views.[62] He recommended that the party should become a strong democratic movement with a leader with the power to carry out its tasks. He thought it wrong that vice-chairmen were elected by the party instead of appointed by the leader, that this allowed the chair to hide behind the inefficiency of these other elected members. Drysdale believed there were just three people who could lead the party: himself, James Lees and Billy Wolfe. By implication, Drysdale did not see Donaldson as the right person to be chair, a point confirmed in other correspondence in which he said so

---

59   Ibid., 11 March 1967.

60   James Kellas, 'Scottish Nationalism', in *The British General Election of 1970* by David Butler and Michael Pinto-Duschinsky (London: Macmillan, 1971), p. 450.

61   *Scots Independent*, 18 March 1967.

62   NLS, Acc. 6038, SNP, Arthur Donaldson, Box 5: letter from Douglas Drysdale to Arthur Donaldson, 6 February 1967.

explicitly.[63] Drysdale's letter continued by criticising Donaldson for being too neutral in the chair and letting committees make key decisions. He did, however, praise Donaldson for running a system that had brought people of talent up through the ranks of the party. Not everyone agreed with Drysdale. Senior vice-chairman Billy Wolfe wrote to Donaldson to say he did not want a chairman who was a 'paternalistic head of state'.[64]

The Drysdale letter proved to be a prelude to a leadership challenge, giving the SNP annual conference an electoral contest for the post for the first time since 1955.[65] Donaldson won an emphatic victory with 362 votes to thirty-seven.[66] Drysdale was decisively rejected, though his ideas were similar to that which the SNP adopted after devolution. It may have helped Donaldson's re-election that he had the opportunity to present the annual chairman's address to party conference shortly before the vote. He appears to have been on inspirational form. He commented on the continuing membership surge and maintained that the SNP had become a match for its rivals, saying, 'Let us show in this new War of Independence that our amateur politicians are worth half a dozen of their professionals.' The SNP was, he argued, the most representative organisation Scotland had ever had and was a party that was neither left nor right. He built the speech up to a dramatic finish, telling the delegates he was giving them the cry of the soldiers fighting at Bannockburn, 'On them, on them, they fail, they fail.'[67]

In the summer of 1966, there had been speculation that Tom Fraser, the Labour MP for Hamilton, was about to resign to become chair of the South of Scotland Electric Board. The SNP took this speculation seriously and adopted Winnie Ewing as a prospective candidate by the end of August.

---

63   NLS, Acc. 13099, Gordon Wilson SNP politician, Item 1: letter from Douglas Drysdale to Gordon Wilson, dated 5 March 1968. In this letter Drysdale names Wilson as a future chairman.

64   NLS, Acc. 6038, SNP, Arthur Donaldson, Box 5: letter from William Wolfe to Arthur Donaldson, 23 February 1967.

65   Somerville, *Through the Maelstrom*, p. 86 for the previous contest.

66   NLS, Acc. 6038, SNP, Arthur Donaldson, Box 5: annual conference reports, 1967.

67   *Scots Independent*, 10 June 1967. It was common for SNP speakers to attempt to inspire by referring to a previous ultimately successful struggle for Scottish independence.

A year later, Fraser resigned to take up a different chair, the North of Scotland Hydro-Electric Board. The by-election for the Hamilton constituency was called for early November 1967. The seat had been Labour since being created in 1918 and was one of the safest Labour seats in Britain; at the 1966 general election, Labour won 71 per cent in a two-party contest with the Tories.

The man who became SNP election agent at the by-election was Hamilton constituency association organiser John McAteer. A decade later, Glasgow activist Hugh MacDonald wrote of McAteer,

> John was architect of the organisational and political strategy that shattered the Labour establishment within its fortress of Hamilton. In terms of sheer professionalism it was the finest piece of organisation and deployment of forces that the National Party has witnessed. He assembled a team of battle-proven activists with just the right injection of new blood to set the whole campaign going. With John McAteer as election agent and Winnie Ewing as candidate, the chemistry, or maybe it was the alchemy, was just right.[68]

The pages of the *Scots Independent* provided a running commentary of progress. At the beginning of September, the front page proclaimed, 'Scotland Free by Seventy-Three' and predicted Hamilton would be better than Pollok.[69] A week later, the front page forecast victory because the number of SNP members would be swamping the constituency in the last ten days of the campaign. This prediction came true, though possibly more through luck than skill given the inaccuracy of the prediction in the previous edition.[70] By the middle of October, an editorial stated that Labour was in a state of panic in Hamilton.[71]

Donaldson was cautiously optimistic. In a letter written a week before polling day, he wrote, 'The situation is very interesting in Hamilton and

---

68   *Scots Independent*, April 1977, John McAteer obituary by Hugh MacDonald.
69   Ibid., 2 September 1967.
70   Ibid., 9 September 1967.
71   Ibid., 14 October 1967.

quite fluid. We shall do very well and Mrs Ewing may even pull it off. Much depends on how the Doubtfuls decide in the next few days,'[72] referring to canvas return 'Doubtfuls'. Canvassing then involved putting voters into three categories: For, Against, Doubtful. Ewing recollected that every door was canvassed twice, a benefit of the numbers pouring in.[73] Wolfe acknowledged the value of the hundreds of activists that poured in from all over Scotland in the last three weeks of the campaign and described Ewing as someone who projected the party well, making every effort to meet people wherever she could find them.[74]

The SNP won the Hamilton by-election with a majority of 1,779. The SNP share of the vote rose from 0 to 46 per cent, while Labour's fell from 71 per cent to 42 per cent and the Conservative vote from 29 per cent to 12 per cent, narrowly losing their deposit. There was no Liberal candidate. Winifred Ewing became the second ever Scottish nationalist MP, and the first to win with both Labour and Conservative on the ballot paper, with a swing of 38 per cent.[75]

Billy Wolfe watched the result on television and then hired a taxi and made his way to a hotel where hundreds of supporters celebrated and Ewing held court like a 'fairy princess'.[76] In the week after there were reports of people queuing outside SNP headquarters to join the party, and interest in the party was not confined to Scotland alone. National secretary Gordon Wilson described the result as having a phenomenal impact, which altered the party mindset because victory became believable.

> It is remarkable that a one-off by-election victory by a fringe organisation
> should have had the impact it did. But Scotland was stirring and the SNP

---

72   NLS, Acc. 6038, SNP, Arthur Donaldson, Box 5: letter from Arthur Donaldson to supporter John Johnstone, dated 25 October 1967.

73   Ewing, *Stop the World*, p. 10.

74   Wolfe, *Scotland Lives*, p. 105.

75   Craig, *British Parliamentary Election Results 1950–1970*.

76   Wolfe, *Scotland Lives*, p. 106.

was an unique outlet for venting the anger and frustrations engendered by our treatment as a nation at the hands of Whitehall. From now on the SNP was ever present either as a political force or as a potential threat to the Union between Scotland and England.[77]

Douglas Drysdale maintained that public attitudes had changed in just two weeks, that there was a pride in being Scottish marking the beginning of a new era.[78] Arthur Donaldson described Winnie Ewing as a candidate in a million.[79]

There has been much academic comment on the Hamilton by-election. Miller highlighted that Hamilton was different from two English by-elections held on the same day. The Conservative vote in Hamilton dropped but rose substantially in the Leicester and Manchester by-elections.[80] Mitchell wrote that matters were going wrong for the Labour government: wage restraints, an unsuccessful application to join the EEC, a sterling crisis leading to devaluation, and the Labour organisation was weak in Hamilton while Winnie Ewing was bright and confident.[81] He maintained that 'no event in 20th century Scottish politics provoked more awareness of the Scottish dimension than this by-election'.[82] Brand wrote that it was clear a year earlier that things were moving but very few seemed to notice, hence the Hamilton result came as a shock. Brand added, 'This election really marks the arrival of the SNP for the majority of the Scottish electorate as a party with a serious potential future.'[83]

What was the proper perspective of the Hamilton by-election? It was clearly a bigger success for the SNP than Motherwell had been twenty-two

77   Wilson, *SNP: The Turbulent Years 1960–1990*, p. 43.

78   Douglas Drysdale, 'Looking Back to Hamilton', in the *Scots Independent*, 18 November 1967.

79   Ibid.

80   Miller, *The End of British Politics?*, p. 46.

81   Mitchell, *Strategies for Self-Government*, p. 204.

82   Mitchell, 'From Breakthrough to Mainstream: The Politics of Potential and Blackmail', in *The Making of the Modern SNP*, pp. 31–2.

83   Brand, *The National Movement in Scotland*, pp. 261–2.

years earlier. Motherwell had only one opponent among the main UK parties, while Hamilton had two. In Motherwell, Labour had been undefeated for two decades but in Hamilton this number was five. When Hamilton happened, nobody knew how far the surge to the SNP was going to go. At the 1966 general election there had been signs that the SNP was beginning to challenge the Liberals for third place in Scottish politics. If Labour could fail to defend a seat in which their starting point was 71 per cent of the vote, did that mean the SNP was now challenging Labour for first place in Scottish politics?

After the by-election, Winnie received invites from all over Scotland to come and address gatherings of supporters. Arthur Donaldson sometimes played the part of warm-up speaker. One such occasion was in the Caird Hall, Dundee on 1 April 1968. Afterwards, Donaldson received a number of letters with positive feedback, including, 'I thought you were excellent. Never heard your voice so resonant, your logic so convincing ... Winnie is a good acquisition, she has courage and character and such obvious charm.'[84]

Six months after Hamilton, in the council elections of May 1968, the SNP achieved their greatest electoral success of the 1960s. The party achieved high percentages of the vote in all four of Scotland's main cities; 30 per cent in both Aberdeen and Dundee and 35 per cent in Edinburgh.[85] In Glasgow, the SNP got 36 per cent of the vote and thirteen councillors elected, Progressive/Conservative got 35 per cent and eighteen councillors, Labour 26 per cent and just six councillors.[86] The SNP topped the poll Scotland-wide in contested burgh elections, with 34 per cent of the vote compared to 18 per cent and third place the previous year.[87]

The edition of the *Scots Independent* for 18 May 1968 announced 'Scottish

---

84   NLS, Acc. 6038, SNP, Arthur Donaldson, Box 6: letter to Arthur Donaldson from supporter Neil Mathieson, dated 4 April 1968.

85   *Scots Independent*, 11 May 1968.

86   Compiled from data in F. W. S. Craig, *City and Royal Burgh of Glasgow Municipal Election Results 1948–73* (Chichester: Parliamentary Research Services, 1984).

87   Miller, *The End of British Politics?*, p. 47. On p. 134, Miller supplies a table of opinion polls for general election voting intention that shows the SNP in first place from February to September in 1968.

Revolution' on its front page, including a photograph of SNP activists at the Kelvin Hall for the count of the Glasgow results. The article underneath declared that 'many of them new to politics, are no longer willing to allow the running of their country to go by default, that voters, many of them so dissatisfied they have never bothered to vote before – certainly in local elections – have wakened up'.[88] Arthur Donaldson wrote in his weekly column that the SNP's opponents were even more panicked by these council results than they had been by Hamilton because this time there were huge SNP increases everywhere.[89] It had been a remarkable electoral journey for the SNP. In a little over two years, from the general election of March 1966 to the council election of May 1968, they had risen from fourth to first place in the popular vote in Scotland. The question was, would this change be temporary or permanent? It turned out to be a bit of both.

At the council elections of May 1969, the SNP fell behind both Labour and Conservative in the popular vote.[90] It took the SNP until 1974 to finish ahead of Conservative again and until 2007 to finish ahead of Labour. Hence the level of success achieved in 1968 was only temporary, almost like a brief, post-Hamilton euphoria among the electorate. The permanent change was that the SNP had replaced the Liberals as the third party in Scottish politics. Arthur Donaldson did not play a major part in causing these tidal shifts in electoral opinion, but this is not a criticism of him. The main function of the party chairman was to chair the National Executive Committee, not be a national figurehead. It is also not a suggestion that a different chairman would have been better for the party at this time. Winnie Ewing's victory at Hamilton elevated her to the position of unofficial national figurehead – no person in the party could avoid being outshone by her at this time.

The years 1968 and 1969 were years of change in the leadership of the Scottish National Party. Ian Macdonald decided to step down as national

---

88 *Scots Independent*, 18 May 1968.
89 Ibid.
90 Miller, *The End of British Politics?*, p. 47.

organiser so that he could concentrate on being a parliamentary candidate again. By December 1968, the party chose John McAteer as MacDonald's replacement, with a brief transition period when they would both be in post.[91] By April 1969, when Macdonald wrote his last report as national organiser, the party had sixty-nine constituency associations. The remaining two were formed during the next six months.[92] Macdonald's contribution had been considerable; in the words of Peter Lynch, his 'performance as organiser and his impact on the party were to turn out to be quite revolutionary as he built a mass membership and branch network that stretched across Scotland'.[93]

Arthur Donaldson's time as chairman was also coming to an end. On 30 July 1968, he had to appear in court to face an assault charge. At a public meeting on 17 June, he had lost his temper with a member of the audience and struck him on the mouth. The individual in question had been recently expelled from the SNP for campaigning against official party candidates in Dundee during the council elections.[94] Donaldson's defence consisted of arguing that he had been provoked by remarks about his wife. The court imposed a fine of £20 on Donaldson.[95] The level of publicity this case received was small, for example the *Glasgow Herald* ran two reports: on 31 July a page 5 article followed by a page 20 article on 28 August.[96] It may seem strange that a party leader on an assault charge was not a front-page headline. This appears to have been because press and television tended to base their reports on politics around what MPs were doing. From the moment Winnie Ewing got elected, the media was far more interested in her than it was in Arthur Donaldson. This arguably worked in his favour and made the assault fine less of a scandal. Donaldson may nevertheless have been affected by what had

---

91   NLS, Acc. 6038, SNP, Arthur Donaldson, Box 7: minutes of Organisation Committee, 18 December 1968.

92   Ibid., Box 8: National Organiser report to Annual Conference, dated 2 April 1969; NLS, Acc. 11987, SNP Papers, Item 6: NC, 6 September 1969.

93   Lynch, *SNP: The History of the Scottish National Party*, p. 106.

94   NLS, Acc. 11987, SNP Papers, Item 5: NC, 15 June 1968.

95   NLS, Acc. 6038, SNP, Arthur Donaldson, Box 7: letter covering payment to the court 9 September 1968.

96   *Glasgow Herald*, 31 July & 28 August 1968.

happened as, according to Jimmy Halliday, it 'undoubtedly prompted him to retire as Party Chairman'.[97]

On 23 January 1969, it was reported in the *Glasgow Herald* and *The Scotsman* that Arthur Donaldson would step down as SNP chairman at the party's next annual conference.[98] It was not clear why he was choosing to step down. The press speculated that there had been a private deal whereby Donaldson would retire to make way for Billy Wolfe. However, the collection of Arthur Donaldson correspondence at the National Library of Scotland does not include a reference to a deal. What is in the collection is a large level of feedback from SNP supporters.[99] Most of it urged him to allow himself to be nominated as chairman; others thanked him for his years in the chair but accepted that these were now over. One of the letters came from Billy Wolfe informing Donaldson that, as the vacancy had arisen, Wolfe had accepted nomination.[100] Following receipt of this letter, Donaldson changed his mind and decided to allow himself to be nominated for chairman. The reasons he gave were pressure from the party organisation and individual members and he believed the annual conference should have the opportunity to decide if it wanted a younger chair.[101]

Why did Arthur Donaldson apparently resign and then change his mind? It could be his self-confidence had taken a knock after the assault charge and the mail he received in late January and early February made him realise he still had support, which in turn gave him his confidence back. This, however, does not explain the timing of his decision to try to remain chairman, which came immediately after being informed that Billy Wolfe had become a candidate. It was almost as though he could no longer face remaining an unopposed chairman but as soon as the prospect of a contest emerged he was for it and did not mind whether he won or lost. At his age of sixty-seven he

97   Halliday, *Yours for Scotland*, p. 83.

98   *Glasgow Herald*, 23 January 1969.

99   NLS, Acc. 6038, SNP, Arthur Donaldson, Box 8.

100   Ibid., letter from William Wolfe to Arthur Donaldson, dated 2 February 1969.

101   Ibid., letter from Arthur Donaldson to party press officer Alasdair MacDonald, dated 5 February 1969.

was getting ready to step down from several of his activities: he had resigned as a Forfar town councillor in 1968 and was destined to step down as editor of the *Forfar Dispatch* at the beginning of 1970.[102] He even resigned as prospective parliamentary candidate for Moray and Nairn at the same time as the reports he was stepping down as chairman.[103]

The 1969 annual conference was held in June in Oban. Wolfe won 544 votes to Donaldson's 238. This gave Donaldson just a little above 30 per cent of the vote and brought his nine years as chairman to an end.[104]

Wilson wrote to Donaldson and commented on his style of leadership: 'In these years you have allowed your fellow office-bearers to develop their talents by marking out the signposts and by leaving them a wide freedom of discretion. Delegation of this type is the mark of a first class Chief Executive.'[105]

This was a very significant compliment coming from the individual who, in November 1963, had written to Donaldson to ask who was chief executive in the SNP. It can be viewed, along with the Douglas Drysdale compliment about allowing talent to come up through the ranks, as indicative of a chairman adept at encouraging the right kind of people to do more for the party.

Winnie Ewing also sent Arthur Donaldson a letter:

> The fact that the Party voted for Billy was almost certainly in part the realisation of the enormous nature of the burden of fighting a General Election unparalleled in our political history. You are our Elder Statesman and the only one Scotland has, but motivation in voting is a strange and complex activity. The Party is now very full of very new members. At our rate of growth, changes have been so quick and the outcome was in these circumstances perhaps predictable.[106]

---

102   NLS, Acc. 6038, SNP, Arthur Donaldson, Box 6: letter, dated 16 January 1968, for resignation as a town councillor; Box 9: letter, dated 20 December 1969, for resignation as an editor.

103   Ibid., Box 8: minutes for Moray and Nairn constituency association, 30 January 1969.

104   Ibid., Box 9: annual conference reports, 1969.

105   Ibid., letter from Gordon Wilson to Arthur Donaldson, dated 3 June 1969.

106   Ibid., letter from Winifred Ewing to Arthur Donaldson, dated 4 June 1969.

The general election was held in June 1970, just twelve months after the end of Donaldson's chairmanship. On this occasion, Donaldson, in what would be his last appearance as a parliamentary candidate, stood in Galloway. Once again he was the first ever SNP candidate in the constituency. He finished with 21 per cent of the vote and a distant second place behind the Conservative in a four-party contest. The Scotland-wide picture in this general election saw the SNP win just one seat. But the party won 11.4 per cent of the vote, with sixty-five candidates managing to save twenty-two deposits. This was double the Liberals' vote but still a long way behind Labour and the Tories.

The SNP had been through a transformative decade that changed their fortunes for the better. Having a chairman who was a good orator and, in Wilson's words, a first-class chief executive was obviously helpful, but was also not the most important point. Having a perceptive and enthusiastic national organiser like Ian Macdonald was arguably even more helpful, but, again, not the most important point. The key event was the expansion of the SNP as an organisation from less than thirty branches and no constituency associations to over 500 branches and a full complement of seventy-one constituency associations. This was the change that made possible sixty-five candidates instead of just five. Each new branch required a minimum of twenty members, a growth to over 500 means at least 10,000 people came forward to be founder members of an SNP branch. Each new branch required office-bearers, a chairman, secretary, treasurer and quite likely a vice-chairman and an organiser as well. Given the number of branches formed, at least 2,000 and more likely 3,000 people stepped up to the task of being an office-bearer in a local organisation that had not previously existed. These were the people who, each in their own way, and for their own reasons, changed the face of Scottish politics. The local events they organised, whether jumble sales, ceilidhs, or public meetings (possibly with Donaldson as a guest speaker), created an SNP presence in their communities. Some of these activists soon rose to positions of prominence in the party, for example the first chairman of newly formed Lewis branch in 1966 was Donald Stewart, and two years later the first organiser of newly formed High Blantyre branch was Margo MacDonald.[107]

It is important to emphasise that the story of the SNP in the 1960s was not so much the story of a leader but the story of a self-assembling mass movement. It should nevertheless also be noted that this mass movement did not build itself up from nothing, but from foundations that were already present. Ian Macdonald acknowledged this when he stepped down as national organiser: 'In the seven years since I took on this job, both the image and the strength of the SNP have changed beyond all recognition, but it is interesting that this edifice was built on an obviously strong and sound foundation.'[108] Macdonald credits three individuals – Robert McIntyre, Jimmy Halliday and Arthur Donaldson – for setting the nationalist movement on the route of parliamentary democracy at a time when there were distracting alternatives and that, between them, they created the political party that was able to develop so extensively in the 1960s.[109]

Donaldson was not the kind of leader that would have emerged in the three main UK parties. His election time schedules show that, apart from his occasional appearances on television, he was speaking two or three times a day in the constituency he was contesting, not touring the country like a national leader.[110] Though he did travel around Scotland outwith election campaigns in response to the many invitations he received to address gatherings of nationalists. His two greatest contributions to the SNP, therefore, were his commitment to the parliamentary elections route to independence and his effectiveness as a motivator.

Donaldson should also be credited as a builder and, later, rebuilder of his own local branch along with his wife Vi. There had been an active Forfar branch in the middle of the century, and the Donaldsons helped start it up

---

107   *Scots Independent*, 12 February 1966 & 24 February 1968.

108   NLS, Acc. 6038, SNP, Arthur Donaldson, Box 8: national organiser report to annual conference, dated 2 April 1969.

109   Conversation between the author and Ian Macdonald, 18 November 2015.

110   NLS, Acc. 6038, SNP, Boxes 2 & 3.

again in 1966.[111] After the end of his chairmanship and his campaign in Galloway, Arthur Donaldson had more time for involvement in his own area and started to attend the meetings of Angus South constituency association.[112] He also continued to be part of the National Executive Committee of the SNP. He would occasionally take time out, for example, he left Scotland in October 1972 determined to spend at least twelve months with his son in California.[113]

In the general election of October 1974, Arthur Donaldson, as a resident of Angus South, finally had an SNP MP when Andrew Welsh won the seat from the Conservatives. The seat was lost at the 1979 general election and by the 1983 election, following boundary changes, Donaldson was active in Tayside North constituency.

The nationalist movement benefited from Arthur Donaldson's skills as a journalist. In the November 1976 edition of the *Scots Independent*, marking the fiftieth anniversary of the first edition, Robert McIntyre paid tribute to Donaldson for having been editor of the newspaper three times and spending years in the post on each occasion.[114] Earlier in 1976, Donaldson had returned to another aspect of his writing skills: pamphleteer. In the 1950s, a booklet called '100 Home Rule Questions' had been written by David Graham with the assistance of information from Donaldson. The mid-1970s seemed the right time for a similar publication with the same question-and-answer format. The new piece, written by Donaldson, was entitled 'Whys of Scottish Nationalism'. It contained thirty-nine questions covering a range of topics: a brief history of the SNP, devolution, the EEC, economics, defence, oil, and the constitution of an independent Scotland.[115]

Arthur Donaldson continued, into his eighties, to be a figure at the annual

---

111   NLS, Acc. 6038, SNP, Box 1 shows a well-attended Forfar branch AGM in 1950. The re-start was reported by the *Scots Independent*, 14 May 1966.

112   NLS, Acc. 6038, SNP, Arthur Donaldson, Box 10.

113   Ibid.

114   *Scots Independent*, November 1976.

115   Arthur Donaldson, *Whys of Scottish Nationalism* (West Calder: SNP Publications, 1976).

conferences of the Scottish National Party perhaps most memorably at the Ayr conference in 1982. On the morning of 5 June, the SNP discussed whether organised groups within the party should be proscribed. In a debate that included some of the party's most eloquent speakers – including Jim Sillars, Gordon Wilson and Alex Salmond – it was only the Arthur Donaldson speech that brought delegates to their feet for a standing ovation. It was not that his argument was any more persuasive than anybody else's, rather the combination of a forceful delivery for a man of his age and, in the words of Gordon Wilson, 'that even after all the years, Arthur had retained very considerable influence, love and respect at grass roots level'.[116] A year later, at the 1983 annual conference, Donaldson did not put his name forward for re-election to the National Executive Committee.[117] This marked the end of his time as a leading figure in the party.

Arthur Donaldson died in 1993 at the age of ninety-one. Many leading nationalists paid tribute. Gordon Wilson remarked, 'Under his inspired leadership the Party mushroomed in size. He was by far the best orator the SNP has had and could hold whole conferences spellbound.'[118] Donaldson's successor William Wolfe said, 'His vision was expressed in oratory and in the written word with a wonderful blend of human feeling, intellect and pragmatism.'[119] The last word, however, should belong to Andrew Welsh: 'Arthur Donaldson was a foundation stone on which a free Scotland will be built.'[120]

---

116   Gordon Wilson email to the author, dated 23 May 2016, and author's handwritten notes from 1982.
117   NLS, Acc. 11987, SNP Papers, Item 45: NEC, 1983.
118   *Scots Independent*, March 1993.
119   Ibid.
120   Ibid.

CHAPTER 13

WILLIAM WOLFE

CHRISTOPHER HARVIE

Billy Wolfe came to the SNP after being active in the Saltire Society and other cultural affairs, which contributed to him becoming convinced of the need for Scottish independence. He was the party's candidate in the West Lothian 1962 by-election against Tam Dalyell, where he lost, but polled respectably, winning second place. He went on to contest the seat on seven occasions but failed to take the seat, though the by-election put down a marker for the SNP. Under his leadership, the SNP became more professional, including the creation of a new SNP logo, which assisted in the perception of a modern, forward-looking party. He became chair in 1969 after defeating Arthur Donaldson and oversaw the rise of the party's profile and vote, particularly in the two 1974 general elections. He was on the social democratic side of the party, and was convinced that the party had to appeal to Labour voters from the left. He resigned following the 1979 defeat, and would have continued to play a high-profile role, but for remarks leading up to the Pope's visit to Scotland in 1982. He continued to be active in CND and on the margins of the SNP but devoted much of his energy to cultural affairs, including the establishment of the Scottish Poetry Library.

•   •   •

'MILIEU AND ENTOURAGE': WEST LOTHIAN IN 1962

Perhaps it is easier to locate the politics of Billy Wolfe now that parallels can be drawn with the mature German Greens. In many respects he anticipated them, in combinations of anti-nuclear morality, intermediate technology and 'parochial' thinking – which the Irish poet Patrick Kavanagh reckoned superior to 'provincial' thinking, because it was centred in a local economic/ecological 'balance'. This was timely in the years that saw E. F. Schumacher's *Small is Beautiful* (1973) and the anti-nuclear movement, but in Scotland it also went back to a left 'philanthropic' tradition – to the Scots followers of Robert Owen, including the Birkmyres of New Lanark, the 'socialist millionaire' Allans of the shipping line, and the veteran Roland Eugene Muirhead (1868–1964), whose substantial tannery firm Andrew Muirhead and Company (which still thrives) indirectly supported his utopian nationalist projects.

Tom Devine doesn't mention Wolfe in his recent *Independence or Union* (2016), but neither does he mention Hugh MacDiarmid (aka Christopher Murray Grieve), Edwin Muir, Neil Gunn or others, who also felt inspired by elements of the egalitarian romanticism that had hooked James Connolly and Patrick Pearse: something they also had in common with the Plaid Cymru leadership around Saunders Lewis and Gwynfor Evans and its handling of cultural politics.[1] The impact on Wolfe of Evans's campaign for the Welsh-language TV Channel S4C would show that if the wider movement could claw itself back from its 1979 trough, cultural leverage was possible in Scotland through the presentation of the 'second' literary renaissance of the 1980s. In Wolfe's own case the development of the Poetry Library campaign after 1983 didn't just make good the trauma of the St David's Day Referendum; this cooperative enterprise would help pave the way for the cross-party 'Claim of Right' campaign and its 'Tory-free Scotland' outlier. As he wrote in that distinctive jaggy black-ink hand to your author in early 1985,

---

1   See Roy Foster, *Vivid Faces: The Revolutionary Generation in Ireland, 1890–1923* (London: Allen Lane, 2014).

The party seems dominated by darkness now, whereas it shone with light and warmth ten years ago. The Heritage [Society] may develop, but I doubt it. The Poetry Library is of great cultural and psychological importance to the nation, and I want to help it succeed, but it can never be my major effort. The Peace movement will always get my help and support but, again, it is not my main scene. The identity and survival of Scotland is; whether I like it or not, it is my faith.[2]

The Wolfe *Heimat* of Torphichen and Bathgate, where the family business and home were based, personified a *Mittelstand* industry type which could have developed on Baden-Württemberg lines; as after 1980 my new home became – thanks to Thatcher's deregulating of overseas investment – the biggest single recipient of the reinvested UK oil revenues. The late Lothar Späth (1938–2016), the Christian Democrats' 'very model of the modern Minister-President', who funded my professorship, made expert use of this bounty in industrial training, modern languages and public transport, the last being the great 'social saving' on which this industrial investment was based. The workforce travelled on foot or by bike, bus, tram and train. Cars – as much as possible – stayed in the garage, though the *Land* lived by building them.

Wolfe had been civic-minded but not political: active in the family forge and foundry, the Church of Scotland, thirty years in the Boy Scouts, and after 1951 seven in the Saltire Society. He had enlisted in 1942 as an eighteen-year-old and (by then an observer-pilot) wasn't demobbed until 1947. In 1952, he married into the Scots governing elite: to Arna Dinwiddie – 'Maimie' – daughter of the BBC's long-time Scottish Controller, the Rev. Melville Dinwiddie, a direct protégé of John Reith, and they had four children. He only joined the Scottish National Party in 1959, during an election which showed the Unionist Party beginning to lose its grip in Scotland. Three years later, on 6 March 1962, John Taylor, the Labour MP for West Lothian, died suddenly

---

2   Harvie Papers, National Library of Scotland: Wolfe–Harvie, 8 January 1985.

on an overseas visit, and Wolfe responded to an SNP invitation to stand in the by-election.[3]

The new Labour candidate, the young aristocrat Tam Dalyell of the Binns, protégé of that fecund ideas-man Dick Crossman, shared many of the ideas – notably cooperatively owned industry – that Wolfe was becoming associated with. But the seat was changing in 1962 and four factors would politicise its social future: the building of the Forth Road Bridge at South Queensferry (September 1958 to June 1964); the end of subsidised production of shale oil, the county's main industry since the 1850s; the start of building the Bathgate commercial vehicle plant of the British Motor Corporation; and the designation of Livingston as Scotland's fifth new town. In 1962 a backwater, with after 1956 only two railway stations (Dalmeny and Linlithgow) and three smallish towns (Bathgate, Linlithgow and Bo'ness), would quickly be 'modernised'. Upsets could not be ruled out.

All this sensitised Wolfe, a man with a feel for history and poetry, things which otherwise flashed up warning lights in the intelligent, localised and cautious SNP elite. He had been a passive member of the Scottish Covenant movement but was also steeped in the story of his own village, Torphichen, its medieval importance as a centre of the Knights Hospitallers, links with the settlement on Cairnpapple Hill that carried it back to Arthurian times, the nearness of the royal capital of Linlithgow. Wolfe writes of being in bed with flu on the eve of the by-election, reading for the first time Lewis Grassic Gibbon's *Sunset Song* of 1932 (he had earlier heard a broadcast version): an 'awakening' trope often encountered in radical as well as religious memoirs – think of the Welsh *cofiant*, literally 'memorial'. The fact that Gibbon-as-Leslie Mitchell actually took a near 'Labour Unionist' position appeared lost on him – and indeed on the mass of *A Scots' Quair*'s readers.[4]

Talking in 1982 and reviewing his own intellectual evolution, he plugged this locality into the social theories of the 1880s, notably those of the Scot

3   Wolfe, *Scotland Lives*.

4   See 'Glasgow', in Gibbon and MacDiarmid, *The Scottish Scene*, 1934.

John Stuart-Glennie (1841–1910), associated with the social anthropologists Andrew Lang and Patrick Geddes, and common ideas of the 'moral revolution' – the evolution of conscious ethical codes as Karl Jaspers's 'axial world-event' – occurring around 600BC.[5] But another link to the Scottish political past was very recent: Max Aitken, Lord Beaverbrook's visit to Torphichen, his father's old parish, early in 1962. This was, according to his biographer A. J. P. Taylor, part of an old man's romance: persuading the current (and last) girlfriend to 'marry' him in the family kirk. In a 1983 conversation Wolfe was unaware of it – but *there would be politics*. Beaverbrook's *Scottish Daily Express* was then dominant, with a circulation of 650,000; his connections (albeit fitful) to the nationalist cause went back to the 1930s and were still around in the shape of his courtier George Malcolm Thomson.

Wolfe's scratch team, their names redolent of the old Scotland, raised the SNP vote from nothing to 9,450. The Liberals, then in a revival, did poorly at 4,537 and the Conservative vote sank from 18,083 to 4,784: an augury of its long-term future. The *Express* thought so: 'An appalling result. It is a fantastic situation, beyond the comprehension of people from outside Scotland … an achievement the party leaders in London dare not ignore.'[6]

Earlier that year the Liberals had unexpectedly won the London suburban seat of Orpington, disturbing the two-party system but distracting them with hopes of southern success. A manifesto calling for a plebiscite on Scottish self-government had been circulated, signed by figures such as ex-moderators, university principals, rising trade unionists like Laurence Daly, even Tom Johnston himself, had been ignored. No longer. Wolfe took the hint. By December his thirty-year career in the Scout movement was over, and his energies were at the disposal of the party.[7]

5 Conversation with CTH at Torphichen, autumn 1982.

6 Wolfe, *Scotland Lives*, p. 10; McKechnie, *The Best-Hated Man*; *Express* cited in *Scots Independent*, 23 June 1962.

7 Conversation with A. J. P. Taylor, Open University Summer School, Norwich, August 1978; *Scots Independent*, December 1962.

AFTER THE BY-ELECTION: BUILDING A PARTY

This success was fortunate, following shortly on the accession to the party of Ian Macdonald as national organiser, determined after a good performance (18.7 per cent) at Glasgow Bridgeton, the Red Clydesider Jimmy Maxton's old seat, in November 1961. He was out to systematise the SNP's expansion. These two shots at revival came when Scotland was turning away from the Tories and towards Labour. Small-scale, folksy measures – coordinated local membership drives, a party pools system from 1965 – sustained a programme of reasonably predictable expansion.

The SNP Executive made Wolfe policy and publicity vice-chairman in 1964 and party vice-chairman shortly afterwards. His propaganda gift came out in pithy, well-structured pamphlets such as *SNP and You* (1964), in which the 'clootie dumpling' swirl – in yellow and black – perfected by the young designer Julian Gibb, represented the thistle and the St Andrew Cross. This was a distinctive, unaggressive but chalkable party icon, followed not long after by the song 'O Flower of Scotland', written by the Gordonstoun-educated Roy Williamson of the Corries folk group, with help from the 'Slaves' Chorus' in Verdi's *Aida*. After its diffusion in 1967 it soon edged 'Scots Wha Hae' out as the country's anthem.

Electoral success was more elusive, but circumstances favoured the SNP in the longer term. The Tory attempt to find a Commons seat for the former Earl of Home, Premier since May 1963, lighted not on an outer-London suburb but on the heather-clad immensities of Kinross and West Perth. The by-election gave only a lowly vote to the veteran SNP chair Arthur Donaldson on 8 November 1963, though it also saw the political re-emergence of Christopher Grieve, 'Hugh MacDiarmid', as Communist candidate, 'surprised to find there were 128 sane people in the constituency'. This was a mellow old tiger, and his equally eloquent though more tactful son Michael (1933–95), would take over the SNP's resilient ally the *Scots Independent* as editor from 1969.

The weekly's 36-year evolution presented in 1962 a useful if telegraphic summing-up of economic and social facts and debate, with the appropriate nation/party angle expressed. It might have been aimed at the 'Village Politicians' of David Wilkie's painting of the 1840s, with elements of 'Douglas Economics' (Social Credit) tacked on. Now the party oriented itself on supporting a continuing political campaign. Between 1951 and 1964 there were only two elections; between 1964 and 1979 there were four, a volatility supplemented throughout by by-elections and local elections. The SNP had to keep up.

Over this short span the rapid winding-up of imperial commitments (by two 'Gaels' Harold Macmillan and Iain MacLeod) began to activate younger Scots, with university students like Neil MacCormick and Allan Macartney setting up the Federation of Student Nationalists in 1960. Between 1960 and 1965, Ian Macdonald's systematic efforts would increase local branches from twenty-three to 165. Thereafter they shot up to 484 in 1968. The party still performed indifferently in the October 1964 general election, getting only 2.4 per cent of the Scottish vote, but this doubled in 1966 to 5 per cent and doubled again to 11.4 per cent in 1970.[8] This was accompanied by the organisation of an efficient secretariat, and a party National Assembly to discuss policy formation quarterly.

Then, following the success of Gwynfor Evans in taking Carmarthen in July 1966, there emerged a coherent 'nationalist' challenge to Labour. Its dominant Oxford elite (there were only two Scots in Wilson's 1964 Cabinet: William Ross and Tom Fraser) had formally dropped the party's traditional Scottish home rule commitment by 1958, while appeasing the veteran James Griffiths in Wales with a campaign for a Welsh Secretary of State. But look north, and at the very least new political platforms were available at a period when mass communications in print and on-screen (through BBC versus Scottish Television competition) were radically expanding. After a romantic period of pirate transmissions, Wolfe gave the SNP's first TV broadcast on 29 September 1964 during the general election campaign. It reached 1.25 million and generated 1,225 membership applications.[9]

8   Lynch, *SNP*, p. 108; for background see Christopher Harvie, *No Gods and Precious Few Heroes* (Edinburgh: Edinburgh University Press, 2016), Chapter 4.

9   Aberdeen SNP, 'SNP chronology: 1964'.

HAMILTON AND A FALSE DAWN

Afterther their hairsbreadth victory in October 1964, Harold Wilson and his Scottish Secretary William Ross had to square an orthodox but generous Scottish development programme – the *Plan for Scotland*, 1966 – competing with and soon defeated by 'great power' commitments to sterling as a reserve currency, a quandary that Ross's 'village dominie' discipline seemed calculated to inflame.[10]

The Conservatives were even more insecure after two defeats, as Tam Dalyell observed: 'Local election results may be a poor indication of a desire to change the constitution; but however ephemeral they may be, their interpretation by frightened politicians can alter policy.'[11]

But the outcome of this would be the 1967 financial crisis, in which the devaluation of sterling coincided with the remarkable victory of Winifred Ewing in the Hamilton by-election of November 1967. Previous sharp SNP gains in local elections were transformed into a Labour by-election crisis in which one of its safest seats was taken.

Ewing's success was hard-bought, and although it brought publicity, Labour pilloried her in Parliament and put her under merciless psychological pressure, which took visible toll: by 1968, the party was wrapping her in cotton wool. She needed Gwynfor Evans's support, and that of the Welsh Labour maverick Emrys Hughes, Keir Hardie's son-in-law in the House, and Wolfe's in Scotland.[12] There would be notable increases both in SNP membership – with a guessed-at 100,000 – and in party victories in local authority elections. These were qualified by inexperience among the new councillors,

---

10   Ross's *Oxford DNB* entry by his friend and spokesman William, Lord Hughes is – unusually, after the work's revision by Colin Matthew – brief, uncritical and uninformative. But he fares better than his successor Bruce Millan in James Callaghan's *Time and Chance* (Collins, 1987) where he doesn't appear at all.

11   Tam Dalyell, *Devolution: The End of Britain* (London: Cape, 1977), p. 155. No one should underestimate Tam's ability to create a rammy in an empty room. But *Devolution* has weight as argument *and* satire: on form, he was the John Galt of his day.

12   Roy, *The Invisible Spirit*, pp. 481–2. Little of her torment shows up in Ewing's cheerfully anecdotal memoir *Stop the World*.

masked for a while by the failings of the old Labour guard, then replaced by more aggression from an ambitious younger element in Labour who wanted to use the situation as their own political lever.[13] Nevertheless, the leakage of Labour voters to the SNP continued, and changed the latter's character. At the 1969 conference in Perth, Wolfe was elected as chairman of the SNP on a social-democratic, anti-nuclear ticket, defeating the veteran 'freedom first!' Arthur Donaldson by 544 votes to 238.

In response to Hamilton the new Tory leader Edward Heath played with devolution; he regarded inaction as 'politically suicidal … but privately he thought the Assembly would be at worst mischievous, at best a waste of time and money'.[14] Though Labour recovered enough to take Hamilton back in the general election of 1970, Donald Stewart captured the traditionally Labour Western Isles constituency, continuing the parliamentary toehold. He was, however, far removed from the increasingly secular central belt, and the party's new younger membership.

The Tory Secretary of State Gordon Campbell, a former diplomat, inherited the Wheatley Committee's consensual commitment to a new system of local government – nine regional and fifty-three district councils (plus three general-purpose island councils). The result would put traditional burgh and county loyalties – what Wolfe characterised as 'home rule for Bo'ness' – under sentence of death and create opaque new organisations, while the continuing political stress steadily created greater possibilities for a reimagined Scots identity.[15] Wolfe responded by exporting organisation from the SNP to create the Social and Economic Inquiry Society of Scotland, largely powered by 'free spirits' from other parties, sick of being ignored.[16]

Was there any political theory behind this, or was it a pragmatic amalgam? Wolfe wrote an autobiography, *Scotland Lives* (1973), halfway through his party career. Apart from the book *The Fraternal Society* (Random House,

13   Wilson, *SNP: The Turbulent Years 1960–1990*, Chapter 6.

14   Philip Ziegler, *Edward Heath* (London: Harper, 2010), pp. 204 & 516.

15   See the misleadingly titled but atmospheric study of Fraserburgh by Frank Bealey and John Sewel, *The Politics of Independence* (Aberdeen: Aberdeen University Press, 1981).

16   Wolfe, *Scotland Lives*, pp. 50–55.

1963) by Richard Hauser and his wife Hephzibah Menuhin, there is little in the way of an explicit intellectual background, true enough of most Scots politicians. But Wolfe's strength was that he could draw on the culture of the renaissance, then undergoing serious academic study, and ally it to spontaneous protest groups. And in this he was aided by a remarkable upsurge in interest in Scottish distinctiveness if not nationalist politics. Of the seventeen books I recommended in *Scotland and Nationalism* (1977), eight had been published since 1965. These provided nationalist activists and international academics and journalists with a convenient range of boxes to be ticked rather than nationalism as *tabula rasa* to be endlessly and exhaustingly explained.

Helpfully, Wolfe frequently wore the kilt to work, instantly attracting foreign press photographers and reporters to an unexpected warmth and intelligence. He looked well rather than self-conscious in it, and replaced that 'Rose Street' sense of grievance – 'the chip on the shoulder, growing and growing' as the English critic Rayner Heppenstall branded the MacDiarmid generation – with an open and sunny accessibility: 'The nicest man to lead a political party,' as the young Labour activist Gordon Brown commented.[17]

An effort at a darker view was made by two young London publicists, Douglas Hurd and Andrew Osmond, with their *Scotch on the Rocks* (1968). Hurd's architect uncle Robert had been an enthusiastic nationalist until his death in 1964 and the plot was based on one of these role-playing exercises beloved of Whitehall, so had credible elements and an 'instant view'.[18] In fact the novel's nationalist moderates looked more like Willie Ross and Co., and within three years Hurd and Osmond's confected violence would be drowned out by the horrors of Ulster, inept internment, and atrocities on both sides. The fact that few links were ever made between the two northern crises could be put down to the tact of the SNP leadership, going as far as the brief appearance of the socialite Colin Tennant, Lord Glenconner, as an SNP candidate, and the publicity activities of Sean Connery, in his James Bond days, 1962–71.

17   Henry Drucker and Gordon Brown, *The Politics of Nationalism and Devolution* (London: Longman, 1980), p. 11.

18   Wilson, *Pirates of the Air*.

A parallel Wolfe investment paid off handsomely. He made contact with servants of the short-lived Scottish Economic Committee in the later 1930s, notably its main economist James A. A. 'Hamish' Porteous, whose lengthy tract *The New Unionism* of 1935 presented a quasi-corporatist theory of government-driven recovery with debts to both Walter Elliot's centrist Toryism and Roosevelt's New Deal.[19] Following on from this, bright young graduates were brought into the SNP at adviser level and concentrated on issues that would subvert the current dominance of far-from-reconstructed Labour. Gordon Wilson, the unromantic but effective politician who structured much of the reorganisation, was in character almost Wolfe's opposite but had earlier doubled as an unlikely but effective 'pirate broadcaster' and complemented his ideas with well-founded research work, particularly into the growing drilling activity around the Scottish coast that would begin the oil age. Once it got under way, researchers like Donald Bain put Wilson's policy outfit so far ahead in the offshore oil-and-gas game that Foreign Office functionaries used shyly to approach the pair for briefings. Jennie Lee's Open University was set up between 1968 and 1970, becoming operational in January 1971, while projected as perhaps the last 'Great British' scheme, it had already been regionalised and in Scotland it took on almost from the first a nationalistic tone – not least because its Social Science: Politics Staff Tutor was the reliable Dr Allan Macartney.

HEATH, EUROPE AND OIL

Edward Heath had form on devolution: the first Westminster leader to concede in 1968 the possibility of a Scottish Chamber. Was his government, already conscious of the growth of unrest in Northern Ireland, following and modelled on the Catholic attempt to emulate Martin Luther King's USA civil rights campaign: from the 1963 march on Washington climaxing at Selma, Alabama, 1967? Skirmishes were looming between People's

---

19   Wolfe, *Scotland Lives*, 62 ff.; James A. A. Porteous, *The New Unionism* (London: Allen and Unwin, 1935).

Democracy and the sectarian B Specials – a type of party militia familiar from authoritarian states – which the reactions of the Stormont government and its internment policies would convert into a full-blown crisis, peculiarly bloody in 1972–73. Scotland may have escaped its lethal force because no one on either side of St George's Channel wanted to instrumentalise it – or even to know about it.

In the autumn of 1973, the veteran Labour MP for Glasgow Govan, John Rankin, died, and was replaced by yet another aged 'Ukanian' councillor, calculated to dismiss out-of-hand the report of the Kilbrandon Commission. Just off the press, this had already been rubbished by Willie Ross, who called it the 'Kill-Devolution Report'. He ran into Margo MacDonald (examined separately in this book) who won and injected another dramatic shock into the Scottish body politic, and Labour's long complacent dominance, alarming Harold Wilson. The Scottish Labour Party was brought into line, quite brutally, by the trade union barons. From then on the Commission took on its own momentum and, as Tam Dalyell recorded, 'provided an invaluable impetus to the SNP'.[20] At the same time the government would be aware that the calculations of likely income from the oilfields, up sevenfold after the Yom Kippur War of autumn 1973, were likely to be favourable to the Scots.

Heath took the UK into the EEC in 1973, and for the SNP Europe became a bogey in advance of the plebiscite of 1975, although policy towards it had earlier been positive and was subsequently quick to change to the Europhilia it now exhibits. Wolfe shared the party's scepticism, and indeed the line remained explicitly hostile until Jim Sillars launched his 'Independence in Europe' initiative in autumn 1988, after the Conservatives started to become divided, and had it endorsed by the Govan election result, and the overthrow of Thatcher.

The SNP's strong position against the expansion of the EEC, compared by Wolfe to Bismarck's expansion of Germany in 1851–70, was allowed to

---

20   Dalyell, *Devolution*, Chapter 6.

lapse as Conservative hostility to Europe increased under Thatcher.[21] Wolfe's Scandinavian loyalties and business interests obviously tuned the SNP's negativity, but, like other ambiguous rallying calls, it was allowed to fade rather than countermanded. My own experience in Baden-Württemberg from 1980 on inspired more confidence in the decentralised structures of German federalism – and Kenneth Cargill's *Scotland 2000* would essentially try to use the renascent regional economies of the Four Motors rather than either the language communities or the Brussels monolith. But this was a response to the weakness by that time of the SNP, not to its strength.

PARTY GRASSROOTS AND THE WILDERNESS YEARS

The problem that immediately confronted the grassroots after 1974 was the disjunction between them and the MPs. Wolfe's failure to reach Westminster in October 1974 proved fatal to his own career ambitions as the solidarity of the parliamentary group, representing generally conservative rural Scotland, clashed with ex-Labour–SNP local members afflicted with the impact of London austerity in the lowland and coalfield areas. Much of the initiative was taken by the radical left.

Concessions to Labour to finesse the qualified autonomy offered by the 1977 Government of Scotland Bill weakened the SNP's ability to bash Westminster in the longer term. Oxbridge hierarchs on the right and the brothers on the left shrank Wolfe's room for manoeuvre and after the failure of the Scottish Labour Party in 1976–79 he was faced within the SNP by the dynamism of Jim Sillars, and outside it by activists emboldened by a more radical and sometimes militant left political activism.

The early and mid-1980s was to see the SNP in the grip of a kind of nervous breakdown 'due to internal conflicts, electoral irrelevance and organisational

---

21   Wolfe, speech at Perth SNP conference, 1975; and see Valeria Tarditi, 'The Scottish National Party's changing attitude towards the European Union', Scotland Europa Institute, Working Paper No. 112; EPERN Working Paper No. 22.

decline'. Its polling figures generally put it back at 1960s levels.[22] The initiative shifted first to Labour radical left-wingers, then to moderates, and dissidents who, through the Social Democratic Party, strengthened the Liberal centre. The SNP's vote was only partially recovering by the end of the decade when Alex Salmond, newly elected in 1987 for Banff and Buchan, became its leader. Brought up in Linlithgow, he had been influenced by Wolfe as the local chief of the party, for instance in devising lively advisory bodies, but had a cutting edge that Wolfe, now in his mid-sixties and pensive rather than prolific, inevitably lacked.[23]

During this period we had from 1981 to 1984 a lengthy correspondence, now lodged in my papers in the National Library, in which Wolfe remarked: 'It's only in the last twenty years, and in particular the last two, that there has been a substantial support for considering Scotland as a political entity, rather than a national entity, or alongside the latter.'

I responded drawing heavily on the low-key military strategy of 'indirect approach' associated with B. H. Liddell Hart:

> Real success seems to come from dedicated, competent organisers [with] a strategy of meeting definite objectives – producing a bibliography, improving a bus or rail service ... and because they are run mostly by consensus among the members and recognition of the authority that comes from reliability and sheer hard work. We have to envisage our national movement in terms of a network of such organisations which can cross-fertilise with politics, and whose individual enterprises can build up a momentum of success which will sustain political organisation ... equivalent to light attacks on an extended front, to confuse and overextend opponents, and probe the weaknesses of their defences, while we build up our strength.[24]

The Poetry Library campaign, although fricative and significant in giving

---

22   Lynch, p. 161.

23   Lynch, pp. 206–7.

24   Allan Massie, *The Thistle and the Rose* (London: John Murray, *Cencrastus* magazine, 1982), reprinted in Harvie, *Travelling Scot* (Argyll, 2002), pp. 174–84.

a cultural-nationalist slant to the voluntary sector – something that Salmond was always careful to pay attention to – was a retirees operation. In this situation Wolfe's role was initially catastrophic. Retiring from the SNP chair in 1979, he was elected party president in 1980 and tried to mediate between Sillars's 'republican-socialist' 79 Group and the Ewingite centre-right. But he compromised himself with anti-Catholic comments on the occasion of Pope John Paul's visit to Glasgow in late 1982 and resigned.

Other ventures proved more conducive to long-term dividend. Tessa Ransford started the Library project when the cause of autonomy was flat on the floor. It took some of its inspiration from the Welsh recovery from an even worse St David's Day. When Gwynfor Evans talked of a Gandhi-style fast unto death to gain the promised/withheld S4C Welsh TV channel, someone mocked up the myth of two Scottish bards threatening to drink themselves to death in the Gaelic cause. Then, with tact and diplomacy – never underestimate a chartered accountant-politician-poet, allied to a nurse with a mission – Scotland had within months a mind-expanding campaign running its own velvet revolution.

'By leaves (broadly defined) we live': Ransford picked up Patrick Geddes's *slogan* (the right Gaelic word) and added to it her notion of a 'force-field'. This sounded on the mystical side but in fact corresponded to a culture borne by a variety of media 'latticing' a landscape when embodied in eyescanned artefacts from Ordnance Survey maps to bus timetables, which poetry's imaginative force could spring together out of subconscious memory.

> But in times of crisis, when attitudes have to be reassessed, new ways of living together tried out; when power, aggression, status and wealth-seeking are clearly leading the world to destruction, poetry will be valued by more and more people as they begin to relate to their own inner being and to connect with the human centre in others, believing in, building and above all envisioning an ever new and continuing world.[25]

---

25   Wolfe and Tessa Ransford, Poetry Library Appeal leaflet, 29 November 1983.

It clicked with Raymond Williams's principle, 'by measuring the distance, we come home', and, indeed, heralded the opening of the first Library in 1984. Scottish poetry, then and subsequently, travelled, amused enthralled, as far off as *Mitteleuropa*... and still mirrored some of the ideas that Wolfe had spun out of Torphichen a quarter-century before.

The rest of the story was less encouraging. Wolfe returned to Chieftain Industries and the production of a new type of heat-pump as low-energy space heating, but in 1985 his firm was hit by the death on 5 April 1985 – in circumstances never satisfactorily explained – of his co-director, the veteran nationalist Willie McRae. On 13 August 1985, Chieftain's young engineer Angus MacLeod died in a car crash, and Wolfe had to file for bankruptcy; one of a number of collateral casualties of the fall of British Leyland Bathgate. So, what had he actually achieved?

Wolfe was reflective about this. Over a decade previous reflecting on his contribution to the party, and writing just before its breakthrough in the 1974 elections, he saw the nationalists as made of powerful qualities:

> In my eleven years' stent, I have seen Scotland's national party grow and develop. It has not just become larger, it has been like the steel under the hammer. As steel is heated, then forged, then heated again and hammered again in a repetitive process, it is refined and shaped and hardened for exacting and testing work. So it is with the Scottish National Party, heated in the total cultural heritage of Scotland, both historic and current.[26]

As a political organiser from a business background, but also as an army pilot and thus a technologised serviceman, and a youth and culture activist, Wolfe brought a breadth of vision and personal resilience to a party perhaps in 1962 content with a marginal social 'gardening' role in a highly structured, left-leaning country. Only with the establishment of the Scottish Parliament in 1999 would the SNP have a platform and an electoral system that guaranteed

---

26   Wolfe, *Scotland Lives*, p. 167.

a political presence, which it has made much of. But by the new century this pragmatic eye for shaping policy to tap current opportunities, and an awareness of the key importance of coordinating purpose with design and publicity, would be dwarfed by the sheer scale of economic change that Scotland had gone through: from the decline and decimation of traditional industries, to remaking of employment and work.

A personal memory from my own family history might serve as epilogue. Armadale's other and larger foundry, the Atlas, was owned by my father's uncle by marriage James Watt. His son George Harvie-Watt (1903–89) was also a politician, like Wolfe attending Bathgate Academy and George Watson's. He went to London, became a barrister and territorial Brigadier, and in 1937 was elected Tory MP for Richmond, which he represented for the next twenty-two years. Because he followed Chamberlain, Churchill made him his parliamentary private secretary in May 1940, to provide an inside view from the party which had never trusted him.

Harvie-Watt was rewarded with a baronetcy and became head of Consolidated Goldfields. He rode the surge of traditional high politics and London finance where there might instead have been a local career in industry and public banking, within a distinctive regional economic policy. Such choices seem to have distorted Scottish bourgeois society in a way that choked off Baden-Württemberg-style reconstruction, achieved through its *mittelstand*. Sir George's connections with Scotland stopped at his villa in Elie and the Royal and Ancient. But even his contemporary Katherine, Lady Elliot, born a Tennant, and, as widow of the remarkable Conservative centrist, far to Harvie-Watt's left, 'hadn't visited Glasgow in years'.

Wolfe's actively political life in fact paralleled the industrial swansong of West Lothian, the British Leyland truck plant at nearby Bathgate. Opened in 1964, it saw only two decades. Tom Devine wrote that:

> …the forces which killed the development were not only national but global
> in scale. The steep fall in world oil prices following the Yom Kippur war
> in the Middle East triggered the worst economic recession since the 1930s.

> It coincided with the election of a Conservative government under Margaret Thatcher whose priorities were not any longer the maintenance of full employment but the control of inflation and reform of public finances.[27]

Not quite. Yom Kippur was autumn 1973, and the price of oil *went up* sevenfold. Thatcher's 'benefit' from the later Iran–Iraq War (1980–88) was that the pound sterling, its exchange-rate *rising* to nearly five Deutschmarks, cut UK exports, and Scottish manufacturing, by 20 per cent.

'A man runnin for his life woundnae notice it.' As my Huntly granny would say. There wasn't much of a repayment, and over time London's 'commercial historians' made it less and less. Andrew Roberts's *History of the English-Speaking Peoples since 1900* (Weidenfeld, 2006, 736 pages) contains one reference to Scotland; Simon Schama's *The Fate of Empire* (Bodley Head, 2009, 447 pages) has ten, though it has a cover picture of the *Queen Mary* being launched at Clydebank in 1935.

Coming out of a memorable lunch in 1983 (from Bell's Bar to the Royal Bengal) with two German postgrads (Ursula Kimpel and Helmut Schroeder, both still active), Angus Calder and Hamish Henderson, a slightly rueful Wolfe remark has always stuck: 'Sometimes, Chris, I think that the things that will make an independent Scotland marvellous are precisely those that will prevent us ever getting there.' But there's also 'Being Scots and loving the world', the title of a book he never wrote, which fetches up against a Whittier poem from an old Emrys Hughes pamphlet on Keir Hardie: the matrix is there.

> Others shall sing the song,
> Others shall right the wrong –
> Finish what I begin
> And what I fail of, win.

---

27   T. M. Devine, 'Preface', *Bathgate Once More: The Story of the BMC/Leyland Truck and Tractor Plant, 1961–1986* (Edinburgh: WEA, 2012), pp. i–ii.

CHAPTER 14

GORDON WILSON

PETER LYNCH

Gordon Wilson joined the SNP in the 1950s and was involved with 'Radio Free Scotland', a pirate radio station that broadcasted nationalist messages in the 1960s. A solicitor by training, he was National Secretary of the party from 1964–71, contributing to organisational and campaigning successes, notably the groundwork for 'It's Scotland's Oil'. MP for Dundee East from February 1974 to 1987, Wilson became chairman in 1979, following the failed devolution referendum and the loss of nine of the SNP's eleven MPs. This saw a period of bitter internal conflicts, with Wilson as leader aiming to keep the party together. The party's fortunes slowly rose as the decade wore on and the re-emergence of the self-government question. Wilson may have represented an older, more conservative guard in the party by the end of his leadership, but he adroitly steered the party through many difficult circumstances.

. . .

INTRODUCTION

Gordon Wilson's leadership of the SNP took place during one of the most difficult periods in the party's history – and it would not be inaccurate to depict him as a civil war leader of the party during his first four years as leader. He had been prominent in the party when it grew rapidly in the 1960s, then was elected MP for Dundee East during its second growth phase in the 1970s. However, he became leader after the bubble had burst comprehensively with the failure of the Scottish devolution referendum of 1 March 1979 and the SNP's heavy losses at the subsequent general election, so he did not inherit a party in good health. Indeed, an accumulation of events from 1974 onwards created a series of crises within the party that dominated the early part of Wilson's term as leader – these involved internal problems such as indirect leadership challenges, internecine factional conflict, lack of party resources and plunging membership levels, alongside external problems of policy and positioning, electoral attractiveness and competition from the newly formed Social Democratic Party. In short, the political environment for Wilson's premiership was overwhelmingly negative, with serious obstacles at every turn and substantial constraints on Wilson's ability to meet the challenges of the role. As one of only two SNP MPs at Westminster, Wilson also faced the personal challenges of leadership limited by time, travel and lack of staff support while operating as a constituency MP and representative in the House of Commons without the resources of a major party leader. And, as the SNP was most definitely a non-parliamentary party at this time, the absences in London were problematic.

Wilson's political lifespan also largely mirrors that of the contemporary SNP. He joined in the 1950s, when the party was a tiny force in terms of membership, local organisation and electoral presence, became an office-bearer as the party grew in the 1960s and then an MP in 1974 before becoming leader in 1979. In rising to the top of the party, he was able to recognise the time limits on leadership and office within the SNP – standing down as national secretary and then as leader at around ten-year intervals. He was keenly aware that a decade in post was more than enough, through his own experience as well as watching the leaderships of Arthur Donaldson and Billy Wolfe. In Wilson's view staying too long in office led to exhaustion, autocratic decision-making and simply running out of ideas.[1] Resigning as leader in 1990 did not involve an exit from politics. Wilson stood as a candidate at the 1999 European elections and, though he did not seek election during the devolution

---

1   Scottish Political Archive [hereafter SPA] 760: interview with Gordon Wilson.

period, he remained politically active campaigning and writing about the party, its goals and strategies. In recent years, Gordon Wilson completed a number of semi-autobiographical books on his time in the SNP. One covered his early years in the party in the 1950s to early 1960s, when he was instrumental in running the pirate radio station Radio Free Scotland.[2] The second covered his period as a senior office-bearer in the party – including his period as leader.[3] The third covered the development of the SNP after Wilson was leader and the years leading up to, during and after the independence referendum of 2014.[4] This level of biographical activity was accompanied by involvement in creating a think tank with former MP and deputy leader Jim Sillars – Options for Scotland – and playing a role in the Yes campaign during and following the independence referendum.

JOINING UP AND MOVING UP

Wilson joined the SNP at Edinburgh University in the 1950s, where there was an active nationalist club. He was attracted by its anti-colonialism and attitudes to the British Empire,[5] and also in reaction to the siting of a rocket range on South Uist in the Western Isles and its effect on the Gaelic language.[6] He also had a long career in the party before being elected as a full-time politician and before he became leader in 1979. He was a solicitor before and after serving as an MP. His early career in the SNP revolved around participating in running the pirate radio station Radio Free Scotland (RFS), which existed from 1956 to the early 1970s. The station operated intermittently after BBC services stopped broadcasting at 11 p.m. each evening, with some broadcasts coming from Wilson's flat in Edinburgh. In essence, RFS would gatecrash the BBC's TV wavelength when BBC programmes stopped at night to feature news, politics

---

2   Wilson, *Pirates of the Air*.

3   Wilson, *SNP: The Turbulent Years 1960–1990*.

4   Gordon Wilson, *Scotland: The Battle for Independence 2014* (Stirling: Scots Independent, 2015).

5   SPA 760: interview with Gordon Wilson.

6   Kemp, *The Hollow Drum*, p. 99.

and culture with a nationalist slant. As the SNP was locked out of news coverage and access to party political broadcasts, this was one of the few media sources the party could employ, and its activities had the added benefit of generating newspaper coverage for the station and its cause.[7] Out of Wilson the rule-breaker emerged Wilson the rule-maker. Wilson was assistant national secretary of the SNP from 1963 to 1964 – an appointed position on the recommendation of the national secretary – and then national secretary from 1964 to 1971 (where he 'ran the SNP by paper') and executive vice-chairman from 1972 to 1973, when he helped design and launch the SNP's 'It's Scotland's Oil' campaign. His period as assistant national secretary was an important one, as he was given the task of preparing a reorganisation of the party's structures to make it a more effective electoral machine. Wilson's reorganisation created structures that lasted over forty years and were only significantly altered after devolution in 1999. Wilson's review took only three weeks to complete and centred around problems with party bodies like the National Executive, which was overloaded to the point of being dysfunctional, and the National Council and a lack of policy-making in the party as a whole. After 1964, Wilson was responsible for administering the new structures as national secretary in a period in which the SNP mushroomed dramatically as a political force – with thousands of new members and hundreds of new branches across Scotland. He held this post until 1971, when he was elected vice-chairman and became responsible for the oil campaign – arguably the most effective in the SNP's history – and then served as senior vice-chairman (effectively deputy leader) from 1973 to 1974. His prominence saw him chosen as the SNP candidate for the Dundee East by-election in 1973[8] – where oil was an issue – and then elected for the seat in February 1974 with nearly 40 per cent of the vote.[9] He was to hold this seat until 1987. His Westminster career involved roles as deputy group leader, oil and energy spokesperson and joint spokesperson

---

7   Wilson, *Pirates of the Air*.

8   Wilson came second to Labour with 30.1 per cent. The by-election was caused by the resignation of George Thomson, who became one of the UK's first European Commissioners.

9   This situation developed even though Wilson had sought to take a step back from active politics at this time.

on devolution. He was elected SNP leader in September 1979 and remained in office until September 1990: meaning acting as leader for three years when not a full-time politician and aware that he could be challenged at any time as leader, something that became a concern with the rise of Alex Salmond in the mid-1980s, as well as that of Jim Sillars later in the decade.

PARTY LEADERSHIP

For Gordon Wilson, the results would be very limited – he was unable to craft an election-winning strategy. Wilson was not leader in 1979 when the party lost nine of its eleven MPs and 13.1 per cent of its support from the high point of October 1974. He was elected to the leadership after the failed devolution referendum of 1 March 1979 and the general election of 3 May. Both of these events – and especially the referendum – were to create major problems for Wilson in all areas of his leadership that persisted throughout his term in office. He was leader in 1983 when the party's vote share dropped further to 11.8 per cent (-5.5 per cent of support in 1979) and in 1987, when vote share rose slightly to 14.1 per cent (+2.3 per cent) but the SNP lost two seats, including the leader's own seat in Dundee East, while winning back three former seats to give it a net gain of +1. Of course, Clarke's leadership measure only involves general elections. Wilson's electoral performance was certainly limited compared to the possibilities of the post-1999 period of devolved elections, but he did preside over modest recoveries in SNP support at local authority and European elections in this period. In essence, Wilson brought the SNP back from the electoral brink to modest levels of competitiveness.

For example, at local elections, Wilson's leadership saw initial declines in electoral support, followed by recoveries. Support for the SNP at the 1980 district elections fell to 15.5 per cent (down from 24.2 per cent in 1977) and in 1984 party performance was even lower at 11.7 per cent. Support only turned the corner in 1988, when the SNP won 21.3 per cent and 113 council seats. Support for the party followed a similar pattern at regional council elections – 13.4 per cent in 1982 (down from 20.9 per cent in 1978) and up to 18.2 per cent in 1986 before settling at 21.8 per cent in 1990. At European elections, the SNP fared reasonably well – with 17.8 per cent in 1984 and 25.6 per cent in 1989. Westminster by-elections brought very mixed fortunes during Wilson's leadership. A decent performance in Glasgow Central in 1980, with a good second place to Labour on 26.3 per cent, was followed by the Glasgow Hillhead by-election of March 1982 and the meteoric rise of the SDP as Roy Jenkins won the seat with 33.4 per cent and the SNP's support remained fairly static in fourth place at 11.3 per cent. Hillhead was a sign of things to come and helped propel the Alliance and then the Liberal Democrats to succeed in a number of seats in Scotland over the next two decades. The Coatbridge and Airdrie by-election three months later saw the SNP far behind Labour and the Conservatives with 10.5 per cent, though there was a slightly stronger result in Glasgow Queen's Park in December 1982 on 20 per cent. There were no Scottish by-elections in the 1983–87 parliament, but two significant ones for the SNP after the 1987 general election. The SNP's Jim Sillars triumphed at the Glasgow Govan by-election in November 1988, with 48.8 per cent of the vote, while the party increased its vote share in Glasgow Central in June 1989 to 30.2 per cent: which did not turn out to be a second Govan, despite a similar candidate and approach. Notably, these results occurred under Wilson's leadership, but when he was no longer an MP and full-time leader.

PARTY MANAGEMENT

For Gordon Wilson, issues of party management were the dominant problem of the first half of his leadership and had primacy over everything else: vision, election-winning strategy, campaigning and party goals. They were connected with every other role and function of leadership and effectively undermined his tenure in office until after 1983. They were so deep and all-encompassing that they crowded out the space and time to re-establish the SNP after the double election defeat of 1979 – it was impossible to move the party into positive campaigning territory because of the extent of internal conflicts. Wilson was certainly not in control of the party in this period and not in control of events around him either. He was often unable to influence let alone control leading party institutions such as the National Executive Committee and National Council, nor the annual national conference. These institutions were frequent battlegrounds between different groups within the SNP for a protracted period from 1979 to 1983. His efforts were frequently undermined by people in these institutions and, while never challenged directly as leader – which could have occurred on an annual basis under party rules – he could be undermined through annual elections to these institutions so that lots of party decisions on strategy and direction could be seen as proxy leadership challenges. While the party was engaged in a civil war, Wilson's position was an uncomfortable one, being frequently undermined by colleagues, even those who shared his views. Wilson's depiction of his role during this period is instructive, as he sought to reform the post-1979 SNP and return it to electability. Part of this involved trying to reconcile the various factions within the party and get them to work together. As Wilson put it himself, 'I was the conductor of a very discordant band hoping that it would learn to play in tune.'[10]

The internal problems Wilson faced were manifold. They were a consequence of the party's attitude and actions towards devolution from 1974 to 1979, its strategy at the referendum and the 1979 general election, the functioning of the SNP parliamentary group at Westminster, divisions between the MPs in London and the National Executive back in Edinburgh as well as the role of new factions within the party with different views on strategy and ideology. All of these factors fed internal conflict as well as recriminations within the party about its direction and outcomes. The environment also produced factionalism within the SNP, in a very formal way, with the establishment of the 79 Group. This left-wing group had its own membership lists, publicity and activism within SNP branches. It ran formal slates of candidates for internal elections and some of its positions and actions antagonised moderates within the SNP. However, what made the 79 Group position more problematic

---

10   Wilson, *SNP: The Turbulent Years 1960–1990*, p. 210.

was the complexity of the party's internal politics at the time. Not only were there other, more moderate left-wingers in the SNP who didn't associate with the 79 Group – some had joined two decades before, others had migrated recently from the Scottish Labour Party with Jim Sillars – but there were different types of moderates ranged against it, as well as the existence of Siol nan Gaidheal, a group of ultranationalists who appeared at SNP events in semi-military formats. In short, the party leader did not face one faction from 1979 to 1983 but a more complex set of internal factors, and resolving them was difficult. For instance, action against Siol nan Gaidheal was opposed by some to protect the 79 Group – despite the huge differences between the two organisations. At the same time, the entrance of a major political figure such as Jim Sillars into the SNP led to suspicions about his leadership ambitions – with campaign initiatives like the Scottish Resistance of 1981 interpreted as leadership challenges.[11]

The 79 Group was the biggest challenge Wilson faced as leader, not least as it was interwoven with fundamental questions about strategy, positioning and personalities. His strategy was not to try to defeat them – not least as it contained too many talented figures who would be central to the SNP's future. Rather, Wilson sought to wear them down and gradually recruit them into more fruitful roles within the SNP. However, Wilson's gradualist attempts were frustrated by some of the 79 Group's own actions, as well as those of leading figures who might have been his allies. For example, a new faction – the Campaign for Nationalism – was created at the 1982 party conference in Ayr to challenge the 79 Group, and its appearance effectively ruined Wilson's strategy.[12] In response, Wilson had to produce a topical resolution at the party conference to ban all internal groups – an measure that succeeded but did not end divisions within the SNP. Gradually the groups disbanded, but not without a fight, with appeals and expulsions ending in a special National Council in April 1983 – followed quickly by a general election in

---

11   Wilson and Sillars were later to become allies, cooperating in a range of SNP and non-SNP initiatives.

12   Wilson, *SNP: The Turbulent Years 1960–1990*, p. 213.

June, at which the SNP struggled badly. Four years of internal conflict, with
a lot of it concentrated in the last months of 1983, saw the SNP slump to
11.8 per cent at the election, while its new moderate rival, the SDP–Liberal
Alliance, won 24.5 per cent.

The 1983 general election was something of a watershed for a divided SNP.
Constant in-fighting had contributed to electoral decline, but the party then
entered a period of slow recovery as Wilson tried to move the party to adopt
more moderate positions and policies. Internal conflict receded though still
remained strong, with distrust and occasional problems that were throwbacks
to the post-1979 period. Wilson sought to reposition the party on major issues
– building consensus across the various factions and tendencies – and also
appointed a Commission of Inquiry 1983–85 to look into party organisation
and structure. It led to a special conference in 1985 that made minor reforms
to party organisation, but the real gain was in getting leading party figures to
work with each other and focus on organisational and electoral questions.
The 1983–87 period was one of relative peace within the party, though the
period after the 1987 election was more challenging. The SNP sought to
exploit Labour's difficulties over the doomsday scenario in which Labour
was the largest party in Scotland but the Conservatives had a majority over
the UK as a whole, its lack of effectiveness at Westminster, lack of progress
on devolution as well as policies like the poll tax/community charge. Managing the party over the poll tax issue was difficult – some within the party
sought radical action in the shape of non-payment but it raised questions
about legal action against the party and its members. Similarly, progress on
the devolution issue involved participation in the new Scottish Constitutional
Convention, albeit in a convention Labour would dominate and completely
sideline the independence issue.[13] The convention issue was problematic
because a form of convention had been one of Wilson's initiatives since 1980

---

13   In discussions on participation in the SCC, Labour's Donald Dewar made it clear that the convention
      would not discuss independence and that the SNP would need to agree to whatever the SCC pro-
      posed on devolution and to campaign for it too: thus neutralising the SNP and its independence cause.
      See SPA 760: interview with Gordon Wilson.

and because the party was divided on the issue in another echo of the 1979 devolution referendum. The SNP was riding high in the opinion polls following the Glasgow Govan by-election and was conscious of seeing its new popularity disappear through involvement in a Labour-controlled body. The National Executive Committee had to create a small sub-group to negotiate a compromise position on the issue to put before the National Council and the debate over strategy was fraught. Each week, Wilson would receive letters from party members alternately supporting SNP withdrawal from the convention or predicting disaster if the SNP were not part of it.[14] In any case, withdrawal was supported at the National Council, despite a bad-tempered debate. However, there was some disagreement over the timing of withdrawal – which occurred before the European elections and the Glasgow Central by-election and helped Labour campaign against an isolationist SNP that didn't want to work with others to create a Scottish Parliament.

CAMPAIGNING

As party leader, Wilson was at the forefront of SNP election campaigns from 1979 to 1990, though his role declined somewhat after losing his Westminster seat at the 1987 general election. In campaigning terms, he had come to prominence as the director of the SNP's oil campaign in the early 1970s. This campaign was probably the most successful in the SNP's pre-devolution history, with economic and policy support for Wilson from the party's research officer Donald Bain, along with a range of publicity, slogans and graphics. The campaign succeeded because it married the economics of independence to the issue of self-government. It gave the party a key issue that struck a chord with voters and provided the SNP with a substantial media profile ahead of the 1974 general election. The manner in which the oil campaign was sidelined after 1974 rankled with Wilson, and he was central to relaunching it in 1980, focused on Mrs Thatcher and unemployment.

14   SPA 760: interview with Gordon Wilson.

However, that second campaign was nowhere as effective as the first – the SNP had lost focus and momentum – and it is striking that Wilson's biggest campaigning impact as a politician came before he was leader.

Even before he became an MP and leader, Wilson was prominent as an SNP representative in the media. He was frequently the SNP's face on political TV programmes, present at campaign and manifesto launches and in front-line campaigning at all types of elections. What this meant was that he was a highly experienced broadcaster and campaigner before he became leader in 1979. He was also a leader who recognised the need for campaign topics supported by different parts of the SNP – hence the compromise campaigning deals he negotiated over issues like the New Deal and Scottish resistance campaigns in 1981, opposition to nuclear dumping and the poll tax non-payment campaign: all which had to be squared with different groups in party. However, projecting these campaign themes in a hugely divided party was ineffective.

Finally, it is worthwhile remembering that Wilson was an MP and, in 1979–87, part of a two-person group while leader. Time needed to be divided between his Dundee constituency,[15] Scotland and Westminster and, as leader and one of two MPs, he had a huge number of constituency and policy issues to pursue at Westminster, meaning covering multiple ministerial portfolios, raising issues, contributing to debates and trying to initiate legislation. Despite the constraints of leadership and geographical distance, Wilson was an active parliamentarian in terms of speeches, parliamentary debates and occasional attempts to make laws like changes to rules over cold climate payments to Scottish residents (several attempts were made by Wilson to amend this legislation),[16] changes to tenancy arrangements,[17] as well as seeking Scottish control of company mergers.[18] He frequently combined with his colleague

---

15   For example, in 1983, Wilson had to deal with local issues such as the redundancies at the Timex factory in Dundee, the development of Dundee airport, hospital admissions to Tayside Health Board and the condition of Claypotts Castle, among others.

16   See, for example, Social Security (Cold Climate Allowance) Amendment, Hansard, 25 January 1984, Vol. 52, cc.929–31.

17   Leasehold (Scotland), Hansard, 15 December 1983, Vol. 50, c.1190.

18   Control of Mergers (Scotland), Hansard, 5 March 1987, Vol. 111, c.1050.

Donald Stewart and the Plaid Cymru MPs to pursue motions in the House, as well as with opposition members from Labour and the Liberals over issues like higher education, housing, nuclear power, public sector industries, etc. All of this is very far from what you see from a party leader from one of the main parties, with their Cabinets, Prime Minister's Questions, special advisers, etc., with Wilson having to pursue all kinds of issues, large and small.

PARTY VISION

As leader, Wilson sought to reshape the SNP into a more moderate, focused and disciplined party, less isolated from the mainstream on policy and on participation in the political system with its opponents. All of this was impossible until the civil war ended. Before then, the party was consumed by internal disputes that dominated its political activity so that agreeing a new vision and projecting it outwards was next to impossible. For the first four years of his leadership, ideas and vision were obstructed by internal feuding over devolution, independence and ideological positioning, all of which made it difficult for Wilson to move the party forwards. Nonetheless, the political landscape after 1979 was challenging, but not without opportunities. Scottish devolution had been defeated by the technical requirements of the 40 per cent rule,[19] but there had actually been a narrow Yes vote in favour of self-government. The new Conservative government moved to the right and was to become deeply unpopular in Scotland. Labour moved to the left and became unelectable at the UK level. These factors created political space for the SNP to make some progress with its position on self-government as well as advance its social democratic policy stances. However, the party's civil war and internal focus made it impossible for Wilson to exploit these changed conditions. Indeed, in Wilson's view, the internal conflict happened at exactly the wrong time – the SNP became completely internally focused

---

19   Under the terms of the Scotland Act 1978, 40 per cent of the eligible electorate as well as a majority of those voting were required before devolution would be implemented.

just when Thatcherism took hold over Scotland and required strong opposition that the SNP did not provide.[20]

On devolution, the party moved towards fundamentalism in internal elections at the party conference in 1979 and took more hard-line stances over independence – any reconciliation with devolution would have to wait as members rejected gradualism for a time: the party was angry with itself and not listening.[21] It took Wilson four attempts to move the SNP to adopt a more constructive stance on devolution – to seek cross-party support for an elected constitutional convention, which would have put pressure on Labour over home rule. He argued for this issue in 1980, in 1982, on general election night in 1983 and at party conference in 1983 – putting forward early versions of the doomsday scenario, by which Scotland voted against the Conservatives but was rewarded with a Conservative government delivered by votes in England. It was an argument about a democratic deficit that would be cured by devolution, but it took time for the SNP to come to terms with this as it remained angry with itself over devolution and the 1979 referendum (it struggled with this in the second half of Wilson's leadership too). Wilson finally moved the party towards a less obstructive attitude to devolution at party conference in 1983, though here conference still rejected the idea of an elected constitutional convention,[22] and Wilson's success relied upon the manner in which the amendment was written up in the conference minutes:[23] a very technical victory.

This change was part of three different initiatives to make the party more electable and less separatist and isolationist in Wilson's view.[24] Alongside a more moderate stance on devolution, Wilson sought to move the party to support Scottish membership of the EU and NATO. The EU change succeeded, with more positive positions in 1983, 1984 and 1988 as the party came to support independence in Europe and relaunched the party's independence

20   Wilson, *SNP: The Turbulent Years 1960–1990*, p. 202.

21   Lynch, *SNP: The History of the Scottish National Party*, p. 176.

22   Wilson, *SNP: The Turbulent Years 1960–1990*, p. 226.

23   SPA 760: interview with Gordon Wilson.

24   Wilson, *SNP: The Turbulent Years 1960–1990*, p. 226.

goal within a broader European framework, in a period in which Europe was growing and popular through the work of the Commission President Jacques Delors and the 1992 programme to create the single market. The European policy change was aided by consensus within the SNP and Jim Sillars's role in promoting the new policy. However, Wilson did not have any luck with moving the SNP towards reconciliation with NATO and the party position on this issue only fundamentally changed in 2013, in preparation for the independence referendum of 2014. By pushing these issues forward publicly at conference, Wilson adopted a high-risk strategy. He succeeded with two of the three issues but he had failed overall and was aware that his resignation as leader was likely, as his credibility would have been shredded in the party and the media.[25] Who took over the leadership from there was not at all obvious.

Even after peace had broken out between the different strands of the SNP, the issue of devolution and engagement with UK politics remained a toxic mix. For example, in the lead-up to the 1987 general election, Wilson promoted the idea of a formal pact with Plaid Cymru. Wilson pursued this goal in an attempt to make the SNP relevant at the Westminster election – which was to prove a persistent challenge for party leaders until 2015. For Wilson, the pact was intended to generate some positive publicity and raise the profile and possibilities of the two parties should there be a close electoral outcome in 1987: an early version of the progressive alliance that Salmond advanced in 2010 and Sturgeon proposed in 2015. It was also intended to anchor the SNP on the centre-left and put pressure on Labour after the 1987 election – would a minority Labour government seek an alliance with the nationalists or allow the Conservatives back into power?[26] Moreover, what opposition would Labour in Scotland offer if the Tories were re-elected on English votes? However, some within the party were opposed to this modest initiative – both at the NEC and at party conference – concerned that the pact would see

---

25   Ibid.

26   This initiative may have come too early for some in the SNP. The same approach was taken in 2015 with Plaid and the Greens, with devastating effects on Labour in Scotland and across Britain – just ask Ed Miliband.

the SNP support a Unionist government at Westminster.[27] This was another clear reflection of the party's experience from 1974 to 1979 over devolution: its desire for political purity and its nervousness about partisan cooperation.

ACHIEVEMENT OF PARTY GOALS AND OBJECTIVES

G ordon Wilson didn't achieve independence – the party's fundamental political goal – but he did move the SNP away from the precipice and into recovery mode. First, his style of leadership involved ensuring the SNP remained focused on independence – though this often faced challenges within the SNP and the wider political system. Wilson's goal as leader was to take the lead on constitutional issues and argue for independence in order to drag the voters and the other political parties towards independence rather than to minimal devolution.[28] In part, this was a response to what he saw had happened in the 1970s, when the SNP were diverted from focusing on independence and oil – which were intimately related – to devolution during the interminable parliamentary debates and referendum from 1974 to 1979. Second, Wilson's leadership was one of survival and repositioning for the SNP, though this involved some changes in direction. For example, he repositioned a reluctant SNP on devolution from 1980 to 1984 and then on the European Union. These were not one-off changes, but gradual steps that took several attempts to succeed – four attempts to get a more positive position on devolution and three on Europe. Even then, following the success of the Independence in Europe policy and SNP electoral success in 1987–88, Wilson had to move the party towards devolution hostility over the party's participation in the Scottish Constitutional Convention in early 1989, though this position did have substantial support within the SNP. Third, in terms of survival and growth, Wilson's record moved from negative to positive over the lifespan of his leadership. If the question is, did Wilson leave the SNP in

---

27   Wilson, *SNP: The Turbulent Years 1960–1990*, p. 230.

28   SPA 760: interview with Gordon Wilson.

better state than he found it? Then the answer is yes. After initial crises from 1979 to 1983 in relation to electoral support, representation, members and money, the party began to recover to modest levels of support and stability.[29]

CONCLUSION

The first four years of Gordon Wilson's leadership were overwhelmingly negative for both him and the party. He was left to manage a divided party at a time of electoral and organisational decline. He wasn't in control of the party or events and struggled to reshape the SNP. In short, he was leader of a party that did not want to be led. Party crisis management was the dominant focus of Wilson's leadership from 1979 to 1983 and it was mostly unsuccessful until after the conclusion of hostilities at the 1983 general election. Party reality cast a shadow over outlining a vision for the SNP, campaigning, advancing the party's goals and developing an election-winning strategy. From 1983, though, once peace had broken out to a substantial degree, Wilson was able to slowly build consensus within the leadership group and support in the wider party for modest initiatives to improve its electability on issues like devolution and Europe. This was also the period in which the SNP settled on its ideological identity, with a consistent left-of-centre focus on policy and positioning that has continued ever since. In electoral terms, Wilson's leadership success was a very modest one. He presided over the decline of 1983 and then the slight rise in 1987, which also saw him lose his seat at Westminster. However, this stood alongside improved performances at district and regional elections, as well as the Glasgow Govan by-election victory of November 1988 and the rise in support at the 1989 European election. By the time he stood aside in 1990, the health of the party at all levels was improved.

29   Lynch, *SNP: The History of the Scottish National Party*, pp. 164–5.

CHAPTER 15

ALEX SALMOND (ACT I)

MURRAY RITCHIE

Alex Salmond joined the SNP while at St Andrews University in 1973, was prominent in student nationalist politics and played an increasingly significant role in the party thereafter. He was elected MP for Banff and Buchan in 1987, and shortly afterwards, in 1990, he defeated Margaret Ewing as party convener. What turned out to be his first decade as party leader saw him lead the party when it adopted independence in Europe and adopt a more pragmatic position on devolution. The latter included convincing his party to give overwhelming support to devolution in the 1997 devolution referendum. He led the party into the first elections to the Scottish Parliament two years later, when the SNP emerged for the first time as the unambiguous challenger to Labour. He stood down as party convener after ten years in office.

●   ●   ●

U ntil he resigned as SNP leader after the Scottish independence referendum of 2014, Alex Salmond was arguably the most effective politician in the United Kingdom. His extraordinary personal achievement in taking charge of a small, struggling political party and transforming it within a few years into his nation's dominant political force with near monopoly power is unprecedented in British politics. So effective a campaigner was he that he came within a whisker of ending 300 years of union between Scotland and England.

Alex Salmond personifies the modern SNP. He and his party could, after the

2015 general election, be described without exaggeration as a political phenom-enon. No other party leader can come close to wielding the authority Salmond enjoyed in the second of his two separate decades as leader of the party he moulded in his own image – feisty, non-conformist and driven by conviction.

UNDERSTANDING SALMOND: THE JOURNEY OF THE MODERN SNP

To understand Alex Salmond we first have to understand his party and how it achieved such unprecedented success by injecting life and excitement into dreary Scottish politics – because the story of the SNP in post-Second World War Britain is so much the story of its most celebrated and controversial personality. For many years there was a truism in Scotland that politics came alive only when the SNP was on the march. Salmond's achievement was, more than any other individual's, to take an ill-disciplined, fractious and impecunious fringe party and establish it as the dominant force in Scotland's political life – this in a country where Labour had been in control for half a century, effortlessly stacking up mountainous majorities all over the most populous central belt.

To appreciate how this transformation came about we need to go all the way back to 1707 when Scotland – or at least its political elite – surrendered its inde-pendent Scottish Parliament, condemning Edinburgh, the country's beautiful capital, to the status of a political and diplomatic ghost town. Though the state of Scotland was no longer, the state of mind of being Scottish never quite disap-peared from its people. Salmond is one of those who regards himself as Scottish first and British second. His genius was to reawaken this dormant Scottishness as the age of empire and world wars passed into history along with unchal-lenged acceptance of the so-called Imperial Parliament in London. Salmond looked to abandon the British Union in favour of a new and bigger and more modern Union, the European one, and to place Scotland in it as a full member.

After the end of the Second World War – a decade before Salmond was born – Scotland began to change. The long-dormant cause of Scottish inde-pendence flickered into life again, but only briefly, when the Scottish National

Party, formed between the wars by an unworldly group of romantics, poets and intellectuals, caused a stir by winning a parliamentary seat only to lose it again next time around. Yet that exceptional event suggested that there still existed in Scotland a faint but discernible yearning among some voters to have their country's independence restored.

Four years before Salmond arrived in the world another event ignited nationalism in Scotland when some students removed the Stone of Destiny from Westminster Abbey. The return of this symbol of English domination to Scotland was regarded in London as an outrageous crime but was met with glee north of the border and boosted the fringe SNP's credentials, bestowing on Scottish nationalism a sense of mischief and rebelliousness which it enjoys to this day – and which has always been part of Salmond's personality.

In the 1960s nationalism reignited again and this time it could not be written off as another aberration. Out of the blue Winnie Ewing, who was to become the grande dame of Scottish nationalism (pre-Nicola Sturgeon obviously), won a famous victory in Hamilton, a Labour stronghold, thanks mainly, it must be said, to some remarkable complacency and incompetence in the Labour Party. But that Hamilton by-election and Winnie Ewing's stunning breakthrough changed everything. Scotland was suddenly different. Its Britishness, that had held strong throughout two world wars and supported the greatest empire the world had ever known, was suddenly being questioned again.

Ewing duly lost Hamilton soon after, but she had prodded the national psyche and is credited with letting the genie of nationalism out of the bottle. The SNP now presented itself as the first plausible and democratic threat to the Union in 250 years. But, however grand its ambition, it remained a disorganised band facing the complacent partnership of Tory and Labour Unionists who took turns at governing Scotland.

THE MAKING OF THE YOUNG ALEX SALMOND

In the early 1970s, a third shock hit Scotland when the full economic potential of North Sea oil began to dawn on politicians of all parties, not least the SNP, which saw the black stuff as an exciting and powerful propaganda weapon. Just as nationalism began driving Scotland's political re-awakening, a chirpy youngster studying economics at the University of St Andrews in 1973 joined the SNP because, he said, it seemed to chime with his own politics. His name was Alexander Elliot Anderson Salmond.

His political credo was not complicated. Explaining his views much later in what was to become a stellar career, he said, 'Nations are nations if they feel themselves to be a nation. And Scotland overwhelmingly feels itself to be a nation.'[1] His difficulty with Scotland was that while it was undoubtedly a nation – one of the oldest in Europe and independent for half a millennium until 1707 – it was no longer a state. Salmond's entry into politics was motivated by the essence of Scottish nationalism that eschews xenophobia or racial intolerance. Rather, it embodies a mixture of uncomplicated patriotism and a desire to see Scotland recognised as part of the wider world to which the Union now denied it direct access. Winnie Ewing put it her own way after Hamilton: 'Stop the world, Scotland wants to get on.'[2]

The schoolboy Salmond, son of a Labour father and Tory mother, was most influenced, he has said often, by his grandfather, Sandy Salmond, who told him tales of Scottish battles and who did not always show respect for historical accuracy. He might have been taking his cue from Scott's *Tales of a Grandfather*, but quite clearly the old boy was a formative influence on young Alex. At school Alex stood for the SNP in mock elections and at St Andrews he joined the Federation of Student Nationalists and then the SNP.

In those days Salmond regarded himself as on the left, a common enough stance for youngsters in Scotland in the early 1970s shortly after Edward Heath's government had 'butchered' – in the words of the Labour Scottish Secretary, Willie Ross – the Upper Clyde Shipbuilders (UCS). The shock of the UCS disaster, which caused a domino effect on traditional heavy industry across Scotland whose effects are still felt today, provoked the famous

---

1   Statement to Reuters, 1999. Personal note.

2   Ewing, *Stop the World*.

work-in led by shop stewards Jimmy Reid and Jimmy Airlie, a year before Salmond's entry into politics. Both work-in leaders were well on their way to national working-class hero status as resistance to the Heath government spread across the UK. The atmosphere in Scotland then was one of resentment at Westminster's high-handed dogmatism – a gift to the SNP and to Salmond with his talent for spirited protest.

By now the Tories were regarded as alarmingly out of touch with Scottish politics and it was then they began their self-inflicted and disastrous electoral decline north of the border. With the encouragement of Heath they dropped their various identities as Progressives or Moderates or Independents in local government, and as Unionists in the national sense, and began calling themselves simply Conservatives. It was never going to work.

This failure to comprehend the shock UCS caused across the country was exemplified at a gathering in the Central Hotel in Glasgow, where the Heath government was trailing an important announcement by then Conservative Scottish Secretary, Gordon Campbell. The Tories did nothing to dampen expectations that UCS was to be saved.

In the hostile presence of UCS shop stewards, and a coalition of campaigning Labour MPs and their supporters, Campbell unwittingly demonstrated the Conservatives' warped sense of priorities. He rose to his feet and began: 'I am delighted to announce today that we have saved …' As some premature cheering began, he added, 'The Argyll and Sutherland Highlanders.'[3] At that time Salmond was watching events closely as an admirer of Harold Wilson. He had also been struck by Wilson's stated ambition to see the British government taking its place alongside the leaders of OPEC, on the back of Scottish oil, at gatherings of the world's pre-eminent oil producers.

When the Tories were about to lose office Salmond aligned himself with the SNP's left despite the fact that the party in those days was by no means all of the same colour. Most SNP activists were neither determinedly left nor right and they all rubbed along easily enough, united in their one ambition

---

3   Speech to a gathering in Glasgow, 1971. Personal note.

of independence. And they were making progress, assisted by dreams of oil riches for Scotland, as they moved ahead in the polls with the 1974 general election approaching. The SNP proved adept at gathering financial support from new sources, enjoying in a startling propaganda coup when the millionaire businessman Sir Hugh Fraser announced he was now an SNP financial backer, a decision that caused deep dismay among the suffering Scottish Tories.

By now the SNP had shed its reputation among the orthodox parties for being a somehow disloyal challenger beyond the political pale, almost a fifth column in British politics and certainly not one for respectable Scottish voters. In truth it was becoming the sort of party Salmond personified. It was entirely legitimate and democratic with an unblemished record of peaceful campaigning towards the restoration of Scotland's independence. And the campaigning was of a gradualist nature – just like Salmond, whose famous gradualism was an irritant only to the so-called fundamentalists, a small grouping of the impatient who wanted some form of direct action.

Salmond's gradualism was to be demonstrated later as the independence referendum of 2014 approached. All opinion polls showed that if the ballot paper had included a third option – as Salmond wished – for home rule or so-called devo-max within the Union, then it would have won comfortably. That way the Scots could have had most of what they wanted and could still have been British in some form of UK federal or confederal arrangement and Salmond would have embraced that. 'The United Kingdom would not end but it would be different. It would become the United Kingdoms,' he argued.[4] For how long that could have been sustained is, of course, another matter, but Salmond has never been an isolationist as his Unionist opponents like to brand him. His 'Independence – Yes or No' stance in 2014 was forced upon him by the Conservative government of David Cameron.

The SNP celebrated a breakthrough in the two 1974 elections, which saw

---

4   This and all subsequent Salmond and other quotes which aren't separately referenced are from personal comments and interviews.

the defeat of the Heath government and the return of Harold Wilson's Labour government with, significantly for Scotland, a promise of devolution – the direct result of nationalist pressure, according to the SNP. Labour's increasing paranoia in the face of the SNP's challenge simply played into the nationalists' hands. An impatient Wilson embarrassed his own Scottish MPs by ordering them at a special conference to embrace devolution – the first and still the finest example of what Johann Lamont, a future Scottish Labour leader, was later to describe as Labour's 'branch office' mentality.

The Scottish Labour Party duly did as it was told at the famous Dalintober Street conference in Glasgow, where it was forced to set course for an Edinburgh Assembly. The devolution sceptic Willie Ross, plainly uncomfortable, was caught in a media scrum in the street outside and said without a hint of embarrassment, 'I have always been a devolutionist.'[5] Ross's idea of devolution was, of course, himself and the Scottish Office, but his famous loyalty to Wilson encouraged him to become a convert to the real deal.

The SNP, with Salmond happily in tow but not yet with a parliamentary seat, found itself with eleven MPs in the October 1974 election. Suddenly it was a significant electoral force, having taken one third of the Scottish vote. Years of bitter argument with Labour ensued. Michael Foot told Winnie Ewing, 'I am not worried at the SNP's eleven MPs – what worries me is the forty-one second places.'

The eleven quickly made a name for themselves in Westminster as a reflection of the party at home – not greatly organised, disputatious, anti-establishment and fun-loving. It was remarked by *The Guardian*'s Michael White, 'They celebrate Hogmanay every week at Westminster' and one of their number, when his seat was lost, reputedly left the biggest unpaid bar bill in the history of the House of Commons.[6]

Salmond was on the periphery of this entertaining but chaotic party progress and moved quietly at first with his limited influence to bring some order

---

5   Statement to media conference, August 1974, Glasgow. Personal note.

6   Torrance, *Salmond: Against the Odds*.

to the SNP. The man who would later become a healer, suffering critics with great patience, first went through his rebel phase. By now a new name in the campaign for devolution was prominent. Jim Sillars was a charismatic left-wing Ayrshire Labour MP who championed devolution (see chapter on Jim Sillars in this volume). He and Salmond, though not close, recognised each other as political like minds. While Labour prevaricated on the proposed Scottish Assembly – an unduly modest proposal offering a mere talking shop in Edinburgh – Sillars lost patience and broke away to form the much more left-wing Scottish Labour Party (SLP), which proposed full-scale home rule with separate Scottish representation in the then European Economic Community. The new party soon fell victim to hard left entryism and went out of business – a loss that was the SNP's gain.

AFTER THE ANNUS HORRIBILIS OF 1979

S almond was by now building a reputation as a mover and shaker in the SNP but he was still without a parliamentary seat and the profile that goes with it. He threw himself into the devolution campaign and when the 1979 referendum failed, provoking SNP–Labour bitterness which lasts to this day, nationalism suffered a meltdown. Recrimination was everywhere and the SNP spent a decade toiling in opinion polls.

Sillars brought the leadership of his defunct SLP into the SNP, where a group of left-wingers, including Salmond, warmly welcomed them as natural allies. Together Salmond and Sillars moved the SNP farther left and formed their own internal so-called 79 Group. Gordon Wilson, the SNP leader, had it banned and its members, including Salmond, expelled with the support of Margaret Bain, later to run for the leadership against Salmond as Margaret Ewing.

This was Salmond's lowest point. He was out of the party, unable to enter Parliament, and frustrated at the SNP's collapse. Not until the early 1980s was he readmitted with his fellow rebels and it was then, in a new spirit of reconciliation, that he began the long process of trying to mould the SNP into an organised, united, party political fighting machine.

The old left-wing radical Salmond was now settling in as a middle-of-the road nationalist, still left on social issues but rightish and pragmatic on the economy. He developed a habit of being seen with successful businessmen with right-wing economic views and he enjoyed rubbing shoulders with celebrities. He was mainly responsible for attracting enthusiastic public and financial support for the SNP from his new friend, Sean Connery, another Scottish working-class hero, one who had started life as a milkman. This coup provoked much Labour jealousy because Labour saw Connery as exactly the type who should have been one of their natural supporters.

Above all, Salmond was ferociously hard-working, earning himself a reputation for fierce ambition. He took a job at the Scottish Office as an economic adviser where he studied the burgeoning North Sea oil industry although his primary responsibility was agriculture. As oil neared its height of production he moved to a job with the Royal Bank of Scotland where he learned more of the economics of the industry.

Under the leaderships of Billy Wolfe and Gordon Wilson (both of whom are dealt with in individual chapters in this book), the party's slogan 'It's Scotland's Oil' had struck a chord across the country and Salmond eagerly weaponised his oil boom expertise against Westminster as the Treasury continued to gather (and retain) 100 per cent of North Sea revenues. Margaret Thatcher's incoming Conservative government in 1979 merely continued this practice, using the oil bonanza to bankroll its 'modernisation' of the economy and provoking fury in Scotland, still angered by the loss of heavy industry under Heath.

Salmond described the events of 1979 as an *annus horribilis*. He had good reason. The referendum had been a failure, not least because of the notorious 40 per cent rule, which effectively counted non-voters in the No camp. He argued with some justification that the SNP had campaigned harder than Labour for Labour's Scottish Assembly, and had lost nine of its eleven MPs in return.

Salmond had much to be miserable about. The SNP bubble that he had invested many hopes in appeared burst. Billy Wolfe made way for Gordon Wilson, and the party entered a decade of dreadful poll ratings and infighting. By 1981, and still only aged twenty-six, Salmond was now on the party executive working on plans to transform the SNP from being a squabbling shambles into a disciplined political fighting machine. In 1981, he married Moira McGlashan, seventeen years his senior – a marriage that has proved happy and enduring.

Salmond continued to devote most of his time to offering the SNP his ideas for professional organisation and discipline which, he promised, would transform its fortunes. Yet in the midst of this, almost unbelievably now, came his expulsion because of his 79 Group activity. Salmond was never one for direct action and he did not show any eagerness to support the more militant direct action approach of Sillars.

For a while the SNP was a broken force as it descended into civil war. And then in 1983 Salmond and the other rebels were readmitted after the intervention of the respected Neil MacCormick, one of the SNP's more hard-headed and pragmatic activists who was the son of 'King John' MacCormick, a party founder. With peace restored, Salmond acquired a greater sense of tolerance, as did Gordon Wilson, who settled for leading a radical party to the left of centre, but not unduly so, and still with an unbreakable commitment to independence.

Salmond and Sillars manage to work reasonably well together and in the 1987 general election Salmond won Banff and Buchan with a majority of 2,441, knocking out the Tory incumbent, Albert McQuarrie, MP since 1979, who in a fit of pique refused to shake hands with his successor, denouncing him as 'scum'. By now Salmond was making an impact on the party's media coverage with his efforts in the role of deputy convener for publicity. Later that year Salmond became deputy leader. Sillars, with Salmond's support, went on to celebrate a famous by-election victory in Glasgow Govan the following year where he overturned a large Labour majority. It seemed all of a sudden as if the future was Scottish nationalist, but it didn't turn out that way – at least for quite a period!

Most of the 1980s were unkind to the SNP. This was the era of the poll tax, which the Thatcher government introduced first in Scotland. When Sillars emerged from his count in Govan his supporters outside were chanting: 'We don't pay the poll tax, Labour pays the poll tax.' Labour, confounded by how to react to the poll tax, did indeed resist it and its MPs toured Scotland denouncing it – but at the same time they were advising people to pay it lest the party was accused of supporting law-breaking. The SNP loved Labour's confusion. Salmond and the SNP had no such qualms and cooperated unofficially with Tommy Sheridan's Militant Tendency's poll tax refuseniks, although Salmond himself was careful to keep out of legal trouble. He happily condoned the 'Can Pay, Won't Pay' poll tax resistance – the party's campaign fronted by Kenny MacAskill – but kept his distance from the more wild talk.

SALMOND BECOMES PARTY LEADER

The ferocity of debate over the poll tax helped consolidate his growing prominence in Scottish politics and when Gordon Wilson stepped down as party leader Salmond promptly announced his candidacy, setting himself up for a contest with Margaret Ewing, the popular MP for Moray and by marriage now one of the influential nationalist Ewing dynasty. Sillars chose to support Ewing, who was on the soft left, causing some strain with Salmond but not yet any lasting enmity.

Salmond and Margaret Ewing had very different personalities although had cooperated smoothly on the left of the SNP. Ewing was loved in the SNP, where she was known as a convivial old-style nationalist given to mixing politics with fun and some memorable partying. Salmond was not yet revered but was admired and respected as an impressive political operator. To the disappointment and even surprise of some traditionalists in the SNP, Salmond won easily by a margin of more than three to one (486 to 186) but to observers at the time his success was less of a surprise than it would have been at the start of the contest. His growing reputation as a debater to be feared by his opponents won the day, after which the SNP would start the transition from growing movement to overwhelming political force.

For a while, Salmond and Sillars, now recognised in the early 1980s as the main players in the struggling SNP, worked happily together. But in truth the two were oil and water. Sillars, a superb political campaigner, appeared unable to thole not having his own way and became an increasingly contrary and detached figure. Salmond showed patience, but not enough to dent his own ambition. He and Sillars broke eventually. Sillars became a constant critic of his former old comrade, given to remarking, 'I am in the SNP but not of it.'[7]

Sillars remained a so-called fundamentalist and Salmond a patient gradualist. The difference was not always semantic. In his 79 Group days, Sillars had supported and taken part in direct action, getting himself into minor trouble with the police. Salmond made the right sounds but was more cautious, avoiding Sillars-style prosecution. He continued to argue that law-abiding gradualism was the way forward – win elections, gain a presence in a Parliament and then persuade the legislature to move with democratic legitimacy for independence. When the fundamentalist–gradualist divide resurfaced and reached damaging heights during the leadership of John Swinney, also a gradualist, one of the leading fundamentalists of the day was asked what precisely was the difference between the two camps. He replied somewhat unconvincingly, 'We shout louder.' Margo MacDonald, by now married to Sillars, was more thoughtful: 'There is no difference in ambition, merely in tactics,' she said. After one particularly stinging attack by Sillars on Salmond's gradualist style, Salmond responded wearily, 'Sometimes I think on the night of independence when the people are celebrating along Princes Street there'll be Jim in a shop doorway shouting "we're getting our independence the wrong way".'

SALMOND THE WESTMINSTER POLITICIAN AND
PARTY LEADER

S almond now had a profile in Scottish politics but it was his entry to the Commons that gave him the platform he wanted. There he demonstrated

---

7   Statement during TV debate, 1999. Personal note.

his talent for attracting national media attention, notably when he made his first significant parliamentary intervention. When Nigel Lawson, the Tory Chancellor, was delivering his Budget in 1988 he was famously interrupted – against parliamentary convention – by Salmond protesting about proposed tax cuts. For his trouble Salmond was 'named' by the Deputy Speaker and expelled temporarily from the chamber – an outcome he had eagerly planned and invited because of the inevitable publicity. His intervention made headlines; suddenly he was a player in British and not just Scottish politics. At the same time he had made the point that one SNP MP had shown more guts in opposition than Labour's 'feeble fifty' MPs put together.

Labour's furious condemnation of Salmond's intervention and the publicity it had earned the nationalists was a measure of the official opposition's embarrassment. Salmond's impertinence paid off in other ways, too. The SNP jumped in the polls.

But for most of his (first) period in the Commons Salmond was powerless to change much. He spent most of his time organising the party and looking to the day when devolution would present a strong chance of handing the SNP real power. Salmond had long taken the view that in modern democracies opposition parties eventually have their turn at governing. He saw a Scottish parliament or assembly as such a possibility and put much effort into planning for the day it would arrive.

With the prospect of devolution coming ever closer, Salmond pushed his gradualism (and his luck) when he let it be known that he was taking on the fundamentalists with his Declaration of Devolution. On a visit to Brussels he briefed his MEPs that the party had to settle the argument once and for all by embracing devolution as a stepping stone to the real thing. The days of bravely holding out – probably hopelessly – for independence through direct action and extra-parliamentary activity were over. Likewise, the day when the SNP could credibly argue that a majority of MPs was a mandate for independence. The SNP endorsed his initiative and began readying itself for the 1997 devolution referendum.

With Labour and the Lib Dems in the vanguard, Salmond led the SNP into the campaign that produced an overwhelming endorsement of Labour's plan. Later Salmond could boast that his embrace of devolution and his party's support had contributed half a million Yes votes to the landslide victory. Along the way he had enjoyed conducting a war of words with his own hometown MP, Tam Dalyell, the combative Union supporter, who had predicted that a Scottish Assembly, never mind a powerful Parliament, would put Scotland on a 'motorway to independence with no exits'.

Salmond happily said that he hoped Dalyell was right because he saw the Parliament as a building block to independence. 'If the Scots get a devolved Parliament and see how constitutional change works to their benefit, they'll obviously want more of it,' he argued.

He enjoyed irritating Labour MPs with his claim that Labour had only grudgingly proposed devolution because of its fear of the SNP. 'Labour's devolution bus runs on SNP petrol,' he was fond of saying. There was much truth to this. Norman Buchan, one of Labour's left-wing and 'off-message' MPs, had remarked, 'We are only offering devolution to appease nationalism.' Salmond teased Labour with claims (probably true) that Tony Blair and Donald Dewar had adopted the word 'devolution' because they could not bear to talk with a more inspiring vocabulary which included 'self-government' or 'home rule'.

HOPE POSTPONED? DEVOLUTION DOG DAYS

Salmond now prepared to lead the SNP into the first Scottish Parliament elections in 1999. He took the view that the Parliament would serve the SNP well on two fronts. It would provide a significant parliamentary presence for his party and although it would probably be in opposition (he admitted this only privately), given the Unionists had chosen the voting system, it would also offer the prospect one day of the SNP winning power.

With the SNP now enjoying a period of peaceful excitement as the Scottish Parliament loomed, Salmond led his forces to a close contest in the opinion polls. But the optimism of the early stages was shattered at its high point by an opinion poll by System Three for *The Herald*. This so-called superpoll consulted 3,000 people – three times the normal sample – and to everyone's astonishment, not least Labour's, it showed the SNP, in the words of *The Herald*, 'in freefall'. 'We had no idea we were so far ahead,' said Labour's Jack McConnell. Until that moment the result had been in some doubt – but not in the mind of Alex Salmond. I recall having lunch with Salmond and his wife Moira in one of his favourite Edinburgh restaurants, after which Moira drove us back to the city. On the way she took a wrong turn and drove through a no-entry sign into a one-way street, prompting Salmond to remark with a smile, 'Don't worry – I'll fix it because I'm going to be First Minister of Scotland.'

This amusing cockiness is a famous part of Salmond's engaging and sometimes infuriating personality. It seems to attract admirers and irritate critics in equal measure and has given him his deserved reputation as a Marmite politician. His admirers and even his opponents greatly respect his abilities but his critics dislike what they see as arrogance. But Salmond seems merely to revel in the attention he attracts from all quarters. 'The more they criticise me the better they ken me,' he likes to say when under attack.

On this occasion, however, his optimism about the election took a sore knock with the disastrous superpoll. His cockiness did not quite desert him at that moment of crushing disappointment, however. Asked if the SNP was about to be humiliated in the first Scottish Parliament elections, he demonstrated his defiance by quoting the Scottish naval rebel John Paul Jones: 'I have not yet begun to fight.'[8]

Salmond's cheeky-chappie style was seen again to great effect in the 1999 campaign, when he walked uninvited into the STUC Annual Congress in Glasgow. The oldest joke in Scottish politics is that the STUC is the political wing of the Scottish Labour Party, with a history of embarrassing the party with its strong commitment to workers' rights and old-style socialism. In 1999, it was experiencing a particularly awkward relationship with Tony Blair's New Labour. Salmond had always hankered after STUC support, and his unannounced arrival at the Congress, accompanied by a media scrum,

---

8   Press conference, Edinburgh 1999. Personal note.

forced Donald Dewar to enter (in a foul temper) through a back door. The ruse had the desired effect. Salmond was received with civility, even some warmth. He held court, worked a roomful of unreconstructed trade union hard cases, and walked off grinning in triumph, mission accomplished. It was a classic display of SNP impudence, the sort of thing Labour, with its long dominance of Scottish politics and 'ownership' of the trade unions, deeply resented. But years and years of such semi-guerrilla activity contributed to political mountains moving, including the trade union movement's commitment to Labour in Scotland.

Salmond has been accused of being a compulsive 'Smart Alex' and sometimes his talent for winning debates and TV studio arguments can fail him. In the first Holyrood election he promoted the SNP's 'Penny for Scotland' brainwave, which, he calculated, would outflank Labour's offer of a one-penny cut in income tax. Salmond argued that keeping the rate uncut would show the Scots were prepared to make a small sacrifice if it assisted the national economic interest and in particular the protection of the NHS and education. Labour shamelessly presented the decision to decline a one-penny cut as a one-penny increase. The SNP plan failed. To this day there is still a debate about whether it damaged the SNP vote, but there is little argument that it did not help. John Swinney's view was that its effect was 'neutral' – which is probably about right. But the effect was not lost on Salmond, who has never since toyed with tax increases. For all his proclaimed social democratic credentials, he is cautious, even, more right than left on taxation and economics.

He failed also to gain much credit for his stand against the NATO bombing of Belgrade, another example of his eagerness to wrong-foot opponents by playing the rebel opposing received wisdom and playing up his 'outsider' credentials (explored further in the chapter on Salmond, Act II). So anxious was he to condemn Labour's support for the bombing that he denounced it in terms that rebounded immediately. 'It is an act of dubious legality but above all one of unpardonable folly,' he said, predicting the NATO action might make matters even worse for the people it was meant to help.[9] Labour's response was crushing. Robin Cook, Foreign Secretary, denounced Salmond as 'the toast of Belgrade', a cruel rebuke that resonated across British politics. To this day it is still cast up to Salmond by some of his critics in the heat of argument and the famous Salmond grin of defiance never quite seems an adequate response.

As expected, Labour emerged as the largest party in 1999 and went into coalition for the first of two terms with the Lib Dems. Salmond, now MSP for Banff and Buchan, had to be content with leading the main opposition to Labour and a group of thirty-five SNP parliamentarians. There were birth pains in how Labour adapted to the new Parliament. Donald Dewar, Scotland's First Minister, mixed a diffident style of leadership with unsuccessful attempts to bully the Lib Dems. Tensions between the two parties were sometimes acute and in the opposition SNP there was uncertainty. Salmond promised strong but responsible opposition but the nationalists took the best part of the first parliament to grow accustomed to the new constitutional settlement.

Several factors were at work. First, Salmond adored the theatre and drama of Westminster and had thrived in its sense of occasion and abrasive exchange. The Scottish Parliament was a very different creature: made for multi-party politics and supposedly a striving after consensus. Second, while the previous, bitter tensions within the party were in the past, the SNP was undergoing a major transformation into a party with a large parliamentary group, researchers and public monies supporting the infrastructure of modern politics. This was virgin territory, and required the evolution of a different party culture and leadership. Third, the SNP was a party with independence as its ultimate goal, which left often questions of strategy: whether to criticise devolution or work with it for further change. Salmond chose the latter.

The spirit of consensus did not survive the first Scottish Parliament by-election, held in Ayr in early 2000 at the height of the controversy over Section 28 and the question of how to deal with homosexuality in the school curriculum. Salmond's SNP mounted a furious assault on Labour-held Ayr, which

---

9   Press statement, March 1999. Personal note.

let the Tories in to claim a remarkable victory. The bitterness between Labour and the SNP only deepened. It was an event which marked the near death of consensus politics in the new Scotland and a return to Westminster-style confrontation, which grew more pronounced after the death of Donald Dewar.

By now Salmond was gathering a reputation for rubbing shoulders with the rich and powerful. He remained close to Sean Connery and was now backed by the SNP's so-called Millionaires for Independence, a group of successful business figures. One, Jim Mather, became an SNP MSP (he had been the defeated candidate in the Ayr by-election) and Salmond remains on good terms with all of them. Which is more than can be said for his relationship with other tycoons. His dealings with Donald Trump turned out to be disastrous when they famously fell out over Trump's golf course in Aberdeenshire. Salmond came in for criticism by rather shamelessly seeking editorial support from Rupert Murdoch and for letting it be known he was on good terms with the royal family.

In September 1997, he had found himself on the losing side when the SNP debated the monarchy at its Rothesay conference. The party became the first major force in British politics to look down the road of republicanism when it voted against its pro-monarchy leader's wishes. The party expressed a desire for a referendum sometime in the future on whether to keep the Queen or her successor but Salmond let the idea die quietly. His opposition did not go unnoticed in high places. Shortly after the Rothesay vote, he received an invitation to meet a concerned Prince of Wales – an event that attracted some attention, which Salmond did nothing to play down in the Scottish media. Salmond typically reciprocated years later when the extent of the Prince of Wales lobbying of government was revealed via the release of his 'black spider' letters to ministers – with Salmond, rare among politicians, publicly defending the prince. Yet, the decision of the royals to rub shoulders with Salmond in such circumstances alarmed the established Westminster parties, who saw the event as a worrying form of recognition of the SNP as a legitimate and respectable political force.

As the years passed, Salmond seemed to persuade enough SNP members

that they could have independence without going to the electorally dangerous extent of abolishing the monarchy – at least not yet. His argument was
that Scotland could not have a republic without independence. But it could
have independence without a republic and so independence should be the
priority. No one argued much.

Salmond stood down from the leadership in July 2000 after it became clear
he would be in opposition for a long time ahead. His reasoning, that he had
done his ten years and that was enough for anyone, was never convincing.
Perhaps he looked ahead and saw long years in which the electorate would
weary of him, ever the bridesmaid singing the same old predictable song of
opposition for the sake of it to the point where familiarity led to boredom.

Some observers, including this one, always suspected he was merely taking
a break – he was only forty-five years old – until he saw his chance of returning
to the Scottish Parliament as First Minister. It was almost as if Salmond was
now as big as the SNP itself. With time on his hands, he took up a column
in *The Herald*, offering racing tips (at which he was rather good) and which
enhanced his reputation as a gambler. Rumours spread to the effect that he
had stepped down because of gambling debts. Various tabloids investigated
his private affairs. One in particular, with a loathing of the SNP, had a team
of reporters working for six weeks probing Salmond's finances. They produced nothing. When he resigned, Salmond left the field open to his chosen
successor, the popular and less abrasive John Swinney.

Alex Salmond had already proven himself a successful politician, who
had played a critical, if not central, role in the transformation of the SNP
into a professional party, which was the only credible alternative to Labour,
was unambiguously on the centre-left, and in which the old divisions of the
1970s and 1980s were firmly behind them. But there was still much work for
the party to do to be taken seriously as a viable government, let alone actually
hold the offices of state. And in the summer of 2000, as Salmond departed
from the leadership of the party, few would have guessed that we had just
witnessed the first act in what was to prove a major drama – one which fundamentally reshaped the SNP and Scottish politics.

CHAPTER 16

JOHN SWINNEY

DOUGLAS FRASER

John Swinney was active in the SNP from joining at fifteen. Prior to being elected national convener, he served as national secretary and senior vice-convener (deputy leader). He gained considerable knowledge of the party's internal workings during this period. He was elected MP for North Tayside on his second attempt in 1997 and won the equivalent seat two years later in the first elections to the Scottish Parliament. He comfortably won election as party convener the following year, succeeding Alex Salmond. Defined by electoral results, Swinney's leadership was a failure (the party went backwards in three national elections). But he instituted significant organisational changes, including one-member-one-vote for the leader and deputy leader, a national membership list and reform of candidate selection that provided the base for the successes that followed. After stepping down, with the arrival of the SNP in office in 2007, he was to fit into the role of a senior Cabinet minister much more comfortably, and became a vital element in projecting SNP competence in government, becoming Deputy First Minister in Nicola Sturgeon's administration from 2014.

• • •

Ask John Swinney about his time as leader, and he immediately starts defining it by its failings. He can be modest that way. Others accused him of various shortcomings during his time as leader of the Scottish National Party, but he has a longer list than most.

The statistics help tell the story. The leader resigned after the European elections of 2004, at which the party's vote share had fallen by 7.5 percentage points to only 19.7 per cent. That was less than two points ahead of Conservatives. (From the perspective of 2016, it may be seen as more significant that the Labour vote fell to 26.4 per cent, its lowest since 1910, and a warning of what was to come.)

Nearly four years at the helm of a party going through a bigger change than that faced by all his predecessors combined, the SNP had gone backwards in three national elections. Five turbulent years in the newly devolved Scottish Parliament had entrenched Labour in power in coalition with Liberal Democrats. Those who had feared that devolution would be a trap for the independence movement were, it seemed, on track to be proven right.

The day after resigning in June 2004, he spoke at the party's headquarters in Edinburgh:

> Many voters are telling us we have not yet answered their key question, why independence? We are not yet seen as an alternative government in waiting, and despite my best efforts over the past four years, I accept that many people still not don't have a clear understanding of what the SNP stands for, over and above an independent Scotland. As leader of the Scottish National Party, I take full responsibility for the fact that we have not made as much progress in these areas as I would have liked.[1]

It is hard, from the perspective of 2016, not to see the Swinney leadership in the context of the subsequent rollercoaster of success. But few seriously believed, back then, that such was the trajectory on which the party was set. That Alex Salmond was seen as the necessary replacement, bringing with him ten years of leadership experience, points to the scale of challenge that Swinney had faced. No one else seemed ready or able. Salmond's return, to a much reformed and less punishing job as party leader, showed that the party reforms and strategic adaptations pushed through during these

---

1   BBC News online, 22 June 2004.

years were a painful but necessary period of transition and maturing, without which the subsequent electoral breakthroughs would have been very
unlikely, if not impossible.

Appearing to be weak, in that he faced public criticism and dissent from
SNP MSPs, was the platform on which Swinney could demonstrate the need
for discipline. A challenge to his leadership in 2003 appeared also to show
his lack of authority, yet it helped to strengthen his leadership position at the
time. It proved to be the last battle for the party's fundamentalists against its
gradualists – a fault line that had been put to rest in most party members'
minds, but was yet to be removed from the minds of a vocal minority, still
stuck in the ideological undergrowth and unaware that that war was over.

If John Swinney's leadership was a failure, it may have been a necessary
one. It was certainly a difficult time for the party, and a difficult task for its
leader. He returned to Holyrood, with a new role of party elder statesman
aged only forty, and a vital part of the transition to government in 2007 and
beyond. He speaks, in retrospect, of his inability to project his personality as a leader and potential First Minister. But as a loyal Cabinet minister,
campaign director, and later Deputy First Minister, his air of uncharismatic
competence would be a vital asset and reassurance, when reassurance was
exactly what voters sought. Having resigned, his career was far from over. In
government, Swinney would find a level which could play to his strengths.

INFLUENCES

A s a government minister, John Swinney spends a lot of time in chauf-
feured cars. The drive from home to St Andrew's House in Edinburgh
is around two hours. So for four hours a day, he is working on papers and
on the phone. It is an important part of his working day. He returns to his
Tayside base almost every evening – too late to put his young son, Matthew,
to bed, but in the right place to get him up in the morning and take him to
school. Elizabeth Quigley, whom he met when she was a political correspondent for the BBC at Holyrood, has multiple sclerosis. She continues to work

as a broadcaster and her mobility challenges give the MSP further reason to get home each evening.

John Swinney was only five years older than Matthew when he first got the politics bug. Born in 1964, he grew up in Corstorphine, a middle-range, middle-class area on the west side of Edinburgh. His father owned and ran a car repair garage across the city in Morningside. His son recalls a fierce work ethic. Swinney Senior didn't do politics. He wouldn't tell anyone how he voted. Swinney Mater didn't do politics either, except that she had strong feelings about the importance of education and the value of the comprehensive ideal. It rubbed off on her son, as John made his way through Forrester High School and on to Edinburgh University to study politics, and also to immerse himself in politics.

Back in 1974, there were two general elections. Edward Heath went to the country in February, as a showdown with the National Union of Mineworkers. 'Who runs Britain?' asked the Tory leader. 'Not you,' replied the electorate. Labour, led by Harold Wilson, entered government as a precarious minority. Britain was entering a new era of multi-party politics. The Liberal Party, under Jeremy Thorpe, won 6 million votes that year, though failed to make a breakthrough. But, by breaking through in a more focused campaign, not only in Scotland but in established areas of activism, the Scottish National Party would end 1974 with eleven MPs. Harold Wilson ended the year with a majority, but a slender one. The SNP were a presence – though often seen as an irritation – that Labour could not afford to ignore over the subsequent five years.

John Swinney recalls watching the ageing big beasts of 1970s Westminster politics, and thinking that they had nothing to do with his life. New voices, with more familiar accents, were appearing on TV, asking why Scotland couldn't run its own affairs. And he agreed. Why not? A year before, the OPEC embargo had shown how powerful small countries with oil could be. And rich. A year later, oil would start to flow from the North Sea. 'It's Scotland's Oil,' said the SNP campaign posters.

To those of us negotiating the early teenage years in Edinburgh through the decade that style forgot, our identity as Scots was a defining characteristic. Economically, Britain was often described as 'sick'. Politically, it was ripe for a severe shake-up under Margaret Thatcher. At least as significant, and much more so for our contemporaries, Scotland had a boxer and sprinter and a football team of which we could be proud.

Hubris runs deep in the Scottish psyche. Our hopes can go up like a rocket and fall to earth like a stick. And those are the same words used by John Swinney, the Deputy First Minister, when he recalls the next year's general election. From eleven MPs, the SNP was cut down to only two. The inevitable march towards independence had turned out to be not so inevitable after all. Labour blamed the SNP MPs for being 'like turkeys, voting for an early Christmas', when they pitched Jim Callaghan's government into an election. That episode is covered in other chapters of this book. For our purposes, it is worth noting as the point at which John Swinney applied to join the party – aged fifteen, buying political stock when the price was low.

He had, over these years of Labour government, become a sort of journalist. An enthusiastic member of the Boys' Brigade, he poured his energies into a publication about big global issues of war and poverty. With him was another lad with a fascination for politics and current affairs, but whose nationalist politics were to be sealed some years after Swinney's. His name was Peter Murrell. More than twenty years later, he would be recruited by Swinney to become the SNP's chief executive, a key ally to the leader in driving through party reforms and professionalising the party campaign machine. Once in SNP headquarters, Murrell would meet and marry Nicola Sturgeon.

This was a small, close-knit band of nationalist brothers and sisters. And because the older generation of brothers had been scunnered by the disappointment of the 1979 election, the Swinney generation, and the Sturgeon one nearly ten years behind, were to find their way cleared. Alex Salmond was twenty-four in 1979. His generation included Mike Russell, Bruce Crawford and Kenny MacAskill. But many others fell away. The internal wrangling about the party's direction after the 1979 defeat led to an internal faction, known as the 79 Group, eager to pull the party away from its conservatism and to adopt a clearly left-wing positioning with which to challenge Labour. Salmond, MacAskill and the others were reinstated. Still at school, John Swinney was outside the fray, but looking on. He recalls a national council meeting in December 1982 at the Mitchell Library in Glasgow, where Matters Arising from the Minutes of the previous meeting took more than six hours. He learned to dislike disruption in the party. His formative years saw him attach to loyalty and discipline as key ingredients in the party's future success.

Those, then, were among the formative experiences by which the teenage John Swinney became vice-convener for the SNP's youth wing. In 1986, aged twenty-two, a few weeks before his university final exams, Gordon Wilson asked him to become national secretary. This followed another hugely disappointing election result at Westminster. Even though Labour had done disastrously against Margaret Thatcher's Conservatives in 1983, Michael Foot's weakness in England had not translated into SNP strength in Scotland. There were still only two SNP MPs, with Gordon Wilson representing Dundee East. Swinney's thoroughness and organisational skills had been noticed. Swinney was seen as the party establishment's choice against Kenny MacAskill, then on the fundamentalist wing, and he still recalls the 292 to 220 margin of victory.

After graduation, he went to work for a small business consultancy in Glasgow, Development Options, overlapping with Alex Neil. In 1992, Swinney became a business strategist for the finance house Scottish Amicable. His memory is of two contrasting experiences which inform his view of business and the economy now – one of a small business, like his father's, in which the work you do has a direct bearing on the income by which people are paid each month: the other a large organisation in which he would advise at board of director level, and see the decisions they took cascaded down through the organisation for implementation through its distribution network. Already holding national office in a party with very limited resources, such employment made for a busy time in his twenties, and even more so after his first two children were born. He was divorced from his first wife, Lorna, in 1998.

In 1992, after six years as national secretary, Swinney moved on to the SNP executive's vice-convenership for publicity, which was already established as a stepping stone for leadership in the party. This is a demanding and influential role in campaigning, putting the occupant very close to the leader. John Swinney was running his own constituency campaign at the time, having won the nomination to fight the Westminster seat of Tayside North. This looked a safe Conservative fortress occupied by Bill Walker, a man whose measure of his own importance was not widely shared, even by his own Tory colleagues. The constituency comprised ten SNP branches, each a minor fiefdom, and together, recalls Swinney, an 'anarchic ragbag'. One of the more powerful ones was managed, with the thorough, ordered efficiency of Ian Grant, a former senior forestry official, while his wife, Ianswythe, provided the firebrand inspiration and energy. They took the young candidate under their wings, taught him what he needed to know to secure the candidacy, and continued to mentor him until both died in early 2016.

They were among the senior party figures who went back to the 1950s and the surge in nationalist support around the national plebiscite, the campaign to elect John MacCormick rector of Glasgow University and the Stone of Destiny episode. John Swinney had a profile at an early age, and in a depleted party, he got to know such stalwarts. It's a generation now departing, but to Swinney, he had the opportunity to make the link with those whose formative years, and whose experience of difficult times with little progress for the cause, were from the years before he was born. It may have been an important grounding in the history and roots of a party which has changed immensely since Swinney rose to the leadership team.

TOWARDS DEVOLUTION

The election in 1992 included few target seats for the SNP. Tayside North was one of them. John Swinney moved from a senior position within his party to a more public national role. But that year, there was to be no breakthrough. Scottish Conservatives stemmed the tide of politics, at least temporarily, holding the seats they had, gaining one back from by-election loss and winning Aberdeen South. John Swinney, then aged only twenty-eight, watched the more urban votes from around Perth swing in his favour. But the country votes remained solidly Conservative. He resolved to spend much of the next five years driving up from his job in Glasgow, and later Stirling, to walk up as many farm tracks as possible, to persuade farmers they could count on this young business analyst from Edinburgh. When the Tory vote ebbed away on a political spring tide in 1997, Bill Walker was soundly defeated. This was not a seat where Labour had put in much effort. But, nationally, the first landslide for Tony Blair saw fifty-six out of seventy-two Scottish seats returned for Labour MPs. The SNP had only six. A Scottish Parliament might be coming, but it looked like it would be delivered on Labour terms.

That's apart from the Lib Dem determination to secure a more proportionate voting system. To ensure cross-party support for its devolution proposals, Labour had conceded that much. It would provide a toe-hold on which Tories could re-engage with the Scottish electorate, although slowly. The list system, countering the over-representation that came from the constituency vote, was to become vital to the SNP's future. But as John Swinney was already MP for Tayside North, he could campaign confidently to win that seat also at Holyrood. As the brightest of the new bunch at Westminster, he had become the party's deputy leader after MEP Allan Macartney died in 1998. He was also the finance spokesman at Westminster, and a vital part of Alex Salmond's leadership team. While trying to hold down his job in Scottish Amicable before the 1997 election, Swinney had been part of the inner team involved in running increasingly demanding local council elections and by-election campaigns in Monklands East, Perth and Kinross and Paisley South. With Salmond away at Westminster, they resolved that the party needed a core team at head office, with a more professional and consistent approach, better equipped to take on by-elections as they cropped up and to plan for national campaigns. That's when they recruited Mike Russell to the new post of chief executive. The young Kevin Pringle – who would become a valuable part of the SNP's future disciplined messaging – became head of communications.

The landslide for Tony Blair and the Labour Party in 1997 was followed only four months later by the referendum on devolution. The previous summer, Labour had been in turmoil over its approach to the vote. The outcome was to cement an expectation that constitutional change should be firmly rooted in a democratic, referendum mandate. That would come to have profound implications for Britain's place in Europe, but before that, for the SNP's preferred route to independence. Having been uncertain about how to handle the 1979 referendum, the SNP had little choice but to side with Labour in the September 1997 vote. But the case for doing so had to be carefully made within the nationalist ranks. Under Alex Salmond, it would also be steered into recognising that independence would require a referendum. A majority of Scottish MPs would no longer be the trigger, not least because it looked an impossibly high target. Fighting an electoral campaign, which opponents could define as being for or against independence, was no way to maximise parliamentary support. Yet, for die-hards in the party, that devolutionary route, followed by a referendum condition, looked like two traps, into which the SNP was falling.

The 1999 campaign was a long way short of the professional standard to which the leadership aspired. It was poorly resourced and haphazardly run. For the SNP, it was a hard lesson in what it meant to be as social democratic as Alex Salmond declared the party to be. Having squeezed public finances hard, Gordon Brown, as Chancellor, began to ease back in the Budget that March. He announced a one-penny cut in the basic rate of income tax. Salmond and Swinney, along with media adviser Kevin Pringle, immediately met in their Westminster offices to decide on their response. Two months out from the first parliamentary vote, they had to make a decision very quickly. So they announced there would be a 'Penny for Scotland' pledge and campaign, reinstating Brown's penny cut and making the case for a higher level of public spending in Scotland. They were falling into a Labour trap. The making of the 'Penny for Scotland' policy lacked the time to explain it, nor any detail, for some weeks, of how the money would be spent. Nationalists would later conclude that they looked like they were making policy on the hoof. While a modest amount of tax would be raised, they were vague about how to spend it, offering a list of the main public services that might benefit. If the tax and spend position was vague with these devolved tax powers, it made it all the more difficult to make the case for the full powers of independence. The SNP downplayed its independence goal in a ten-point policy pledge card, and was tormented by a brutal but effective campaign from Labour, asserting 'divorce is an expensive business'. So effective was this approach that Labour continued to use the same device for many years, failing to notice when it ceased to work on voters.

The election delivered thirty-five SNP MSPs to Labour's fifty-six. For the SNP, it was a disappointing result, winning only seven constituencies and having to rely on regional list seats. Yet this was a party that had gone from six MPs 400 miles away at Westminster to thirty-five salaried MSPs, funded by the taxpayer to employ parliamentary staff. Overnight, it had more parliamentarians than it had had across its entire history. With intense scrutiny from the media, it was an uncomfortable place for all the early participants in the Scottish Parliament, and particularly so for those whose nationalist politics were uncomfortable with the compromise of devolution.

Looking to the subsequent elections, however, was daunting. Labour was heading for another Westminster landslide in 2001, and the SNP had to fashion a new type of campaign for Westminster seats, while its focus and energy was in Edinburgh. Voters were clearly differentiating between their willingness to support the SNP in the Scottish Parliament, and being much less willing to do so in the House of Commons. At the Scottish Parliament, the assumption was that Labour, with the Liberal Democrats, could expect to retain power for the foreseeable future. Alex Salmond, after ten years as leader, and with voters seeing him as too abrasive, was telling his deputy that he had become the obstacle to the party's further progress. To outsiders, however, it was a surprise in July 2000 when Salmond announced his departure. To Swinney, as heir apparent, the prospects looked difficult, and aged thirty-six, it had probably come too early. He had taken on the enterprise committee convenership, and sought to define a new way of doing politics by working closely on a shared agenda with

Henry McLeish when the latter was Labour's enterprise minister. But with the leadership open, Swinney was clearly the frontrunner. Only Alex Neil stood against him, coming from the left of the party and the fundamentalist wing. It was in decline and finding it hard to swallow the strategy of achieving independence through a referendum. Swinney beat Neil in the conference vote, by a two-to-one margin, declaring in his victory speech, 'I stand here as the first leader in the history of the SNP who has a hard headed opportunity to lead our party into government and our country on to independence.'[2]

INTO LEADERSHIP

The first challenge facing Swinney, three weeks in as National Convener, was striking the right tone after the sudden death of Labour leader and First Minister Donald Dewar. Dewar's replacement was Henry McLeish, who presented an unusual challenge to the opposition leader. Whereas Swinney has a politician's precise use of language, McLeish did not. In weekly question time encounters, Swinney would attempt to nail down McLeish. It was too often like trying to nail jelly to the wall. Labour was struggling with inexperience and division. Henry McLeish took the populist route into an expensive commitment to free personal care for the elderly, against the wishes of his own Health Minister, Susan Deacon, but with the support of Liberal Democrats and the SNP. Such shifting alliances did not make the leadership role any simpler for John Swinney, but it should have opened an opportunity for the SNP. When that did beckon, and Henry McLeish stumbled into a 'muddle, not a fiddle' over his office expenses in 2001, it could have been John Swinney who pressed home the charge of incompetence. But it was not. Tory leader David McLetchie got the credit for that political scalp, when McLeish had to stand down.

Labour elected Jack McConnell to be its next leader and Scotland's First Minister. He was an easier opponent for Swinney to gauge, yet the SNP leader remained cautious and perhaps too methodical in his approach to opposition.

---

2   *The Guardian*, 25 March 2001.

Week by week, he would build cases against the Executive administration, citing examples of inept public services. It could unsettle McConnell, but it lacked the punch that got Swinney's reputation out from the chamber to connect with voters more widely.

McConnell set about streamlining the administration, taking more populist approaches on crime and policing, and choosing his battles with the Labour government in London. Swinney had learned from the 'Penny for Scotland' experience that this was no time to push for redistribution, particularly as the spending taps had been turned on at Westminster and there was less mileage to be had for the opposition from a sense of unjust application of spending restraint.

While the powers of the Scottish Parliament and the previous work experience of MSPs meant that attention focused on public services, both McConnell and Swinney chose to steer their parties gingerly towards more emphasis on economic growth. It was one arena in which the SNP leader had a lot more confidence than Labour's. This was supported by a boardroom and media blitz, led by finance spokesman and economist Andrew Wilson with Jim Mather, a businessman-turned-MSP, who together went out to make the case for more fiscal powers at the Scottish Parliament, and to impress on potential supporters that the SNP was a business-friendly party. That would become a vital step towards the platform and wider credibility that won power for the SNP in 2007, with economic growth highlighted as 'The Purpose'. However, ahead of the 2003 election, it vacated the territory of redistribution through higher tax, leaving little difference with Labour and an opportunity for the Scottish Socialist Party.

The energies of the new SNP leader were being taken up with internal party management. The 1999 election may have been disappointing, but it meant a parliamentary group on an unprecedented scale. Swinney's regret now is that he did not move faster on reforms necessary to modernise the party. But this was a new political terrain, with a large, inexperienced group of parliamentarians, still feeling their way. By-elections offered opportunities for the SNP, but they made little headway. In Ayr, it was won by a Conservative, regaining a toe-hold in Scottish politics. In the MP and MSP seats vacated by Donald Dewar, the SNP was the main challenger. It registered its worst by-election result since 1978.

Looking ahead to the 2003 election, the party went through a calamitous selection process. With few constituencies and limited hope of gaining them, the emphasis was on the list selections. Small numbers in party branches could make big differences to the votes. Some, who had sought to raise their profiles, were punished for getting above themselves and for failing to show true, unwavering allegiance to the independence cause. Andrew Wilson was one who paid a heavy price for raising the issue – now a mainstream view – that the SNP should embrace Scots' cultural Britishness. Mike Russell was also put down the list by others who worked the internal branch system better than him. Margo MacDonald was punished by the party selectorate for trouble-making. Swinney was under pressure to protect his new MSPs, but declined to take action. He could see how much damage was being inflicted. And having failed to take action for an ally such as Mike Russell, he could not then back MacDonald. There was a high price to pay. Both were knocked down the party lists. Losing his seat in 2003, and from outside the parliamentary party, Russell would later take revenge on Swinney's leadership through his media writings. Margo MacDonald, having been openly, sharply and damagingly critical of the Swinney leadership, left the party to become an independent MSP. From that position, she was twice re-elected as a Lothian list MSP. She became something of a national treasure, and not only made her peace with John Swinney but they became good friends.

Those around Swinney recall that too many reforms had been neglected under Salmond. He had gone a long way towards closing down the gradualist–fundamentalist argument within the party, though some still fought on. Ian Blackford was party treasurer and an outspoken critic of Salmond, including the leader's use of party expenses.[3] Salmond and Swinney moved to oust Blackford and took the opportunity to bring Kenny MacAskill in from the

---

3   *The Herald*, 13 June 2000.

'woad-wearing' firebrand fundamentalist wing. He became the new party treasurer, beginning the long journey to becoming a party insider, one of its more thoughtful cooperators across party boundaries, and eventually the Justice Secretary.

In interviewing John Swinney, one sentence stands out as defining both the man's strengths, and his limitations: 'What I've always been driving for is the presentation of coherence.' From the incoherence after 1979, the seat-of-the-pants by-election campaigns of the 1990s, the 'anarchic ragbag' of branch structures and the free-flowing, speak-your-mind culture of the first cohort of MSPs, that was his struggle with the party. That drive for coherence would continue as the defining characteristic of his time as a government minister.

Having declined to take the opportunity to assert his leadership after the second Labour Westminster landslide of 2001, at which the SNP tally fell from six to five, the 2003 election added a further disappointment. Not only did some of the brighter SNP MSPs fail to return, but the party had failed to see the threat from the Greens and Scottish Socialist Party. The SNP was knocked back from thirty-five seats in 1999 to twenty-seven. This became known in the media as 'the rainbow Parliament' due to its seven Greens, six SSP and three independents. To significant numbers in the SNP, the loss of seats to these other parties showed that they had to embrace the same positions, particularly as the nationalists were still failing to break through in traditional working-class constituencies. Tommy Sheridan had charisma, and could reach these voters. John Swinney did not; he was seen as too cautious and too middle-class.

His approach to the 2003 election had been to find coherence in the platform, in a disciplined message and in being prepared. He wanted the spending commitments in his manifesto to add up, and the priorities, messages and values to be consistent. It was a dry pitch – 'realise our potential' – which left the heather (to which he had changed the party colour) unlit. Opposition to Public–Private Partnerships may have put Swinney on the side of majority opinion, but it was never likely to be the motivating cause with which to galvanise voters behind him. What he now concedes is that, for all his coherence, he lacked the personal characteristics to punch through the final stages of the campaign: 'The exuberance didn't come naturally to me. My style didn't give us enough reach.'[4] Just as William Hague had led the Conservatives into the 2001 Westminster campaign as an intelligent leader, well-liked within the political and media village, exposure to the broader electorate in the final weeks of the campaign was a painful experience. So too with Ed Miliband at the helm of Labour's 2015 Westminster election campaign. These leaders appeared geeky, speaking a political language which turned off voters, and lacking the leadership qualities voters wanted to see. In the Holyrood contest, Jack McConnell was projected as more personable and in touch with real people's lives, focusing his campaign on measures to combat anti-social behaviour. The battle in 2003 was being fought on the inside pages of the papers, as the Iraq War dominated the front-page headlines. That had met with widespread opposition before it started, but by the time of the Scottish election campaign there was more interest in the 'shock and awe' of how war was being fought. As voters went to the polls in Scotland, President Bush was on a US Navy aircraft carrier, triumphantly declaring 'Mission Accomplished'. Closer to home, the Holyrood Parliament building project had fired up widespread anger at its mismanagement and cost overruns (which quickly dissipated after its completion) and the SNP had not been able to distance itself from that. The early years of sometimes chaotic political mismanagement and disunity within parties, covered in detail across the media, had tarnished the opposition as well as the governing parties.

With twenty-seven seats from the 2003 result, and Jack McConnell's Labour group back in power with Liberal Democrats, it was then that John Swinney set about the party reforms he believed to be necessary for the SNP – transforming it from a 'party of protest to a party of government'. But before getting there, he faced a challenge from a Glasgow activist, Bill Wilson, who claimed to be speaking for grassroots members who feared the party was being 'New Labourised' – a reference to Tony Blair's reforms within the Labour

---

4   From interview with the author, June 2016.

Party. Wilson was an intense and geeky scientist who had been an activist in Glasgow but was barely known across the membership. If Team Swinney had sought out someone it could swipe aside as a token opponent, it could not have chosen better. However, Wilson spoke for the disaffected in the party when he said that both the SNP and the independence cause were being ill-served by Swinney's centrist tendencies, that the leadership was not listening, that party reforms were intended to strip the grassroots of their powers, and that the independence message was not being given sufficient priority. He brought back the battle over the strategy of offering the national electorate a referendum on independence. Wilson argued that as soon as the SNP was installed in power, it should immediately begin negotiating for independence. His candidacy emerged the day before John Swinney and Elizabeth Quigley got married. At the time, Wilson seemed to some a stalking horse for others to follow, but the challenge lacked much traction and no significant figure came forward to take on Swinney.[5] By the time of the final party hustings at the conference in September 2003, Wilson was arguing that progress had rarely been won by reasonable people: 'Progress comes from people who refuse to be reasonable, who stand up and say, this is our argument, this is our position.'[6] For John Swinney, the event was notable for an uncharacteristically rabble-rousing appeal for the party to put 'the big question – are you for independence, yes or no? – and then tell the Brits to get off'.[7] The leader secured 84 per cent of the conference votes – 577 to 111. He called for an end to the 'corrosive re-running of past contests' and stated, 'This is the moment when this party draws a line, this party moves on, and I expect every single member of the party to move on today.'[8]

A special Aberdeen party conference, in April 2004, was called to consider several reforms, to end what the leader then termed the 'bureaucratic tyranny'

5   BBC News online, 25 July 2003.

6   BBC News online, 27 September 2003.

7   *The Scotsman*, 27 September 2003.

8   BBC News online, 27 September 2003.

of rules that the party had failed to update for twenty years, so that the SNP could be 'liberated' to fight for independence. There was to be one-member-one-vote in selecting candidates and list rankings, and in elections for the leadership, which had until then been elected by conference delegates. To avoid a repeat of Bill Wilson's campaign, there would be a higher hurdle to mount challenges to the leadership, requiring 100 nominations across twenty constituencies. The new constitution would aim for independence rather than the more ambiguous 'self-government', and the leader would relinquish some of the more time-consuming party management tasks, with the creation of a separate business convener role, chairing the National Executive and handling head office. The previous September, conference had approved a central membership register in place of the opaque branch membership lists. And with that, central control of finances would take power from the branches and help turn around the woeful underfunding of SNP campaigns through the introduction of membership direct debits. Many small fiefdoms were under threat, so it was time to call in loyalties that had been a long time being built up. 'These people had seen me grow up,' recalls Swinney. 'I confronted them, and said, "I need you to do this."'[9]

In swinging support behind the reforms, he was helped by yet more disloyalty. Mike Russell wrote in *Holyrood Magazine* that a poor result in the European elections would mean 'the writing will be on the wall for Swinney. He could not lose ground in three successive elections without a visit from the men in grey kilts. In terms of Scottish party leaders, he has the most to lose.'[10] Swinney learned of this when on an open-top bus in New York, marking Tartan Week. He wouldn't speak with his former ally until their re-election in 2007, when Russell came to Swinney's office to make peace. Just ahead of the Aberdeen conference in April 2004, Campbell Martin was one of the MSPs whose flirtations with the SSP would also infuriate loyal members. By recommending that voters either abstain or back other parties in order

9   From interview with author, June 2016.

10   *Sunday Herald*, 4 April 2004.

to contribute to the ousting of Mr Swinney, the West of Scotland list MSP gave his leader the opportunity to show he could and would crack down on dissent. Martin faced disciplinary measures. He was at first suspended and then expelled, a few weeks after John Swinney's resignation.

RESIGNATION

Mike Russell had been right. The 'men in grey kilts' had prevailed – a reference to the Conservative tradition of faceless grey-suited party grandees telling an incumbent leader that the time had come to move on. This was played out in public after a weekend at home with his wife, deciding to quit and then repeatedly changing his mind. Having decided to fight on, Swinney drove to Forfar on Monday morning, bought a copy of *The Courier* and read of another party grandee telling him to go. It may have been Jim Sillars, he vaguely recalls. He phoned Elizabeth and told her he was resigning and to get in touch with friends to accept their invitation to join them on holiday.

He appeared liberated. Aged only forty, he could take a back seat for the first time in nearly twenty years. Alex Salmond trounced his opponents, Roseanna Cunningham and Mike Russell, in the subsequent leadership election, with a promise to put 'head, heart and soul' back into party campaigning. The implication was that John Swinney had been too much about the head. He had not communicated the heart and soul expected by the membership, which were also found missing by the wider electorate. Whereas Alex Salmond had quit the leadership in 2000, while looking ahead to a tough few years of adjustment, reform and tricky elections for the SNP, he returned to the leadership in 2004 facing a more benign set of circumstances. The Labour Party was embroiled in internal Downing Street battles and the fall-out from the Iraq War. Its Scottish leader, Jack McConnell, had chosen managerialism over vision, and it lacked a compelling narrative with which to regain power in 2007. Salmond was refreshed by four years out of the leadership, and took over a party which was also refreshed. It was tired of dissent, and willing to follow him. Bellwether by-elections began to swing its way.

There was another factor that may have helped the transition from Swinney to Salmond. The returning leader could make people fear him. John Swinney was known by friend and foe to be one of the most decent men in politics. Was he, in plain language, too 'nice' to be a successful leader? He is uncomfortable with the word. His initial reaction is to say how tough he can be. But he concedes that he is more interested in working through an argument than, in footballing terms, playing the person: 'I don't deal with people in a personalised way. I treat people well.' After a long conversation, he observes that we haven't mentioned 'faith', and that it is an important explanation for his behaviour and his motivation. 'Do unto others…' he begins, and trails off. The point is made, but not laboured.

INTO GOVERNMENT

That was the same style that John Swinney took with him into St Andrew's House when the SNP made the move into government. By 2007, Alex Salmond was fronting a team with a reputation for competence in opposition. The SNP campaign machine was slick, professionalised, disciplined and far better resourced than it had ever been. It had secured business credibility with significant endorsements. It owed a lot to the groundwork John Swinney had put in, with his boyhood friend Peter Murrell running a professional operation from head office as chief executive, facilitated by investment in the most modern of political campaign databases.

Entering government, the new First Minister already had Nicola Sturgeon as his party deputy, and heiress apparent. But he turned to John Swinney to take on the biggest role in government. His title was Cabinet Secretary for Finance and Sustainable Growth. Apart from managing the money, that included enterprise, the enterprise agencies, relations with business, inward investment, energy, transport, infrastructure, tourism, local government, planning, Scottish Water and climate change. In a slimmed-down Cabinet structure, it would require exceptional time management and delegation skills. To that end, it was telling how quickly Swinney grasped the mindset of his civil servants.

He could have made an excellent civil servant himself, and realised that clear and consistent expectations would get the best results from them.

The portfolio put Swinney at the heart of managing the budget process for a minority administration, doing deals with other parties to get legislation through, and taking opportunities to wrong-foot his Labour opponents in the process. With Jim Mather as junior minister, he pushed through a radical change in the shape and role of enterprise agencies. He managed a new type of relationship with local authorities, giving them more spending autonomy through a concordat, and beginning a prolonged freeze of council tax. As budgets tightened, he sought flexibility to move marginal funds into infrastructure spending, notably on major roads and the Queensferry Crossing. After the 2014 referendum, he took the lead for the SNP in negotiating the Smith Commission deal on additional powers. Although he signed up on their behalf, his own colleagues quickly sought to distance themselves from it – a discord that seemed to do him no political harm at all. Having done the deal, he was well placed to negotiate the complex details of the fiscal framework with the Treasury. This was to modify the block grant for the Scottish Parliament, to reflect the additional taxation powers. Swinney pushed Whitehall ministers a significant distance and avoided a settlement that could have been very harmful for Holyrood's budgets.

One of his most significant contributions was in writing a Cabinet memo about budget planning, which was leaked to the 'Better Together' campaign in March 2013, a year after its circulation within St Andrew's House. This was to warn fellow ministers of the constraints they faced, on difficult choices ahead, and on the limitations within their plans for independence. The more eye-catching elements were about the volatility of oil revenues and demographic challenges, with talk of the affordability of pension commitments. Asked if he regrets it being made public, Swinney regrets only the way it was interpreted and used against the SNP and the pro-independence campaign: 'what they admit in private, but won't tell voters'. That is not to say he regrets the message got out that the SNP had a fiscally prudent Finance Minister with an eye to the long term.

With additional taxation powers being introduced after the 2016 vote, Nicola Sturgeon carried out a Cabinet reshuffle that split finance gatekeeping from spending briefs. It put John Swinney into the First Minister's top priority area of education, along with skills. That includes the role of a significant shift in the way education is run, risking battles with some powerful lobbies within it, including councils and teacher unions, of trying to present the SNP administration as decentralising to communities, while facing the charge that its instincts are centralising. It also put him in the position of having to refresh party and government thinking, while mid-administration, challenging and changing some of its previous decisions, which is rarely an easy thing to do. The 2016 manifesto was controlled by the party leader, but those around Swinney are in no doubt that his imprint was firmly on it. If Nicola Sturgeon's instincts are to tackle inequality with redistribution and to focus on public services over private sector growth, her deputy has been close by to make sure that the more cautious, business-oriented, middle-class middle ground is protected. With the party now representing every part of Scotland except the northern isles, his is a voice that keeps the rural, formerly Conservative SNP heartlands represented at the Cabinet table.

But before that came the referendum on Scottish independence. Less than two years later, and now as Deputy First Minister, John Swinney doesn't choose to distance himself from economic arguments within the White Paper that failed to convince enough voters that they were credible, or that a heavy price might have to be paid. The White Paper, 'Scotland's Future', was full of assertions for what might be possible. And true to his guiding principle of party loyalty, that is what John Swinney went out to argue for. But for a man whose style remains cautious, seeking to reassure rather than to bluster, it was much more from the Salmond playbook than Swinney's. When the time comes for the SNP to revisit the question of its policy on currency, on shared services with the rest of the United Kingdom, on membership of the European Union and on the costs of transition, John Swinney is well placed both to be the main influence on the revised policies, and to be the reassuring figure sent out to explain it to the public. If and when that time comes, he won't wish to repeat the experience of being asked thirteen times in a BBC Radio Scotland interview what the costs of transition to independence would be without being equipped with one of his 'coherent propositions' as a reply.[11]

CONCLUSION

In the twelve years since John Swinney left the leadership of the Scottish National Party, he has put to rest any party doubts that he was not a true believer in the independence cause. Those doubts dogged him in his four years as leader. The weaker his leadership authority became, the more stridently he had to ramp up his independence rhetoric. He has become more comfortable in his role as the SNP Cabinet's cautious bank manager. And some of the more reckless commitments within the White Paper have vindicated that caution.

From experience going back to 1979 when he joined, he brought to the task an overriding loyalty to the party and an emphasis on discipline within its ranks. He had to contend with the setbacks of a particularly difficult time for the SNP, and some of his choices made the task harder. On the main battleground issues of public services and redistribution, the SNP had not staked out a position much different from Labour's. Swinney steered cautiously into the centre ground while leaving the left flank exposed. He led the party into three consecutive national elections, each of which registered a declining share of the vote. He explained that the party was stuck mid-way between being a party of protest and a party of government. And he poured his energies into securing party reforms, while drawing criticism which would only demonstrate the damage that internal divisions can do a party's public standing and credibility.

That must be counted as part of the explanation why internal party discipline by SNP ministers, MSPs and the wider party, once in power, would be a defining characteristic. The party reforms bequeathed to Alex Salmond a modern, more streamlined, much better funded party. The one-seat margin of victory in 2007, by which the SNP could claim the momentum with

---

11   *Daily Record*, 29 May 2014.

which to form an administration, can be attributed to many factors. But John Swinney can take credit for several of the more compelling ones. The factor in which he takes most (understated) pride is that he believes he has helped Scots become more confident about themselves.

He was also ideally placed to take a powerful role within the new administration. Having been in the leadership, and with no interest at all in returning to it, he carried status in the party, while being no threat to his successors as leader. That factor should not be under-estimated. Heads of parties and governments are often surrounded by those who would replace them. But those with no intention of doing so tend to have more influence. That was true also of William Hague, in the first administration headed by David Cameron; of Sam Galbraith in the early years of Labour–Liberal Democrat Executives in Edinburgh; and as Margaret Thatcher said of her sounding board, Willie Whitelaw, who would counsel her in her early years as Prime Minister: 'Every Prime Minister needs a Willie.'[12]

At the time of writing, John Swinney has served thirty-seven years in the party, eighteen of them in national leadership positions, including two as deputy leader and four as leader. He has been an MP or MSP for nineteen years, and has been a senior figure in government for nine. He is now aged fifty-two and across politics, long commutes, parenting, cycling and distance running in the Angus countryside, shows little sign of flagging. Where does he go from here? The Swinney story could still have a long way to go.

---

12   *The Guardian*, 2 July 1999.

CHAPTER 17

ALEX SALMOND (ACT II)

JAMES MITCHELL

Alex Salmond's return as leader in 2004 was as unplanned as it was sur-prising for all involved, himself included. Yet, it also marked a critical point in the evolution of the party and leadership. The election of an SNP govern-ment in 2007 and Alex Salmond as First Minister was a watershed, and provided the answer to how the SNP should strategically respond to devo-lution: with competence and an attitude of positivity. A second, even more emphatic victory resulted in 2011, producing majority government, and an independence referendum, which although was narrowly lost, confirmed the SNP's dominance in politics. Salmond announced his resignation for the second time the morning after the vote, passing the baton to his deputy, Nicola Sturgeon, and returning to Westminster in 2015 as part of an SNP group of fifty-six MSPs.

. . .

In June 2004, Alex Salmond ruled out standing for the leadership of the SNP, declaring, 'If nominated I'll decline. If drafted I'll defer. And if elected I'll resign.' A month later, he announced he was standing. What happened in the intervening weeks tells us much about the first SNP First Minister of Scotland. He had served a decade as leader from 1990, during which he had taken it from fourth place in terms of seats and votes to become a serious challenger to Labour as Scotland's main party. He had moved his party from ambivalence, and at times hostility, to devolution to embrace it wholeheartedly.

Had his career ended in 2000, when he stood down as leader, he would have been assured a strong place in nationalist history and a significant, though not major, place in modern Scottish politics.

His emphatic denial that he would run for the leadership was not so much aimed at ending journalistic speculation than sending a clear signal to those inside the SNP who were putting pressure on him to stand again. When he stood down from the SNP leadership four years before, he did so after an exhausting period at the top of his party. In the interim, he stood down from Holyrood and returned to Westminster. He was enjoying life as an ex-leader, especially focusing on international politics and frequently called upon by the London media for interviews. He would have missed the limelight – Salmond had been a big fish in the small Scottish pond but his return to London at least meant he was a small fish in a large pond – but it came without the pressure that he had endured as party leader. Having been an MP since 1987, he had been socialised into the ways of Westminster and had struggled to acclimatise to Holyrood. He had never mastered First Minister's Questions against Labour First Minister Donald Dewar, for example, and always seemed more at home in the House of Commons, a place he had initially described as 'alien' when he took up his seat in 1987.

There was speculation that Salmond had mistimed his announcement to stand down from the leadership in 2000. Donald Dewar was dead within a fortnight of the election of Salmond's successor. While Salmond had struggled in exchanges against Dewar, few believed that Dewar's successors would have been a match against Salmond. But it was too late, he had missed his chance. Or so it seemed.

Those pressing him to stand included some who had been close to him over many years and who were as much, if not more, Salmond loyalists as SNP supporters. While media speculation died down after his announcement that he would not stand, the internal pressure within the party did not abate. Angus Robertson MP, Duncan Hamilton and Andrew Wilson were among those urging him to stand, but Salmond was clear that he wanted Nicola Sturgeon, whom he had known since the late 1980s, to replace him.

He had always had a keen eye for young talent and encouraged those with potential, using the limited patronage available to the leader of a small minority party. Sturgeon's performances in the media, as well as her staying power, had impressed him, and his admiration for her had grown over time.

What finally convinced him to stand was his concern that his preferred candidate would lose. He had never been close to Roseanna Cunningham, who was contesting the leadership against Sturgeon. Sturgeon and Cunningham had once been politically inseparable and while their close friendship was tested when each decided to stand for the leadership, it seemed likely that it would stand the strain. But what happened next would take many years to mend and never returned to past intimacy. Salmond was aware that there was growing support for Cunningham, but it was when he heard that Peterhead branch in his own Banff and Buchan constituency had decided to support her over Sturgeon that he decided he had to stand. Though Cunningham and Salmond had both been members of the 79 Group, they had significant political differences. The Group had adopted three key positions at its founding conference: independence, socialism and republicanism. Salmond never shared Cunningham's republicanism and his socialism was never very convincing. Sturgeon was more in his pragmatic social democratic mould.

Three people had already thrown their hat in the ring. As well as Sturgeon and Cunningham, Mike Russell had been nominated, though he was no longer a Member of the Scottish Parliament. Salmond's relationship with Russell had previously been comparable to Sturgeon and Cunningham's, and Salmond had appointed him to the newly created post of SNP chief executive in 1994 and then to a frontbench position in the first Scottish Parliament in 1999. But Russell was another SNP MSP who had lost out in internal reselection battles in 2003.

A number of matters needed to be addressed before Salmond could stand. He had to consult his wife, discuss his decision to stand with Nicola Sturgeon, inform his constituency party, and ultimately, he had return to Holyrood. Moira Salmond was enjoying the relative privacy of life after years of losing her husband to the demands of leading the SNP. She supported him in his decision to contest the leadership, though, aware that he would always regret it if he did not stand. But, again, she did not intend to play a public role.

Salmond reached agreement with Sturgeon that she would remove herself from the leadership contest and stand for the deputy position with his support. There has been speculation on the agreement with suggestions that Salmond might stand aside in her favour at some future point in time but each knew well the dangers of Granita-style misunderstandings and myths. Sturgeon knew her prospect of leading the party would depend on how well she performed in partnership with Salmond rather than any agreement reached at this time. To Salmond's surprise, she asked for time to consider the proposal and agreed within a day. She had initially planned to stand for the leadership with Kenny MacAskill as her running mate for the deputy post, so agreement to stand for the deputy position required that MacAskill stand aside. Sturgeon and MacAskill had never been particularly close and MacAskill had long since abandoned any leadership ambitions and was simply keen to be part of a future SNP government. He recognised the Salmond–Sturgeon combination as a winning formulation. He had observed at close hand the damage caused by the rift between Salmond and Jim Sillars over a decade before and was keen to prevent any similar development.

Salmond's constituency party was enthusiastic and letting them know first made it easier to collect signatures for nomination. He announced his decision at a regular monthly constituency association meeting and asked those present to keep it to themselves. It was a mark of his constituency association's loyalty, and the Scottish media's central-belt focus, that news never leaked. When he was adopted as SNP candidate in Banff and Buchan more than twenty years before, the incumbent Tory MP had dismissed the young pretender from Scotland's central belt as the 'laddie from Lithgae' but Salmond was now firmly rooted in the area.

Salmond was no longer an MSP, having stood down from Holyrood in 2003. It was agreed that Sturgeon would lead the party in Holyrood until his return. If the SNP failed to win the next election then Salmond would likely resign and, assuming she put in strong performances in Holyrood, then she could expect to become leader. Salmond/Sturgeon offered a dream team for many in the SNP frustrated at the lack of progress and fearful that George Robertson, former Scottish Labour leader, had been right when he had suggested in 1995 that devolution would 'kill nationalism stone dead'. The contest was transformed. What was assumed to be a fairly open election was now a foregone conclusion and the prospect of Salmond's return energised the party. Had either Cunningham or Russell known that Salmond intended to contest the leadership, either might have been inclined to stand for the deputy position. But pulling out would have been difficult.

He announced his decision to contest the leadership and casually explained that he had changed his mind. It was with 'surprise and humility, but with renewed determination' that he was 'not just launching a campaign to be SNP leader' but 'launching my candidacy to be the First Minister of Scotland'.[1] A decade later, Jim Murphy copied the line when he announced his decision to stand for the leadership of Scottish Labour. From the start, Salmond intended to present himself in statesmanlike form. The style adopted in his first period as leader was being consciously replaced. This repackaging would be a challenge for a politician socialised – and expert in – the politics of guerrilla tactics and adversarial oppositional politics.

The contest was fairly straightforward. The entire membership had a vote for the first time in the party's history due to changes to the party's constitution brought about by John Swinney. One-member-one-vote resulted in Salmond winning 75 per cent of members' votes, with over 80 per cent of members participating in the election. Cunningham won 15 per cent and Russell 10 per cent. Sturgeon won the deputy post with 54 per cent of the vote while the remaining vote was split reasonably evenly between two other candidates.

Sturgeon proved the most effective performer at First Minister's Questions of any party since the establishment of the Parliament, and while she was busy causing difficulties for Labour in Parliament, Salmond concentrated his efforts

---

1   http://www.theguardian.com/politics/2004/jul/16/scotland.devolution

on building support across Scotland, making particular use of television studios. John Swinney had been attacked internally for backsliding on independence but Salmond came in for no serious criticism on this front, despite no evidence of a change in SNP strategy. The mood inside the party had changed. The SNP on the whole again believed it could win, though still some doubts remained.

The first major test came a year later at the UK general election. The number of Scottish seats in the House of Commons had been reduced from seventy-two to fifty-nine to take account of devolution. Fewer seats and new boundaries in all but three constituencies muddied the waters as far as straight comparison with previous elections was concerned. This worked to the SNP's advantage. Its share of the vote fell by 2.4 per cent to 17.7 per cent but it increased its seats from one to six (it had been calculated that under the new boundaries the SNP would have won only four seats at the previous election). Alex Salmond held his Banff and Buchan seat comfortably though with a slight fall in vote share. The post-election spin, however, was that the SNP had advanced. The real turning point came with the Moray by-election in 2006, caused by the death of Margaret Ewing, whom Salmond had defeated for the leadership in 2000. The SNP ran an efficient campaign and Richard Lochhead, who had formerly worked for Salmond, increased the SNP majority. Salmond used the result to energise and convince the party membership that victory was possible at the following year's election.

TEAM SALMOND

Machiavelli maintained that the 'first opinion of a ruler's intelligence is formed on the quality of the men he has around him'.[2] Over his career, Salmond has inspired loyalty from a core of close confidants and friends. Some of them have been parliamentary colleagues but mostly they have been advisers, often criticised for their laddish tendencies, though this is by no means true of all of the group. Geoff Aberdein, Stephen Noon and Kevin Pringle had

---

2   Machiavelli, *The Prince*, p. 124.

formal roles and worked for Salmond over many years. Salmond would speak to a wider body of people, testing out ideas and opinions, especially with those who would offer robust criticisms. He knew his weaknesses. His written style was poor and much that appeared under his name has been written by others. Mike Russell performed this function in his early years. Duncan Hamilton, former MSP and later special adviser, gave Salmond some of his lines as speech writer. Jennifer Erickson, an American economist who later became director of a Washington DC think tank close to the Obama administration, was economic adviser to Salmond in opposition and government. She and Andrew Wilson put together the impressive team of economic advisers that included two Nobel Laureates. All of these people worked long hours, happily relinquishing credit to the 'boss'. Each viewed working for Salmond as exciting, a great learning experience, albeit exhausting and more demanding than anything they had done before or since. The most common word used to describe the experience was 'privilege', though not everyone who had worked for him found it so positive.

Being SNP leader while an MP was, of course, not new for Salmond, but the existence of Holyrood ensured that his deputy had a far more significant role than any of those who served as deputy during his first period as leader. His absence from Holyrood allowed Sturgeon to redefine the role of deputy leader to suit herself, just as Salmond had defined the roles of each of the national party offices he had previously held. His return to the leadership brought back some key Salmond courtiers: Kevin Pringle and Stephen Noon, in particular, had remarkable access to the leader.

In his first term as leader, Salmond had given little thought to his succession but this time round it was clear, unforeseen developments apart, that he wanted Sturgeon to succeed him. If a deal was done – as has been the subject of much journalistic speculation – it was never acknowledged by either and would likely have been denied had he ever concluded that she was the wrong person to succeed him. He would go out of his way to praise his deputy in speeches and conversations. The SNP had been described as a 'one-man band' in the earlier period, which irritated Salmond but also appealed to his ego as it suggested that he had no equal inside his party.

He was keen to project a more collegiate image of leadership, more in common with how the party had understood the concept until he had first assumed that role in 1990. He was assisted in this in having far more established full-time politicians in 2004. Collegiality was fine because there was no doubt that he would be *primus inter pares*. In 1990, he had been one of only three SNP MPs and the SNP was ambivalent at best in its attitude to devolution, struggled to gain media attention and rarely set the agenda. Under his leadership, it had engaged in political guerrilla tactics: stunts that the large established parties frowned upon. Towards the end of his first term, he had fought the first election to the Scottish Parliament, hoping to become First Minister. Salmond was the political upstart in the eyes of opponents, a compulsive and opportunistic attention-seeker. It had then proved difficult to make the transition to a type of leadership that would be required of a First Minister in the eyes of the electorate.

He returned to the leadership of the party with a larger and more experienced supporting cast, a solid base in Holyrood. It was still some way short of becoming the largest party but it could now seriously aspire to be an alternative party of government. Alex Salmond's objective was clear: he was seeking office as First Minister at the head of an SNP administration. The hope was that the Liberal Democrats would join a coalition if the SNP became Scotland's party, but when that did not happen, Salmond made a virtue of necessity and formed a minority SNP government. Expectations were that this inexperienced team would not last the course and that there would be another election before the formal four-year set parliamentary term was over.[3] Salmond knew the scale of the challenge ahead and told a close associate, 'Enjoy it. We'll be out in six months.'

Finding a seat in Holyrood proved easy. His old Banff and Buchan Holyrood seat was held by Stewart Stevenson, a friend of many decades, and Salmond held the equivalent seat in the Commons. His base was in north-east Scotland and a couple of possibilities arose. The SNP had been in third place

---

3   *Edinburgh Evening News*, 21 June 2007.

at the previous election in Gordon and second to Labour in Aberdeen Central. On paper the latter looked like the best bet and when Salmond chose to stand in Gordon, and also headed the regional list, there was speculation that he was hedging his bets. If he failed to win Gordon then the SNP would probably fail to become the largest party. He could then resign at some suitable point from the regional list without causing a by-election, as list vacancies were filled by the next person on the party list. He was still a Member of the Commons so would be in the same position that he was before the election. The speculation was only partly correct. It was a calculated bet and would have allowed him to bow out again from Holyrood if the SNP failed to become the largest party, but Gordon was the best prospect. Gordon was number twenty on the SNP's list of target seats and the party needed an additional twenty seats to win. Salmond liked this: 'I win, we win.' Boundary changes meant that a sizeable part of Gordon had been in his old Banff and Buchan constituency and many of the local issues that he had campaigned on since 1987 were common to both, and he knew the area well. Councillor Stuart Pratt, who had been his election agent in every contest since 1987, would lead a formidable and trusted team of local activists. Salmond's north-east base would once more prove to be the solid foundation of his support.

Salmond won Gordon with a 2,062 majority over the Lib Dems, but more significantly the SNP finished narrowly ahead of Labour in both seats and votes: forty-seven to forty-six in the former; and 32.9 per cent to 32 per cent in the constituency vote and 31 per cent to 29.2 per cent in the regional vote. The narrowness of the result belied its historic nature: this was the first nationwide victory by the SNP in its history; and likewise it was the first Labour defeat at either a Scottish Parliament or Westminster contest since the 1950s.

The result imposed a self-motivating discipline on the SNP and its group of parliamentarians. And while the result imposed pressures on the SNP, in another respect, it reduced some of the expectations public opinion had of the first ever SNP Scottish government. Labour, on the other hand, found itself in opposition, struggling to come to terms with defeat. Labour's turmoil provided a consistent aid to Salmond's tenure as First Minister.

His first Cabinet was half the size of the previous one headed by Labour's Jack McConnell and consisted of five other members with whom he had worked closely over many years. There was a core group of Salmond, Sturgeon and Swinney. The six Cabinet Secretaries were joined each week by Bruce Crawford, Minister for Parliament Business, whose job it was to ensure that the SNP government was not defeated in the Holyrood chamber. Crawford forged deals with the various opposition parties, identifying how far the government could push its proposals without falling foul of the combined opposition. The Tories had signalled that they would give constructive support to whichever party was the largest in key votes but would oppose any effort to pursue independence. But there were occasions when Tory support was not given and deals had to be done with other parties. Concessions to the other parties that were essential for the survival of the government were acknowledged from the start and relatively easy with Labour given the degree of broad agreement across non-constitutional matters.

It was a cohesive group and civil servants were surprised at the changes in Cabinet government. Whereas previously most decisions had been taken outside Cabinet and special advisers had in some cases been as important as ministers, the SNP minority government appeared to operate as a textbook Cabinet should. Cabinet Secretaries engaged in fulsome debate but maintained collective responsibility. Contrary to what might have been expected given his dominance of the party, this was not a First Ministerial government. Salmond gave ministers considerable autonomy though he led on a number of matters.

He was particularly concerned with the Scottish government's lack of capacity in two areas close to his heart – energy and the economy. The old Scottish Office, his first employer on leaving university as a member of the government Economic Service in 1978, had strengths in these areas and he was keen to see these built up again. At times he was frustrated by an old guard in the civil service but equally determined not to rock the boat, recognising that he needed the officials on his side. In 2010, when the opportunity came to appoint a new Permanent Secretary, he was keen to see an outsider get the job. Sir Peter Housden's appointment was approved. Housden had been Permanent Secretary for the Office of the Deputy Prime Minister and then the Department for Communities and Local Government and had a career in English local government before joining the UK civil service. Salmond henceforth developed a constructive relationship with him and the service, and though critics thought that Salmond was politicising the civil service, it was simply the case that he understood, not least from his own experience, how it worked.

He stood by Education Secretary Fiona Hyslop as long as he could when she became the focus of criticism. She was only removed from her post as Cabinet Secretary for Education and Lifelong Learning when she faced a motion of no confidence – which was bound to pass given parliamentary arithmetic – but he gave her an alternative ministerial post outside Cabinet and then brought her back following the SNP's victory in 2011. There were changes at junior ministerial level but these were fairly minor. The message was clear: he would stand by colleagues under pressure and expected this support to be recip-rocated. Old virtues were evident in his willingness to forgive and move on. Kenny MacAskill and Salmond had had a turbulent relationship back in the pre-devolution days but Salmond had always recognised MacAskill's talents and appointed him Justice Secretary. Mike Russell and Roseanna Cunningham were given junior ministerial posts, and Russell was eventually made a Cabinet Secretary, replacing Hyslop, though each had had significant differences, the former more recently than the latter. The degree of continuity of membership of the government was striking. All six members of his original Cabinet were still in place, though not all with same portfolios, when he demitted office seven years later. His approach to government was, ironically, to act as a convener, giving considerable leadership roles to Sturgeon and Swinney.

His second period as leader necessitated a wholly different approach. Attracting attention from the political fringe had required tactics and styles that would be inappropriate for someone seeking and holding office as First Minister. The outsider had to learn to become an insider, but old habits, as they say, die hard, and he would occasionally lapse into styles that were more appropriate to his first term, especially when the adrenalin was pumping in the aftermath of elections. He enjoyed the occasional return to being the anti-establishment politician and in this sense he remained a classic outsider as political leader in much the same way as Margaret Thatcher.[4] This was frowned upon by his opponents, but this time they could add that he was behaving in a manner that was not in keeping with his office. But it served him well in maintaining his outsider status.

SALMOND'S NATIONALISM

In his younger days, critics inside the 79 Group had referred to him as 'slippery Salmond', so difficult was he to pin down politically. Salmond had little interest in ideology. His support for the 79 Group was more to do with party positioning. He believed that the SNP needed to be more than a party of independence and that 'standing up for Scotland' required elaboration. His view was that if the SNP failed to define its position on the left–right spectrum then its opponents would do so. The 79 Group message was clear about where on that spectrum it wanted the SNP to be placed, even if he had serious problems with republicanism and reservations about socialism. Apart from the constitutional question, Salmond would have fitted comfortably into the social democratic wing of the Labour Party. He understood the tensions between encouraging entrepreneurial behaviour leading to economic growth and the distribution of wealth consequences that followed. For him, the issue was not a case of either/ or but about balancing wealth creation and distribution. He could show irritation, sometimes verging on contempt, for those who sought simple solutions and posed as left-wing by advocating using tax in crude ways.

His upbringing in a Presbyterian household in Linlithgow, a small town east of Edinburgh, might have led to socially conservative views. In some respects

---

4   Anthony King, 'The Outsider as Political Leader', in Larry Berman (ed.), *The Art of Political Leadership: Essays in Honor of Fred I. Greenstein* (Lanham, MD: Rowman & Littlefield Publishers, 2005); Michael Foley, *The British Presidency* (Manchester: Manchester University Press, 2001), pp. 68–70; Hugo Young, *One of Us: A Biography of Margaret Thatcher* (London: Pan Books, 1989).

this was true. He was a friend of Scotland's most senior Catholics during both periods as leader. His views on abortion and the importance of the family were moderately conservative but his views on gay rights were liberal. During his second period as leader, Alyn Smith SNP MEP requested a meeting with Salmond to discuss a personal matter. On hearing that Smith was about to publicly come out as homosexual, Salmond expressed surprise that he needed to be informed and even a little irritation that a personal matter that was of no concern to him as leader had taken up some of his busy schedule.

Salmond brought a sharp mind to leadership but it was of a clever rather than an intellectual kind. He was a problem-solver, often reaching a decision intuitively and speedily. Enquiry had to serve a purpose. His politics were innate, born of experience rather than extensive reading and deliberation. He was, however, rigorously analytic in his thinking, though this was more in the sense that he was a rational calculating machine than someone who engaged with big ideas. Independence was the only 'big idea' for him. He had insisted he was an 'economic nationalist' in his early years in politics but this was less a statement on how he thought than a response to criticisms that nationalism was emotional. In these early years, it made many suspect that his nationalism was shallow and conditional. If the figures did not add up, it was assumed, then Salmond might easily defect to Labour. By the time he returned to leadership he had grown in confidence and references to 'this historic nation' had replaced 'economic nationalist' in his language. Quite simply, Scotland was the community to which he belonged and felt allegiance. This was not a matter of dispute and therefore hardly a matter of speculation, least of all for someone least likely to engage in introspection.

Salmond would often be the key figure in meetings who would bring the discussion back to independence and he insisted on it being mentioned in election leaflets, though little was done preparing a detailed case for independence until the 2011 election. The focus instead was on winning elections, the pre-requisite for a referendum. More thought had gone into working out the details of independence during his first period as leader than in the period from 2004 to 2011.

Optimism has had to be a characteristic of all SNP leaders. As Eisenhower noted in a discarded draft of his memoirs, 'Without confidence, enthusiasm and optimism in the command, victory is scarcely obtainable.' Optimism and pessimism, as the American President knew, were 'infectious and they spread more rapidly from head downward than in any other direction'.[5] Salmond had rarely lacked optimism, fuelled by seeing his party move from the fringe to centre stage, and that optimism was now needed to believe that polls showing an overwhelming majority against independence could be turned around.

Salmond shares Eisenhower's conscious resolve to project optimism regardless of circumstances: 'I firmly determined that my mannerisms and speech in public', wrote Eisenhower in his wartime leadership, 'would always reflect the cheerful certainty of victory – that any pessimism and discouragement I might ever feel would be reserved for my pillow.'[6] Defeats and setbacks were turned into victories, and the hope that an independent Scotland was possible was kept alive. In this respect, vision, message and strategy merged in Salmond's approach to politics. 'Yes we can' was an SNP slogan in 1997, more than a decade before Obama adopted it in his first presidential campaign.

WINNING INDEPENDENCE BY GOVERNING COMPETENTLY

The party was relieved that Salmond was back and those who felt independence had been downgraded appeared content that there was no sign of it moving up the party's agenda. The message from the leadership was that the party needed to demonstrate its competence and that this would somehow translate into support for independence.

This was an old issue for the SNP. In the 1960s, Dr Robert McIntyre had taken the view that the SNP needed to show it could govern and encouraged the party to contest local elections. He had been stung by criticisms that the SNP couldn't

5   Stephen E. Ambrose, *Eisenhower: Soldier and President* (New York: Simon & Schuster, 2003), p. 82.
6   Ibid.

'run a sweetie shop' and set out to disprove it.[7] McIntyre himself served as Stirling's provost for a decade (see Richard Finlay's chapter in this book). The existence of the Scottish Parliament offered a more significant means of demonstrating competence, showing that the SNP could run a country. Convincing voters that the party was competent and that it had sufficient talent was important. The SNP worried that if voters saw Labour as incompetent this would undermine the case for independence by suggesting that the pool of talent was limited to one party and so it had to be careful about how it articulated its opposition.

This marked another significant change from his earlier period in office, reflecting the changed context of Scottish politics. When he had first been elected leader, Scotland had no Parliament and was governed by the Conservatives under Margaret Thatcher. The 1980s had seen considerable economic and social upheaval as traditional industries declined and the Scottish economy underwent significant change. Riding the wave of opposition to the government in London had seen the SNP compete with Labour to be the strongest opponent of Thatcherism. The emphasis had been on Scotland's economic decline. The politics of opposition had been the politics of despair. The SNP had forged a positive message around 'independence in Europe' but this sat uneasily alongside the message that the London government was turning Scotland into an economic basket case. The emphasis was unambiguously on optimism in his second period as leader.

Showing that devolution worked was thought likely to lead to increased support for independence, though critics suggested that voters might conclude that there was no need for more powers. The sense of unity and purpose contrasted with Labour's lack of ambition and tired image, having been in office since 1999. Labour made leadership an issue in the 2007 election when First Minister Jack McConnell questioned whether Salmond was fit to hold office. But this was counter-productive. Survey findings showed Salmond comfortably ahead in the public's estimation as a credible First Minister.[8]

7   Ibid.

8   R. Johns, D. Denver, J. Mitchell and C. Pattie, *Voting for a Scottish Government: The Scottish Parliament Election of 2007* (Manchester: Manchester University Press, 2010), pp. 47–56.

Opponents in other parties and the press set out to attack Salmond, hoping that damaging him would leave the SNP with little to offer. But, once again, the style of criticism showed limited understanding of public opinion. Portraying Salmond as an arrogant bully helped his image as a strong leader, and his advantage increased considerably by the time of the 2011 elections, when Salmond had served as First Minister and he faced Labour's Iain Gray.[9] Like other strong leaders, he polarised opinion.

The decision to release Abdelbaset Al-Megrahi, the only man ever convicted for the Lockerbie Bombing, in August 2009 on compassionate grounds proved the most controversial and high-profile decision of his leadership. Salmond and Kenny MacAskill, his Justice Secretary, were clear that the process should be above reproach and expected a backlash but were surprised by its scale. The Scottish government was brought to the attention of the media across the globe and while the Scottish government was attacked by senior US politicians, it also put Scotland on the map. Scottish public support swung behind the government and the whole episode contributed to the sense that Salmond and his ministers were capable of operating at this level and willing to ignore US demands.

Relations with London needed to be handled carefully. Salmond was portrayed by opponents as someone who would seek conflict with Westminster, but was keen to demonstrate a willingness to work constructively while standing up for Scotland when necessary. The opportunity to portray London as the uncooperative partner was an unexpected gift. Prime Minister Blair's refusal to congratulate Salmond on becoming First Minister contrasted with the Prime Minister's willingness to congratulate Ian Paisley on becoming First Minister in Northern Ireland. Salmond exploited this with heavy sarcasm, 'He never phones, he never writes,' he complained at First Minister's Questions. Everyday relations between London and Edinburgh operated efficiently, constructively and well away from the media spotlight.

---

9   C. Carman, R. Johns and J. Mitchell, *More Scottish than British: The 2011 Scottish Parliament Election* (Basingstoke: Palgrave Macmillan, 2014).

The occasional flashpoint allowed Salmond to play the role of David taking on Goliath. UK government allowed him to continue to be the outsider.

Relations improved after David Cameron became Prime Minister in 2010. The Conservatives did not have Labour's sense that Salmond and the SNP had usurped Labour's entitlement. Cameron's 'respect agenda' involved making a conscious effort to be constructive. Salmond viewed the Tories' vulnerability on the 'Scottish question' and hoped to convince the new Prime Minister that he should offer a more advanced form of devolution than the Calman Commission had proposed. He thought that David Cameron might see the opportunity to propose a measure of fiscal autonomy and claim this as evidence that the Tories were no longer the party that had opposed devolution. He attempted to build up support for fiscal autonomy, encouraging individuals and groups to press the case over the course of the summer and into autumn of 2010. Early meetings suggested that Cameron was interested in the idea but by late 2010 his interest had waned. Polls suggested that Labour's support was on the rise and that they might win the 2011 election. There was little reason, therefore, to placate the Scots. Many in the SNP were worried about the polls, although the one consistently positive message to come out of them for the SNP was that, when it came to leadership ratings, Salmond easily outpolled Iain Gray, Labour's then leader. Salmond took little comfort from this, however, reminding those who suggested that this meant the SNP would win that parties could lose with the most popular leader, citing Jim Callaghan in 1979. He took more comfort from the interpretation of the polls that suggested that voters were operating in the shadow of the UK election and that SNP support would pick up when voters turned their attention to who should govern Scotland from Holyrood. This required emphasising the economic potential of independence without undermining confidence by over-stating the weakness of the Scottish economy. He wanted to associate himself and his cause with Scottish success and there appeared to be no greater Scottish success in the early years of the new millennium than the Royal Bank of Scotland, his old employer. Shortly after winning the election in 2007, he wrote to Fred Goodwin stating that it was in the 'Scottish interest for RBS to be successful, and I would like to offer any assistance my office can provide' in support of the ill-fated RBS bid for Dutch bank ABN AMRO.[10]

While opponents have exaggerated Salmond's links with the bank, this was aided by his keenness to create that impression himself. His initial reaction to the collapse of the bank was little different from those in government across the world. He searched for an explanation but did not want to confront the possibility that any blame might be found at the door of RBS. His defence later was that he had assumed that the Financial Services Authority had performed its duties properly. The ensuing economic and fiscal crisis undermined the optimism felt necessary for voters to switch to independence. Salmond had referred to the 'arc of prosperity' that took in a number of small European states. This would be mocked after the collapse of these economies, though Salmond's irrepressible nature combined with his uncanny knack of shifting ground was evident when he delivered a lecture at Harvard University in 2008.[11] The 'arc of prosperity' was still relevant, as evidenced by the UN Human Development Index that placed Ireland, Iceland and Norway in the top five countries in the world. These were small, dynamic trading nations with flexibility to claim a major stake in the knowledge economy. He predicted that they would bounce back more effectively than some of the larger economies. It was the case for optimism in difficult times.

THE INDEPENDENCE REFERENDUM

The policy of holding an independence referendum once elected to government had initially been motivated by considerations of party management. The leadership had wanted to placate hardliners while not scaring off voters who might be inclined to vote SNP but less keen on independence. The lesson had been learned from Labour's 1997 referendum on devolution. Without an overall majority in 2007, there was little prospect of

10   Ian Fraser, *Shredded: Inside RBS, the Bank that Broke Britain* (Edinburgh: Birlinn Ltd., 2015).

11   Alex Salmond, 'Free to Prosper: Creating the Celtic Lion Economy', speech at Harvard University, 31 March 2008. [http://www.gov.scot/News/Speeches/Speeches/First-Minister/harvard-university]

a referendum until Wendy Alexander, Labour's leader at the time, challenged the SNP to 'bring it on'. However, it soon became clear that Alexander did not have the backing of her party, including Prime Minister Gordon Brown. Salmond was bemused by Alexander's proposal and was not convinced that she was bluffing, assuming instead that this had the support of Brown. He was convinced, though, that Labour was in more of a mess than he had imagined.

One of Alexander's initiatives was more successful. She convinced the other opposition parties to work with Labour and come up with a more advanced scheme of devolution than then existed. A commission was set up under Sir Kenneth Calman that deliberated and produced proposals separate to and as an alternative to the SNP government's 'National Conversation', which was launched in 2007. This National Conversation had set out the SNP's independence proposals and alternatives and it was hoped might stimulate a debate on the constitution. It was as much as anything an attempt to show to party members that the SNP government had not lost sight of independence while acknowledging that its scope to do much on this agenda was limited. The SNP may have been in office, but it was still only fulfilling the function it had long performed at points of peak electoral support in the past. It was forcing others to respond to the threat and moving the constitutional debate forward while still not coming close to achieving independence.

By the time of the 2011 election, the likelihood of a referendum seemed a distant prospect. After four years in office, support for independence remained much as it was when Salmond became First Minister and fewer voters saw independence as a major issue. The SNP won an overall majority because it was seen as competent.[12] Indeed, had the constitution been at the front of voters' minds then it is likely that the SNP would not have come close to winning so well. An independence referendum was on the agenda because independence had not been an issue in the election. The referendum campaign effectively began as soon as it became clear that the SNP had secured an overall majority, something the electoral system had supposedly been

---

12   Carman et al., *More Scottish than British.*

designed to prevent. Even if London refused to allow a referendum, it was clear that it had become a major issue.

Salmond was well aware that support for independence was well behind support for the union, and he also knew the difference between risk and uncertainty. He was not afraid of the former and would measure up probabilities, but he shied away from the latter. He was well aware of the classic distinction drawn by Frank Wright in his seminal book *Risk, Uncertainty and Profit*, published in 1921, that risk involved future events with measureable probability while uncertainty involved situations when some future event was incalculable or unclear. His fondness for a flutter on the horses was widely interpreted as a willingness to gamble on an uncertain future, but few really examined his gambling technique. It was the case that he usually came out on top but often without his horse winning the race. Victory, for Salmond, was defined in terms of what was possible. He was not frightened of making difficult decisions but when it came to gambling he preferred to hedge his bets. He resurrected his aim of getting fiscal autonomy – some measure of devolution lying beyond what already existed but short of independence – on the agenda. The SNP government held a consultation including whether there ought to be a third option on the ballot paper. Had that succeeded, then the likelihood is that the referendum would have been a more predictable affair, with most voters supporting the middle option. Salmond would have been able to claim to have advanced the cause. As it happened, London dug in its heels. This would be a straight fight between the status quo and independence. In the last week of the referendum campaign, it was David Cameron who looked like the gambler. When he had agreed to a referendum Cameron had assumed that it would be relatively easy to defeat independence.

It was a mark of his confidence in Sturgeon that she led the campaign until the final stages. Some thought was given to him standing down as First Minister and campaigning as party leader. The idea would have been a return to before 2007, when Nicola Sturgeon took charge in Holyrood and he would campaign across Scotland, but it was rejected. Salmond's role in the referendum was vital given his status as First Minister but he was keen not to be the defining feature of the campaign. It was felt essential to send a strong message that it was still business as usual. This also meant that accusations that the SNP were neglecting their everyday duties in government could be refuted. He intervened at key stages and his involvement was ramped up from the launch of the independence white paper, setting out the SNP government's vision of independence, in November 2013. The campaign for independence combined the two Salmond styles. With overwhelming opposition in the press, he knew that the campaign needed to reach the public via alternative routes and gave free rein to local campaigns, imaginative stunts and the creation of a variety of groups for independence. This meant ceding control of much of the campaign but left him to focus on his strengths in dealing with the broadcast media. Two campaigns ran in parallel, therefore, with some of Salmond's core team working in both and maintaining some degree of consistency. The emphasis throughout was on being the underdog, though this approach was abandoned in the run-up to the first set-piece debate between Salmond and former Labour Chancellor of the Exchequer Alistair Darling, who was leading the pro-union cause. Salmond did not meet the hyped expectations, while Darling confounded critics and acted in an abrasive, challenging manner, which defined much of the debate. But that served Salmond well in the second debate, where, with lower expectations and a much stronger performance, Salmond emerged the clear victor overall. But, while the debate's main function was to galvanise support, it also galvanised opposition.

As election day approached, the polls began to close. Opponents of independence finally agreed to offer an alternative to both independence and the status quo. What was titled 'The Vow' was as close as anything was likely to be to the 'more powers' option Salmond had wanted in the first place, though by this stage he would have preferred a straight contest between independence and the status quo.

The result was a disappointment, though he could take comfort from the increase in support for independence and a record 85 per cent turnout.

He would subsequently maintain that 'The Vow' had reversed the trend towards independence. He conceded defeat gracefully and announced that he would stand down as SNP leader and First Minister. Anyone imaging that this was Salmond bowing out of politics, however, was mistaken. Salmond had always known that he would have to resign if defeated, that if he had held on as First Minister then he would have become the focus of demands for his resignation and the defeat would define the SNP government and his career. By resigning, he would allow the SNP and the independence campaign to move on. 'The Vow' would also prove useful.

Within days of the referendum, he was working out how to ensure that he could extract as much as possible from the defeat. Nicola Sturgeon was assured victory in the SNP leadership contest had one occurred and Salmond would stand for Gordon at the next election to the House of Commons. It was broadly the same seat he held in Holyrood and the long-standing incumbent Liberal Democrat Member had announced he was standing down. Salmond calculated that if almost all of those who had voted for independence voted for the SNP then the party could sweep the board across Scotland, since the 55 per cent who had voted against independence would be split between the other parties. In order to take full advantage of the referendum, Salmond considered having 'Yes Scotland' rather than SNP candidates in the election. This would allow those who had been active in the referendum but not SNP members to stand. Sturgeon, however, disagreed. Instead, the SNP relaxed its rules on who could stand as candidates, allowing a number of new recruits to put themselves forward. Eight months after defeat in the referendum, the SNP achieved the best result of any party since the extension of the franchise. While the Scottish Unionist Party and Liberal Unionists combined had won 50.1 per cent of the vote in Scotland in 1955 at a time of the two-party system, the SNP won 50 per cent of the vote on its own, gaining fifty-six (95 per cent) of Scotland's seats. Salmond had insisted that the SNP would hold the UK government's 'feet to the fire' and that the 'dream would never die'. It was classic Salmond, the ever ebullient politician who was able to turn defeat into victory.

CONCLUSION

Sidney Hook famously distinguished between 'eventful' and 'event-making' leaders. Things happen to the former and the latter make things happen. Alex Salmond belongs emphatically in the event-making list of political leaders.[13] For this he was and is likely to remain a hero for many in the SNP, though by the same token he inevitably became a focus of opposition that might otherwise have been less virulent. Indeed, few Scottish politicians have experienced such sustained levels of invective. Rumours would be circulated that he had massive gambling debts and much else besides. Had any of this been true then the considerable effort and investment made by the tabloid press to find evidence of Salmond's misdeeds would surely have uncovered this or else he was remarkably skilful in covering his tracks. At the height of the MPs' expenses scandal, journalists became excited when it appeared that a major scandal had finally been uncovered. House of Commons expenses were being paid to a nursery in Plymouth in 2008. Salivating journalists were working up stories about Salmond's love child until it was noticed that a mistake had been made and the expenses claim related to a different MP.

Alex Salmond was viewed by opponents as an upstart leading an upstart party. He stood down as leader having brought Scotland closer to independence than at any time before, creating the conditions that led to the SNP becoming the dominant party in Scotland to an extent unrivalled since full adult enfranchisement. Sixteen- and seventeen-year-olds got to vote in the Scottish referendum and would vote in subsequent Holyrood elections. The Scottish government's capacity and focus on the economy and energy, especially renewable energy, were enhanced. Its international reach, within the limits of devolution, was developed, and he ensured that Scotland had a presence on the international stage as never before with inward investment at record levels. He handled crises skilfully, from the Glasgow airport terrorist

13   Sidney Hook, *The Hero in History: A Study in Limitation and Possibility* (New York: John Day Company, 1943), Chapter 9.

attack, to the economic crisis, to the proposed Grangemouth refinery closure, which threatened a key part of the Scottish economy. He took particular pride in abolishing tuition fees. But, ultimately, his key achievement as SNP leader was to take Scotland closer to independence than ever before. This legacy ensured that the SNP achieved the highest share of the vote for any single party since full adult enfranchisement when the SNP won fifty-six of Scotland's fifty-nine seats in the Commons.

In his biography of Joseph Chamberlain, Enoch Powell had written that 'All political lives, unless they are cut off in midstream at a happy juncture, end in failure, because that is the nature of politics and of human affairs.' Salmond's career as leader of the SNP ended in failure as measured by the exceptional standards he set himself when he was first elected to the House of Commons in 1987, but few would interpret his leadership other than as remarkably successful.

CHAPTER 18

NICOLA STURGEON

MANDY RHODES

Nicola Sturgeon joined the SNP while still at school and came to the attention of Alex Salmond, then leading the party, while still a law student at Glasgow University. She was the youngest SNP candidate at the 1992 general election and went on to contest the Glasgow Govan Westminster constituency and then the Scottish Parliament seat. She was elected as an SNP list member for Glasgow in the first elections to the Scottish Parliament in 1999 and eventually won the Govan constituency in 2007. She initially intended to stand for the leadership when John Swinney resigned in 2004 but instead made way for Alex Salmond and successfully contested the deputy leader position. In 2007, she became Deputy First Minister and Cabinet Secretary for Health and Wellbeing. She led the SNP campaign in the independence referendum until the final few months while holding the post of Cabinet Secretary for Infrastructure, Investment and Cities. She was returned unopposed as SNP leader, and thereby First Minister, following Alex Salmond's resignation after the referendum. In the wake of the referendum, under her leadership, the party achieved its best Westminster election result when it won fifty-six of Scotland's fifty-nine seats with a 50 per cent share of the vote. In May 2016, the SNP lost its overall majority but still comfortably retained its position as Scotland's largest party.

• • •

Saturday 2 January 1971 is remembered as the darkest day in Scottish footballing history. Around 80,000 people left for the traditional Old Firm Ne'erday match at Ibrox that morning, but sixty-six Rangers fans would never return – crushed to death on Stairway 13 at the Copland Road end of the ground. At the start of the match, few could have predicted the horror that was to follow. No one is quite sure what happened as the fans left the stadium, but it seems likely that someone fell, creating a domino effect, a barrier collapsed and thousands of people were trapped in a desperate battle for life. The disaster, which saw 140 casualties and sixty-six dead, changed Scottish football for ever.

Four decades on, thousands of people gathered at the ground on 3 January 2011 to mark the disaster. Rangers players, past and present, including John Greig, the captain on the day of the tragedy, Celtic manager Neil Lennon, Rangers' assistant manager Ally McCoist and Celtic's chairman and former Home Secretary John Reid, were joined by family and friends of the dead as well as Scotland's religious leaders and leading politicians. Among them was Labour's then leader Iain Gray and the SNP's Deputy First Minister Nicola Sturgeon, whose constituency of Glasgow Govan covered Ibrox.

Addressing the service, Rangers' chief executive Martin Bain said the disaster was an 'unimaginable horror'. It was a grim occasion and, looking back now at pictures from that day, Nicola Sturgeon appears tired and pale. Some images show her with her eyes tightly shut and, while the occasion was undoubtedly sombre, she looks to be in real pain. The cause of which was something beyond the commemoration.

In fact, as she sat on the terraces that day, Sturgeon was going through her own very personal anguish. She was miscarrying a baby. The Deputy First Minister should have been at home in her bed, being looked after by her husband, Peter Murrell, and not sharing in what was a public grief. But that day on the stand at Ibrox, as the photographs confirm, was where her personal and professional worlds collided and the latter won out. It was her public duty to be there, so there she was.

Over the years there has been much speculation among commentators about the fact that Sturgeon has not had children. In interviews she would be constantly asked when she'd be starting a family, questions that she deftly deflected before moving the conversation on. Nevertheless, assumptions have been made and opinions have been formed. I knew only by accident – a slip of words over lunch – that being childless had not been an entirely conscious choice for Sturgeon and it has made me reflect on how much female political leaders, in particular, wrestle with what they expose of themselves and why.

Sturgeon is, despite outward appearances, an intensely private person and our relationship has been a slow burner. Not long after the 2011 election, in which the SNP won by a historic majority, we had been having lunch, going over the politics and then talking about a mutual friend who had lost a baby, when intuitively I realised that Sturgeon was referring to herself. She chose, as is her prerogative, to not to talk about the miscarriage publicly, and I have respected her need for privacy in an increasingly public world, but with the passage of time she has become less adamant that it stays a secret and has allowed me to refer to it now.

It is important because it says something about the pressures on and the conjectures made about women in leadership positions. Crucially, it also says something about the impact that all of that scrutiny and speculation has had on her and how she manages it.

In December 2010, Labour was polling way ahead of her own party. There were serious questions about whether the SNP could hang on to power – they had formed a minority government in 2007, having beaten Labour by just one seat – and Sturgeon knew she had a fight on her hands and that the next few months would be a struggle.

She would have been almost forty-one and six months pregnant going into the formal election campaign and, while clearly happy about being pregnant, she would also have been anxious about how it might affect not just the election campaign but also her role in any future Cabinet. And while these are normal feelings for any woman with a career to think about, for someone as politically programmed as Sturgeon, who would also never have wanted something as personal as a pregnancy to see her accused of exploiting a personal situation for political gain during an election, they would have been paramount.

Being prepared and in control is what has powered Sturgeon – turned the gauche, unsmiling teenager who first stood on a platform for the SNP at the age of sixteen, finding herself dubbed the 'nippy sweetie', into the powerhouse politician, beloved by the masses, that she is now. Being vulnerable and powerless are not positions Sturgeon likes to be in.

Why does any of this matter in the context of political leadership? It matters because Sturgeon is cognisant of the responsibility that she has as a role model. Because, as the first woman to be First Minister, she is acutely aware that some young girls will look at her and think that as a woman you have to sacrifice part of your life to climb the career ladder. And in that respect, it is important to understand that being childless was not always a conscious choice for Sturgeon. She is also aware that women in politics are afraid to show vulnerability, as if revealing emotion in the male-dominated world of politics is seen as a weakness that would reflect adversely on their ability to lead. And that, too, is wrong.

It also puts into some context the repeated accusations that she has had to endure, both in and out of the parliamentary chamber, that, as a political leader without children, she could not understand some of the concerns that parents might feel about the impact of her political decisions.

'Speaking as a mother' is a phrase frequently used by politicians with the presumption that being a parent gives you a shortcut to authenticity and normality. As if not being a mother makes you less of a person – abnormal. Week in, week out at FMQs, Johann Lamont would start off her questions to Sturgeon with what political commentators dubbed her 'mum-isms'. One very senior female Labour politician once described Sturgeon to me as 'ruthlessly ambitious', all because she assumed that, given that she had no children, she had put career first.

For a female politician, being childless becomes a much more defining characteristic than it ever does for a man. Sturgeon herself has posed the question about how many interviewers have ever asked Alex Salmond why he didn't have children. And the answer is, of course, very few. Mainly because they made assumptions – rightly or wrongly – about his wife, who is seventeen years his senior.

During the UK Labour leadership contest, the former Labour minister Helen Goodman wrote a column for the Huffington Post in which she said that she supported Yvette Cooper for leader because, 'As a working mum, she understands the pressures on modern family life. We need a leader who knows what challenges ordinary people face day to day, and who is committed to helping them.'[1] And during the EU referendum, Tory MP and party leader hopeful Andrea Leadsom constantly referred to being a mother, as if that enough were a qualification to fight for a particular future for the UK.

In July 2015, the *New Statesman* magazine ran an article entitled 'The Motherhood Trap' and on the front cover pictured Sturgeon along with Theresa May, Liz Kendall and Angela Merkel standing by a cot, empty bar a ballot box. It asked the question, 'Why are so many successful politicians childless?'[2] Sturgeon later praised some of the content of the article but had initially tweeted, 'Jeezo … we appear to have woken up in 1965 this morning.'

And as Isabel Hardman wrote in response, in a blog for *The Spectator*, 'Being a parent does not automatically mean you will understand even other parents. You will still need empathy in order to put yourself in the shoes of a single mother living on benefits if you are married and running a house on two salaries.'

The article cited research that showed 45 per cent of female MPs were childless compared with just 28 per cent of men and raised a fundamental question about how we perceive our female politicians. However, it also made fundamental assumptions about why women may or may not have children.

For Leadsom, it was a bargaining chip that also led to a headline in *The Times* claiming she had said in an interview with one of its journalists that she had an advantage over Theresa May in the Conservative leadership contest

---

1   Huffington Post, 6 July 2015.

2   Helen Lewis, 'The Motherhood Trap', *New Statesman*, 16 July 2015.

because she was a mother and therefore had more of a stake in the country's future. While she denied she had ever said that, and that it had been the journalist that had constantly referred to it as an issue, the ensuing media storm ultimately led to her withdrawing from the contest, leaving May to become the party leader and the next Prime Minister.

May, who has been married for more than thirty years, had previously talked of her sense of loss at not having children, but has only gone as far as saying it was something that just didn't happen. She said she and her husband, Philip, sought happiness from other things in their lives that they were 'blessed with'.

For Sturgeon, there have been moments, for instance, during her appearance on Radio 4's *Desert Island Discs* in 2015, when it seemed that she was almost on the verge of making public what was clearly a very private matter, but at the last minute decided against it.

Instead, on questions over why she and Murrell did not have children, she said,

> That can be hurtful if I am being brutally honest about it, because people make assumptions about why we don't have children. The assumption that people sometimes make is that I have made a cold, calculated decision to put my career ahead of having family, and that's not true. Sometimes things happen in life, sometimes they don't.[3]

Sturgeon hasn't been public about her own circumstances before because, clearly, while the miscarriage was a highly personal experience that will always be with her, it is not something she wants to be defined by. She is acutely self-aware and knows how things like this can be viewed or even manipulated.

Despite her overwhelming public popularity, Sturgeon retains a very definite personal boundary. And despite the outward appearances of being incredibly comfortable with the cult of personality; the selfies, the informality

3   *Desert Island Discs*, Radio 4, 15 November 2015.

on Twitter, the public shows of affection and so forth, when it comes down
to actually talking about herself or sharing intimacies, even with close asso-
ciates, she is much less comfortable.

She is naturally quite shy, a bit of an introvert – this is the woman who admits
that as a child she hid under a table at her own birthday party. She wasn't
unpopular at school but neither was she in with the in-crowd. She describes
her younger self as perhaps a little too serious; others say she was achingly
shy. She has few lifelong friends and most of the people that might describe
themselves as close – and whether she shares that view is debatable – are of
and from the party, so the fact that so many people now think they know her,
when actually they know very little about her, is quite illusory.

Ironically, as Sturgeon's public appeal has grown exponentially, her closest relationships have diminished to a handful: her husband, her family and,
to some extent, Health Secretary Shona Robison, who is often quoted as a
close friend. There is no real inner circle – something that she is attracting
criticism for – and the Sturgeon/Murrell combo at the top of the party has
led to some misgivings internally that there is no real avenue for criticism,
constructive or otherwise, of the party leadership.

Sturgeon and Murrell are very self-contained as a couple. They have known
each other since she was eighteen, when they met on party youth weekends
which he organised. They started going out properly in 2003, having become
particularly close during that year's election campaign, when they were living in adjacent flats on Edinburgh's Royal Mile, lent to them by other party
members. They can sit for hours in silence just reading, rarely socialise with
others as a couple and spend their holidays alone together at his parents'
time-share apartment in the Algarve in Portugal. She doesn't seek his counsel on major political decisions, in fact, she says that most decisions that she
takes on a day-to-day basis he will know nothing about. However, crucially,
she says she can't imagine doing the job without him. And while he often
doesn't even know where she is or what she is doing, she does utterly rely
on him for fundamental practicalities like cooking and driving (unusually,
she has never learned to drive). She credits him with being one of the most

important counterbalances to her because, she says, he is in many ways her complete opposite. She talks of him as almost an extension of herself. He is, clearly, her rock and he adores her.

In fairness to Murrell, he is also a very significant SNP player in his own right. He was chief executive of the party even before they started going out together and has a longer history of party involvement than his wife. He was first employed by Alex Salmond in his constituency office in 1987, then worked for the SNP MEP Allan Macartney before moving to the chief executive role at SNP HQ. He has never sought a public role or profile but he is responsible for the party's organisation, has presided over its exponential growth in membership and electoral success and clearly supports his wife to the hilt. He is also extremely personable and can be very funny.

Indeed, despite her reputation as being a bit frosty, Sturgeon has a quick wit and a risqué sense of humour, and she laughs a lot more than she is ever credited for. One profile described her as someone that you wouldn't see on a girls' night out, but that is just not true. In fact, she is very much a woman's woman – depending on the woman – and can talk as enthusiastically about shoes and fashion as she can about fighting inequality.

She is an incredibly private person doing a very public job and has become adept at giving the impression of being just like you and me, elevating 'being normal' to an art form, which has in turn given her the authenticity that is undoubtedly the secret to her more recent mass popularity. Paradoxically, she is more at ease, it seems, with strangers, where she is not having to give of herself, than she is with closer acquaintances, where more personal investment might be required.

She is a formidable woman. She is intelligent – a lawyer by training – and a veteran politician in her forties. She joined the SNP at sixteen and was quickly tipped as 'one to watch' and has pretty well grown up as a politician in the full glare of the media's eye, unable to escape the unfortunate and not entirely justified label of being a 'nippy sweetie'.

She was, in her younger political days, and by her own admission, a 'bit po-faced' and if there is one bit of advice she would give her younger self it would be to smile more. And, despite much commentary to the contrary, there was never any one big make-over, just a simple evolution over time and with maturity. She reflects on the person that was dubbed the 'nippy sweetie' as 'probably not being the real me'. She felt this persona was one she believed fitted better into the political arena. Of her younger, frostier days, she says, 'It's a cliché, but all the things that are seen as positives in men can be seen as negatives in women.'[4]

THE FORMATIVE YEARS

Sturgeon was born in July 1970 and grew up in a terraced council house – which her parents later bought under the right-to-buy scheme – in the village of Dreghorn in the west of Scotland. Her emerging interest in politics played out against the 1980s backdrop of the Thatcher government. The local impact of Tory policies was stark: rising unemployment, closures of heavy industry, a widening gap between the rich and poor and clear evidence of deeply ingrained poverty. She says she became aware of 'a sense of hopelessness' among her school friends and even then believed independence was the route to make change happen.

Asked if she thought any of her teachers would have identified anything in her back then that would have indicated where her future would lie, she says that she doubts it, but she remembers feeling that she would not necessarily take a conventional path in life. She couldn't identify exactly what that would be but thought she might grow up to be something like a famous children's author. She remains a voracious reader.

She joined the Campaign for Nuclear Disarmament in her early teens and followed this up with membership of the SNP at sixteen, joining in a fit of pique after her English teacher, who was also a Labour councillor, presumed she would be a Labour supporter.

The introverted but determined teenager was soon campaigning vociferously on the doorsteps in the 1987 general election for her local SNP

---

4   Interview with Nicola Sturgeon, March 2016.

candidate, Kay Ulrich. She was discovering something in herself that felt entirely comfortable, while others say they watched as she just blossomed. And while Ulrich failed to win the seat for the SNP, this did not deter the young Sturgeon. Fuelled by a hatred of Margaret Thatcher, which she says has been 'the motivation for my entire political career', she ploughed her energy into the Young Scottish Nationalists, joining its national executive when she was still seventeen and at school. She went on to study law at Glasgow University, where she gained a 2:1 and enjoyed an active political life in the SNP.

Eradicating poverty through independence remained the driving force behind her political consciousness and it became even more focused when, as a young lawyer, she worked in the law and money advice centre in Glasgow's impoverished Drumchapel, where she said her views about the unacceptability of poverty in a country as rich as Scotland were consolidated.

In 1991, aged just twenty-one, she was selected as the SNP's candidate for the Glasgow Shettleston seat, making her the youngest candidate in the 1992 general election, and although she was beaten by almost 15,000 votes by Labour, it became only the first of seven consecutive electoral defeats.

TOWARDS PARLIAMENT

In 1992, 1994 and 1995, she failed to win seats on local councils, then in 1997 she fought Glasgow Govan in the general election, losing again to Labour. Undeterred, she contested the seat again in both 1999 and 2003, eventually securing it in 2007. However, she did enter the Scottish Parliament in 1999 on the list vote.

In 2004, following John Swinney's resignation as leader after a poor set of results in the European election, Sturgeon stood against Roseanna Cunningham for the SNP leadership. Cunningham, nineteen years her senior and a very close friend for more than a decade, may have felt betrayed when Sturgeon announced she would run against her, but when Alex Salmond, who had quit as leader in 2000, then announced that he too would be running, but with Sturgeon (who by now was on course to lose to Cunningham) as his deputy, any friendship Cunningham and Sturgeon had previously enjoyed disappeared overnight. The rift, despite Cunningham now sitting at Sturgeon's Cabinet table, has never healed.

Salmond and Sturgeon were subsequently elected as leader and deputy leader but, with Salmond still an MP in the House of Commons, Sturgeon led the party in Holyrood until 2007, when Salmond was elected as an MSP. She was seen as a formidable opponent to then First Minister Jack McConnell, and he now credits that time in opposition for Sturgeon as the period that helped her understand the need to form coalitions and work across parties to get results. He believes it was this experience that stood her in good stead for government when the SNP won the 2007 election by just one seat and formed a minority administration.

Sturgeon was formidable in opposition. She made few friends across the political divide and it was therefore viewed with some satisfaction by some in the opposition when in 2010 it was discovered she had written a letter of support for one of her constituents who was due to be sentenced for benefit fraud. She referred to the crimes, including a previous conviction for stealing £60,000, as 'mistakes' and appealed to the sheriff for alternatives to custody. Labour said it was a resignation matter and revealed a lack of judgement. But Sturgeon managed to silence them all with a full, complete and humbling apology to the Chamber.[5]

What was most striking about the episode was that she committed what Salmond would probably consider to be the cardinal political error: publicly admitting to being wrong. The incident seemed to indicate a change in manner for Sturgeon that she claims was shaped by her time as Scotland's Health Secretary from 2007 to 2012, when she realised people appreciated action more than politics.

In the Scottish Parliament election of May 2011, the SNP ran a campaign based on 'team, record, vision'. Sturgeon's personal record as Health Secretary was pivotal to that and her high profile was key. She promised the health budget would be protected and that the NHS in Scotland was safe in the

---

5   BBC News, 24 February 2010.

SNP's hands, unlike, she said, south of the border, where it was being disman-
tled, first by Labour and then by the Conservatives. She also made 'big ticket'
pledges over free prescription charges and, on what became a very personal
quest, to introduce minimum pricing on alcohol. The result was that the SNP
won a historic majority in a parliamentary system designed not to let that
happen. Sturgeon had, as ever, given it her all and as usual had taken nothing for granted. She won her seat easily with a majority of more than 4,000.
Years of electoral defeat have meant she assumes nothing, but even she was
surprised to see the SNP overtaking Labour as the largest party in Glasgow.

The victory also meant that an independence referendum was now a reality
rather than just a point for debate and Salmond was to put his deputy at the
forefront of that independence campaign during a reshuffle in 2012. It was
an astute move by the First Minister. His deputy already had a formidable
reputation at home in Scotland but had also been very positively exposed to
the much wider UK stage in 2009 for her capable handling of the swine flu
outbreak. Salmond was also acutely aware that while his popularity remained
high, support for him and for independence among women was relatively
low – Sturgeon could fill that gap.

She also knows policy detail better than Salmond. After all, she spent five
years running health, the largest department in the Scottish government,
before spending two years as Cabinet Secretary for Infrastructure, Cities
and Investment, as well as steering through the Edinburgh Agreement and
paving the way for the eventual referendum. Salmond, on the other hand,
despite all his political experience and prowess, has never run a government
department other than that of First Minister.

And it was with that spirit that she took on the high-octane role of the
minister responsible not only for investment and infrastructure, but also for
the constitution. For a woman who joined the SNP while at school because
she believed 'heart and soul' that independence was the only way Scotland
could fulfil its potential, this was a dream transfer. And, by all accounts, when
she took the lead in terms of getting the process moving along, her modus
operandi was one of being constructive, efficient and to the point.

Conservative MP and then junior Scotland Office minister David Mundell
said that there had been a 'cathartic' moment when the tone and character of
the inter-governmental discussions changed from one of prevarication and
'dancing on the head of a pin' to one of consensus and resolution, and that
was when Nicola Sturgeon became involved.

Salmond stood down as leader within hours of the No vote in the referendum, saying it was time for a new generation, and then Sturgeon unexpectedly
took the party to a whole new level. Until her coronation, there were many
political commentators who believed the SNP was a one-man band. And that
man was Alex Salmond. However, after losing the referendum, the party has,
ironically, only risen in popularity. Today, under Sturgeon's watch, the SNP is
now the third largest party in Britain. And in a Westminster general election
campaign, which would normally pay scant attention to the SNP, the party
was at the centre of every other party's rhetoric and the subject of much media
commentary and debate. It was variously blamed for trying to get into government on Ed Miliband's coat-tails as well as making a Tory win inevitable.
Sturgeon herself became the favourite in the UK leaders' televised debates,
with viewers across the country asking why they couldn't vote for the SNP.
Her name was also the most Googled during the broadcasts. Her critics may
have called foul, saying she got away with murder because she wasn't being
scrutinised on her record in a devolved Scottish government or the fact that
she wasn't even a contender for Westminster, never mind No. 10, but the end
result was that she presided over a landslide victory in Scotland for the SNP.
Her party reduced Labour, the Lib Dems and the Conservatives to just three
seats north of the border, with Sturgeon's party taking fifty-six of the fifty-
nine seats at Westminster.

And what could be more humiliating for a prospective leader of the UK
Labour Party than to be asked on live television what characteristic they
wish they shared with the leader of a party that wants to break up Britain?
But, a year on from a decisive independence referendum that saw the Labour
Party campaign shoulder-to-shoulder with the Tories to save the Union and
then get decimated in a general election, that is exactly the question that

Liz Kendall, Yvette Cooper, Andy Burnham and Jeremy Corbyn were asked as part of their first televised debate in their party leadership contest.

Burnham said he admired Sturgeon for being a plain talker and an effective campaigner. Kendall talked about being a woman and Cooper observed that she couldn't manage Sturgeon's heels. It was left to veteran left-winger Corbyn, at that point a rank outsider, to point out that what he shared with Sturgeon was opposing Trident and the Iraq War. He added that Scotland's First Minister had been 'very effective in putting forward a message that resonated with people'. And with the SNP leader firmly setting the bar for the UK Labour leadership contest, it was only Corbyn who had the good grace to recognise Sturgeon's skills as a politician.

She is a much more empathetic politician than Salmond. She has an acute emotional intelligence that he doesn't have and while both want independence, she has a much clearer vision of the kind of socially just Scotland she wants to create and also how to get there. It is this that plays well to the new, more impassioned, left-leaning Scots who joined the party in their droves post the referendum. So, when Scottish Conservative leader Ruth Davidson warned her party that Sturgeon would take the SNP lurching to the 'left', it was not a description that unduly upset her.

The independence referendum ignited something deep inside Scotland, no matter what side of the argument you were on, and so with that rebirth of a nation, it seemed apt that it was a woman who then took charge. In accepting the role of First Minister, Nicola Sturgeon, a working-class woman from Ayrshire, referred to her eight-year-old niece, Hannah, and said she hoped her appointment sent a strong and positive message to girls across our lands – that there should be no limit to their ambition or what they can achieve. 'If you are good enough and if you work hard enough,' she said, 'the sky is the limit – and no glass ceiling should ever stop you from achieving your dreams.'[6]

These were heartfelt words and gave succour to those who believe the issue of gender equality needs to be ramped up a notch and that quotas need

---

6   Nicola Sturgeon, First Minister Acceptance Speech, 19 November 2014.

to be embedded within law. No one can deny that Sturgeon has achieved high office through anything other than merit. But she brings a realpolitik to the role of First Minister, so, while her predecessor was an impressive and sometimes divisive figure, whose skills as an artful tactician stood him and his party in good stead on the road to a referendum, it has been left to Sturgeon to capture the mood of a nation and govern for all.

She put poverty and inequality at the heart of her government and has shown by example on gender by creating a 50/50 split Cabinet of men and women. What is remarkable about Sturgeon's story is how little her ideas have changed since she was a teenager. Almost thirty years of political experience have done little to lessen her ideals, although her left-wing rhetoric has been toned down to a degree and she would describe herself more as a social democrat than as a socialist. And while she does talk a lot more about gender equality now than she ever did before, she did campaign in the 1990s for the party to introduce zipping[7] for the list candidates. She may have lost that vote then but has since seen the party change the rules to encourage more women to stand.

> Equality means a huge amount to me, gender equality in particular means
> a huge amount to me and while I can't change everything as First Minister,
> I made a decision before I was in the job formally that I was going to use
> the fact of being the first woman First Minister to make as much change
> or try to influence as much change, as I can. I can't look to other people
> to make that change if I'm not prepared to make it myself.[8]

And while strategically she knows that putting gender equality at the core of her policy making is a good move politically, she also believes in it. She is acutely aware that women have become the shock absorbers of austerity, that low-pay, zero hours contracts, part-time work and the prohibitive costs of childcare mean many women can't afford to work at all. She knows that women have paid a far

---

7   Whereby men and women are ordered alternately on the list.

8   *Holyrood Magazine*, 15 January 2015.

higher price, proportionately, than men for the so-called welfare reforms, and that with more women than men working in the public sector, they are also doubly hurt by the cuts in public service spending – with more still to come. She also knows that gender inequality became a touchstone for a political awakening during the referendum year and if now, with a woman First Minister leading the country for the first time, is not the time to enshrine equality, then when?

As Scotland's first female First Minister, and as one of the world's most powerful women – she is ranked fiftieth on the influential Forbes list of 100 most powerful women – Sturgeon has lifted the issue of gender equality from a fringe subject that most politicians paid lip service to but did little to address, to one at the very heart of her own government.

She has presided over a remarkable rise in SNP membership, from 25,000 before the referendum to nearly 120,000 today. She has the highest approval ratings of any party leader and has led her party to a historic third term in government in the May 2016 Scottish Parliament election. Sturgeon is most definitely her own woman and a very different First Minister and politician to the man who has mentored her for all her political career. Salmond changed the course of Scottish history because without him there would not have been that referendum, but Sturgeon now has the opportunity to make that history matter. She has emerged from the EU referendum as the only political leader to look as if they know what they are doing. She has filled a political vacuum at Westminster by standing up for Scotland in the best way she can – heading to Brussels to ensure that European political leaders are left in no doubt that Scotland voted to stay within the EU.

Sturgeon stands out from other professional politicians, not only because she is a woman, but because she appears authentically Scots; state-educated, working-class, left-leaning and believably human. While Salmond can adopt a chumminess that can as quickly be turned off, Sturgeon takes longer to get to know but is genuinely warm.

Within weeks of her becoming First Minister, she had to deal with the tragedy of the Glasgow bin lorry crash and the news that the Scottish nurse Pauline Cafferkey had contracted Ebola while working in Sierra Leone. She handled both with great dignity and with emotion, expressing a heartfelt sorrow that a nation could empathise with. In a world where politicians are so aware of their public persona and often frightened to show real feelings, never mind do ordinary things, Sturgeon appears natural even in difficult circumstances. 'If I ever get to a point in this job where I am scared to show human emotion I think I will give it up, because that's the point where you are absolutely not being yourself and it is critically important to me that I remain "me",' she says.

> Now as a politician you have to on many occasions keep your human emotions under check in a way that is about representing the nation, particularly in times of tragedy, but politicians are human beings and we share the same reactions to these things as anybody else does. I think we should be forgiven for showing how we feel.[9]

There is no doubt that for women, particularly, in politics, in the quest for authenticity there is a balance to be struck between being genuine and revealing too much. Sturgeon understandably protected herself in the early days with steel-plated armour, which many interpreted as evidence of a cold nature. As she has grown more comfortable with herself, however, she hasn't completely shed the armour but she has had the confidence to reveal more and, as a result, her popularity has grown. Politicians might not like to show vulnerability, but in terms of public appeal, it works.

An interesting question in the context of equalities, her role in that and whether women can 'have it all', is whether Sturgeon could have achieved all that she has if she had had children. 'If the miscarriage hadn't happened, would I be sitting here as First Minister right now? It's an unanswerable question. I just don't know,' she says.

> I've thought about it but I don't know the answer. I'd like to think 'Yes', because I could have shown that having a child wasn't a barrier to all of

---

9   Ibid.

this, but in truth, I don't know. Having a baby might have so fundamentally changed our lives that things would have taken a different path, but if somebody gave me the choice now to turn back the clock twenty years and say you can choose to start to think about this much earlier and have children, I'd take that, but if the price of that was not doing what I've gone on to do, I wouldn't accept that, no.

CHAPTER 19

WINNIE EWING

ROBBIE DINWOODIE

Winnie Ewing was a lawyer who was prominent in the Glasgow Bar Association. She shot to Scottish and UK prominence when she won the Hamilton by-election in 1967 – a result which altered perceptions of the SNP for good. While she lost her parliamentary seat at the subsequent election, she returned to Parliament in February 1974 when she defeated Tory Secretary of State Gordon Campbell. She was the first SNP politician to be represented in the indirectly elected European Parliament in 1975 and was elected to it in 1979 for the Highlands and Islands, serving until 1999, being universally known as 'Madame Ecosse'. She was elected to the Scottish Parliament in 1999, and served as Presiding Officer on its opening day, as its oldest member. She remains the only SNP member to have served in three different Parliaments. Ewing's contribution to the SNP has been incalculable, and while never formally being leader, she has been part of its collective leadership for nearly five decades.

．　　．　　．

When a politician comes to be on first-name terms with voters, it can be a significant breakthrough, often an indication of a widespread public recognition factor or a sign of being held in high esteem, although sometimes it can be a marker of notoriety. Remarkably for a small political party that has only really emerged as an electoral force in recent decades, the SNP has produced three women who have achieved this rare distinction: Winnie Ewing, Margo MacDonald and Nicola Sturgeon. A case could be made too for Roseanna Cunningham and, more recently, Mhairi Black, the youngest of the landslide Westminster intake of 2015. The pioneer among these was Winnie Ewing, who also became known by the sobriquet Madame Ecosse – a nickname being another sure-fire indicator of voter recognition and, by extension, campaigning prowess.

Despite never having been national convener of the Scottish National Party, Ewing merits inclusion in this book on political leadership as a result of her achievements spanning five decades of her nation's politics, a record in public life encapsulating the highs and lows of her party's fortunes. Twice she has been her party's sole representative in parliaments, at Westminster and in Europe. During the time she was crafting her public image as Madame Ecosse as a Member of the European Parliament, she kept the light of Scottish nationalism shining in the darkest of times, when her party slumped to near electoral extinction. She helped to shape Scotland as a part of the United Kingdom, which began to define itself differently in relation to Europe. Her longevity meant she formed a bridge between her father's era of the romantic Labourism of the pro-home rule Independent Labour Party and the Red Clydesiders through the evolution of re-emergent post-war nationalism of the second half of the twentieth century and into the modern day's nuanced civic nationalism and social democratic pragmatism which has allowed the party to supplant the Labour Party's decades of hegemony in Scotland.

She left two giant footprints on the base camps of Scottish self-determination. Her daring seizure of the Labour stronghold of Hamilton in the by-election of November 1967, seen as the springboard for SNP advance in modern times, prompted her joyous, unrehearsed outburst: 'Stop the world, Scotland wants to get on.' And then, some four decades later, the happenstance of her being the most senior among the first intake of MSPs to the new devolved institution in Edinburgh afforded her the opportunity to declare: 'The Scottish Parliament, adjourned on the 25th day of March, 1707, is hereby reconvened.' These two quotes alone would justify Ewing's place in any political lexicon or modern history of her nation.

Ewing also prompts a persistent and intriguing question with relevance not just to Scottish politics and identity but to the United Kingdom and England, in particular in terms of their relationship with Europe. It is this: why has there been a Madame Ecosse but never a Monsieur Rosbif? The epithet – originally intended by political foes to scorn what they saw as her airs and graces, but adopted with pride and enthusiasm by Ewing herself – was employed by her to build her peak public persona on her identification with Europe. No English or Welsh politician has done that, or, perhaps more accurately, has dared to do that.

There have been many facets to Winnie Ewing. To her foes she was a Tartan Tory who sent her children to elite schools, a diva, a champagne-drinking socialite and – an ill-defined and, in her case, absurd term – a narrow nationalist. But her adoration of and pride in her father's ILP roots, her overt internationalism and her commitment to Europe, to Ireland and to human rights, speak to a different narrative. Her friends would concede a stub-born streak and a theatrical tendency to hog centre stage; her opponents would admit charm and a brilliant public campaigning vigour; and during her party's turbulent schisms between fundamentalist, all-or-nothing purists seeking a single leap to independence versus gradualists prepared to take self-determination a step at a time via devolution, it can be argued that she was a steadying, even unifying influence.

Each of the strands of Ewing's life build towards a broader picture of her importance to Scottish nationalism: the secure upbringing that encom-passed both her father's Red Clydesider beliefs with a strong streak of cultural nationalism; her breakthrough in Hamilton in 1967 and subsequent appall-ing treatment at Westminster at the hands of many Scottish Labour MPs; the determined streak which saw her take on and beat an incumbent Con-servative Secretary of State for Scotland in Moray and Nairn; her years as Madame Ecosse in Europe, fighting successfully for a better deal for the Highlands and Islands; her willingness during her MEP days to defy her party's line on Irish issues; her realisation of a dream as an MSP 're-convening' the historic Scottish Parliament; and, above all, through the bad times for her party, the manner in which she prevailed as a public face of the SNP, representing a thread of political doggedness encapsulated by simply being 'Winnie'.

*   *   *

L et us begin at the end, and a journey in March 2016 to the picturesque Quarrier's Village, south-west of Glasgow, where Winnie Ewing is living in a retirement home. Her television is tuned to 24-hour news rather than game shows or shopping channels, her bedside cabinet is piled with books, there is an SNP sticker in her window and recently donated artworks are proudly on display. Frail but feisty would be a fair description. When a woman is approaching her eighty-eighth year it can be hard to tell if she has just got misty eyed, but it was there, I'm sure, and it wasn't when she talked about Scottish nationalism, or the faltering European dream. It came when I asked a standard question often put to nationalists: if Scotland had become, or had always been, independent, what party would you be in? The received wisdom of others had informed me, with confidence, that Winnie Ewing would have been an old-style Liberal. But that's not what came across at all. Referring to her experience of getting to know Labour opponents first-hand in the 1960s, she said,

> By this time the Labour Party wasn't really how I expected it to be. I was very attracted by my father's description of the Independent Labour Party and I met all his old friends of his age. They weren't like the people in the Labour Party I came to know. I don't know whether I am being romantic about it but when I was first in the Commons there were still members who had known my father and they hadn't moved much. I felt quite at home with some of them. It was quite helpful for me to have these old guys who were friendly to me.[1]

---

1   Interview with Winnie Ewing, 21 March 2016.

No hint of the derided Tartan Tory in these words. Nor was there when she told Hugh MacDonald of *The Herald*, the morning after the independence referendum in 2014: 'This was just the first chance. This is a movement and it will continue. There is a desire for more fairness for less fortunate people that cannot be addressed under the present system. The English Parliament will not consider it.'[2]

Similarly, to quote her wider ambitions for an independent Scotland,

> We would decide which treaties should bind us and which obligations we would willingly enter into. We would not be dealing in the instruments of death, peddling them to whichever dictators suit our purpose. We would be peacemakers, not aggressors. We would welcome those who wish to come here, or who are forced to do so because of persecution in their own lands. We would uphold not just the rule of law, but justice as well.
>
> We would have compassion for those of our own citizens who were less favoured by fate and less able, and we would create on such foundations a just society, ambitious and enterprising yet also gentle and forgiving. None of our old people would by dying of hypothermia in the most fuel-rich nation in Europe, and none of our young people would be leaving school without hope and without the basics of education. We would see the right to work as being as basic as all other rights and we would nurture our precious cultures – all of them.[3]

None of this sounds terribly Tartan Tory, the jibe she was later to face from within Labour ranks. Nor should it, given her origins.

Winifred Margaret Woodburn was born on 10 July 1929, with twin brothers eleven years older than her and a sister eight years her senior who considered her spoiled.[4] All of this rings true to her later public persona, as does

---

2   *The Herald*, 20 September 2014.

3   Ewing, *Stop the World*, Preface, p. xiii.

4   Ibid., p. 17.

an admission that at an early age the young Winifred 'started to nurture the-atrical ambitions'.[5] Her father, George Woodburn, emerges as an intriguing figure, a turner to trade who had the talent to be a professional baritone singer but lost a hand in an industrial accident, which denied him a potential stage career. He used his £500 compensation to set himself up as a paper merchant and, as a result, 'his children got a university education'.[6]

The key to this was that although Woodburn was a proud product of working-class Bridgeton in Glasgow's East End, his new family home on the city's South Side was full of music, books, and political and cultural refer-ences. His youngest child absorbed not only these Scottish cultural influences but political ones too. George Woodburn not only saw the Red Clydesiders off to Westminster at Central Station in 1922, he similarly saw off members of the International Brigade as they left to fight in the Spanish Civil War.[7] He encouraged in his youngest child a free-thinking scepticism, and he fully upheld the belief that a university education was worth it for its own sake, not just as a vocational stepping stone.[8]

Her mother, Chris Anderson, a blacksmith's daughter forced out of edu-cation at the age of thirteen to care for siblings when her mother died, also cuts an impressive figure, loving literature, theatre and cinema in spite of her curtailed life opportunities.[9] As a result the Woodburns put in place all the cultural markers to inculcate in their younger daughter a profound sense of Scottishness, and yet her father was initially appalled when his youngest child turned to nationalism. Her sister had been secretary of the Socialist Club at Glasgow University, and married the club president, but Winnie in her own words 'strayed' and joined the Student Nationalist Association while study-ing history with a view to becoming a teacher. She recalled,

---

5   Ibid., p. 19.
6   Ibid.
7   Ibid., p. 20.
8   Ibid., p. 37.
9   Ibid., p. 21.

When I first told him I wasn't joining the Labour Party he said, 'You're a traitor to the working class.' That's what he said to me. And I said, 'I'm sorry, but your Labour Party doesn't have people in it I recognise any more and I'm joining the Scottish National Party.' I wasn't popular with my father. However, I went ahead and never regretted it.[10]

There was a postscript to this two decades later, recounted in Ewing's autobiography. 'The story of our different politics – my father's and mine – has a strange and touching ending.'[11] George Woodburn died three months before his daughter's by-election triumph in Hamilton in 1967 and she discovered among his personal effects an SNP membership card dated just a fortnight before his death, a near-deathbed conversion from his socialist faith.

Her university years, during which she switched to study law, saw a romance with a fellow student who had served in the Second World War, and whose subsequent alcohol problem would perhaps now be diagnosed as post-traumatic stress disorder. He was a Catholic and Ewing took instruction in that faith during their engagement before it was broken off. Her reminiscence of the period remains a testament to the unusually broad-minded nature of her upbringing, as she recalled, 'Prejudice about religion was new to me and I was more than a little shocked to realise the real reason behind the normal question at a law apprenticeship interview, "What school did you go to?"'[12]

On graduating, she served her legal apprenticeship and became a law lecturer before demonstrating her internationalism by qualifying for the English Bar and then studying at the Hague Academy of International Law. During this time she also had relationships with a Dutch lawyer and a former Luftwaffe pilot who had become a lawyer in Hamburg.[13] It was as if she were conducting an apprenticeship as a European citizen. She met and married

---

10 Interview with Winnie Ewing.

11 Ewing, *Stop The World*, p. 36.

12 Ibid., p. 39.

13 Ibid., pp. 48–9.

accountancy lecturer Stewart Ewing and their honeymoon took them to Rome, Florence, Venice, Rimini, Milan, Zug and Heidelberg, stopping over in The Hague, Amsterdam and Rotterdam on the way home to Glasgow via Oxford and Cambridge.[14]

She may not have realised it but already she was in training as Madame Ecosse, learning Dutch and German and cultivating a network of friends across Europe. She and Stewart started a family, with children Fergus, Annabelle and Terry arriving and the parents juggling, in a manner more like the pattern of some decades later, family and career responsibilities. But still, between handling criminal cases and being active in the Glasgow Bar Association, Ewing would holiday abroad or in Scotland in an open-top car.

All of this meant that she cut an unusually glamorous figure: articulate, cosmopolitan, stylish and manifestly worldly. Although she had spoken at only a small number of party events, there was a logic to her receiving an approach in the early summer of 1966. 'I gave these visiting activists from Hamilton a generous dram and said that as I had three young children, I couldn't possibly go to London.'[15] Note the confidence. Not that she could not find the time to stand as an election candidate, but that it would be impossible because she assumed she would win. Her husband gave her a nudge, she changed her mind and accepted, and the following year Labour incumbent Tom Fraser was appointed head of the North of Scotland Hydro-Electric Board, prompting the by-election.

It was a very modern by-election campaign, the SNP's first to receive the vocal backing of actor Sean Connery, and broadcaster Ludovic Kennedy spoke at her final hustings. In the euphoria of her victory she famously declaimed: 'Stop the world! Scotland wants to get on!' Ewing insists that this phrase simply shot into her head in the excitement of the moment and had not been rehearsed in advance.[16] It was to propel her, not just to the

---

14   Ibid., pp. 52–3.

15   Ibid., p. 8.

16   Interview with Winnie Ewing.

Westminster Parliament and misery in these gothic corridors, but to a later general election victory and on to her defining period as a Member of the European Parliament.

*   *   *

Ewing's triumphant journey to Westminster on the 'Tartan Express' train chartered by the party soon turned to a grim experience as the sole SNP MP and a woman in a resolutely male world. She makes clear in her autobiography the misery of this time, bullied verbally in the Chamber and tearooms by Scottish Labour MPs, stalked through the creepy late-night corridors of the Palace of Westminster by one in particular, and derided at every opportunity. She recalled in interview,

> I had a hard time when I was alone in the House. I was treated very badly by those from the Labour Party in Scotland. I think they were quite pleased I was a woman because they thought it would be easier for them to treat me badly. It was a totally male place and the women were very few.
>
> It's an eerie place. At night, lights start going off and it was absolutely horrible. I had the friendship of one or two Old Labourites who knew my father – that was the thing, I had a very honourable background. They just couldn't adjust to that.[17]

There were exceptions, but rarely from the embittered Scottish Labour ranks. Her chief befriender was Emrys Hughes, the Welsh-born rebel Labour MP for South Ayrshire, son-in-law and biographer of Keir Hardie, who had known Ewing's father.

> It was a cruel place to me. Emrys Hughes was my protector, and a considerable protector at that. He knew my father had been a brave, early supporter

---

17 Ibid.

of the ILP who had put money in when we hadn't a lot of money. Word got round that I had connections but these were all with people who were past figures. He was amazing because he didn't give a damn for anybody. He said, 'If you get fed up just seek me out and sit beside me.' He was always surrounded by people who thought the world of him. For all the friends I could have wished for no better than Emrys Hughes.[18]

Hughes was also surrounded by party colleagues who loathed his willingness to befriend enemy nationalists, as he had done the previous year with new Plaid Cymru MP Gwynfor Evans after his victory over Labour in the Carmarthen by-election. He even taunted Scottish MPs by saying of Evans and Ewing: 'Behold, my two illegitimate children!'[19] Perhaps a more curious exception to the mistreatment was Prime Minister Harold Wilson, who appeared to harbour no grudge against Ewing for her by-election victory and whose displays of respect and courtesy to her are acknowledged in her autobiography.[20] But the great bulk of Scottish Labour MPs gave her little respite, drawing attention to every absence from the Chamber and making no allowance for the fact that she was her party's sole representative. The physical stalking of her by a particular MP stopped only after a complaint to the Leader of the House. There were jibes during debates that 'The Honourable Lady should be on at the London Palladium,' was 'a parasite'[21] and even that she 'should see a psychiatrist', the latter cited in her book[22] but not recorded in Hansard. But it was Fife MP Willie Hamilton who deployed in the Chamber a particular toxic term, already in use within Labour since Willie Ross used it at the previous year's Scottish conference,[23] interrupting

---

18   Ibid.

19   Ewing, *Stop The World*, p. 75.

20   Ibid., pp. 91–2.

21   Hansard, 3 November 1969.

22   Ewing, *Stop The World*, p. 72.

23   Christopher Harvie and Peter Jones, *The Road to Home Rule: Images of Scotland's Cause* (Edinburgh: Polygon, 2000), p. 90.

Ewing as she opened her own adjournment debate in 1969 to say, 'The Hon. Lady is a Tartan Tory.'[24] As Gerry Hassan observed,

> It is no mere coincidence that 'Tartan Tory' arose not only in the period where the SNP appeared as an electoral force, but also when the Scottish Conservatives began to decline and disappear as a serious threat to Labour. It was easier for Labour, having defeated one opponent which was 'Tory' to pin the same label on a new upstart.[25]

Her first term at Westminster was not quite unrelieved misery. Part of her job involved representing Caledonia on the London and Scottish social and cultural scenes, and she took this to heart, with a couture to match. Historian Owen Dudley Edwards, who was active in the SNP at that time, recalls,

> Winnie liked to be Queen Winnie and people fell into the business of treating her mildly like one. One of the things Winnie was good at was telling funny stories about herself. Stewart [Ewing] had his own sense of humour and told a story about the time shortly after Winnie had been elected in 1967, and the Queen's portrait by Annigoni was put on display. There was a ceremony to which the Ewings were invited. Winnie and Stewart were given very prominent positions, television cameras flitting around them, particularly in proximity to the Queen and Duke of Edinburgh. Then the television cameras wandered away, the audience and the Queen wandered away, Winnie wandered away. Stewart stood there looking at the portrait and behind him a voice said: 'Well, Mr Ewing, how does it feel?' It was the Duke of Edinburgh doing a boys-together joke, and a bloody good one too.[26]

---

24   Ewing, *Stop The World*, pp. 71–2.

25   Hassan, *The Modern SNP*, pp. 31–2.

26   Interview with Owen Dudley Edwards, 10 March 2016.

Back in the Mother of Parliaments, Ewing continued to have a miserable time, traduced daily, overworking to compensate, losing weight. Would a man have been treated this way? Isobel Lindsay suggested not: 'Whoever had won the seat would have been the target for intense hostility and remorseless scrutiny but Winnie presented another challenge to the Westminster club. She was a feisty young woman who had a successful legal career and a family – so this was a double offence.'[27] When the 1970 general election came along the SNP did well in Hamilton but not well enough to hold the by-election gain. Dudley Edwards recalls her sardonic reaction to that year's party conference: 'I will now return to the simple, quiet, protected life of a Scottish criminal lawyer.'[28] Arthur Donaldson, introducing her at that conference, said, 'If she never does another thing, she has done enough.'[29]

*   *   *

Although Ewing pledged to herself never to return to the horrors of the Palace of Westminster, having been in the political trenches she discovered on her return to civilian life something even more intolerable: 'boredom beyond belief'.[30] While re-building her legal caseload she remained active within the party and was approached by a delegation inviting her to contest Moray and Nairn, not to win it as such but to draw Tory defences towards incumbent Secretary of State for Scotland Gordon Campbell and thus open up neighbouring seats to attack from the SNP. She wrote, 'I was not expected to win, but I could not help thinking that as I had won a Labour seat, why not try to win a Tory one too? Facing, and possibly beating, a member of the Cabinet would add icing to the cake.'[31] Or, as Dudley Edwards put it:

---

27   Hassan, *The Modern SNP*, p. 95.

28   Interview with Dudley Edwards.

29   Ewing, *Stop The World*, pp. 121–2.

30   Ibid., p. 121.

31   Ibid., pp. 128–9.

She decided to go for the big one. She looked around at Tory Scotland, noted that the Tory Secretary of State for Scotland was Gordon Campbell, and decided she was going to contest Moray and Nairn. That's what she did, go for the big one. She decided that if they had done her down, by God, she was going to get her own back. And she did and won it. She stopped being Winnie of suburbia and started being Winnie of the Highlands.[32]

Soon, she bought a small house on the square in Lossiemouth, birthplace of Ramsay MacDonald and, to her mind, 'a friendly and egalitarian place, much to my taste'[33] and returned to her natural forte of campaigning. The by-election victory of Margo MacDonald in Govan in 1973 foreshadowed a fresh SNP surge, and although this heavily redrawn Glasgow seat could not be defended in February 1974, the party did make its greatest general election breakthrough to date. Ewing took the scalp of the Scottish Secretary, this time heading for Westminster as part of a group of seven MPs. She made a tactical decision to take a back seat when the portfolios were being allocated, preferring to expend her energy on defending her constituency seat. Making a decision which was to prove iconic, she accepted a motley group of responsibilities which, along with law and defence, included Europe, an outlandish spread of briefs of interest to no one else among that 'magnificent seven' spring intake. 'My second term as a Westminster MP was in total contrast to my first,' she recalled.

The personalised cruel attacks and the continuous heckling that I had suffered from so greatly between 1967 and 1970 came almost completely to an end. Of course, there was still overwhelming opposition to us politically and resentment at Scotland and its demands, but I was no longer on my own and our group was too clever, too tough and too good on its feet to be targeted maliciously.[34]

---

32   Interview with Dudley Edwards.

33   Ewing, *Stop the World*, p. 133.

34   Ibid., p. 141.

Something else had changed too. North Sea oil had begun to flow and with it the arguments over the economic case for Scottish independence – arguments which were to be turned on their head four decades later during the referendum debate.

It was inevitable that, following the hung parliament of the spring, Harold Wilson would seek an improved mandate and at the October general election the SNP saw another surge. Having gone from an 11 per cent popular share to 22 per cent, the autumn saw the dizzy heights of 30 per cent and eleven seats. They were now dubbed by the press 'The First XI'.

A Westminster staff tip-off about discounted wine being sold off allowed them to become known as the champagne party but the joyous times were not to last, as Labour's pledge to enact the Kilbrandon Commission on devolution began to unwind and the fight to push legislation through a reluctant Westminster turned into legislative trench warfare. This stalled progress, and growing friction between the MPs and the party in Scotland led to internal division. George Reid recalls the 1974–79 term as characterised by 'constant struggles over power and purpose' between the MPs in London and the party in Edinburgh, adding, 'I did admire Winnie's ability to carry the party in Scotland and in this sense she was a unifying force.'[35]

The tensions were heightened by what Ewing called 'the biggest political swindle of the century'[36] – Labour MP George Cunninghame's amendment imposing the 40 per cent threshold on the 1978 devolution referendum. This, combined with a degree of voter weariness and something recognisable as 2014's Project Fear, meant this threshold was never likely to be met. Ewing wrote:

> When I look back on it I am surprised that such a weight of opposition did not have more effect. Yet despite the obstacles and one of the roughest winters for years, the people voted 'Yes' by a clear margin of 4 per cent. And they voted in greater numbers than they did at the EEC referendum.[37]

---

35 Correspondence with Sir George Reid, April 2016.

36 Ewing, *Stop the World*, p. 160.

37 Ibid., p. 163.

The failure to reach 40 per cent not only led to the bringing down of Callaghan's Labour government and the rise of Margaret Thatcher, but the SNP was reduced once more to two Westminster seats and shifted to the political margins, the vote in the RAF bases in her constituency contributing to Ewing's defeat.

*   *   *

Ewing's career, however, had already taken a different turn. In the 1975 European referendum the SNP campaigned against EEC membership on the grounds that Scotland should negotiate its own terms, but the result was 67.2 per cent to 32.8 per cent in favour. It was at that time an appointed European Parliament. At short notice the SNP were invited to fill one space. The obvious contenders were Ewing, who held the European brief, and George Reid, the SNP member of the Parliamentary Assembly of the Council of Europe, but he had already been disciplined by the Westminster party for attending a meeting of the European Movement and saying the SNP should be a social democratic party committed to EU membership. Winnie was nominated as the SNP's MEP and we will never know whether Reid might have become Monsieur Ecosse.

To say Ewing took to Europe would be putting it mildly. As Owen Dudley Edwards put it,

> She thought European and thought it in a very natural way. Winnie came from a generation that buzzed around Europe, they did a lot of inter-university debating and things of that nature. So for her Europe was a good, exciting place where all sorts of things were happening. It was an interesting alternative to London's own obsessions with itself. She automatically thought of Europe as her friend.[38]

---

38   Interview with Dudley Edwards.

Bizarrely, the moment Ewing got to the European Parliament, she was forced to face once again the treatment meted out by Labour in the wake of 1967. Disputes over seating arrangements were followed by a year of targeted attacks by Willie Hamilton and Tam Dalyell, resulting in a call from the President of the European Parliament to the Speaker of the UK Parliament calling the attack dogs off. But by then she was learning a more important lesson, from her Irish friends from the north and south, skilled in the ways of attracting European funding.

She had always been a natural admirer of all things Irish and had been prepared to resist her party's caution on this – a reticence based on both fear of comparison with Irish nationalism during the Troubles and an element of Protestantism in the party's past. Ewing's affinity for Ireland trumped that. The first time came in 1969, when she was invited to appear on an Irish television discussion programme and ended up arranging to visit her 'hero'[39], President Éamon de Valera. Six years later the only way she could get to Dublin to attend his funeral was to charter her own aircraft. 'I had to fly back the same day to a meeting in Scotland at which I discovered that I was the subject of some criticism within the SNP for having attended the event. Nonetheless, I did not regret going for a moment and I do not regret it now.'[40] She was to compound the felony.

She tells one story of being asked to intervene at a reception to bring together politicians of the north and south.[41] And, magnificently, she did not flinch when approached by a group of mothers and wives of Northern Irish Republican prisoners seeking to present a petition on rights.

> I explained how awkward it would be for me to undertake this task, being both a Scottish member and a nationalist, for the press would be merciless. Surely there was an Irish member who would help? But there was not, for even those who were there had made themselves scarce.

---

39   Ewing, *Stop the World*, p. 95.

40   Ibid., p. 156.

41   Ibid., p. 176.

Ewing defied a direct order from headquarters because she saw it as a human rights issue, and took the petition to EU President Simone Veil, who accepted it by pointing to her own past as a prisoner of the Nazis. An SNP politician being prepared to take up the cause of relatives of Irish Republican prisoners would have been a huge story in that or any other day, but Ewing claimed the incident passed unreported because of the D-Notice system.[42] The Ministry of Defence points out that system is voluntary and editors themselves make the final decisions, adding: 'The system's object has always and only been to avoid the inadvertent public disclosure of specific information which would lead directly to national security damage and lives as risk; a public petition to the European Parliament would certainly not fall into that category, whatever its contents.'[43] However, the story here was not the petition or its contents but – at the height of the Troubles – the involvement of a Scottish politician.

Ewing went on to be elected as an MEP in her own right in 1979, serving another twenty years and, learning lessons from the likes of the DUP's Ian Paisley and the SDLP's John Hume, fighting hard for funding. Dudley Edwards said:

> She did get a great deal of money for the Highlands and Islands and many people's lives were a lot happier because of what she did. In evangelising Europe in Scotland she was Madame Ecosse and we were all to think like Europeans because of her. On the party executive in the early '80s anyone who raised the slightest question about Europe was cut to pieces by her.[44]

*   *   *

Madame Ecosse came home from Europe in order to seek election to the new Scottish Parliament, becoming a regional list member for the

---

42   Ibid., p. 178.

43   Air Vice-Marshall Andrew Vallance, Secretary, Defence and Security Media Advisory Committee, in correspondence, June 2016.

44   Interview with Dudley Edwards.

Highlands and Islands, and fate handed her a magnificent swansong, the right to open proceedings. Ewing believes that the procedures were agreed on the understanding that veteran Glasgow Tory Bailie John Young was the Father of the House and would deliver an apolitical opening to proceedings. But the parliamentary clerks checked the birth dates and found that Ewing was the Mother of the House and it fell to her to deliver the first words of the modern Scottish Parliament. 'It came as a terrible shock to Labour, and to me. They were furious but I was delighted, of course. I'm sure they had someone else in mind. It was a very happy moment, a piece of good fortune,' she recalls.[45]

Her speech that day spoke of words she had always wanted to say or hear others say, her preamble also telling: 'This is a historic day and, after a long time in politics, I am aware that we owe a debt to many who are not here and who did not live to see the promised land.' She named politicians of all parties in that roll call and added a coda which is rarely reported but gets to her essence. 'My last hope is that everyone who was born in Scotland, some of whom, like me, could not help it, and everyone who chose Scotland as their country, will live in harmony together, enjoying our cultures but remaining loyal to their own.'[46] In many ways, that was the best aspect of the speech.

*   *   *

In politics, imponderables proliferate. The possibilities outnumber the probabilities. Had the SNP adopted a stale, pale male for Hamilton in 1967, would he have won? Probably not. Having adopted Ewing, did her victory advance the political tide for her party? Undoubtedly. James Mitchell called it 'the beginning of a new era in Scottish Politics', adding, 'Westminster and Whitehall exhibited signs of panic and no event in twentieth-century Scottish politics provoked more awareness of the Scottish dimension.'[47] However, it

---

45   Interview with Ewing.

46   Ewing, *Stop the World*, p. 292.

47   Hassan, *The Modern SNP*, pp. 31-2.

was also another in a series of false dawns. As Mitchell put it, 'The Hamilton by-election of 1967 was an important milestone in the party's development. But contrary to the hopes of SNP members, it did not bring the party into the mainstream.'[48] The point about the ebb and flow of the SNP tide, however, was its wider impact on Westminster's willingness even to contemplate the Scottish question. Thus, the shock of her Hamilton victory – along with that of Gwynfor Evans of Plaid Cymru in Carmarthen the previous year – pressured the two main Westminster parties into a fresh bout of constitutional activity. Edward Heath made his Declaration of Perth committing the Conservatives to devolution in 1968 and a year later Harold Wilson's Labour government established Kilbrandon. When the oil-fuelled surge came for the SNP in 1974, Ewing was at the heart of the breakthrough. She served in a group that pushed Westminster into holding a devolution referendum, which under all other UK electoral rules would have been successful. When the next political downturn came she was already forging a new career in Europe and, arguably, sculpting a new Scottish attitude to the EU. As Dudley Edwards put it,

> Winnie Europeanised the party. She made us look at Europe as the place where the party was a success. Westminster by that stage had become the graveyard of the SNP vote and Winnie offered a new destiny in the European Parliament. And this was down to her chutzpah and, in fairness, to her charm. I think the SNP was very lucky to have her.[49]

And when the Scottish Parliament was won, one of that gathering's new grandees was handed the opportunity to proclaim it, not as some mere devolved assembly, but as a reconvening of the sovereign Scottish Parliament 'adjourned' in 1707. It was a fitting climax to a political career and a life that bridged Labour's home rulers of the early twentieth century and saw

---

48   Ibid., p. 31.

49   Interview with Dudley Edwards.

her party emerge after the referendum disappointment of 2014 to a Westminster landslide the following year. As the book *Transition to Power* put it, the SNP's most 'significant success during the period up to devolution was that it had survived'.[50] Winnie Ewing was at the heart of that survival. At the 2015 general election, Labour, in common with Conservatives and Liberal Democrats, were reduced to the single-member status she had endured in 1967, a scarcely imaginable turnaround.

---

50   Mitchell, Johns and Bennie, *The Scottish National Party*.

CHAPTER 20

MARGO MACDONALD

ISOBEL LINDSAY

Margo MacDonald trained as a physical education teacher. She and her first husband ran a pub in Blantyre, Lanarkshire. She stood for Parliament for the first time, aged twenty-six, in Paisley in 1970, describing herself then as a housewife, and won 7 per cent of the vote before successfully winning the Glasgow Govan by-election in November 1973. Even though she lost the seat in the February 1974 election, this was the beginning of a life in the public eye, associated with the SNP and wider nationalist movement. She was elected senior vice-chairman (deputy leader) that year when Gordon Wilson, recently elected as an MP, stood down from that post. In that role she was responsible for strategy and became the party's best known member outside Parliament. She was defeated as deputy leader following the 1979 general election, partly blamed for the SNP's setbacks that year. She became a member of the 79 Group and resigned from the party in 1982, when the SNP banned internal groups. She returned to the SNP in the lead-up to the establishment of devolution and was elected as a Lothian list MSP in the Scottish Parliament in 1999 but stood as an Independent after being effectively deselected in the run-up to the 2003 elections. In 2003–14 she achieved almost a national treasure status, as she championed such issues as assisted dying, and battled with Parkinson's disease. Margo, as she was known to everyone, was one of the public faces most associated with the SNP over the last forty years, even though she was only an MP and MSP for the party for little over four years. Her passion, zeal and independent mind made her a natural campaigner, but less a successful party politician.

•   •   •

There are two distinct periods in the narrative history of Margo's contribution to, and relationship with, the SNP and the wider nationalist movement. The first is the 1970s, when she played a major part in the project coordinated by then leader Billy Wolfe of entrenching the SNP as a social democratic party with a pragmatic approach to the devolution/independence debate.

Central to that objective was the encouragement and promotion of a new generation of activists into leading positions. Margo was one of those and contributed significantly in projecting that image of the party. That project fell apart with the repeal of the Scotland Act in 1979 and one of the outcomes of that traumatic period was Margo's exit from formal political involvement throughout most of the 1980s and 1990s. By the time of her election to the Scottish Parliament in 1999, both the party and wider political scenes had changed.

Margo inherited a bitter feud second-hand which affected her relations at Holyrood, and after becoming an independent MSP assumed the role of a celebrity more than that of a politician – universally known, colourful, individualistic, with a strong personality and a big emotional life story. She contributed to the wider nationalist movement but became known for her work on specific non-party issues. She contributed to the identity of the Scottish Parliament but was not in a position to contribute to the development of the SNP. It is the wider historical context that so often determines the achievements of leaders. We don't know if Margo would have achieved more if she had retained her Govan seat in 1974, if there had been a genuine cross-party referendum campaign in 1979 in which she would have had a leading role, or if she had not had the baggage of hostility to Alex Salmond that excluded her from any shadow ministerial position.

THE SNP AND LEADERSHIP

Apart from those on the political right, most of those with a theoretical or applied interest in politics have an ambivalent attitude to the importance of political leaders. The Marxist and social democratic traditions are based on an interpretation of political change driven by socio-economic developments, dismissive of 'heroes' as initiators and drivers of change. Yet in practice the whole left spectrum loves its heroes, at least when they are long departed. We see this in Scotland with the love of the 'Red Clydesiders', and UK-wide with the deification of Nye Bevan – all of them controversial figures in their own time. But, interestingly, leaving aside the exception of Clement Attlee, this is not just about practical achievements, and in fact left-wing heroes are often associated with failure. There has to be something other than, or at least in addition to, achievement – personality, risk-taking, big ideas, challenge. The political right is not only comfortable with the great person interpretation of political history; it has a similar interpretation of economics. The justification of great concentrations of wealth and power is social Darwinism – special talents rise to the top or inherit cultural characteristics to fulfil leadership roles. The right love the dominant leader and deference is in their DNA. There is an ideological consistency here.

Where does a nationalist movement fit in its relationship to leadership? A civic nationalist party is built around broadly based social, economic and cultural issues. In the case of the contemporary SNP it is also on the centre-left of the spectrum. Nineteenth- and twentieth-century independence movements have produced big heroic figures – in Italy, in Ireland, in Poland, in the anti-colonial struggles. But not the Scottish movement.

It would be a fair assumption that few SNP members know who the founding fathers of their party were. Little has been made of them since the big SNP expansion of the late 1960s. This is not because there were not big, colourful figures. Few could be more colourful than Cunninghame Graham. Add Roland Muirhead, Compton Mackenzie, Eric Linklater, John MacCormick, Wendy Wood. Of course, they did not get killed for the cause and led comfortable lives, but surely that is not the only reason. Oddly and interestingly for the SNP, unlike other movements, the past century has been another country. The only heroes quoted tend to be Maxton and Maclean, not the party founders. The modern SNP's orientation has been to the present and the future with just a nod to *Braveheart*.

SNP members have shown considerable loyalty to leaders over the past fifty years. All of the national leaders have gone at a time of their own choosing. SNP leaders have had the advantage of their members' solidarity in the face of external hostility and the big prize of independence ahead of them. But no matter how good any party leader is, they can't buck the underlying political and economic situation in which they are placed. No matter how gifted the leader, the SNP was always going to struggle in Westminster elections in the 1980s. Scottish electors had a priority – to get rid of the Thatcher government. The SNP couldn't replace her in Downing Street. Nor in the first Scottish Parliament term was the SNP likely to win because Labour had delivered devolution and giving them a chance seemed the obvious thing to do. The context of the 1960s and 1970s was right for the SNP. But for a movement, winning seats is not the only thing that matters. Margo showed that she had the ability to win but the importance of her contribution was in giving independence a face that in all its complexity was remembered and was one of us.

THE EARLY YEARS

For some, early experience is of marginal significance in understanding adult achievement. For others, the adult cannot be fully understood without understanding it. That experience for Margo was traumatic and created some of her later strengths and weaknesses. Until adolescence she had the status of being the eldest child of a local GP who was professionally well-regarded, living with both parents and two siblings in a large villa in the industrial town of Hamilton. She had successful entry to the county's academically best senior secondary school when there was still a selective system. Domestically, life was more difficult than the outside image – a father who was a heavy drinker with a nasty temper and an able and charming mother who had to hold things together under stressful circumstances.

When she was thirteen, her father left the family to live with a woman who had been his patient, and was no longer able to work as a doctor. Soon afterwards, he violently evicted his family from their home and his alimony payments were small and irregular. In the 1950s, there were few organisations to go to for help. They moved to a small flat and later to a house in East Kilbride new town. Their financial circumstances were very difficult and her mother had to return to nursing although she had health problems. Margo experienced a huge change in social status and considerable disadvantage and it is not difficult to translate this to the political context. But as in the way she coped with illness in her last years, there was a cheerful face and no obvious sign of stress in the context of school. She enjoyed socialising, was popular, was middling academically and excelled at sport. She went on to qualify as a physical education teacher, married her school boyfriend who ran his family's pub, and had two daughters. She didn't return to work but was under pressure to help run the pub.

Had the biography been different, would there have been the eventual involvement in politics, the intuitive identification with the disadvantaged and marginalised? Always there were communication skills and enjoyment in socialising, but this was combined with a strand of insecurity that needed regular reassurance and could edge into distrust.

INTO THE SNP AND GOVAN

Margo joined the SNP in 1967 around the time of the Hamilton by-election, which was her home constituency. It was a period of massive and unprecedented growth in membership and branches. The big trigger was the success in winning one of the safest Labour seats in Scotland and the impact of the candidate. Winnie Ewing was a clever, attractive, young Glasgow lawyer who with her team ran a bold, confident campaign. This was not politics as usual. But Hamilton and the huge gains in local government elections six months later was the culmination of several years of slow but significant growth in SNP support in by-elections in Bridgeton, West Lothian and Pollok.

Why the 1960s? There were some structural and some political factors.[1] This was the second highest period of net migration loss in the century

---

1   Finlay, *Modern Scotland.*

(interestingly the highest was in the 1920s – the period that saw the formation of the National Party in 1928). Average earnings in Scotland were substantially lower than in the Midlands and the south of England and although unemployment was not high, it was significantly higher than in England. The old working-class communities had been radically changed with new housing estates and new towns. For many, the Labour government was not seen as meeting Scotland's needs. For a small but active minority who had been very involved in the anti-nuclear movement, the Wilson government had betrayed its promises and proceeded with the British Polaris programme at Faslane. The SNP looked like a new political opportunity. Margo fitted the profile of the new members. She was young. She was rooted in neither the old working class nor the established middle class but with an intermediate class status. She had social concerns and aspirations but was not ideologically rigid. Her decision to join coincided with some frustrations in her personal life. She was under some pressure to continue working behind the bar rather than planning a return to teaching. She wasn't using her abilities and training so politics offered a stimulating new challenge.

The big membership expansion – as with the recent post-referendum surge – brought in many thousands of people with no background in the SNP or in party politics. Suddenly every election local and national had to be contested. As in the contemporary party, many found themselves as candidates after very short membership. Margo was selected to fight the Paisley parliamentary seat for the 1970 election. This was a time of few opinion polls but there were indicators from the failure to win the Gorbals and South Ayrshire by-elections and poorer local election results. Getting 11 per cent of the Scottish vote and only one seat, that of Donald Stewart in the Western Isles, would have seemed real progress five years earlier but was a huge disappointment after the high expectations of the post-Hamilton period. Winnie Ewing lost her seat and Margo's result was similar to everyone else in the central belt. The SNP was written off by the commentariat, but not for long. Most of the new activists like Margo remained committed and soon a close second result in the Stirling by-election and a very effective oil campaign saw a strong upward swing. It was the SNP rather than Labour who appeared to be the beneficiaries of the unpopular Heath government and dramatic events like the Upper Clyde Shipbuilders sit-in campaign in 1971.

When the Govan by-election came up, it was thought it might be winnable, but as a very safe Labour seat needed a candidate who could add a strong personal appeal to the underlying upward trend in support. It was a male-dominated culture with shipbuilding and other heavy industry still influential although in decline – so choosing a young woman as a candidate was a bit of a risk. It had worked in Hamilton but, although mainly working-class, that was a more socially mixed constituency. Govan was a solidly working-class community, still with much poverty and bad housing. The Labour candidate was an old left-winger with strong Govan roots. But Margo could communicate and socialise in any situation and sounded like the future not the past. Winning the seat was important because it was a Labour seat, because it reinforced at a crucial time the message that the SNP could win and because it gave the SNP that memorable and attractive face that had a centre-left identity. It was fortunate that there were two elections on the same day; the other in the Edinburgh New Town area. The SNP was third with 18 per cent and it might have been interpreted as a downward trend just a few months before a general election. Ted Heath's 'who governs Britain' challenge to the miners in February 1974 produced big successes for the SNP but in a bitter twist Margo lost Govan by just 571 votes.

AFTER GOVAN AND THE EU REFERENDUM

Coping with the defeat post-Govan was very painful, especially given the success for the party as a whole. The February result was impressive, with 22 per cent of the vote and seven seats. This was followed in the October election with over 30 per cent of the vote, eleven seats and a good second in many more Labour seats. Meanwhile, between the two elections the Labour Party in Scotland had been pressured to change its anti-devolution position by the UK leadership, who were concerned about losing their solid Scottish bloc, and support for an elected Scottish Assembly became the policy of the new government. The SNP appeared to be in an especially promising position given that the Wilson government had an overall majority of only three.

Because only three out of the eleven seats had been Labour, some, including Margo, expressed concern that the SNP's campaign had been insufficiently targeted at working-class Labour voters. The results were more complex than this. Labour had only gained 36 per cent of the Scottish vote. The Tory seats were not necessarily won by former Tory voters but by an anti-Tory alliance coalescing around the SNP. But the Labour vote was concentrated and could deliver a disproportionate number of seats. There was no strong case for suggesting that the narrow loss of Govan was because the overall campaign was insufficiently focused on the working-class voter. What was surprising was how high the SNP vote was, and how low the Labour vote, given that general elections are seen as choosing whether Tory or Labour will form the government.

The immediate future for Margo had to be within the party structure in Scotland and she was elected at the 1974 annual conference as senior vice-chair, a position she held until 1979. She had been in one of the vice-chair positions since 1972. While there were several years of complex relationships ahead, particularly between the leadership in Scotland and Westminster, in 1975 the big issue of the EEC referendum presented itself. Margo was put in charge of the campaign. There were differences within the SNP on the issue. While no one was contesting that the party's position should be for a No vote, the reasons differed. For some, like Winnie Ewing, Stephen Maxwell, Donald Stewart, Billy Wolfe and probably a majority of both the National Executive and the Westminster group, the opposition was to the nature of the EEC as a centralising force, removing the potential for Scottish control over fishing and agriculture and as facilitating big multinational business. (Donald Stewart joked that it was designed so that countries would take in each other's washing machines.) For others, like Gordon Wilson and Margo, the opposition was to lack of Scottish representation not to the EEC as such and they preferred to leave open the prospect of membership if Scotland became independent. There was some tension around where the emphasis in the campaign should be, but this was kept internal and unlike the other parties they appeared united around a No vote. The outcome was disappointing. There was a 58 per cent Yes vote in Scotland and it didn't help the SNP's credibility being on the losing side but because of the big divisions in the other parties, the failure to take Scotland with them was not as damaging as it might have been. There was not a blame game around this so it did not damage Margo; there was massive establishment support for a vote to remain so it was not seen as a fault in the campaign.

THE DEVOLUTION LEGISLATION

Before examining her role in the tortuous saga that was the process of getting a Scottish legislature Bill through Westminster, the personal becomes intertwined with the political. Margo ended her marriage in 1976. She and her husband had increasingly grown apart. He continued to be a sports-loving publican while she had become a celebrity politician. While she and Jim Sillars did not marry until 1981, their close political relationship started some years earlier and that became significant for both of them. Jim was first elected in a very bitter by-election contest with the SNP in 1970 (see the chapter on Jim Sillars for more details). He was a very able and articulate MP and strongly opposed to devolution but he changed his mind a few years later after, as he explained, his experience of Westminster. He, with three other MPs, became active promoters of a much stronger Scottish Assembly than the Wilson and then the Callaghan governments were proposing. Increasingly frustrated in the Parliamentary Labour Party, he and a number of other Labour figures started a new party – the Scottish Labour Party – in 1976. There was initially very enthusiastic support and huge media coverage (a number of leading journalists were supporters) from people on the left who were coming round to independence, or at least a version of devo-max, but could only identify with an explicitly socialist party. Within a couple of years, the SLP had disintegrated with bitter infighting. Meanwhile, the SNP saw several strands of internal tension develop – gradualist/fundamentalist, left/right and the location of decision-making whether Scotland or Westminster. Margo was involved with these issues.

The prospects in 1974 looked good,[2] Labour had changed policy on Scottish devolution and had a manifesto commitment. They had a majority of only three, which was soon lost in by-elections, so that suggested that the eleven SNP MPs could have considerable leverage. But there was no real interest or enthusiasm in the Parliamentary Labour Party. On the contrary, there was considerable hostility, and the support which it was assumed would come from the Liberals turned out to be very problematic. The first Bill was introduced at the end of 1975. It conceded most of the Scottish Office powers but with many restrictions that undermined autonomy. But it was a legislature and it was directly elected – the two absolute essentials for the SNP. The reasoning was that even if the powers were too limited, that could be changed later providing it had democratic legitimacy and the principle was established that it could make laws.

The hostility was so strong at Westminster that there was a determined cross-party attempt to sabotage it with the tabling of 350 amendments. The Wilson government could not get it through without a timetable motion and a combination of Tory, rebel Labour and Liberal votes defeated the Bill early in 1977 because it did not offer proportional voting. There was no certainty that another Bill would be introduced. For the minority in the SNP who were hostile to devolution, this was a confirmation of that position; for all of the SNP it was a confirmation that you could not trust any of the Westminster parties. Another Bill was, in fact, introduced in November 1977 after a Lib–Lab pact, despite the fact that it still did not include any proposals for voting reform.

The seemingly endless manoeuvring around the devolution proposals created increased impatience on three dimensions. One was about gradualism versus fundamentalism. Overlying this was a centre-left and centre-right dimension, but some of this was less about intrinsic policy positions than a tactical one about which social groups and issues should be the main focus of campaigning. The third area of disagreement was to what extent the SNP

---

2   For the devolution saga, see Marr, *The Battle for Scotland*, Chapter 4.

should develop a full policy portfolio like other political parties or whether it should choose to be primarily a single-issue campaign. There was an established majority opinion on these issues among the leadership and the membership. The SNP would support a staged route to independence, it was a centre-left social democratic party and it would engage with the whole spectrum of policy issues. Margo was part of this consensus and helped to reinforce it during the '70s. But there were critical voices; if this consensus didn't produce results, the critics were in the wings.

Margo was not a dedicated participant in the policy development process. It was Billy Wolfe's idea before he became chair to introduce the National Assembly into the constitution. The intention was to provide a place for more detailed policy debate that would be smaller than annual conference or National Council. With the prospect of a Scottish Assembly the need to be prepared with a strong manifesto was broadly accepted and many candidates and key activists engaged enthusiastically. Margo was only an occasional participant in policy debates. She had a broad-brush interest in some areas, was supportive of having a full policy portfolio but wasn't by choice a detailed policy person, and that provides part of the answer to the later 'what if' question. What, had relations been different, would Margo have made of a ministerial or shadow minister role?

The divisions among the Westminster group were greater than in the National Executive. They ranged from a mainstream social democratic gradualist like George Reid to a right-wing fundamentalist like Douglas Henderson. Things were particularly difficult when the majority of the group decided to vote against the Aircraft and Shipbuilding Nationalisation Bill. They had a specific reason for doing so but it was seen as damaging in industrial seats, especially when one of the MPs was seen to tear up a telegram from the STUC. As senior vice-chair Margo had some responsibilities to liaise with the Westminster group but it was not the most ideal of combinations. There was some resentment with the National Executive for trying to influence Westminster decisions but Margo was not the best person to build cooperative relationships. She had personal antagonisms towards some in the group that she was not good at hiding. It was mutual. Billy Wolfe then took on more of the liaison work.

With the 40 per cent amendment passed, there was a majority in the Westminster group who were intent on voting against the government at the end of the Queen's Speech in autumn 1978. There was a clear instruction given by the NEC not to do this. While no one was disagreeing that the 40 per cent rule was an attempt to sabotage devolution, opinion polls suggested that it was still possible to win a referendum and if it was SNP MPs who were seen to bring down the government, this would be a gift to the opposition, with no guarantee that any new government would proceed with the Act. With a majority in the group insisting on voting against, this was a low point in Westminster/Edinburgh relations and reinforced Margo's negative views of the MPs, but she was certainly not alone.

THE SECOND HAMILTON BY-ELECTION AND THE REFERENDUM

The Garscadden by-election in March 1978 was expected to be won by the SNP but they got just 31 per cent of the vote. However, the death of the Hamilton MP Alex Wilson meant a by-election in May 1978. It looked like destiny, an opportunity to regain momentum. But as so often happens, destiny took a wrong turn. This was a decade after Winnie's historic victory in Hamilton. Another strong, vibrant woman would surely be the ideal candidate, especially since it had for years been the constituency in which Margo had lived. A win in Hamilton would send a clear message to those Labour MPs who were trying to sabotage the Scotland Bill and would give a great lift to the referendum campaign, which was expected within a year. It turned out so different.

The Labour candidate, George Robertson, was competent but not inspiring. He was on the right of the party but was pro-devolution. By the late '70s the Labour organisation had improved significantly but it did not out-perform the SNP. While Margo's failure to win – she got 33 per cent – was not blamed on her as a candidate, it didn't strengthen her position. Hard-working activists get few rewards and being on the winning side is one of them. The result was not about her, yet nor about local issues; it was about the wider political situation. A good candidate and a good organisation can give some advantage in the right political context but it rarely bucks the wider political trends. The similarity of the SNP vote in Garscadden and Hamilton, both strong Labour seats, was a pointer to the direction of change.

June 1978 had a Callaghan government that seemed to be making some economic progress, a Scottish Assembly appeared to be in prospect and the years of tedious manoeuvring had taken away much of the dynamic. The breakaway Scottish Labour Party had disintegrated unpleasantly. At UK level there was a new Tory leader, Margaret Thatcher, who was divisive and had no great appeal in Scotland. Many commentators thought that had Callaghan chosen to have an autumn election he would have had a good chance of getting an overall majority, but he ducked it, to the relief of the SNP. A lost deposit in October in the Berwick and East Lothian by-election was another negative sign, although as a Tory–Labour marginal it was never going to be a good result. A general election could be almost a year away, however, and there was still plenty of time to build support before Assembly elections assuming a successful referendum. Some hoped that Jim Sillars and other leading figures in the SLP might at this point join the SNP but when, knowing the close relationship, Margo was asked informally about this, the response was that it wasn't the right time.

Irrespective of the signs of decline of support for the SNP, the limited polling evidence still suggested a big majority for a Yes vote.[3] A poll in April 1978 by Mori for *Weekend World* had 63 per cent Yes, 27 per cent No and 10 per cent undecided. Officially only the Tory Party was opposed and there were some well-known pro-devolution Tory rebels. The majority of the press were also on the Yes side.

Margo was given the lead in the party's referendum campaign and what should have been an upbeat experience with historic significance turned into

---

3   See John Bochel, David Denver and Alan Macartney (eds), *The Referendum Experience Scotland 1979* (Aberdeen: Aberdeen University Press, 1981).

the opposite – a catastrophic failure. This was not because of what the SNP did or didn't do but because of the context of the campaign and the deep divisions on the Labour side. Neal Ascherson has written one of the best accounts of the atmosphere around the referendum.[4] There were a minority of party members who were unenthusiastic about devolution and did little work in the campaign but it wouldn't have mattered if they had. The issue was caught in a perfect storm. If a genuine cross-party campaign had got off the ground, Margo would have been good in that context. She was not particularly tribal and had the personality to work with people in other parties, at least for a short period. While she played a central role along with Jim Sillars in the Yes for Scotland campaign, this was mainly made up of a collection of individual enthusiasts without substantial institutional participation. Helen Liddell, Secretary of the Labour Party, had ruled out any cooperation with the SNP. There was no possibility of the kind of cross-party campaign that emerged in 1997. The SNP was open to cooperation with others but focused on its own activities. It was other events that dominated the months leading to the referendum.

The Callaghan government, having been in a favourable position in autumn 1978, decided to continue with a tough incomes policy that had for several years imposed tight wage restraint while inflation was starting to rise again. Private sector workers had various options for evading this through, often phoney, productivity deals, but this was not an option for most public service workers who had seen their relative earnings decline. The unions withdrew their cooperation with incomes policy and a series of long public sector strikes started. The disputes became increasingly bitter. Add to this an exceptionally bad winter – very cold with long periods of snow in Scotland. Callaghan's notorious supposed comment 'Crisis – what crisis?' on returning from an overseas visit was a gift to the press. The result was that by March the Labour government who were responsible for the Scotland Act had seen its support slump.

---

4   Neal Ascherson, *Stone Voices: The Search for Scotland* (London: Granta Books, 2002).

Another factor was the change in Conservative leadership. Heath had shown some sympathy towards devolution, but Thatcher was virulently opposed. While there were still some prominent Tories in Scotland who supported an Assembly, not only was the party machine opposed but Thatcher used her media supporters to launch a full-out attack. The recent change in ownership of the *Scottish Daily Express*, which still had a high Scottish readership, shifted the paper overnight from a pro-devolution position to one of extreme hostility. The Labour Party was deeply divided at all levels. There were few real enthusiasts; as well as some MPs, many local councillors saw an Assembly as a threat to their powers. Some trade unions, notably the Transport and General Workers' Union and the Mineworkers, did put resources and effort into the campaign.

With industrial conflict, very bad weather, Labour Party divisions on the ground, sub-optimum member activity by the SNP – this was not the context for maximising the Yes vote or the turnout. The press overall should have been an advantage but the No papers were assertive and strident while the Yes papers were low-key and more even-handed, perhaps sensing the direction of the public mood. The polls did show a shift. Yes had gone down to 49 per cent with 26 per cent No in early February but by late February Yes and No were equal at 42 per cent.[5] The result was a 52 per cent majority for Yes but with a 64 per cent turnout it failed the 40 per cent hurdle. In the days after the vote the enormous disappointment was focused on demands that the Act should be implemented because there was a majority in support. With the prospect of a No Confidence vote at Westminster, a meeting of the National Council was called to decide the parliamentary group's position. The MPs were divided. Margo moved a resolution on behalf of the NEC supporting a No Confidence vote if there were no substantial concessions by the government. National Council backed this overwhelmingly. The gamble was that since the government would be faced with almost certainly losing an early election, they would find a way to proceed with the Assembly. The other argument was that there had to be an election by October anyway and it was better to fight an early election on the Scottish democracy

---

5   See Bochel et al., *The Referendum Experience Scotland 1979*.

issue. Michael Foot apparently thought that the SNP would not have the nerve to bring Labour down and would ensure that a couple of their MPs would abstain. In the subsequent election the SNP held only two of their eleven seats and their vote was down to 17 per cent. Jim Sillars and John Robertson also lost their seats under the breakaway Scottish Labour Party banner.

POST-REFERENDUM TRAUMA AND THE 79 GROUP

After the general election the SNP had a lengthy period of bitter conflict in which Margo played an important role and ended by resigning from the party. Ian Bayne gives a detailed account of events.[6] A decade of huge effort and great promise had ended in abject failure and lots of people were looking for scapegoats – but there were a few to choose from. For many the enemy was devolution, which had compromised the principle of independence and diverted attention to the preparation of plans for an Assembly rather than campaigning. But the other main critique was that there had not been a bigger Yes vote and election vote because the SNP did not have a clear socialist identity and had not gained sufficient support among the industrial working class. The 79 Group was established as a pressure group within the party to change this. Jim Sillars joined the party at this point but made it clear that he was joining because he could now join a socialist group within the SNP. There were many long-established members like Stephen Maxwell who joined the 79 Group, and young activists like Alex Salmond and Kenny MacAskill, but Margo and Jim were central to the high profile of the group and some argued that it facilitated Jim's membership since he had previously said that he would never join a party that was not socialist.

Neither the fundamentalist/traditionalist faction nor the 79 Group based their positions on any objective evidence of why the Yes majority was not higher. A referendum study showed that the two lowest socio-economic groups were

---

6   Ian O. Bayne, 'The Impact of 1979 on the SNP', in Tom Gallagher (ed.), *Nationalism in the Nineties* (Edinburgh: Polygon, 1991).

65 per cent Yes voters while the two highest groups were only 35 per cent Yes.[7] Nor was there any evidence that people voted No because they wanted to go to independence in one jump. People were looking for excuses that fitted their ideological positions and these ideological differences were combined with strong personal antagonisms, as with Margo and Winnie and Robert McIntyre (who was actually a gradualist), who had a strong distrust of Jim Sillars and interpreted the 79 Group as primarily a power base for him. While the Group was much broader than that, it was a plausible interpretation for some. Gordon Wilson, now the party leader, tabled a resolution at annual conference to proscribe all formal groups. He assumed that faced with expulsion, people would step back. Sillars did. Margo resigned from the party in protest and six others including Alex Salmond stuck in their heels and were expelled, later reduced to suspension. For the next fifteen years, Margo was not involved with the SNP except through whatever influence she might or might not have had with her husband, who continued for some years to play a major role. She focused on building a career in broadcasting and press and was a natural broadcaster.

GOVAN AGAIN AND THE CONSTITUTIONAL CONVENTION

Jim Sillars's success in winning the second Govan by-election in November 1988 created a new burst of confidence but it also triggered events which, although Margo was not directly involved, had important implications for her future position in the SNP. Alex Salmond and Kenny MacAskill had been very much Sillars's close allies a few years earlier. Salmond in particular was very loyal to him. At some point, for some reason, this changed and it came into the open on the issue of the Constitutional Convention.

The cross-party Campaign for a Scottish Assembly had produced the 'Claim of Right for Scotland' recommending the establishment of a Convention to prepare detailed consensus proposals for a Scottish Parliament.

---

7   Bochel et al., *The Referendum Experience Scotland 1979*, p. 142.

To demonstrate democratic authority, invitations to participate would go to all Scottish MPs, MEPs and representatives of every local council and major civic organisations including political parties. The SNP National Executive had approved participation in this in July. So had the Liberal Democrats, and by later in the year the Labour Party. Inter-party negotiations took place in January and appeared successful. Shortly after this, without consulting the Executive or National Council, Gordon Wilson, Jim Sillars and Margaret Ewing held a press conference to announce that the SNP would not participate and claimed that this was supported by all office-bearers. Alex Salmond was the senior vice-chair and Jim Sillars had been asked to discuss the issue with him, which he failed to do. So the second most senior office-bearer was not informed of a major decision and heard it first from the media. This was the first indication for many that the relationship had broken down. This was reinforced when, astonishingly, Jim Sillars backed Margaret Ewing as party chair in opposition to Alex Salmond. By this stage in her career Margaret was closely identified with the traditionalist grouping in the party. Margo's later relationship with the party leadership has to a considerable extent to be seen as a continuation of Sillars's bitter hostility towards Salmond. She may have had different reasons of her own but this is unknown. There were no obvious policy disputes at this stage although there might have been some tactical ones. The hostility seemed more personal than political.

BACK IN THE SNP AND HOLYROOD

Margo rejoined the SNP in the mid-'90s and, after the big Yes vote in the 1997 referendum, put herself forward for the Lothian regional list. The order of party list candidates is selected by individual members in the SNP. Given her political reputation from the 1970s and her years of broadcasting and press work in the Lothian area, it was expected that she would be well-placed on the list and would be elected. She came top of the list, though the hostility to Salmond and some others in the leadership continued. Had this not been the case, might Margo have been given a shadow ministerial job?

And would she have suited that role? There was a long period in which she had not been a party member and had been able to say what she thought without restraint. She had been free to pick up the issues that interested her without bothering about party priorities or the views of colleagues. She was probably happiest in that role and this was attractive to many voters who were tired of 'suits on message'. However, a party has to manage and maintain some element of coherence. Whether, given the responsibility, Margo would have focused on a particular central policy area in depth and stuck with it is very uncertain.

The biggest issue she took on in the first term was the cost and suitability of the new Parliament building and, on a specific issue like this where she could make a difference, she was tenacious in her pursuit and it was a popular position at the time. She introduced a Bill in 2002 for the establishment of prostitution tolerance zones but this was unsuccessful. Even to outsiders, however, she did seem rather semi-detached from the SNP group, often making critical comments that made no attempt at diplomacy. She was formally disciplined by the group at one point for publicly criticising them for not supporting a debate on the medical use of cannabis. Had all of this been only about a specific policy issue or issues, it would have been less damaging but it seemed more like a general anti-leadership position. When Salmond stood down in 2000, she unsurprisingly backed Alex Neil, an old SLP colleague of Sillars's, for the leadership in opposition to John Swinney.

When the selection process started for the 2003 elections, it can be assumed that the leadership team would not be unhappy to see her go, despite the fact that her high profile was a positive for the party. She came fifth and would have had no chance of re-election. Obviously she was very angry and claimed senior figures in the party had been lobbying against her, which was likely to be true, but that kind of lobbying is not always guaranteed to work. This was a decision made by individual members and it may have been that enough of them had their own doubts.

Nevertheless, what seemed the end of her political career turned out to be a new opportunity. Margo stood on the list as an independent and won. Needless to say, relations were even more bitter at this stage, made even worse by her health issues. She had been diagnosed with Parkinson's in 1996 but did not make this information public. It was made so by a source in 2002 and she accused an unnamed person in the SNP of doing so in order to undermine her; this was denied. In the 2003 'rainbow Parliament' her position was made more comfortable due to the big expansion of small parties. She also won the next two elections. She seemed happier as an independent member – 'I find it liberating to be able to work with a wide range of folk without any party affiliation getting in the way.'[8] There was no sign of improvement in relations after Salmond's return as leader, and then First Minister, until a little thawing at the very end.

There was great disappointment when, despite a lot of work and eloquent advocacy, her Assisted Suicide Bill failed despite substantial public opinion on her side. She also failed in her attempt to be elected Presiding Officer in 2007. The years at Holyrood did not produce much by way of concrete achievement and yet the paradox is that many people would think of her as one of the more effective MSPs.

IN MEMORY

There is much that will be remembered about Margo that is non-political, notably the courage and strength of character with which she coped with her illness. She continued to work and to attend events even in the advanced stages, when mobility was extremely difficult. She faced this with the same outward cheerfulness and lack of self-pity that she had shown in her early teens in coping with terrible family circumstances. There was success in her private life, with a close relationship with two daughters, grandchildren and a good second marriage.

In relation to the SNP, her major contribution was in the 1970s. In relation to the wider independence movement, she continued till the end to be one of the faces that reassured the public that Scottish independence was a civic nationalism, concerned with social justice and inclusiveness.

---

8   Anne Simpson, 'Face to Face interview', *The Herald*, 23 September 2006.

The other politician who comes to mind as being similar in many respects to Margo was Mo Mowlam, the Labour MP, who also had to cope with terminal illness. Historical circumstances gave her a key role in a specific project – the Northern Ireland peace agreement. For Margo, different historical circumstances might have produced opportunities for greater achievement. However, she will be remembered, and that can be said of few politicians.

CHAPTER 21

JIM SILLARS

GERRY HASSAN

Jim Sillars joined the Labour Party and was elected as Labour MP for South Ayrshire in 1970, before setting up a breakaway Scottish Labour Party in 1976, which saw him lose his seat in 1979 and join the SNP the following year. He became a prominent figure and campaigner in the party, sensationally winning the Glasgow Govan by-election in 1988. Despite much promise, however, he failed to hold the seat in the 1992 election. Sillars subsequently withdrew from politics, but came back to play an active public role in the 2014 independence campaign. While Sillars never came near leading the SNP, his public life and trajectory symbolises the often-problematic relationship between the nationalist and Labour movements.

. . .

One of the great post-war Scottish political talents – a leading force in Labour and then influential figure in the SNP and wider nationalist movement (in between setting up his own fledgling party, the Scottish Labour Party) – has undoubtedly been Jim Sillars.

He has through the years been lauded across the political spectrum. He was praised in his early years by Labour, noted by Tories as star quality, and in the SNP seen as a potent force, earning praise from the likes of Alex Salmond as 'the most talented politician of his generation'.[1] Arnold Kemp,

---

1   *New Statesman*, 10 March 1995.

former editor of *The Herald*, described him in 1993 in the following terms: 'He has everything: he is a brilliant debater and skilful parliamentarian, a pungent writer, a trenchant propagandist; he has passion and sincerity.'[2]

Sillars's political life can be divided into four distinct acts. All are filled with drama, bathos, elements of exuberance, tragedy and defeat. There has even been a powerful emotional strand to his public life, most obviously seen in the love and affirmation of his long-term partnership with another elemental force in nationalism – Margo MacDonald – who earned a similar reputation for independence of mind (covered in this volume by Isobel Lindsay).

These four acts entail different sets of characteristics. The first involved being a rising star in Labour and the trade union movement; second, setting up his own Scottish Labour Party in the mid-1970s; and third, becoming an SNP member and politician. The most recent period during the independence referendum could be seen as Sillars's Indian summer, where he refound his voice as a high-profile, adept campaigner and populiser – still in the SNP, but increasingly appealing to a constituency outside it. In each of these phases, in true theatrical style, there are mini-acts, sections and sub-stories.

Sillars's odyssey covers many of the dynamics and drivers of post-war Scottish politics. It has addressed how Scotland gives expression to its increasingly asserted centre-left values, alongside what is the appropriate balance and relationship between socialism and nationalism. What are the prospects for steering and shaping the economy in Scotland, and what is the most practicable political vessel for advancing all of these goals: the labour movement, a new party, or the SNP?

This has been a political life that says much about Scotland's centre-left, progressive and anti-Tory politics, and the ebb and flow of fortunes between the country's two main parties of power, Labour and SNP. In all of the above and all of his politics, Sillars has been a rare, if not unique, force. He has been prepared to think, take risks and follow his instincts and principles – sometimes with harmful consequences to both himself and colleagues.

---

2   Kemp, *The Hollow Drum*, p. 154.

FORMATIVE LABOUR YEARS

Jim Sillars was born in Ayr on 4 October 1937 to Matthew, a railwayman, and Agnes, a carpet weaver. He attended Newton Park School and Ayr Academy, where he was, by his own account, unmotivated. After formal education, he worked briefly in the building trade as an apprentice plasterer before joining the railways and with it the National Union of Railwaymen (NUR), experiencing first-hand the 1955 rail strike. The following year, 1956, he joined the Royal Navy, which included a period in Hong Kong. This is where Sillars's own political education really began and when he started to think about issues for himself. He was shocked by the realities of Hong Kong colonialism, found himself drawn to the Chinese 'Great Leap Forward' but resistant to the allure of Maoist ultra-leftism after reading the philosopher Bertrand Russell. Sillars, like the generation before in the Second World War, found the communal atmosphere of the armed forces the ideal debating society and became an avid reader of books, making up for the opportunities he had missed in school.

In 1960, after buying himself out of the Royal Navy early, Sillars returned to Scotland and became a fireman, joining the National Fire Brigades Union (NFU) and the Labour Party. Two years later, in his mid-twenties, he became secretary of the local constituency Labour Party and part-time election agent, as well as an elected member of Ayr Town Council.

Labour was returned to office in October 1964 under Harold Wilson. Sillars was a Wilson supporter and a believer in democratic socialism and the politics of centralism, which he described as 'democratic centralism'. This was a period where, post-1959, as Scotland moved away from the Tories and towards Labour, the party had, in Sillars's words, 'a good conceit of itself'. After Wilson was re-elected in March 1966, trouble began to emerge with deflationary measures introduced in July of that year. Sillars defended these, but found the party loyalist case unconvincing, saying to himself, 'I made a private promise never again to sin my soul.'[3]

---

3   Sillars, *Scotland: The Case for Optimism*, pp. 20 & 21.

This was only the beginning of Labour's troubles, however, as it postponed for as long as it could the devaluation of the pound, undermining its own plans for economic growth and modernisation. This turbulence brought problems to party heartlands such as Scotland and Wales, and witnessed the first serious upsurge of support for the SNP and Plaid Cymru. The SNP polled well in the Glasgow Pollok by-election in March 1967 and, in November, Winnie Ewing sensationally won the previously impregnable Labour seat of Hamilton. Nothing would ever be quite the same again.

Sillars's reaction was on his own account affected by a speech Winnie Ewing gave at Ayr racecourse, where she attacked not just Labour politicians, but Labour voters. This led Sillars to produce, with Labour MP Alex Eadie, a fifteen-page pamphlet, 'Don't Butcher Scotland's Future', followed up with a shorter leaflet, 'Exposed: The Truth About the SNP'.[4] This was the pre-internet age, where printed material, argument and facts were often hard to get hold of, and the Sillars-led initiative answered a need among Labour members for counters to the nationalists' positive case. It was robust, unionist and still firmly of the democratic centralist mindset. It argued that Scotland gained from the union, and that Scotland was 'subsidised' by England and would have difficulty 'going it alone'.[5]

Sillars was now being noticed and was in demand as a speaker at local Labour parties. In 1968 he began working at the STUC as Head of Organisation and Social Services, and that year it endorsed the idea of an elected Scottish Assembly. In March 1970, after winning the South Ayrshire Labour nomination, he easily held the seat with a 20,807 majority over the SNP in a by-election, part of a wider picture of the SNP surge subsiding post-Hamilton.

In the June 1970 general election, the Conservatives under Ted Heath were returned with a national majority of thirty seats, whereas in Scotland, Labour won forty-four seats to the Tories' twenty-three. This was the beginning of what later became known as 'the Doomsday scenario': a UK Tory government elected on English votes, while Scotland voted Labour. This troubled Sillars, as can

---

4   Alex Eadie and Jim Sillars, *Don't Butcher Scotland's Future: The case for reform at all levels of government* (no publisher, 1968); *Exposed: The Truth about Scotland's Future* (no publisher, 1968).

5   Eadie and Sillars, *Don't Butcher Scotland's Future*.

be seen when he pointed this out to Heath in the new parliament: 'Scotland voted overwhelmingly for Labour [and] it is claptrap for him and his Ministers to say that they have a mandate for cutting Scottish public expenditure…'[6]

This period is the genesis of Sillars's first public revision of his position on Scottish self-government. With Labour MPs Alex Eadie, Harry Ewing and John Robertson (the latter to become along with Sillars the other Scottish Labour Party MP), a 'group of four' pro-devolution MPs formed, who began lobbying for the party to adopt a supportive policy to home rule. Their pamphlet 'Scottish Labour and Devolution' was to be published in 1973, but had to wait due to the events of March 1974, by which time Wilson and Labour were back in office as a minority government.[7]

Scottish politics were in an era of fast change. The end of 1973 had seen the publication of the long-awaited Kilbrandon Report on the Constitution, while the Glasgow Govan by-election had seen Margo MacDonald, later to marry Sillars, overturn a Labour majority and win the seat by 571 votes. The atrophy of the local Labour Party came as a shock to Sillars, and caused him to reflect on the nature of the party as a whole. In the campaign, Sillars asked the Labour candidate Harry Selby to remove a burnt-out car, to which Selby memorably replied: 'I know about that car, we used it to stand on when drumming up support for rent demonstrations.' Willie Ross on polling day drove around declaring through a loudspeaker: 'Now's the day and now's the hour for Govan to kick out Tory power.'[8] The reality of Glasgow Labour and its lack of responsibility for decades of party rule seems to have made a lasting impact on Sillars, aided by Margo's victory.

BREAKAWAY

Post-February 1974, Scottish politics was changed by the arrival of the SNP at Westminster in sizeable numbers and Labour's need to protect

---

6   Sillars, *Scotland: The Case for Optimism*, p. 34.

7   Alex Eadie, Harry Ewing, John Robertson and Jim Sillars, *Scottish Labour and Devolution: a discussion paper* (no publisher, 1974).

8   Ibid., p. 43.

its seats north of the border. This meant the party had to shift from the anti-devolution stance it adopted in the 1950s and had reaffirmed since. This happened at a special Labour conference at Dalintober Street, Glasgow on 16 September 1974, with the trade union block votes organised by Alex Kitson. This cleared the ground for Scottish Labour to stand on a manifesto in October 1974 promising a Scottish Assembly, with party materials committing to creating 'Powerhouse Scotland' and 'an Assembly with economic teeth'.[9]

Labour was elected in October 1974 with a narrow majority of three, while bitterly divided between left and right on Europe and devolution. The publication of the White Paper on Scottish devolution at the end of 1975, with its commitment to an Assembly with limited powers and very few economic responsibilities, appalled Sillars, and began his exit from the party. On 18 January 1976, Sillars, fellow MP John Robertson, Alex Neil and others launched the separate Scottish Labour Party: a brave but foolhardy exercise that they had not planned for, but instead instinctively stumbled into.

Sillars's short-lived Scottish Labour Party attracted great interest, column inches in papers and comment, but it was born fatally flawed – lacking long-term planning, strategy or support, rent asunder by bitter internal divisions, including Trotskyite entryism, and hamstrung by the inequities of the first-past-the-post electoral system (not just for Westminster, but for the fledgling Scottish Assembly). Still, some of the notices for Sillars were over-the-top eulogies. Neal Ascherson wrote a profile, 'Jim Sillars: A future Prime Minister of Scotland?', and noted that a man who is 'going to change his mind in the stiff orthodoxies of Scottish political life needs a bomb-proof opinion of himself' – an accurate description of his greatest strengths and most profound flaws.[10]

Tony Benn had a long-term respect for Sillars, but in a conversation with

9   Henry Drucker, *Breakaway: The Scottish Labour Party* (Edinburgh: Edinburgh University Student Publications Board, 1978), pp. 30–31.

10   *The Scotsman*, 1 November 1975.

him post-breakaway he reflected on this mix, and how Sillars had allowed the favourable media comment to turn his judgement:

> Sillars is a proud man with charisma and appeal; he knows how to use the press, and of course has been taken up by the media. He thought he would be Prime Minister of Scotland, but actually the press are only interested in him because he split the Labour Party.

He concluded: 'It shows how easy it is to go wrong, mainly by being misled by a sense of your own importance.'[11]

There followed two years of tortuous parliamentary manoeuvrings leading to the Scotland Act 1978 getting on the statute book, Labour having lost its majority at the end of 1976, while Sillars and Robertson were often more supportive of devolution than many Labour members. The 1979 referendum campaign saw Labour divisions come to the fore, and the party ruling out forming an umbrella campaign with devolutionists in other parties. Labour's anti-devolutionists had an energy and zeal, and Sillars was one of the few tried and tested campaigners who was prepared to travel the country making the case.

The vote was narrowly won for an Assembly, but did not pass the 40 per cent threshold of the electorate legislated for, leaving Labour unsure what to do. Sillars and pro-devolutionists suggested they bring the Repeal Order of the Scotland Act forward (as the legislation specified) and vote it down, but this would expose Labour divisions, and Jim Callaghan was unwilling to do so. Instead, a vote of no confidence, first tabled by the SNP, then superseded by a Tory one, was debated, which the government lost 311 to 310; the SNP voted with the Tories, Sillars with Labour. In the resulting election, Thatcher was returned with an overall majority of forty-three, Labour in Scotland won forty-four seats and Sillars lost in South Ayrshire to a young Labour Turk called George Foulkes by 1,521 votes. Thus signalled the end of one chapter in Sillars's life.

---

11   Tony Benn, *Conflicts of Interest: Diaries 1977–80* (London: Hutchinson, 1990), p. 173.

POST-1979 AND THE SNP YEARS

S illars's failure to be elected in 1979 left the Scottish Labour Party project stillborn and, after a period of reflection following the May 1980 council elections, he joined the SNP. He did so reassured by the establishment of an internal SNP pressure group, the 79 Group, with its three principles: social-ism, independence and republicanism, which had been formed in the wake of the party's 1979 defeat. Some thought the group had been formed with the aim of making the shift of Sillars to the SNP easier, but this wasn't the case.

The SNP's radicals mirrored similar moves in British Labour post-1979 as a new generation challenged an older, more conservative establishment. Both were to be ultimately unsuccessful, but precipitate bitter party civil wars and permanently change their parties. Sillars joined the SNP as he neared thirty-three and was therefore older than most of the impatient and eager left-wingers in the 79 Group, which made him a natural authority figure.

At the 1981 SNP annual conference, Sillars became vice-chair for policy, the 79 Group won five seats on the party executive and he gave a powerful address on standing up to the Thatcher government which saw a motion on civil disobedience passed. This was his first-ever address to SNP conference, and it was an emotive one: 'Sacrifices there will be. People will be hurt … it will be unpopular at first … We have to be prepared to accept that the cell doors will clank behind some of us.'[12] Gordon Wilson, party leader, astutely gave responsibility for the campaign to Sillars. On 16 October 1981, Sillars and five other party members broke into Edinburgh's former Royal High School building, which was to have been the site of the Scottish Assembly. A small protest was held, but it was all a bit amateurish, even an embarrassment, and the rally the next day had to be cancelled. 'Scottish Resistance' this was not.

The following year at SNP conference, the party leadership responded by forming a pressure group, the Campaign for Nationalism in Scotland, and as a result a motion was put forward to proscribe organised political

---

12   *The Scotsman*, 29 May 1981.

groups, with the intention of closing down the 79 Group, which was carried 308 to 188. Subsequently, the 79 Group disbanded, but reformed as the Scottish Socialist Society, inviting people from other and no parties to join. This was seen as disobeying the party and, on 21 September, seven members of the 79 Group were expelled, including Salmond.

The SNP didn't enter 1983 in good heart or shape, and while it retained the two seats it had kept in 1979, its vote continued to decrease nationally. The only upside was that, with the re-election of the Thatcher government, the gauntlet was now thrown down to Scottish Labour to protect the country from its worst excesses, thus providing a line of attack for the nationalists. This was the period when 'the Scottish question' reignited from its post-1979 slumber, and the catalyst was the Thatcher government's poll tax: planned and tried out in Scotland, which made the question of 'no mandate' a central one.

Sillars produced a pamphlet, 'Moving On and Moving Up in Europe', in 1985, calling for a rethink of the party's position on Europe, which was as an argument to prove influential.[13] He also wrote his part-autobiography, part-manifesto, *Scotland: The Case for Optimism*, in this period, published in 1986.[14] It is a revealing, candid read, filled with Sillars's remorseless energy and drive, detailing his inability to play the game in Scottish Labour of swallowing your pride and principles and keeping quiet. His journey to independence and the SNP is portrayed as the logic of a man always thinking about and questioning the big issues: the nature of capitalism, socialism, democracy, and the European Union. It is Sillars's most personal and persuasive book, particularly in the autobiographical parts, and reading it even years later it sparks with insights and reflections.

The 1987 election saw Sillars stand for the first time as an SNP candidate in the Linlithgow constituency against one of his old sparring partners, Tam Dalyell, and poll respectably, behind Labour by 10,373 votes. More significantly, Thatcher won a third term based on English votes and MPs, as Scotland decisively moved against the Tories. North of the border, the Tories

---

13   Jim Sillars, *Moving On and Moving Up in Europe* (Edinburgh: SNP Edinburgh Branch, 1985).

14   Sillars, *Scotland: The Case for Optimism*.

saw their parliamentary representation more than halved, while Labour returned fifty MPs ('the fighting fifty' or 'feeble fifty' depending on politics), and the SNP, while losing their two seats, won three former Tory seats, seeing Alex Salmond elected for the first time.

The SNP annual conference that year was held to the backdrop of 'The Real Choice: Independence or Thatcher' and party spirits on the rise. Labour had little idea what to do with its mandate, publishing a Scottish Assembly Bill that went nowhere and facing the challenge of the poll tax, on which the SNP could embrace non-payment. All of this tied into the revival of the constitutional question.

In 1988, 'independence in Europe' became SNP policy, significantly aided by Sillars's own long-term thinking. This was to turn out to be the apex of his influence, and the period where he and the rest of the party leadership most found themselves travelling in the same strategic direction. The European question had long been a major factor in Sillars's political odyssey, from the moment the UK joined in January 1973. Indeed, in June 1973, he told Tony Benn that 'he had become a convinced Scottish nationalist'; a few months later, in October 1973, he said to Benn that if the UK stayed in the European Community then 'he would become a Scottish nationalist member'.[15] It is also pertinent to note that Sillars launched his Scottish Labour Party in 1976, once the European referendum was out of the way, and for the time being resolved.

GOVAN VICTORY

Later, in 1988, Labour MP for Govan Bruce Millan became a European Commissioner, forcing a by-election, and Sillars was chosen as the SNP candidate. The nationalist campaign was run by Salmond and filled with excitement and energy, whereas Labour's was the exact opposite: a picture similar to Margo's Govan victory in 1973. Sillars was described on the ballot paper as 'Scottish National Party: Anti-Poll Tax Candidate' and he turned a 19,509

15   Tony Benn, *Against the Tide: Diaries 1973–76* (London: Hutchinson, 1989), pp. 46 & 73.

Labour majority into a 3,554 SNP one – a 33.1 per cent swing. Tony Benn, who had previously admired Sillars, reflected, 'There had been no socialist politics in our campaign – just the idea that if you keep your head down you'll win.'[16]

Sillars arrived at Westminster on the tail of another SNP bandwagon and a wave of high expectations. These were dramatic times in Scottish politics, with ongoing discussions about setting up a Scottish Constitutional Convention involving all the opposition parties at an advanced stage. Post-Govan, Sillars oscillated in tone and content: pre-Govan, he had savaged Labour for its inaction on the constitution. In the campaign, he acted in a nuanced way to appeal to and win over floating Labour voters, and immediately after he won was conciliatory, reaching out 'the hand of friendship to like-minded people in the Labour Party in Scotland'; and then changed again, likening Donald Dewar to an 'Uncle Tom'.[17]

Post-Govan, the SNP was on the up, in January 1989 hitting 32 per cent in the polls, only 4 per cent behind Labour on 36 per cent – representing the party's best showing since 1977. At this point the SNP Convention team, made up of Gordon Wilson, Margaret Ewing and Jim Sillars, decided not to participate in the Convention, but when they took party soundings, Sillars didn't mention this to Salmond when they spoke. The reasoning was that Salmond would be for remaining, but, in so doing, the Sillars–Salmond relationship, which had been close until this point, was changed for ever. The SNP put out a press release that weekend: 'Scotland lost out in 1979 because of a rigged referendum. It is our view that the SNP cannot take part in a rigged Convention which can neither reflect nor deliver Scottish demands.'[18]

The post-Govan mood of euphoria was burst, the Convention went ahead without the SNP and most of the party rallied around the leadership. But something had shifted: gone was the high spirits of Govan; in its place, a widespread, disgruntled mood. The party polled respectably in the Glasgow

---

16   Tony Benn, *The End of an Era: Diaries 1980–90* (London: Hutchinson, 1992), p. 553.

17   Quoted in *The Observer*, 24 September 1989.

18   SNP Press Release, 29 January 1989.

Central by-election of June 1989, but didn't worry Labour, and it won a decent 25.6 per cent and two seats in the European elections, finishing ahead of the Tories but way behind Labour.

Gordon Wilson stood down as leader in 1990 and there were expectations that Sillars would stand. Instead, Margaret Ewing faced Salmond, with Ewing initially the favourite. She was disadvantaged by a number of factors: one was having two campaigns, an 'official' one and the 'Left Caucus' one of Sillars, while a second reason was complacency and lack of any real agenda. Sillars displayed his growing hostility towards Salmond, writing,

> David Owen is a superb performer on television. None can match him for style. Yet he and the party that wrapped itself around his style and personality is no substitute for the policies, the strategy, and the unity that comes from a collective leadership based on the depth of experience.[19]

Salmond won by 486 to 186, in part making explicit the earlier Sillars agenda of differentiating between the Labour establishment and its members: 'The SNP must never forget that our enemy is not the Labour rank and file but its grey Scottish leadership.'[20] This victory produced another watershed in the Sillars–Salmond relationship, which has some similarities to that of Blair and Brown in 1994, when the former, as the junior in the relationship, stood and won the Labour leadership. Until this point, Sillars had seen himself as being the senior, even the mentor, and Salmond his protégé; others disagreed even before the 1990 contest. One view put forward by Sillars's supporters is that, had he stood in 1990, he would have won, but again others reject this. Sillars did judge, after deciding that he would not stand, that he would be able to aid Ewing winning, block Salmond and, perhaps, consider running in the future. All of this was altered for ever by Salmond's victory, leaving Sillars with a sense of personal bitterness over the next two decades.

---

19   *The Scotsman*, 14 August 1990.
20   Ibid., 7 August 1990.

Salmond's first year as leader was a relatively quiet one. Thatcher had resigned as Prime Minister in November 1990 and the poll tax's abolition was announced. There was the expectation of an imminent UK election, and the party was drifting. At the 1991 SNP conference, Sillars defeated Alasdair Morgan for the deputy leadership by 279 to 184, while Alex Neil announced without any advance warning to the leadership that Scotland would be independent by 1 January 1993, translated into 'Free by '93', with Salmond seeing this as the work and style of Sillars.

The 1992 general election saw the SNP damaged by their own expectations. First, an opinion poll put support for independence at 50 per cent, then *The Sun* came out for independence, and in a debate of all four party leaders in the Usher Hall, Edinburgh, Salmond got the better of Donald Dewar, shadow Secretary of State for Scotland. In the pre-election period, Sillars claimed, 'The days of being patronised, lectured to, bullied and insulted are over.'[21] Yet, while the party increased its vote from 14 per cent to 21.5 per cent, it didn't increase its previous tally of three, and Sillars lost his Govan seat to Labour's Ian Davidson by 4,125 votes. 'Free by '93' became 'three MPs in 1993', and Salmond later reflected that it had been 'an object lesson in how to turn a campaign triumph into a perceived defeat', aided by Sillars being 'obsessed with securing "the mandate"' for independence.[22]

That year, 1992, represented Sillars's second parliamentary defeat, and as in 1979 he was left exhausted, out of pocket and with significant debts. Post-election, in an STV interview, he bitterly observed that 'The great problem is that Scotland has too many ninety-minute patriots whose nationalist outpourings are expressed only at major sporting events.'[23] Sillars's phrase 'ninety-minute patriots' was to pass into the popular lexicon and be used as a dismissive term about Scottish nationalism. He went further, saying that a profound 'honesty' was lacking in the SNP in 'those who have marched

---

21   Ibid., 30 January 1992.

22   *Scotland on Sunday*, 14 September 2000.

23   *The Herald*, 24 April 1992.

along the Con-Convention road, brains clogged with rhetorical trash about "claims of right"'.[24] Thus, Sillars exited Scottish politics for a period.

AFTER PARLIAMENT

The period 1992–97 was characterised by the growing unpopularity of John Major's Tory government, from 1994, the advent and success of New Labour and the expectation of a Scottish Parliament (as distinct from an Assembly). Sillars played no major role in politics and the party, concentrating on business interests and serving on the Scottish Enterprise Board after being appointed by Michael Forsyth, Tory Secretary of State for Scotland. When Labour won emphatically in 1997, it legislated for an immediate referendum on Scottish (as well as Welsh) devolution, frontloading it, rather than, as in 1979, leaving it to the fag-end of a parliament.

Critical to winning a referendum was bringing the three non-Tory parties together, Labour recognising that to win well it needed Liberal Democrat and SNP cooperation. The SNP endorsed a Yes-Yes vote and cooperation with the cross-party campaign, 'Scotland Forward', with Gordon Wilson and Jim Sillars the only significant public dissenters – the latter arguing to little effect for mass abstention. Sillars offered faint praise of Salmond's role in the referendum, calling him 'brilliant' and then observing, 'It never seems to have struck the SNP that when your generals are given medals by the other side, they've probably been firing at the wrong targets.'[25]

The Scottish Parliament elections saw the return of a Labour–Lib Dem Executive and Donald Dewar as First Minister, and while Sillars took no active part, his wife, Margo MacDonald, was elected as one of thirty-five SNP MSPs. Salmond didn't adjust to the ethos of the new parliament, and the role of opposition to Labour, and there was growing unease in the party. However, it still came as a surprise to most when, in July 2000, he announced

---

24   *The Scotsman*, 25 April 1992.

25   Ibid., 8 May 1999.

he was standing down as leader. This gave Sillars yet another opportunity to take a pop at his former protégé, declaring he would refuse to 'join in the hypocritical praise that will be heaped upon Alex Salmond now that he has snuffed out his political life at the top'.[26]

John Swinney was comfortably elected leader against Sillars's ally Alex Neil, but the party still found progress difficult, and in the 2003 Scottish elections went backward in votes and seats. There then followed a *kamikaze* leadership challenge to Swinney by Bill Wilson, which was resoundingly defeated, and before this a very public debate about the role of a pre-legislative referendum on independence, played out in the columns of *The Scotsman*'s letters page.

This began with Bill Wilson criticising the policy of a pre-legislative referendum on independence, which had become the party's position in 2000. Salmond replied, which led to Campbell Martin, then an SNP MSP, answering; Salmond retorted: 'Our referendum policy was devised to allow Scotland a democratic way out of that unionist trap, a straight vote on the principle of national freedom.'[27]

Sillars replied, asking, 'If the SNP cannot command an absolute majority of seats, how is it to get the referendum on principle through the Parliament?'[28] Salmond wrote back: 'The answer is that there may well be MSPs who support independence, but not the SNP, and others who do not agree with independence but favour the issue being settled by the people.' He then got personal with Sillars: 'I recognise the zeal of the convert … His talent could have been really important for Scotland's cause. What a pity that he wasted it.'[29]

This was just the beginning. Sillars pointed out that 'May well be' might also mean 'May well not be'.[30] Salmond's response went after Sillars: 'In a previous letter, I pointed out he has been both fiercely unionist and passionately nationalist. I missed out his pro-devolution and anti-devolution phases, his pro-Convention

26 *Scottish Sun*, 18 July 2000.
27 *The Scotsman*, 6 September 2003.
28 Ibid., 9 September 2003.
29 Ibid., 12 September 2003.
30 Ibid., 16 September 2003.

and anti-Convention periods and his bewildering conversion from anti-European to Euro enthusiast and now to reborn Eurosceptic,' before signing off, 'Perhaps if his talk had even a smidgeon of consistency, then I might believe that he plans any action at all beyond a long, self-indulgent girn.'[31] After two more exchanges, Sillars got the last word in the exchange: 'Mr Salmond seems to believe his policy will keep Westminster out of the independence issue. How naïve.'[32]

In reality, Salmond was to get the last word. In 2004, Swinney announced his resignation as leader and after initially not considering standing, Salmond put his hat in the ring in a 'dream team' with Nicola Sturgeon as his deputy. Sillars and Salmond were now far apart, and Sillars was publicly dismissive of his once-ally's return: 'After ten years of Alex's leadership, and his continued manipulative dominance, the party Gordon Wilson led in his final years … has been turned into a poisonous cabal, operating with one controller…'[33] There was only going to be one winner and result, and Salmond was triumphantly re-elected leader.

In 2007, the SNP won its first ever national election and Salmond became First Minister. This didn't change Sillars's low estimation of Salmond, hitting out at 'Scotland's first ever experience of the cult of personality'.[34] He intervened by writing a pamphlet in November 2009 calling for a change from 'the SNP concentrating on tactical non-independence approaches to voters'.[35] 'The UK is still the English State,' he argued, and 'Scots have long forgotten how to think in State terms', which the SNP had yet to counter.[36] When the SNP polled poorly in the 2010 Westminster election, Sillars called for change: 'What the election result should produce for the SNP is a revolution. A revolt by the party to bring the present leadership to heel, or replace it…'[37]

---

31   Ibid., 18 September 2003.

32   Ibid., 26 September 2003.

33   Ibid., 16 July 2004.

34   *Holyrood Magazine*, 29 June 2009.

35   Jim Sillars, *Thoughts on getting to the only sensible choice for Scotland: Independence* (no publisher, 2009), p. 1.

36   Ibid., pp. 4 & 5.

37   *The Scotsman*, 10 May 2010.

His critique was all-encompassing of a party for the first time in its history in office: 'The party is a vacuum the leadership fills with banalities. The SNP has members, branches, and meets all together on occasion, but to no avail. To blind faith they allow themselves to be led down silly paths.'[38] At the same time, Sillars commented that he and Salmond hadn't spoken since 1992, but 'If Salmond needed me to help tomorrow, I wouldn't hesitate to help.'[39] Little did Sillars realise that the success of Salmond's nationalist project would reignite his public role.

THE LAST ACT?
THE INDEPENDENCE REFERENDUM

In 2011, the SNP and Salmond won an overall majority in the Scottish Parliament based on a mandate for an independence referendum. Sillars for once was full of praise: 'Alex Salmond is now in the world of the politics and the art of the possible, not the politics of perfection.' He quoted at length his own pamphlet on independence of two years previous: 'Small size nations and larger ones too, are often constrained on policy due to the proximity of a near or larger state, whose own state interests limit those of its neighbour … Scotland does not lie outside spheres of influence.' The SNP had to be strategic and understand geo-political sensibilities:

> Leasing the Trident base? Jings, crivvens, help ma Boab. Never! is likely
> to be the first reaction of party members … We must, if we are serious,
> look through the English end of the telescope. Scottish independence, in
> the old model and old policies, threatens English state interests, and if so
> threatened, they will fight to keep us in the Union …[40]

---

38   *Holyrood Magazine*, 15 May 2010.

39   *Sunday Times*, 16 May 2010.

40   *The Scotsman*, 14 May 2011.

This didn't last long, and soon Sillars reverted to his role as the most out-spoken critic of the leadership. In February 2012, he savaged the state of the party: 'The SNP MSPs, and the membership, has tasted power and likes it. None more so than the First Minister.' Sillars doubted whether Salmond really wanted to hold a single-question referendum, for which he had the mandate, and was deeply suspicious of the manoeuvres concerning the merits and prospects of a two-question vote. Defeat in a single-question referendum would be 'a grievous blow', but there wasn't 'an SNP mandate for a second question'.[41]

Over the course of the next two and a half years of the independence referendum, Sillars was a tireless critic of the SNP, Salmond and the Yes Scotland campaign. He attacked the lack of campaigning and information being produced by Yes Scotland, saying, 'the Yes leadership report card to date reads "nice people, intelligent, mean well, but need to do better"';[42] savaged the nature of the SNP as 'totalitarian' and defined by 'dumb loyalty'; and expressed dismay at Salmond's style of leadership: 'For too long Alex Salmond has exercised unfettered authority. But like all human beings he does not walk on water.'[43] With Gordon Wilson, he criticised the SNP's pro-EU stance, suggesting it was 'damaging to the prospects of a Yes majority' and reducing Scotland to that of 'a beggar at the Brussels gate'.[44]

The publication of the Scottish government's long-awaited White Paper on independence in November 2013 was criticised in a number of areas, such as the currency and EU membership, and conflated a Yes vote with that of 'an endorsement of Alex Salmond or his government'.[45] He even went as far as to question the mandate of the Scottish government to call itself such, and to open post-vote negotiations. The SNP saw itself as '"the democratically

41   *Daily Record*, 15 February 2012.

42   *The Scotsman*, 29 January 2013.

43   Ibid., 26 October 2012.

44   Ibid., 7 November 2012.

45   'Scottish left talks independence in Edinburgh', *The Targe*, 8 December 2013. Available at http://thetarge.co.uk/article/current-affairs/0164/scottish-left-talks-independence-in-edinburgh

elected Government of Scotland". That's not true.' Instead: 'Alex Salmond is First Minister of an administration elected to divide up a bloc grant…'[46] Such irrevocable fundamentalism took one nowhere helpful, but a political cul-de-sac, and close to a Westminster sovereigntist politics: the opposite of the intention.

The long campaign of the referendum opened up many possibilities of public events and engagement, with a plethora of initiatives filling an appetite for political discussion unseen in decades. Into this arena Jim Sillars emerged as one of the attractions of the independence campaign. He debated with opponents such as George Galloway, and produced a book, *In Place of Fear II* (so named in tribute to his hero, Labour minister Nye Bevan's *In Place of Fear*).

In debate with Galloway, the atmosphere and content had the air of a left-wing revivalist meeting from years ago. Sillars said of the contemporary SNP: 'They call themselves "social democratic" which most people will find very hard to actually define, but it takes them away from the Tartan Tory idea that was flung at them for many years.'[47]

In Place of Fear II invoked Nye Bevan's radicalism and that socialists 'must be able to think and do what the establishment says we must not think and cannot do'.[48] Sillars believed that 'Scottish socialism will be renewed by the challenge of independence', and that

> the socialist movement in Scotland has never been able to pursue its policies here because no matter how we vote in the elections in which lie real power, those for the Westminster government, the Scottish tail can never wag the southern dog … How many times are the Scots willing to go to the polls, vote for the government they want, and end up with the government they rejected? Happens in the UK. Cannot happen in an independent Scotland.[49]

---

46   *Daily Record*, 3 January 2013.

47   *Newsnight Scotland*, 25 March 2014.

48   Jim Sillars, *In Place of Fear II: A Socialist Programme for an Independent Scotland* (Glasgow: Vagabound Voices, 2014), pp. 5–6.

49   Ibid., p. 13.

His distinctive voice found new audiences in the independence referendum. Sillars gave encouragement to a younger generation of left-wingers in the Radical Independence Campaign and elsewhere. The tragic death of Margo MacDonald in April 2014 brought out the best in Sillars when he spoke for a country beyond Yes and No at a moving memorial ceremony in the Assembly Rooms, Edinburgh: 'I bring a message from Margo to all engaged in the campaign: 'There will be harsh statements on both sides, the debate will be fierce, there will be verbal wounds inflicted, but if we conduct ourselves in the run-up to 18 September the Margo MacDonald way, the division will be much easier to heal.'[50]

There was even a brief rapprochement with Salmond towards the end of the referendum, but it didn't last. As Yes went briefly ahead in the polls, the British state pulled out all the stops, including numerous corporate threats, leading Sillars to say: 'This referendum is about power, and when we get a Yes majority, we will use that power for a day of reckoning with BP and the banks.'[51] It was an unfortunate phrase, in a heated, charged atmosphere, which he regretted, later admitting it 'was a mistake ... That was an error on my part.'[52]

Post-referendum, Sillars showed his pent-up frustration and disappointment on his Twitter account @NaeFear, writing: 'Let Yes assert new indy rule – no more ref – majority votes and seats at Holyrood 2016 enough', followed by: 'What's this about a waiting a generation – indy remains on agenda now' and then: 'Queenie intervened for No as she did in 1979. So no more softly-softly – we go for Republic'.[53] Some of the motivation must have been as much, if not more, directed at the continued cautiousness and carefulness of the SNP post-vote than the forces of anti-independence.

A sequel to *In Place of Fear II* followed in *In Place of Failure*, which

50   *STV News*, 25 April 2014.

51   *The Scotsman*, 12 September 2014.

52   *The National*, 16 September 2015.

53   @NaeFear, 21 September 2014.

addressed how to maintain the spirit and hopes of the referendum and bring the question back as quickly as possible. Sillars revisited his criticism of Yes Scotland and the White Paper on independence, writing of the problem which left Yes campaigners being identified with the SNP: 'What leapt from its pages was an SNP programme for "change no change".'[54]

Sillars gave his support to moves for the Radical Independence Campaign to create a new left pro-independence party, RISE, which stood in the 2016 Scottish elections. Sillars sent a note of support to the inaugural conference, making the case for the new force, stating about the Labour Party that 'you cannot breathe life into a political corpse'.[55] In the run-up to the vote, publicly, as an SNP member, he made the case for voting SNP in the constituency vote, RISE in the regional vote. This caused some controversy, with public calls for Sillars to be expelled, which came to nothing. Similarly, RISE, despite not insignificant publicity, polled a derisory total, finishing behind Tommy Sheridan in Glasgow and nationally.

His response to the re-election of a Nicola Sturgeon SNP government in May 2016, but one which was short of an overall majority, was that 'Independence parties won, the Unionists lost, in the overall vote' and that the rise in the Tory vote wasn't that noteworthy, arguing, 'It is a pity that the SNP was not bold enough to ask for another referendum mandate.'[56]

Sillars contributed to the EU referendum, penning another pamphlet on why Brexit was the solution for both Scotland and independence, writing, 'We on the Yes side are being asked by the SNP to campaign in favour of an EU that, during the referendum campaign, told us to get stuffed, and if the UK remains in, will tell us that again when we come to the second independence referendum.'[57] The EU, in relation to Scotland, was even less democratic than Westminster: 'The question at the heart of this referendum is simple:

---

54   Jim Sillars, *In Place of Failure: Making It Yes Next Time* (Glasgow: Vagabound Voices, 2015), p. 23.

55   *The National*, 4 December 2015.

56   *Holyrood Magazine*, 9 May 2016.

57   Jim Sillars, *The Logical Case: Why ScotLeave.EU makes most sense* (no publisher, 2016), p. 2.

do we want to continue being governed by an organisation we do not elect and cannot reject or do we want to bring democracy home, in exactly the way generations of nationalists have urged us to?'[58] It was a typically Sillars position: contrarian, challenging, even to positions he had been consistently identified with in the past, but why would anyone expect any different?

A CONSISTENT AND CONTRARIAN VOICE

The political life of Jim Sillars is inarguably one of the longest and most varied of anyone who has risen to senior rank in the Scottish nationalists. What lessons, if any, can be learnt from such a full public life?

First, there is the incessant drive and energy that has defined Sillars and nearly everything he has done. Never for him the quiet life of politics for advancement or office. Instead, it has always been about the big questions – of who holds power, accountability and issues of democracy and economy. Second, he has been an inveterate political activist and thinker, penning books, memos and pamphlets in a way that shames many of today's managerial class of politicians in all parties.

What kind of politics and Scotland has this been about? The one constancy has been the belief in socialism: the ideology that first drew Sillars into politics, and which he has held since. Sillars's socialism is shaped by ideas encountered at an early age, when he was inspired by Nye Bevan, leader of the Labour left in the 1940s and 1950s. There was never a detailed programme to Bevanism, amounting instead to an ethical socialist outlook, and that is close to a description of Sillars's politics. Moreover, a constant pillar of his politics since joining the SNP and supporting independence has been to say, 'I am not a nationalist, I am a socialist.'[59]

One strand of Sillars's socialism has been about how it understands modern societies and social change. There is in this a powerful romanticising

---

58   CommonSpace, 9 May 2016.

59   *Daily Record*, 24 January 2016.

of the near-past, and the age of a more organised, political working class. This was evident in Sillars's Scottish Labour Party, where he misunderstood the nature of working-class Scotland in the view of Henry Drucker in his study of the party, *Breakaway*: 'They mistook South Ayrshire for Scotland. Before he set up his own party, Sillars was adored by his constituents. He had an intense following in the Doon Valley. The Doon Valley is the epitome of the old Scotland. It is an area of small towns and mining villages.'[60] Such areas were historically characterised by class loyalty and solidarity but, by the 1960s and 1970s, this was severely weakening, as was the hold of Labour.

Years later, Sillars still spoke wistfully of the culture of South Ayrshire: 'It was a welcoming wonderful, rich world, a place of self-education, discussion and debate', yet at the same time, in the period Sillars represented the area, change was already underway, as he in retrospect acknowledged: 'The self-sustaining, supporting world of Labour was slowly eroding and disappearing.'[61] Yet, the hold of a radical nostalgia has never disappeared on the left, and Scottish left in particular, aided by the phenomena of Thatcherism and New Labour, both of which didn't translate well into Scotland.

In a debate on the thirtieth anniversary of Margaret Thatcher becoming Prime Minister in May 2009, Sillars, along with former Labour MP Brian Wilson, made the case against Thatcherism, while Tory politicians Malcolm Rifkind and David McLetchie made it for. The most passion shown was about the pluses and minuses of council house sales, which Wilson spoke about as producing 'social apartheid' and an 'underclass', while both he and Sillars spoke about the policy that began in 1980 in the present, as if history could be reversed. So pronounced was this that Rifkind criticised them for their continued 'left-wing paternalism'.[62] Irrespective of the complex issue of the consequences of council house sales, Rifkind was able to claim that Sillars, Wilson and the Scottish left were incapable of learning from

---

60   Drucker, *Breakaway*, p. 144.

61   Hassan and Shaw, *The Strange Death of Labour Scotland*, pp. 217 & 238.

62   Gerry Hassan, 'The Legacy of Thatcherism North of the Border Thirty Years On', *Open Democracy*, 5 May 2009, available at http://www.gerryhassan.com/short-journalistic-essays/the-legacy-of-thatcherism-north-of-the-border-thirty-years-on/

history and were still wedded to municipalism and statism. This might sound unfair, coming from someone who was one of Thatcher's Secretary of States for Scotland and who presided over the poll tax, but a big strand of the Scottish left, in and out of Labour, has been traditionally highly authoritarian and centralist.

Sillars has been a rare iconoclastic voice on the Scottish left and within nationalist circles, a constant contrarian railing against orthodoxies. Former Labour organiser Jimmy Allison wrote in 1995, 'If Jim Sillars was the SNP leader he would be giving the Labour Party establishment in Scotland something to think about.'[63] He proved too immune to the disciplines and constraints of party politics for that ever to be tested, and Scottish Labour ended up in a state of collapse anyway. Two years previous, John Pollock described him as 'a classic personality type. They're marvellous in certain circumstances. They're great in wars, at the high point of battles, a lot of energy, a manic force. But it goes hand in hand with enormous egotism and things go into reverse in a dramatic way.'[64]

One area worthy of comment has been the significant political relationships in his life. In his formative years, he looked up to Willie Ross, Wilson's Secretary of State for Scotland, but disappointed him by showing too much independence of thought. In the 1980s, his relationship with Alex Salmond, where Sillars was the senior figure, initially proved more successful, but turned into a twenty-year war of bitterness, where Sillars did most of the sniping. The exception is his 33-year partnership and marriage to Margo MacDonald, which was an exemplar of love, affection and care, with Jim in his later days being Margo's carer, as she struggled with Parkinson's disease. All of the above illustrate the many qualities of Sillars's character. The personal element of politics – how to rub along with and win over people, make friends, alliances and avoid creating enemies is key to successful politics – and, unfortunately for Sillars, despite his many talents, he often fell significantly short in this respect.

---

63   Jimmy Allison, *Guilty by Suspicion: A Life and Labour* (Glendaruel: Argyll Publishing, 1995), p. 130.

64   Kemp, *The Hollow Drum*, p. 164.

There is, with all the obvious differences, some element of commonality between Sillars and another prominent Scottish politician and serial rebeller: George Galloway. They are from different generations: Sillars born in 1937 and Galloway in 1954. Both were from an early age seen as shining Labour stars and were even spoken of as future Scottish Labour leaders. Both were autodidacts, never going to university at a time when more and more Labour colleagues were beginning to do so. Each was a gifted orator, capable of arousing great passions and emotions in both admirers and detractors.

Both rebelled against the conventions of Scottish Labour and wider Labour politics, while in many respects continuing to be defined by its politics and values. Galloway, despite being expelled from Labour in 2003, has continued to yearn to return to the party. One of Sillars's motivations for independence was to allow the Scottish Labour Party to return to its radical roots and be true to itself, rather than Westminster. This comparison can only be taken so far, for a principled and moralistic sense of duty has always informed Sillars through the decades, whereas Galloway has been flexible in the extreme on such things. Yet, it can be said that the transformation of working-class Scotland and the decline of the old South Ayrshires of this world has made such politicians possible: a culture of political entrepreneurs yearning for an age of greater solidarity and collectivism, which would have made their emergence difficult, if not impossible. This is a politics of 'radical nostalgia' found on parts of the left: the conservative left-wingers dreaming of turning the clock back to a world before Thatcherism, and not recognising that individualism, less deference and social control made the emergence of serial rebellers such as Sillars, Galloway, and even Jeremy Corbyn and John McDonnell in British Labour, more possible.[65]

In the history of Scottish politics, Jim Sillars will be remembered as one of the most challenging and thoughtful politicians, with a consistent independence of action and thinking. At significant points in politics – the 1970s

---

65   See on the Scottish left and Thatcherism: Gerry Hassan, *Caledonian Dreaming: The Quest for a Different Scotland* (Edinburgh: Luath Press, 2014), Chapters 8–9.

devolution debate, the 1980s transformation of the SNP, the Govan victory, and in the independence debate – he played a formative role, in the first three at the centre of events, and in the last from the margins, carving out a distinct positon and constituency.

Sometimes he was significantly ahead of the curve, in, for example, the 'idea' of the Scottish Labour Party and 'independence in Europe', while at other points, harking back to a Scotland – in class, economics, politics and socialism – that no longer existed with an almost evangelical sense of certainty. Timing is, if not all in politics, critical, and there was something often misjudged in when and where Sillars floated his various projects.

If there has been one continual tension, it was his inability to muster the skills to play successfully the game of party politics, and in so doing, failing to find a long-term vehicle for his ideas. He was a product of weakening party loyalty and tribalism, which made possible his series of distinctive acts, but which also prevented him from fully realising his ideas. Jim Sillars was a product of another political world, who challenged and provoked the politics of an older Scotland, but ultimately was unable himself to fully adapt to the political environment he helped to create.

CHAPTER 22

DONALD STEWART

EILIDH MACPHAIL

Donald Stewart was a Hebridean born and bred and represented his home constituency for seventeen years in Parliament. He joined the SNP in 1936 after becoming convinced of the arguments for Scottish independence. He stood unsuccessfully for the SNP, before finally winning the Western Isles in 1970: the first seat the SNP ever gained at a UK general election, and succeeded in holding it for the next four contests until his retirement in 1987. He was leader of the SNP parliamentary group from 1974 to 1987, including the turbulent 1974-79 parliament, and post-1979, when the party was reduced to two MPs. A long-time champion of the Gaelic language and culture, Stewart was a social conservative, a tendency that spoke to a significant part of Scotland. He was also, in his demeanour and politics, deeply shaped by the importance of public service and public duty.

· · ·

Donald Stewart famously described the Scottish National Party as 'a radical party with a revolutionary aim'. He himself could not be described as a radical, with his time as leader of the parliamentary party and as party president characterised by his calm, laid-back, undramatic approach, always charming and courteous, but all the while unflinching in his beliefs and his commitment to both Scottish independence and his constituency of the Western Isles. Although his political stance was revolutionary, he did not look, act or talk like a revolutionary, and he was quick to emphasise that the SNP had always opposed any road other than the democratic one.[1]

Donald Stewart was born on 17 October 1920 in Stornoway, a place he claimed was 'a grand place for boys to grow up in'.[2] The son of a ships engineer, he was educated at the local secondary school, the Nicolson Institute in Stornoway, leaving at the age of sixteen to take a job as a junior clerk in a local solicitor's office. Aware that his parents could not afford to send him to university, he was keen to leave school as soon as possible and begin earning. He did acknowledge later that, 'looking back, I would rather have had a university education than not, but – as the Gaelic expresses it – "it wasn't put out for me" so I have never wasted any time bemoaning the lack of it.'[3] Despite the lack of university education, as fellow MP Winnie Ewing noted, he was 'largely self-educated and read voraciously' becoming a 'fountain of knowledge' who 'had enormous charm and enormous recall – he never forgot anything or anybody'.[4] As she describes, he was 'extremely well read – he could summon up at any time the right quotation from poets, playwrights and all manner of writers, thinkers and politicians from many countries and could recall an apt joke for every occasion'.[5]

From his first job in a solicitor's office, he went on to work for Kenneth Mackenzie Ltd., a leading Harris Tweed manufacturer, in their office. Two years later, with the start of the Second World War, he was called up to the Royal Navy, opting for the signals branch where he spent five years, serving on HMS *Celandine*, a lower-class Corvette escorting Atlantic convoys. After the war, he returned to the Harris Tweed industry, re-joining his old company, where he remained until his election to Parliament twenty-five years later, by which time he had become a director of the company.

He got his first taste of political life becoming a councillor in what was the

---

1   'Obituary: Donald Stewart', *The Times*, 24 August 1992, p. 13.

2   Stewart, *A Scot at Westminster*, p. 11.

3   Ibid.

4   Ewing, *Stop the World*, p. 124.

5   Ibid., p. 154.

Stornoway Town Council in 1951, in which he served for almost twenty years. He served as elected provost of Stornoway from 1959 until 1965 and again from 1968 until his election to Parliament in 1970. His time in local government – as a councillor, provost, a magistrate and Honorary Sheriff – and as a board member of the Stornoway Trust Estate, not only afforded him political experience and a strong local profile but also gave him a keen awareness of the issues facing the Western Isles electorate. As he says in his own modest way, 'I went to the House of Commons fairly conversant with the main concerns of my constituency ... I was armed in some part to do battle on behalf of my electorate, and although realising that I was entering new terrain, I felt that I would not be entirely defenceless on some vital issues.'[6]

As Stewart describes in his memoirs, his support for independence and his dedication to a national movement to advance this was also a product of his early years in the Western Isles. From hearing of the struggles of Wallace and Bruce in his school days, he became convinced of the case for an independent Scotland during the general election in 1935, when Sir Alexander MacEwen fought the Western Isles in the nationalist cause. His involvement with the Scottish National Party began shortly after this, at the early age of sixteen, when in 1936 he wrote to the SNP headquarters in Glasgow expressing his wish to join the ranks and asking for details of the party's aims and policies. As he noted himself, 'In those days to meet another nationalist was almost as unusual as the Livingstone/Stanley encounter in Africa.'[7]

At the same time, he also became a convert to socialism and, thinking he could 'achieve two ends in one – a Socialist Scotland – by joining the Labour party', he did so in 1937. This was short-lived, with him leaving only two years later, having become disillusioned with the lack of conviction of the leadership and his distaste for the influence of the union bosses.[8] During his time in the navy, he regained his interest in the nationalist cause, then becoming

6   Stewart, *A Scot at Westminster*, pp. 12–13.

7   Ibid., p. 14.

8   Ibid., p. 16.

a member of the SNP, regularly reading their pamphlets and the party paper, and becoming inspired by the orations of fellow nationalists Oliver Brown and Douglas Young. When Dr Robert McIntyre won the Motherwell by-election for the SNP in 1945, he said he could 'still recall [his] feelings. Here at last was the dawn of a new day for our country. The nation was poised for independence once the war ended. Alas, it was to take another twenty years before a similar victory was achieved.'[9]

It was Donald Stewart himself who achieved one of the next striking victories for the SNP. Following the success of Winnie Ewing at the Hamilton by-election in 1967, the nationalists had hoped to build on this in the general election of June 1970. The party fielded a record number of sixty-five candidates in the seventy-one Scottish constituencies and forty-two of them lost their deposit. In a bigger blow, Labour regained Hamilton with an 8,582 majority.[10] As Winnie Ewing herself describes it, it was 'a bitter blow. As the night went on it seemed as if we would once again go back to having no voice at Westminster. But then something wonderful happened.'[11]

Donald Stewart had been campaigning as the SNP candidate for the Western Isles against the sitting Labour MP, Malcolm K. Macmillan, who had held the seat for the previous thirty-five years. Stewart felt that they had campaigned in a strong challenge to Labour and were confident of a good showing, although he claimed that 'only the most optimistic entertained the possibility that we could beat Malcolm Macmillan'.[12] Fellow campaigners remember how Stewart insisted on being driven to every small village in the islands. They recall him arguing for his cause using the case of the *Torrey Canyon*, the ship which had run aground off the south coast of England in 1967, telling voters, 'If the *Torrey Canyon* had run ashore on the Outer Hebrides, the British government wouldn't have given us one bottle of Parazon

9   Ibid., p. 18.

10   Richard Sharpe, 'Nationalists gain seat', *The Times*, 20 June 1970, p. 2.

11   Ewing, *Stop the World*, p. 120.

12   Stewart, *A Scot at Westminster*, p. 9.

to clean it up.'[13] His approachable nature and personal standing in the community, along with increasing disenchantment with the sitting MP's perceived absence from the constituency, combined to contribute to his success and he drew votes from both traditional Labour and Conservative supporters. As Brian Wilson, former Labour MP and one-time electoral opponent of Donald Stewart in the Western Isles, noted, 'Having cut a popular figure in local government, as Provost of Stornoway ... Donald was uniquely qualified to take advantage of a mood for change.'[14]

Due to the geographical spread of the Western Isles, at that time it was necessary to collect the ballot boxes by boat and so the result was announced almost twenty-four hours behind the rest of the UK. As *The Times* reported it,

> The SNP sprang the biggest surprise of the general election in Scotland late tonight by winning the Western Isles seat held by Labour for the past thirty-five years. Mr Donald Stewart, aged forty-nine, Provost of Stornoway, Lewis and a leading opponent in Scotland of British standard time, converted a Labour majority of 5,733 in the 1966 election into a nationalist majority of 726. Mr William Wolfe, chairman of the SNP, said tonight, 'we are absolutely elated. We could have no better member for the SNP in parliament than Donnie Stewart. We have lost one seat and we have won one. We are delighted that we have someone in parliament who knows many of the real problems of Scotland and we can build on this.'[15]

The result brought joy to the SNP ranks after a poor showing. A number of leading members of the party had gathered that day in Ewing's house, in a depressed mood, but Stewart describes how, on telling the party's chairman, Billy Wolfe, 'I'm in', he 'could hear the room erupt in hysterical delight.'[16]

---

13   Interview with author, Rae and Nellie Mackenzie, 8 February 2016.

14   Brian Wilson, 'Genial Nationalist from the Isles', *The Guardian*, 24 August 1992, p. 31.

15   Richard Sharpe, 'Nationalists gain seat', *The Times*, Saturday 20 June 1970, p. 2.

16   Stewart, *A Scot at Westminster*, p. 10.

As Ewing recounts, 'He said in his usual witty style: "I've toppled him over, the load from the Isles."'[17] On taking calls from all over Scotland and beyond that evening, Stewart felt that 'it was clear that our win had revived the party's spirits and hopes.'[18] It was the first time that the party had won a seat at a general election and Donald Stewart himself claimed that 'it ended the taunts that the SNP could make a showing at by-elections but that faced with forming a government, the public would revert to the established parties'.[19]

As the sole SNP representative at Westminster, Donald Stewart had a tough role to get to grips with during his first term in office. He was helped to settle in by Winnie Ewing, who herself had previously been the sole elected member for the party and who he considered a 'faithful friend'.[20] He went on to form good relationships across party boundaries and he spoke fondly of the many 'characters' and 'odd-balls' on all sides of the Commons, particularly in the 1970s. He had the combination of gravitas and a great wit and developed a reputation as a great raconteur himself, with many humorous anecdotes in his memoirs about members of all parties. Isobel Lindsay suggests that at the time he was seen by the political and media establishment as a 'pleasant "character" who was acceptable in the Westminster club'.[21] Sandy Matheson, who went on to follow him to high office in the local council, agrees that he commanded respect across Westminster, from the policeman at the gate up to Cabinet members, but argues that while he became part of the Westminster system of government, he never became part of the Westminster establishment.[22]

During his time in office, he was, as *The Times* describes, 'careful to avoid becoming simply a figurehead in a nationalist crusade. His primary concerns were the appalling social conditions of the Western Isles: unemployment (with 25 per cent of the working population on the dole), emigration, alcoholism

---

17   Ewing, *Stop the World*, p. 79.

18   Stewart, *A Scot at Westminster*, p. 10.

19   Ibid.

20   Ibid., p. 115.

21   Isobel Lindsay, 'The SNP and Westminster', in *The Making of the Modern SNP*, p. 96.

22   Interview with author, Sandy Matheson, 16 February 2016.

and costly transport.'[23] He brought forward a Private Member's Bill to improve the position and status of the Gaelic language and made a number of interventions on behalf of fishermen. He was also influential during his early period in office, along with the Liberal MP for Inverness-shire, Russell Johnston, in amending the plans for local government reform, so that for the first time there was a single authority to cover all of the Western Isles. It has been suggested by Brian Wilson that this may have been a 'mixed blessing, but the overall contribution to the self-confidence and economy of the islands has been considerable'.[24] Stewart himself felt that the creation of the council had been good for the islands and also made his job as an MP easier.[25]

Stewart was certainly revered in his native islands, and he was re-elected with increasingly large majorities at each election until his retirement in 1987. Sandy Matheson describes him as effectively the 'father of the Western Isles as a single political unit' and someone who had a profound influence on the development of the islands in the 1970s, due to his assistance in promoting the Arnish construction yard, the Western Isles Development Board and the Gaelic language.[26] Voters in the islands felt that the 'Western Isles was enjoying a good name at the centre of power'.[27] Such was the esteem with which he was held, at the 1979 election the local Labour candidate went to the house of the Labour election agent in Barra, only to find an SNP poster in the window, which was surreptitiously removed and replaced by a Labour one on hearing who his visitor was![28] Wilson summarises: 'In the Western Isles, his outlook, demeanour and identification with local causes fitted a large proportion of his constituents like a glove and he saw off various challenges – including my own – with ease.'[29]

---

23   'Obituary: Donald Stewart', *The Times*, 24 August 1992, p. 13.

24   Brian Wilson, 'Genial Nationalist from the Isles', *The Guardian*, 24 August 1992, p. 31.

25   Donnie MacInnes, 'Donald looks back', *Stornoway Gazette*, week ending 5 December 1987.

26   Interview with author, Sandy Matheson, 16 February 2016.

27   Ibid.

28   Ibid.

29   Brian Wilson, 'Genial Nationalist from the Isles', *The Guardian*, 24 August 1992, p. 31.

In Westminster, during the period 1970–74, apart from a brief spell from 1973 when he was joined by Margo MacDonald following her win at a by-election, Donald Stewart was a 'one-man band' for the SNP. While this may have had its challenges, it also suited him. As he joked himself, 'It was not as difficult as it might appear, and in fact it had distinct advantages. At any given moment I knew (a) where the parliamentary party was, and (b) how it intended to vote.'[30] Members of the local constituency association remember how, unlike current politicians who send regular email updates, Stewart very much took his own path, noting that 'consultation wasn't really his thing'.[31]

This significant freedom from the confines of party loyalty allowed him to largely plough his own path, reflecting his own strong moral values, which mirrored the values of many of his constituents at the time. *The Times* suggested that 'his conservative nationalism suited both the Calvinism of the northern islands and the Catholicism of the southern ones. As well as favouring Scotland's breakaway from England, he opposed easy divorce and abortion and supported capital punishment.'[32] He was also very much in favour of the abolition of nuclear weapons. Stewart is described by friends as being a 'small "c" conservative' and many of his views were derived from his Free Church of Scotland background and upbringing. As Wilson illustrates, 'While he never pushed religious views down anyone's throat, he was unswerving in his beliefs, and despite how unfashionable they may have been, he stuck to them all.'[33]

Stewart went on to win two out of every three votes cast in the following election in February 1974, when he was joined by six other SNP MPs in the House of Commons, the so-called magnificent seven, and at the October 1974 election this number rose to eleven, the 'first eleven'. As the longest-serving

---

30   Stewart, *A Scot at Westminster*, p. 115.

31   Interview with author, Rae and Nellie Mackenzie, 8 February 2016.

32   'Obituary: Donald Stewart', *The Times*, 24 August 1992, p. 13.

33   Brian Wilson, 'Genial Nationalist from the Isles', *The Guardian*, 24 August 1992, p. 31.

parliamentarian and a figure who commanded respect, Donald Stewart was the obvious choice for leader of the parliamentary party in 1974, and he was elected unanimously by his fellow MPs without a ballot.[34] Stewart continued in some ways where he had left off, still preferring to follow his own path and keep up his strong cross-party relationships. Winnie Ewing noted that the new parliamentarians often dined together after parliamentary sessions, with Stewart attending only occasionally, such was the demand he was in by members of all parties in the House of Commons.[35] His wife Chrissie claimed that it 'was a shot in the arm to Donald that he now had ten colleagues'.[36] There was also some safety in numbers, with Ewing remembering that Stewart had made it a 'strict rule from the beginning that none of us [SNP MPs] drank alone, fearing if we did so then we could be misquoted or compromised by those who wanted us to fail'.[37]

The role of parliamentary leader at this time was not an easy one for Stewart: with eleven MPs, among them some strong characters, and a lack of clear party policy or shared ideology on all issues, it was now harder to ensure party coherence. Tensions surfaced within the parliamentary group at times for both political and personal reasons. As Lindsay notes, the personal problems in the parliamentary group were endemic in all the Westminster parties, brought about by the culture; however, these were 'more visible in a small group' and had 'some impact on [SNP] group morale because it caused some embarrassment to those whose behaviour was impeccable'.[38] Friends of Donald Stewart recollect that fellow parliamentarians often turned to Donald and his wife for support in these times, because of the kind of people they were, with Mrs Stewart seen almost as the 'mother of Parliament' and as a counsellor to many of the parliamentary group.[39] Winnie Ewing describes

---

34 'Obituary: Donald Stewart', *The Times*, 24 August 1992, p. 13.

35 Ewing, *Stop the World*, p. 154.

36 Stewart, *A Scot at Westminster*, p. 118.

37 Ewing, *Stop the World*, p. 154.

38 Lindsay, 'The SNP and Westminster', in *The Making of the Modern SNP*, p. 98.

39 Interview with author, Rae and Nellie Mackenzie, 8 February 2016.

444   SCOTTISH NATIONAL PARTY LEADERS

Donald Stewart in a similar vein: 'To the SNP Members in the Commons he was our father figure, our counsellor, and someone who could uplift our spirits with a formidable force of wit.'[40]

There were political tensions to be managed, too, between the parliamentary group and the party's National Executive Committee back in Scotland, who were unused to having such numbers of elected representatives. *The Times* described the situation thus: 'Through Donald Stewart, member for the Western Isles and party leader, the outriders in London keep in touch with the body politic in Edinburgh but the accent has shifted distinctly southwards.'[41] The party chairman at the time, Billy Wolfe, emphasised after the February 1974 election how the parliamentary group and the party institutions at home discussed tactics closely, though the group in Parliament had complete freedom of decision.[42] The parliamentary group did vote against the wishes of the NEC on the 1976 Aircraft and Shipbuilding Nationalisation Bill and tensions also arose due to differing views on devolution and votes of confidence against the minority Labour government.[43]

Devolution had become the key issue for the SNP during this time. The development of the Scottish oil industry, and the party espousal of the 'It's Scotland's Oil' slogan, had given a boost to the independence cause in the mid-1970s. The rise in popularity of the SNP had contributed to the pressure on the Labour Party to promise, just prior to the October 1974 election, the creation of a Scottish Assembly, and the parliamentary group had hoped to capitalise on this and the weakness of the minority Wilson and Callaghan governments. However, the SNP itself was divided on the issue, as was the parliamentary group, between those who wanted independence, nothing less, and those who accepted that devolution and a Scottish assembly was an acceptable step on the way to this end goal.

---

40   Cited in Stewart, *A Scot at Westminster*, p. 124.

40   Cited in Stewart, *A Scot at Westminster*, p. 124.

41   'The man who put wheels on the Scottish bandwagon', *The Times*, 26 March 1974, p. 14.

42   Ibid.

43   Lindsay, 'The SNP and Westminster', in *The Making of the Modern SNP*, p. 98.

Donald Stewart fell into the latter camp, using a speech in Parliament to outline

> in deliberately undramatic style, the step-by-step process towards independence: first the passage of a Bill setting up an elected Scottish assembly which would in turn create an irresistible demand for control over industry, then a fixed share of oil revenues and then budget control. Scotland, he emphasised, wanted full sovereignty with control of borders, oil revenues and a separate defence force. 'One day', he predicted, 'we'll wake up and find that, without quite realising it, we've been given the whole cake.'[44]

The acceptance that the party needed to first get a Scottish legislature delivered was the majority view in the party as a whole and among the MPs, and was a priority for the NEC.[45]

The enthusiasm for devolution in Scotland led to a backlash at Westminster. Many hours were devoted to the issue and to the passage of the Scotland Bill, leading to bitterness from other MPs, with Stewart stating that the 'antagonism in the House of Commons [...] was palpable'.[46] Even the Queen made a rare foray into politics, passing a thinly veiled comment on the issue in 1977, when the time being spent on the Scotland Bill in the House of Commons was at its height. Speaking to both Houses of Parliament, she commented, 'I cannot forget I was crowned Queen of the United Kingdom.' Winnie Ewing felt it was 'a clear and obvious political rebuke to the SNP and to the hundreds of thousands of Scots who supported the party', but Donald Stewart calmly responded to the press afterwards that 'if he ever had to make the choice (and he hoped he never would) between the Queen and the freedom of Scotland, he would choose the freedom of his country'.[47]

---

44 'Obituary: Donald Stewart', *The Times*, 24 August 1992, p. 13.

45 Lindsay, 'The SNP and Westminster', in *The Making of the Modern SNP*, p. 99.

46 'Obituary: Donald Stewart', *The Times*, 24 August 1992, p. 13.

47 Ewing, *Stop the World*, p. 143.

The devolution issue dragged on and there was a 'growing weariness in Scotland with the whole process'.[48] The parliamentary group in Westminster was also feeling the strain, with Ewing describing how 'night after night, the SNP group would troop through the voting lobbies becoming more and more disenchanted with the matter and the way in which it was being handled'. As leader of the parliamentary group, Stewart had to try to motivate his colleagues: Ewing describes how 'Donnie did a superb job in keeping the morale up, but it was soul destroying to see the great opportunity for change being gerrymandered in this way.'[49] Stewart had a very keen sense of humour and Ewing tells of how, one night after a particularly terrible House of Commons defeat on the Scotland Bill, Stewart instructed the group to stay on the Commons benches while he regaled them with a joke about John Wayne and the group left the chamber laughing, much to the surprise of their political opponents.[50] In doing so, he knew it sent an important image to their antagonists.

The Scotland Bill dragged through Parliament facing numerous amendments aimed at weakening its powers, culminating in the need for a positive referendum result requiring the support of more than 40 per cent of the electorate in order to create a Scottish Assembly. The SNP faced a problem at third reading stage, with a number of the parliamentary group in favour of voting against the Bill. Stewart remarked that it was a position that could be argued for, since the Bill was now 'even sorrier in appearance than at first showing', describing it as 'anaemic'.[51] However, it was felt that it was 'a start on a first degree of decision-making returning to Scotland' and so the entire parliamentary group supported it. As Donald Stewart reflected ruefully in 1978, 'You've got to go one way or the other. There are only two lobbies in the House of Commons. I sometimes wish there were three.'[52]

---

48   Ibid., p. 158.

49   Ibid.

50   Ibid.

51   Stewart, *A Scot at Westminster*, p. 120.

52   Brian Wilson, 'Genial Nationalist from the Isles', *The Guardian*, 24 August 1992, p. 31.

This was pertinent again in autumn 1978, when the majority in the parliamentary group wanted to vote against the government in a confidence motion, contrary to the wishes of the SNP's NEC. There were divisions in the parliamentary group; two of them did not vote with the others and the motion was unsuccessful.[53] Following the defeat of devolution in the referendum in 1979, despite a slim majority voting in favour, the issue of a confidence motion arose again. While there was some reluctance within the parliamentary group this time, given the prospect of an immediate election, there was support from the wider party and the NEC, who felt it was the only way to salvage anything out of the Scotland Act.[54]

Stewart himself was rather reluctant to support a no-confidence vote, as he was personally quite close to Jim Callaghan, and the confidence vote was one occasion when he would have quite liked that third 'lobby'.[55] Indeed, he claimed that 'in better times, he [Callaghan] would have made an outstanding Prime Minister'.[56] He met with the Prime Minister on the eve of the vote and describes how he had a 'friendly talk in which he [Callaghan] appeared relaxed and even fatalistic as I made clear the intention of the SNP to vote against the government unless the Scotland Bill was submitted on a vote of confidence basis'.[57] They both knew that this would not happen and, despite Callaghan's taunt that the SNP were 'turkeys voting for an early Christmas', the SNP went on to vote unanimously against the government. As Wilson suggests, 'As far as Donald was concerned, Labour's inability to deliver a Scottish Assembly was the crucial factor and he led his troops accordingly – a few of them much against their own better judgements.'[58] In fact, Stewart himself had some reservations, according to Tam Dalyell, Labour MP at the time. He suggests that it was Stewart's fellow MP,

---

53   Lindsay, 'The SNP and Westminster', in *The Making of the Modern SNP*, p. 99.

54   Ibid.

55   Brian Wilson, 'Genial Nationalist from the Isles', *The Guardian*, 24 August 1992, p. 31.

56   Donnie Macinnes, 'Donald looks back', *Stornoway Gazette*, week ending 5 December 1987.

57   Stewart, *A Scot at Westminster*, p. 89.

58   Brian Wilson, 'Genial Nationalist from the Isles', *The Guardian*, 24 August 1992, p. 31.

Douglas Henderson, who had persuaded his more cautious colleagues to support the censure motion and that Donald Stewart had later told Dalyell that he 'deeply regretted caving in to Henderson's impetuosity', in Dalyell's words, given that the party was left with only two seats at the subsequent election.[59]

Given his declared socialist views, Stewart must also have regretted that this decision led to the following eighteen years of Tory government. However, despite declaring himself 'on the left politically', he had argued that if he had to choose between the Tory and Labour Parties as Secretary of State for Scotland, he would opt for a Tory, as he felt that a Tory Secretary of State was more sympathetic and helpful to his rural constituency. He found that in his time representing the Western Isles, the 'big developments in [that] area were initiated by Tory Secretaries'.[60] He had mixed views on many of the leading Tories at the time, outlined in his memoirs, with some receiving praise (he described Alick Buchanan-Smith as 'utterly trustworthy' and Enoch Powell as the 'outstanding Parliamentarian of the 1970s and '80s') while others received fairly scathing criticism (Margaret Thatcher he viewed as 'an inverted Midas whose touch turned everything to dross' and Michael Heseltine was described as an 'eyes blazing with insincerity' type).

While he had respect for individuals within the Labour Party, such as Tony Benn ('his impact on the Parliamentary scene was tremendous and a staggering achievement'), Donald Dewar ('rational and fair') and John Smith ('a politician of a high standard and a nice man'), he was highly critical of the path the Labour Party had taken. He noted in his memoirs in the early 1990s that 'I cannot help, as a one-time member, being struck by the distance the party has travelled from the ideals and aims of Socialism'.[61] He was particularly scathing of the party's support for the financial sector: 'So far has the sell-out of Socialism gone that Labour has supported the bailing out of

59   Tam Dalyell, 'Douglas Henderson: Obituary', *The Independent*, 18 September 2006, http://www.independent.co.uk/news/obituaries/douglas-henderson-416599.html [accessed 10 February 2016].

60   Stewart, *A Scot at Westminster*, p. 105.

61   Ibid., p. 66.

Stock Exchange gamblers who had had a poor year at Lloyds after years of piling up profits.'[62] One can only imagine what he would have to say about the current financial crisis.

From his comments on his fellow MPs, it is clear that what Donald Stewart valued most in others was integrity and strong beliefs, and he particularly admired those who had the courage of their own convictions regardless of party loyalty. He acknowledged that 'no matter how divergent their views from mine, I have always had a salute for the men of independent mind, the 'out-of-step', the thumbers-of-noses at party brass'.[63] It could be said that this was how he himself approached his own role and position within his own party.

So how did Donald Stewart's views fit within the party at the time? The SNP had lacked a clear ideological direction itself, with its membership united mainly by the desire for Scottish self-government. In 1974, eight of the SNP's eleven seats had been won from the Conservatives, but the SNP election manifestos in 1974 had proclaimed the SNP as a social democratic party and proposed a range of social democratic policies.[64] In the 1970s, the party had begun to focus more on producing detailed policy positions and Billy Wolfe's election as party leader in 1969 was seen as an endorsement of this approach[65] as opposed to one that would stay neutral on policy (and ideology) until there was a Scottish Parliament in place to make detailed policy.[66]

Donald Stewart was not in favour of this approach, arguing that 'a broad national movement should not be confined to a "specific philosophy of Left and Right"'.[67] In a speech to the SNP's annual conference in Rothesay in 1980, referring to the guideline laid down by one of the party's founders, Stewart argued, 'Scotland free can take a left road or a right road – but it will

---

62   Ibid.

63   Ibid., p. 58.

64   Lynch, *SNP: The History of the Scottish National Party*, p. 133.

65   Miller, *The End of British Politics?*, p. 47.

66   Peter Lynch, 'From Social Democracy back to No Ideology? – The Scottish National Party and Ideological Change in a Multi-level Electoral Setting'.

67   Peter Hetherington, 'Independence before ideology, Scots MP tells nationalists', *The Guardian*, 2 June 1980, p. 2.

be a Scottish road. That is the fundamental aim – Scottish independence.'[68]
He was also highly critical of the left-wing 79 Group, which had formed with
the intention of moving the party to the left, and which included many future
prominent members of the party, including Alex Salmond, Margo MacDonald and Jim Sillars, the former Labour MP who had joined the party at that
time. Stewart felt that this might jeopardise the struggle for Scotland's independence by putting narrow ideologies before party unity, making a speech
'designed to reinforce more fundamental nationalist elements in the party
who believe that it should strongly resist any political philosophy until independence is achieved'.[69]

One issue that did require a policy position to be taken by the party was
that of the European Union. Stewart was a firm opponent of the UK's membership of the European Economic Community (EEC), as it was at the time.
He had been opposed to the UK's membership in 1972, and in the great debate
on the Common Market and subsequent referendum in 1975, he continued
to campaign against UK membership. He felt uncomfortable, as someone
who had served in the war, as he put it, 'to line up with continental countries,
some of whom had been in the enemy camp'.[70] He was highly sceptical of
the trade benefits, critical of the scale of fraud as he saw it, and very much
against the Common Agricultural Policy and Common Fisheries Policy,
which he felt did tremendous harm to his own constituency. Indeed, he
expressed his satisfaction regarding the rejection of the EEC by his constituency, the Western Isles, one of only two constituencies that had voted no,
and it had been 'particularly emphatic [...] where on a turnout of just over
50 per cent, the "no" votes totalled 8,109 (70.5 per cent) with 3,393 (29.5 per
cent) voting yes'.[71] As usual, he used the opportunity to extol the virtues
of his homeland:

---

68   Ibid.

69   Ibid.

70   Stewart, *A Scot at Westminster*, p. 66.

71   'Western Isles and the Shetlands vote "No"', *The Times*, 7 June 1975, p. 1.

The Western Isles are a stronghold of feeling against the Common market. [...] This decision is by no means parochial. The people are well educated, as our rates of educational success show. They are well travelled as merchant seamen. They are well able to make a sound judgment on the merits of the issue.[72]

The Scottish National Party campaigned for a 'No' vote in 1975 and Donald Stewart was one of the most vehement proponents of this stance. His view was that 'it seemed illogical (to put it mildly) for a nationalist striving to regain power for the people of Scotland, to hand over power to a faceless European bureaucracy'.[73] Stewart argued at the time of the referendum that 'people had suffered enough from government from London and had no wish to replace it with government from Brussels' and expressed the intention that 'when a Scottish government is set up it will carry out the decision to pull out of Europe'.[74] However, in the mid-1980s, the party's stance on Europe changed considerably, and the campaign for 'Independence in Europe' was adopted in 1988.[75] By then, Donald Stewart had stepped down as president of the party and retired from Parliament, yet he never wavered in his hostility to the European Union.[76]

Donald Stewart has been described as 'the father of the modern SNP'[77] and held significant posts within the party, as leader of the parliamentary group from 1970 until his retirement in 1987 and party president from 1982 to 1987. What was his legacy as leader over this period? Mitchell argues that he 'preferred Westminster and the Western isles over mainland Scotland. There was no lack of charisma, enthusiasm or ideas, but an absence of discipline and means to

72   Ibid.

73   Stewart, *A Scot at Westminster*, p. 50.

74   'Western Isles and the Shetlands vote "No"', *The Times*, 7 June 1975, p. 1.

75   Eve Hepburn, 'Degrees of Independence: SNP Thinking in an International Context', in *The Making of the Modern SNP*, p. 193.

76   Brian Wilson, 'Genial Nationalist from the Isles', *The Guardian*, 24 August 1992, p. 31.

77   Andy Collier, 'Legend', *Independence: The SNP Magazine* (Glasgow: Saltire Magazines/Scottish National Party, 2015), 34 (September/October 2015): 22.

channel the party's abundant energy in a clear direction.'[78] His approach to leadership was to lead by the carrot rather than the stick, and to lead quietly by example rather than by pushing, cajoling or over-powering. As Sandy Matheson describes, he was not an authoritarian, 'up and at them' figure. By putting forward his own case calmly and politely, and standing his ground with principle, he hoped that others would follow.[79] Friends have suggested that as a leader he was good at calming troubled waters if there was friction.[80] He was renowned for his plain-talking approach and calm demeanour, a leadership style perhaps better suited to the role of a chairman than a strategic political leader.

No profile of Donald Stewart is complete without further acknowledgment of the important role played by his wife, Chrissie, who accompanied him to London during his time in Parliament. Such was her importance, Sandy Matheson argues that, 'As good a man as he was, Donald Stewart would not have been the man he was without Chrissie.' She was ever-present at his side and 'if Donnie missed a trick she quietly picked it up and ran with it'.[81] She was said to be instrumental in the creation of a family room in the House of Commons, where she met with the wives of fellow MPs, helping to build up their network of friends across the political spectrum. As Wilson suggests, 'Donald's popularity in parliamentary circles was matched by that of his wife Chrissie.'[82] Winnie Ewing hailed Chrissie as the parliamentary party's twelfth member and 'our secret weapon'.[83] Sandy Matheson described them as 'a formidable political partnership, renowned for their inherent generosity and welcoming hospitality',[84] while friends in the constituency, Rae and Nellie Mackenzie, suggest that they were a unique team, where you got 'two for the

---

78   James Mitchell, 'From Breakthrough to Mainstream: The Politics of Potential and Blackmail', in *The Making of the Modern SNP*, p. 34.

79   Interview with author, Sandy Matheson, 16 February 2016.

80   Interview with author, Rae and Nellie Mackenzie, 8 February 2016.

81   Interview with author, Sandy Matheson, 16 February 2016.

82   Brian Wilson, 'Genial Nationalist from the Isles', *The Guardian*, 24 August 1992, p. 31.

83   Ewing, *Stop the World*, p. 125.

84   Interview with author, Sandy Matheson, 16 February 2016.

price of one'.[85] Chrissie Stewart's significant role was recognised when they were the first to be awarded the honour of Freemen of the Western Isles in 1988 in recognition of their service to the community.

Stewart was appointed as a Privy Councillor in 1977 but on his retirement in 1987 turned down the offer of a seat in the House of Lords.[86] As always, he refused to put political expediency before principle, based on his belief in the undemocratic nature of the institution and his feeling that the existence of the SNP in the Lords would set the party firmly within the British establishment. Fellow party members such as Winnie Ewing disagreed with his stance, but Stewart was firm in his view that 'a decision by the Scottish National Party to accept the offer of a Lords seat will signify that the party has opted for squatting in a British lay-by in preference to advancing along the road to Scottish independence'.[87]

Instead, upon his retirement, Donald Stewart was happily at home in the streets of Stornoway, smoking his ever-present pipe. He died, aged seventy-one, in August 1992, following a heart attack. Glowing tributes were paid to him upon his death, reflecting the esteem in which he was held by both supporters and opponents, who reflected on him as a man of integrity and conviction. *The Independent* described him as 'the most popular member of the Commons'[88] and Alex Salmond paid tribute to him as achieving 'the rare distinction of being universally respected by political friend and foe alike'.[89] Perhaps, as his sister suggests, his career is best summed up in the words from *The Independent*: 'In his public life he evinced modesty, honesty, trustworthiness – qualities almost unique in a modern politician. He set his style on his party and his cause which he advanced mightily, securing for it a permanent and respected place in Scottish politics.'[90]

---

85   Interview with author, Rae and Nellie Mackenzie, 8 February 2016.

86   Ewing, *Stop the World*, p. 154.

87   Stewart, *A Scot at Westminster*, p. 78.

88   'Obituary: Donald Stewart', *The Independent*, 25 August 1992.

89   *Stornoway Gazette*, 25 August 1992.

90   'Obituary: Donald Stewart', *The Independent*, 25 August 1992.

BIBLIOGRAPHY

Allison, Jimmy, *Guilty by Suspicion: A Life and Labour*. Glendaruel: Argyll Publishing, 1995.

Ambrose, Stephen E., *Eisenhower: Soldier and President*. New York: Simon & Schuster, 2003.

Ascherson, Neal, *Stone Voices: The Search for Scotland*. London: Granta Books, 2002.

Barker, Rodney, 'Legitimacy in the United Kingdom: Scotland and the Poll Tax', *British Journal of Political Science*, 22 (1992): 521–33.

Bayne, Ian O., 'The Impact of 1979 on the SNP', in Tom Gallagher (ed.), *Nationalism in the Nineties*. Edinburgh: Polygon, 1991.

Bealey, Frank and John Sewel, *The Politics of Independence*. Aberdeen: Aberdeen University Press, 1981.

Beers, Laura, *Your Britain: Media and the Making of the Labour Party*. Cambridge, MA: Harvard University Press, 2010.

Benn, Tony, *The End of an Era: Diaries 1980–90*. London: Hutchinson, 1992.

— —, *Conflicts of Interest: Diaries 1977–80*. London: Hutchinson, 1990.

— —, *Against the Tide: Diaries 1973–76*. London: Hutchinson, 1989.

Bircham, Josh and Grant Costello, *We are the 56: The Individuals Behind a Political Revolution*. Glasgow: Freight Books, 2015.

Birnie, Clive M., '"New deal" or raw deal? Public Administration and Economic Development in the Highlands and Islands of Scotland, 1929–1939', unpublished MSc thesis, University of Edinburgh, 2003.

Bochel, John, David Denver and Alan Macartney (eds), *The Referendum Experience Scotland 1979*. Aberdeen: Aberdeen University Press, 1981.

Bogdanor, Vernon, *The People and the Party System: The Referendum and Electoral Reform in British Politics*. Cambridge: Cambridge University Press, 1981.

Bold, Alan (ed.), *The Letters of Hugh MacDiarmid*. London: Hamish Hamilton, 1984.

Bowd, Gavin, *Fascist Scotland: Caledonia and the Far Right*. Edinburgh: Birlinn, 2013.

Boyce, D. George, *Nationalism in Ireland*. London: Routledge, 1995, 3rd edition.

Braatoy, Bjarne, *The New Sweden: A Vindication of Democracy*. London: Thomas Nelson, 1939.

Brack, Duncan, et al. (eds), *British Liberal Leaders*. London: Biteback Publishing, 2015.

Brand, Jack, *The National Movement in Scotland*. London: Routledge and Kegan Paul, 1978.

Brown, Alice, David McCrone and Lindsay Paterson, *Politics and Society in Scotland*. London: Macmillan, 1998.

Bryant, Chris, *Parliament: The Biography (Vol. II – Reform)*. London: Transworld Publishers, 2014.

Buller, Jim and Toby S. James, 'Statecraft and the Assessment of National Political Leaders: The Case of New Labour and Tony Blair', *The British Journal of Politics and International Relations*, 14/4, (2012): 534–55.

— —, *National Statecraft and European Integration: The Conservative Government and European Union, 1979–1997*. London: Bloomsbury, 2000.

Butler, David and Anthony King, *The British General Election of 1966*. New York: St Martin's Press, 1966.

— — and Uwe Kitzinger, *The 1975 Referendum*. London: Macmillan, 1976.

de la Calle, Luis, *Nationalist Violence in Postwar Europe*. Cambridge: Cambridge University Press, 2015.

Cameron, Ewen A., *Impaled Upon a Thistle: Scotland since 1880*. Edinburgh: Edinburgh University Press, 2010.

— —, 'Gibb, Andrew Dewar (1888–1974)', *Oxford Dictionary of National Biography*. Oxford University Press, October 2009; online edition, September 2010. [http://www.oxforddnb.com/view/article/58792]

— —, '"Rival foundlings": the Ross and Cromarty by-election, 1 February 1936', *Historical Research*, 81 (2008): 507–30.

— —, *Land for the People? The British Government and the Scottish Highlands, c.1880–1930*. East Linton: Tuckwell Press, 1996.

— — and Annie Tindley (eds), *Dr Lachlan Grant of Ballachulish, 1871–1945*. Edinburgh: Birlinn, 2015.

— —, Campbell, R. H., 'The Scottish Office and the Special Areas in the 1930s', *Historical Journal*, 22 (1979): 167–83.

Carman, C., R. Johns and J. Mitchell, *More Scottish than British: The 2011 Scottish Parliament Election*. Basingstoke: Palgrave Macmillan, 2014.

Clarke, Charles and Toby S. James (eds), *British Labour Leaders*. London: Biteback Publishing, 2015.

— —, et al. (eds), *British Conservative Leaders*. London: Biteback Publishing, 2015.

Collier, Andy, 'Legend', *Independence: The SNP Magazine* (Glasgow: Saltire Magazines/Scottish National Party, 2015), 34 (September/October 2015).

Connelly, Mark, *We Can Take It! Britain and the Memory of the Second World War*. London: Pearson Longman, 2004.

Cragoe, Matthew, '"We like local patriotism": The Conservative Party and the discourse of decentralisation, 1947–51', *English Historical Review*, 122 (2007): 965–85.

Craig, F. W. S. (ed.), *British Electoral Facts 1832–1987*. Parliamentary Research Services, 1989.

— —, *City and Royal Burgh of Glasgow Municipal Election Results 1948–73*. Chichester: Parliamentary Research Services, 1984.

— —, *British Parliamentary Election Results 1885–1918*. London: Macmillan, 1974.

— —, *British Parliamentary Election Results 1950–1970*. Chichester: Parliamentary Research Services, 1971.

— —, *British Parliamentary Election Results 1918–1949*. Glasgow: Political Reference Publications, 1969.

Cronin, Sean, *Irish Nationalism: A History of its Roots and Ideology*. London: Academy Press, 1981.

Crowley, D. W., 'The "Crofters" Party: 1885–1892', *The Scottish Historical Review*, 35/120 (1956): 110–26.

Cullen, Stephen M., 'The Fasces and the Saltire: The Failure of the British Union of Fascists in Scotland, 1932–1940', *Scottish Historical Review*, 87/2 (2008): 306–31.

Cunninghame Graham, Jean, *Gaucho Laird: The Life of R. B. 'Don Roberto' Cunninghame Graham*. London: The Long Riders' Guild Press, 2004.

Dalyell, Tam, *Devolution: The End of Britain*. London: Cape, 1977.

Darling, Elizabeth, 'MacEwen, Ann Maitland (1918–2008)', *Oxford Dictionary of National Biography*. Oxford University Press, January 2012. [http://www.oxforddnb.com/view/article/99705]

Denver, David, James Mitchell, Charles Pattie and Hugh Bochel, *Scotland Decides: The Devolution Issue and the 1997 Referendum*. London: Frank Cass Publishers, 2000.

Devine, T. M., *Bathgate Once More: The Story of the BMC/Leyland Truck and Tractor Plant, 1961–1986*. Edinburgh: WEA, 2012.

— —, *Independence or Union: Scotland's Past and Scotland's Present*. London: Allen Lane, 2016.

Dewar Gibb, Andrew, *Scotland Resurgent*. Stirling: Eneas MacKay, 1950.

— —, *Scottish Empire*. London: Alexander Maclehose, 1937.

— —, *Scotland in Eclipse*. London: Toulmin, 1930.

Donaldson, Arthur, *Whys of Scottish Nationalism*. West Calder: SNP Publications, 1976.

— —, *Scotland's Tomorrow: Our Fight to Live*. Glasgow: Scottish Secretariat, 1941.

Douglas, Dick, *At the Helm: The Life & Times of Dr Robert D. McIntyre*. Portessie, Buckie: NPFI Publications, 1996.

Douglas, R. M., 'The Swastika and the Shamrock: British Fascism and the Irish Question, 1918–1940', *Albion*, 29/1 (1997): 72–3.

Drucker, Henry, *Doctrine and Ethos in the Labour Party*. London: George Allen and Unwin, 1979.

— —, *Breakaway: The Scottish Labour Party*. Edinburgh: Edinburgh University Student Publications Board, 1978.

— — and Gordon Brown, *The Politics of Nationalism and Devolution*. London: Longman, 1980.

Dutton, David, *British Politics Since 1945: The Rise and Fall of Consensus*. London: Blackwell, 1991.

Dyer, Michael, '"A nationalist in the Churchillian Sense": John MacCormick, the Paisley By-Election of 18 February 1948, Home Rule, and the Crisis in Scottish Liberalism', *Parliamentary History*, 22/3 (2003): 285–307.

Eadie, Alex and Jim Sillars, *Don't Butcher Scotland's Future: The case for reform at all levels of government*. No publisher, 1968.

— — and — —, *Exposed: The Truth about Scotland's Future*. No publisher, 1968.

— —, Harry Ewing, John Robertson and Jim Sillars, *Scottish Labour and Devolution: a discussion paper*. No publisher, 1974.

Edwards, Owen Dudley, *A Claim of Right for Scotland*. Edinburgh: Polygon, 1989.

Evans, N. and H. Pryce (eds), *Writing a Small Nation's Past: Wales in Comparative Perspective, 1850–1950*. Farnham: Ashgate, 2013.

Ewing, Winifred (ed. Michael Russell), *Stop the World: The Autobiography of Winnie Ewing*. Edinburgh: Birlinn Ltd, 2004.

Finlay, Richard J., *Modern Scotland: 1914–2000*. London: Profile Books, 2004.

— —, *Independent and Free: Scottish Politics and the Origins of the Scottish National Party 1918–1945*. Edinburgh: John Donald, 1994.

— —, 'National Identity in Crisis: Politicians, Intellectuals and the "End of Scotland", 1920–1939', *History*, 79 (1994): 242–59.

— —, '"For or Against?": Scottish Nationalists and the British Empire, 1919–39', *Scottish Historical Review*, 71 (1992): 184–206.

— —, 'Pressure group or political party? The nationalist impact on Scottish politics, 1928–1945', *Twentieth Century British History*, 3 (1992): 274–97.

Fitzsimons, M. A., 'Midlothian: The Triumph and Frustration of the British Liberal Party,' Review of Politics, 22/2 (April 1960): 187–201.

Foley, Michael, *The British Presidency*. Manchester: Manchester University Press, 2001.

Foster, Roy, *Vivid Faces: The Revolutionary Generation in Ireland, 1890–1923*. London: Allen Lane, 2014.

Fowler, John (ed.), *Bannerman: The Memoirs of Lord Bannerman of Kildonan*. Aberdeen: Impulse Books, 1972.

Fraser, Ian, *Shredded: Inside RBS, the Bank that Broke Britain*. Edinburgh: Birlinn Ltd., 2015.

Freeden, Michael, *The New Liberalism: An Ideology of Social Reform*. Oxford: Clarendon Press, 1986.

French Jr, J. R. P. and B. H. Raven, 'The Bases of Social Power', in D. Cartright (ed.), *Studies in Social Power*. Ann Arbor, MI: Institute for Social Research, 1959.

Gallagher, Tom, 'Political Extremism in Urban Scotland 1930–1939: Its Growth and Contraction', *Scottish Historical Review*, 64/2 (1985): 143–67.

Graham, James, The Duke of Montrose, *My Ditty Box*. London: Jonathan Cape, 1952.

Greenstein, Fred, *The Presidential Difference: Leadership Style from FDR to Barack Obama*. Princeton, NJ: Princeton University Press, 2009, 3rd edition.

— —, '"The Qualities of Effective Presidents": An Overview from FDR to Bill Clinton', *Presidential Studies Quarterly*, 30/1 (2000).

Grimond, Jo, *The Liberal Challenge*. London: Hollis & Carter, 1963.

Habermas, Jurgen, *The Structural Transformation of the Public Sphere*. Cambridge: Polity, 1989.

Halliday, James, *Yours for Scotland: A Memoir*. Stirling: Scots Independent, 2011.

— —, *1820 Rising: The Radical War*. Stirling: Scots Independent Publications, 1993.

Hamilton, Ian, *A Touch of Treason*. Moffat: Lochar Press, 1990.

Harper, Marjory, *Emigration from Scotland Between the Wars: Opportunity or Exile?* Manchester: Manchester University Press, 1998.

Hart, F. R. and J. B. Pick, *Neil M. Gunn: A Highland Life*. London: John Murray, 1981.

Harvie, Christopher, *Scotland and Nationalism: Scottish Society and Politics, 1707 to the present*. London: Routledge, various editions.

— —, *No Gods and Precious Few Heroes*. Edinburgh: Edinburgh University Press, 2016.

— —, 'The Moment of British Nationalism, 1939–1970', *Political Quarterly*, 71/3 (2000): 328–40.

— —, 'Labour in Scotland during the Second World War', *Historical Journal*, 26/4 (1983): 921–44.

— — and Peter Jones, *The Road to Home Rule: Images of Scotland's Cause*. Edinburgh: Polygon, 2000.

Hassan, Gerry, *Independence of the Scottish Mind: Elite Narratives, Public Spaces and the Making of a Modern Nation*. London: Macmillan, 2014.

— —, *Caledonian Dreaming: The Quest for a Different Scotland*. Edinburgh: Luath Press, 2014.

— — (ed.), *The Modern SNP: From Protest to Power*. Edinburgh: Edinburgh University Press, 2009.

— —, 'The Legacy of Thatcherism North of the Border Thirty Years On', *Open Democracy*, 5 May 2009.

— — and Eric Shaw, *The Strange Death of Labour Scotland*. Edinburgh: Edinburgh University Press, 2012.

Hennessy, Peter, *Never Again: Britain 1945–51*. London: Penguin Books, 2006.

Herdman, John, *Another Country: An Era in Scottish Politics and Letters*. Edinburgh: Thirsty Books, 2013.

Heyck, T. W. and William Klecka, 'British Radical MPs, 1874–1895: New Evidence from Discriminant Analysis', *The Journal of Interdisciplinary History*, 4/2 (Autumn 1973): 161–84.

Holman, Bob, *Keir Hardie: Labour's Greatest Hero?* Oxford: Lion Hudson, 2010, Kindle edition.

Hook, Sidney, *The Hero in History: A Study in Limitation and Possibility*. New York: John Day Company, 1943.

Hossay, Patrick, 'Partisans and Nationalists: Rethinking Cleavage Formation and Political Nationalism in Interwar Flanders and Scotland', *Social Science History*, 27/2 (2003): 186–7.

Howell, David, *British Workers and the Independent Labour Party, 1888–1906*. Manchester: Manchester University Press, 1984.

Hutchison, I. G. C., *Scottish Politics in the Twentieth Century*. Basingstoke: Palgrave, 2001.

Jamison, Brian P. (ed.), *Scotland and the Cold War*. Dunfermline: Cualann Press, 2003.

Jarvis, David, 'Mrs Maggs and Betty: The conservative appeal to women voters in the 1920s', *Twentieth-Century British History*, 5 (1994): 129–52.

Johns, Rob, David Denver, James Mitchell and Charles Pattie, *Voting for a Scottish Government: The Scottish Parliament Election of 2007*. Manchester: Manchester University Press, 2010.

— — and James Mitchell, *Takeover: Explaining the Extraordinary Rise of the SNP*. London: Biteback Publishing, 2016.

Jones, Peter d'A., 'Henry George and British Labor Politics', *American Journal of Economics and Sociology*, 46/2 (April 1987): 245–56.

Keating, Michael and David Bleiman, *Labour and Scottish Nationalism*. London: Macmillan, 1979.

Kellas, James, 'Scottish Nationalism', in David Butler and Michael Pinto-Duschinsky, *The British General Election of 1970*. London: Macmillan, 1971.

Kemp, Arnold, *The Hollow Drum*. Edinburgh: Mainstream, 1993.

Kidd, Colin, *Union and Unionisms: Political Thought in Scotland, 1500–2000*. Cambridge: Cambridge University Press, 2008.

King, Anthony, 'The Outsider as Political Leader', in Larry Berman (ed.), *The Art of Political Leadership: Essays in Honor of Fred I. Greenstein*. Lanham, MD: Rowman & Littlefield Publishers, 2005.

Klugmann, James, *The History of the Communist Party of Great Britain (Vol. I – Formation and Early Years, 1919–24)*. London: Lawrence & Wishart, 1987, new edition.

Knox, William W., *James Maxton (Lives of the Left)*. Manchester: Manchester University Press, 1987.

— — and Alan McKinlay, 'The Re-Making of Scottish Labour in the 1930s', *Twentieth-Century British History*, 6/2 (1995): 174–93.

Lamont, Archie, *Small Nations*. Glasgow: William MacLellan, 1944.

Lawrence, Jon, 'The Transformation of British Public Politics after the First World War', *Past and Present*, 190 (February 2006): 185–216.

Lowe, David, *Souvenirs of Scottish Labour*. Glasgow: W. & R. Holmes, 1919.

Lyall, Scott, '"The Man is a Menace": MacDiarmid and Military Intelligence', *Scottish Studies Review*, 8/1 (Spring 2007): 37–52.

Lynch, Peter, 'From Social Democracy back to No Ideology? – The Scottish National Party and Ideological Change in a Multi-level Electoral Setting', *Regional & Federal Studies*, 19/4–5 (2009), Special Issue: New Challenges for Stateless Nationalist and Regionalist Parties: 619–37.

— —, *SNP: The History of the Scottish National Party*. Cardiff: Welsh Academic Press, 2002.

MacArthur, Brian, *The Penguin Book of Twentieth-Century Speeches*. London: Viking, 1992.

MacCormick, J. M., *The Flag in the Wind: The Story of the National Movement in Scotland*. London: Victor Gollancz, 1955.

MacCormick, Neil (ed.), *The Scottish Debate: Essays on Scottish Nationalism*. London: Oxford University Press, 1970.

MacEwen, Alexander, 'A dictator for the highlands? The strengths and weaknesses of the Scottish Economic Committee's Report', *Scots Magazine*, 30 (1938–39): 293–8.

— —, *Scotland at School: Education for Citizenship*. Edinburgh: Belhaven Press, 1938.

— —, *Towards Freedom: A Candid Survey of Fascism, Communism and Modern Democracy*. London: William Hodge, 1938.

— —, *The Thistle and the Rose: Scotland's Problem Today*. Edinburgh: Oliver and Boyd, 1932.

— —, John MacCormick and Thomas H. Gibson, *Scottish Reconstruction*. Glasgow: National Party, 1930.

— — and John Lorne Campbell, *Act Now for the Highlands and Islands*. Edinburgh: Belhaven Press, 1939.

Machiavelli, Niccolò, *The Prince*. Harmondsworth: Penguin Classics edition, 1975.

McKechnie, George, *The Best-Hated Man: George Malcolm Thomson, Intellectuals and the Condition of Scotland Between the Wars*. Glendaruel: Argyll Publishing, 2013.

Mackenzie, Angus, 'Self-help and Propaganda: Scottish National Development Council, 1931–1939', *Journal of Scottish Historical Studies*, 30 (2010): 123–45.

Mackenzie, Compton, *My Life and Times, Octave 7, 1931–38*. London: Chatto, 1968.

— —, *On Moral Courage*. London: Collins, 1962.

McKibbin, Ross, *Parties and People: England, 1914–1951*. Oxford: Oxford University Press, 2010.

— —, *The Evolution of the Labour Party, 1910–1924*. Oxford: Oxford University Press, 1984.

Macmillan, Harold, *The Middle Way*. London: Macmillan, 1938.

McNeill, D. H., *The Historical Scottish Constitution*. Edinburgh: Albyn Press, 1971.

MacNeil, Lauchlan, *The Tragedy of Ramsay MacDonald: A Political Biography*. London: Secker & Warburg, 1938.

Manson, John (ed.), *Dear Grieve: Letters to Hugh MacDiarmid*. Glasgow: Kennedy & Boyd, 2011.

Marquand, David, *Ramsay MacDonald: A Biography*. London: Jonathan Cape, 1977.

Marr, Andrew, *The Battle for Scotland*. London: Penguin, 1992.

Massie, Allan, *The Thistle and the Rose*. London: John Murray, *Cencrastus* magazine, 1982.

Maxwell, Jamie (ed.), *The Case for Left-Wing Nationalism*. Edinburgh: Luath Press, 2013, Kindle edition.

Mazower, Mark, *Dark Continent: Europe's Twentieth Century*. London: Allen Lane, 1998.

Miller, William, *The End of British Politics: Scots and English Political Behaviour in the Seventies*. Oxford: Oxford University Press, 1981.

Mitchell, James, *The Scottish Question*. Oxford: Oxford University Press, 2014.

— —, *Strategies for Self-Government: The Campaigns for a Scottish Parliament*. Edinburgh: Polygon, 1996.

— —, Lynn Bennie and Rob Johns, *The Scottish National Party: Transition to Power*. Oxford: Oxford University Press, 2012.

Mitchison, Naomi, *You May Well Ask: A Memoir, 1920–1940*. London: Victor Gollancz Ltd., 1979.

Morgan, Kenneth O., *Britain Since 1945*. Oxford: Oxford University Press, 2001.

Morton, Graeme, *Unionist Nationalism: Governing Urban Scotland, 1830–1860*. East Linton: Tuckwell Press, 1998.

Muir, Willa, *Belonging*. London: Hogarth Press, 1968.

Nicolson, Sir Harold, *Diaries and Letters, 1939–45*. London: Collins, 1967.

O'Day, Alan (ed.), *Political Violence in Northern Ireland: Conflict and Conflict Resolution*. London: Praeger, 1997.

Paton, H. J., *The Claim of Scotland*. London: George Allen & Unwin, 1968.

Pelling, Henry, *The Origins of the Labour Party*. Oxford: Oxford University Press, 1961.

Perman, Ray, *The Man Who Gave Away His Island: A Life of John Lorne Campbell of Canna*. Edinburgh: Birlinn, 2010.

Petrie, Malcolm R., '"Contests of vital importance": By-elections, the Labour Party, and the reshaping of British radicalism, 1924–1929', *Historical Journal* (2016): 1–28.

— —, 'Public Politics and Traditions of Popular Protest: Demonstrations of the Unemployed in Dundee and Edinburgh, c.1921–1939', *Contemporary British History*, 27/4 (December 2013): 490–513.

Porteous, James A. A., *The New Unionism*. London: Allen and Unwin, 1935.

Powell, Jonathan, *The New Machiavelli: How to Wield Power in the Modern World*.
    London: Bodley Head, 2010.

Power, William, *Should Auld Acquaintance*. London: Harrap, 1937.

Roy, Kenneth, *The Invisible Spirit: A Life of Post-War Scotland 1945–1975*.
    Edinburgh: Birlinn, 2013.

Salmond, Alex, *The Dream Shall Never Die: 100 Days that Changed Scotland Forever*.
    London: William Collins, 2015.

— —, 'Free to Prosper: Creating the Celtic Lion Economy', speech at Harvard
    University, 31 March 2008. [http://www.gov.scot/News/Speeches/Speeches/
    First-Minister/harvard-university]

Sillars, Jim, *The Logical Case: Why ScotLeave.EU makes most sense*. No publisher,
    2016.

— —, *In Place of Failure: Making It Yes Next Time*. Glasgow: Vagabound Voices, 2015.

— —, *In Place of Fear II: A Socialist Programme for an Independent Scotland*.
    Glasgow: Vagabound Voices, 2014.

— —, *Thoughts on getting to the only sensible choice for Scotland: Independence*. No
    publisher, 2009.

— —, *Scotland: The Case for Optimism*. Edinburgh: Polygon, 1986.

— —, *Moving On and Moving Up in Europe*. Edinburgh: SNP Edinburgh Branch, 1985.

Smith, Anthony D., *The Ethnic Revival*. Cambridge: Cambridge University Press,
    1981.

Smyth, J. J., *Labour in Glasgow, 1896–1936: Socialism, Suffrage, Sectarianism*.
    Edinburgh: Tuckwell Press, 2000.

SNP, *Re-elect a Scottish Government: Working for Scotland*. Edinburgh: SNP, 2011.

Somerville, Paula, *Through the Maelstrom: A History of the Scottish National Party,
    1945–1967*. Stirling: Scots Independent, 2013.

Stewart, Donald, *A Scot at Westminster*. Sydney, Canada: The Catalone Press, 1994.

Tanner, Duncan, *Political Change and the Labour Party 1900–1918*. Cambridge:
    Cambridge University Press, 2008.

Tarditi, Valeria, 'The Scottish National Party's changing attitude towards the
    European Union', Scotland Europa Institute, Working Paper No. 112.

Thompson, Frank G., 'A different drum: a biographical note on Sir Alexander

MacEwen, Inverness', *Transactions of the Gaelic Society of Inverness*, 60 (1997–98): 108–24.

Thomson, George Malcolm, *Scotland: That Distressed Area*. Edinburgh: Porpoise Press, 1935.

Torrance, David, *Nicola Sturgeon: A Political Biography*. Edinburgh: Birlinn, 2015.

— — (ed.), *Whatever Happened to Tory Scotland?* Edinburgh: Edinburgh University Press, 2012.

— — (ed.), *Great Scottish Speeches*. Edinburgh: Luath, 2011.

— —, *Salmond: Against the Odds*. Edinburgh: Birlinn, 2010.

Tschiffely, Aimé F., *Don Roberto: Being the Life and the Works of R. B. Cunninghame Graham*. Kingswood: Heinemann, 1937.

Vernon, James (ed.), *Re-reading the Constitution: New Narratives in the Political History of England's Long Nineteenth Century*. Cambridge: Cambridge University Press, 1996.

Watson, Dr M. Bruce, 'Foreword', in *Whose Country? An up-to-the-minute plea for the Democratic Government of Scotland*. Glasgow: Scottish National Party, 1947.

Watson, Graham, 'Scottish Liberals and Scottish Nationalists and Dreams of a Common Front', *Journal of Liberal Democrat History*, 22 (1999): 3–13.

Watts, Cedric, 'Graham, Robert Bontine Cunninghame (1852–1936)', *Oxford Dictionary of National Biography*. Oxford University Press, 2004. [http://www.oxforddnb.com/view/article/33504]

Weber, Max, 'Politics as a Vocation' (1919), in Gerth and Mills (eds), *From Max Weber: Essays in Sociology*. New York: Oxford University Press, 1958.

Weight, Richard, *Patriots: National Identity in Britain 1940–2000*. London: Macmillan, 2003.

Wilson, Gordon, *Scotland: The Battle for Independence 2014*. Stirling: Scots Independent, 2015.

— —, *Pirates of the Air: The Story of Radio Free Scotland*. Stirling: Scots Independent, 2011. Wolfe, J. N. (ed.), *Government and Nationalism in Scotland*. Edinburgh: Edinburgh University Press, 1969.

Wolfe, William, *Scotland Lives: The Quest for Independence*. Edinburgh: Reprographia, 1973.

Wood, Wendy, 'We Will Fight No More in England's Wars. Eirich Alba', *Voice of Scotland*, 1/1 (June–August 1938): 15–17.

Wyn Jones, Richard, *The Fascist Party in Wales?: Plaid Cymru, Welsh Nationalism and the Accusation of Fascism*. Cardiff: Cardiff University Press, 2014.

— —, *Plaid Cymru: The History of the Welsh Nationalist Party, 1925–98*. Cardiff: Welsh Academic Press, 2005.

Young, Clara and David Murison (eds), *A Clear Voice: Douglas Young, Poet and Polymath: A Selection from his Writing with a Memoir*. Loanhead: Macdonald Publishers, 1977.

Young, D. C. C., *Hitlerism in the Highlands*. Glasgow, 1944.

Young, Douglas, *The Burdies: A Comedy in Scots Verse*. Tayport: Douglas Young, 1959.

— —, *The Puddocks: A Verse Play in Scots frae the Auld Greek o Aristophanes*. Tayport: Douglas Young, 1957.

— —, *Chasing an Ancient Greek: Discursive Reminiscences of a European Journey*. London: Hollis & Carter, 1950.

— —, *Labour Record on Scotland: Unfulfilled Pledges Exposed*. Carlops: Scottish Secretariat, 1949.

— —, *'Plastic Scots' and the Scottish Literary Tradition: An Authoritative Introduction to a Controversy*. Glasgow: William Maclennan, 1947.

— —, *The International Importance of Scottish Nationalism*. Glasgow: Scottish Secretariat, 1947.

— —, *'Fascism for the Highlands': Gauleiter for Wales?* Glasgow: Scottish National Party, 1943.

— —, *William Wallace and this War (Speech at Elderslie Commemoration, 1943)*. Glasgow: Scottish Secretariat, 1943.

— —, *Quislings in Scotland*. Glasgow: Scottish Secretariat, 1942.

Young, Hugo, *One of Us: A Biography of Margaret Thatcher*. London: Pan Books, 1989.

Ziegler, Philip, *Edward Heath*. London: Harper, 2010.

INDEX

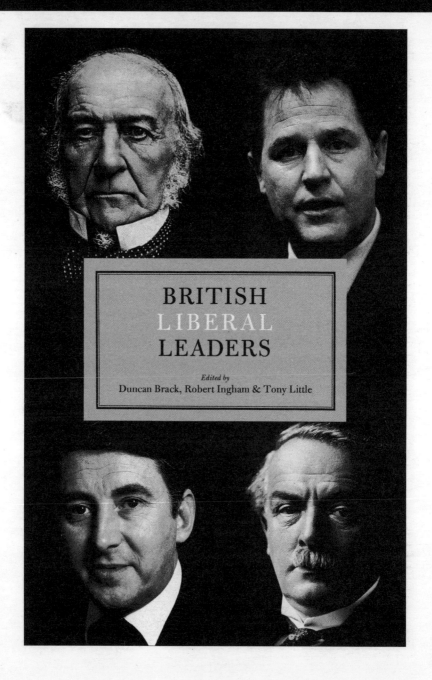